Twentieth-Century Teen Culture by the Decades

• A Reference Guide •

Lucy Rollin

D0075130

Greenwood Press

Westport, Connecticut • London

185 7715

Library of Congress Cataloging-in-Publication Data

Rollin, Lucy.
    Twentieth-century teen culture by the decades : a reference guide
  / Lucy Rollin.
      p.   cm.
    Includes bibliographical references and index.
    ISBN 0–313–30223–5 (alk. paper)
    1. Teenagers—United States—History—20th century. 2. Teenagers—
United States—Social life and customs. 3. Popular culture—United
States—History—20th century. I. Title.
HQ799.U65R65 1999
305.235'0973'0904—dc21   98–51892

British Library Cataloguing in Publication Data is available.

Library of Congress Catalog Card Number: 98–51892
ISBN: 0–313–30223–5

First published in 1999

Greenwood Press, 88 Post Road West, Westport, CT 06881
An imprint of Greenwood Publishing Group, Inc.
www.greenwood.com

Printed in the United States of America

The paper used in this book complies with the
Permanent Paper Standard issued by the National
Information Standards Organization (Z39.48–1984).

10 9 8 7 6 5 4 3 2

Copyright Acknowledgments

The author and publisher gratefully acknowledge permission for use of the following material:

Excerpts from Suzanne Wasserman, "Cafes, Clubs, Corners and Candy Stores: Youth Leisure-Culture in New York's Lower East Side during the 1930s," *Journal of American Culture* 14, no. 4 (1991):43–48.

For Mary Sue, and for Jonathan

If the adults' culture seems to be working all right, the kids help themselves to whatever aspects of it they like. But if it seems stodgy and dated or fails to meet their needs, they are not constrained by it. They can make a new culture.

—Judith Rich Harris, *The Nurture Assumption: Why Children Turn Out the Way They Do; Parents Matter Less Than You Think and Peers Matter More.* New York: The Free Press, 1998.

Contents

Preface

Teen culture is dismissed by some as comprising only music, fashion, and vulgar language, but writing this book has taught me that it is much more. It includes the personal, the aesthetic, the educational, the medical, the economic, the political, and the technological elements of American life—as well as music, fashion, and vulgar language. This book is written for teen and adult readers who want to enter this complex and fascinating territory.

It seems to me that we have a new archetype, that is, the teenager. We have always had the archetype of the *youth*, the fresh, innocent young person untainted by the culture around him (and the archetype is usually male). The *teenager* is the young person, male or female, who is completely immersed in the surrounding culture—its music, its gadgets, its fashions and fads and slang. On the one hand, *youth* are the shining hope of the future, unspoiled, energetic, and ready for the task ahead. On the other hand, *teenagers* are the eager consumers of everything consumable, and for some they are the curse of the modern world, the representation of all that is wrong with us, the ultimate downfall of our country.

This is why I chose to use the word *teen* throughout this book. It seemed to avoid the overglamorizing of *youth*, the sociological tone of *adolescent*, and the negative Fifties overtones of *teenager*, while still suggesting all of the above. As I moved through the large task of writing this book, I realized that the contradictions had not disappeared—which is, I suppose, the sign of a true archetype. The image of the "clean teen" beams out from Sunday supplement articles on teens who succeed in sports and school and politics, who stoutly maintain their belief in the American system, who love and respect their parents and teachers. The image of the juvenile delinquent sneers from behind frightened articles detailing the latest teen-perpetrated crime or the most recent statistics on drug use. It has been difficult to avoid falling into one tone or the other since so many sources sound notes of either praise or alarm.

The idea of "teen culture" in this book means cultural elements associated *primarily* with teens. Therefore, I have not said much about teens who play classical music, who read Shakespeare and Dostoyevsky, who enjoy ballet and modern dance, who go to church weekly with or without their parents, who regularly and quietly participate in politics on behalf of a particular party, who are active in family businesses or businesses of their own, who play baseball or football or soccer. There are plenty of these teens in America today, and there always have been. (And they are often the same people as their apparent opposites. A best friend from my high school could play Chopin superbly, and just as superbly dance the dirty boogie at the local hangout.) I have focused—as much as it is possible to sort this out—on those elements of life created for teens and maintained by teens. In the early decades of the twentieth century, when the idea of a separate teen culture was in its infancy, the connections between teens and adults were closer than they are today. It is important to remember that teens have always partaken of the adult life around them, as well as of the culture of the children around them. One of the difficulties of writing this book has been to keep those boundaries clear enough while suggesting their fragility.

Other difficulties have centered around geography, class, and race. Teen culture in the American South often differs from that in the Northeast or on the West Coast, and the sources rarely address these differences. After midcentury, however, thanks to radio, television, and now computer technology, teen culture has become somewhat more geographically homogenized. Class differences are another story. They seem to be increasing as the century draws to a close. Economically disadvantaged teens are excluded from many elements of what we think of as teen culture. Upper class, middle class, and lower class are admittedly imprecise designations which invite stereotyping, but I have used them, as have most of the surveys in the early and middle decades, when it seemed necessary to make distinctions among family incomes. As for race, one of the constant frustrations of this project has been the whiteness of the teen culture as it appears in virtually all sources on the subject. This is especially true in the early decades, but even in the later ones, the kind of information available on minority teens tends to perpetuate certain unpleasant stereotypes: the greater sexuality of black girls than white ones, the more widespread presence of drug pushers in the black culture, and so on. I have sought out information on minority teens, but it is difficult to find. A history of black teen culture in America is very much needed.

My consultant on sociological issues has informed me that, statistically, eighteen- and nineteen-year-olds are not considered adolescents, but since they are still teens, I have included them in my exploration of teen culture. In the Twenties especially, college students represented wild youth, the beginnings of the consumer culture, and the worship of youth itself which has flowered fully in the late decades. It seemed appropriate to consider them in the Eighties and Nineties, too, because most college freshmen are still supported almost entirely by their parents. They are, to put it another way, still adolescents. I have tried whenever possible to include younger teens as well in my discussions, although often my sources have not made this easy. Postwar teens dated at younger ages than previously, and today, young teens are engaging in sex and drug use to a greater degree than ever before. Adolescence seems to have spread its boundaries very widely.

Dividing the trends and events of the century by decade is of course an artificial exercise. Some decades seem to take on particular characteristics, at least from a distance, usually because of some cataclysmic event such as the stock market crash or the Vietnam war. During my research, I sometimes noticed that trends that appeared in popular literature in a particular decade turned up in scholarly literature a few years earlier. A particular fashion or trend would begin in adult culture and a few years later—perhaps in the next decade—become part of teen culture. I have tried to balance these discrepancies as fairly as possible. Each chapter offers an overview of historical events relevant to teens, treats teens at home, work, and school, then focuses separately on teen fashion, slang and leisure. Since the most distinctive teen culture occupies leisure time, I have treated at length under that heading such topics as dating and sex, movies, music, dancing, and reading. Radio and television are treated as part of home life. Sports and the car seem more important in some decades than in others, and toward the end of the century, computers and electronic gadgets defy categorization as they affect teen life at home, in school, and at leisure. The cellular phone, for example, is practically a fashion accessory by the late Nineties. Of course, it has been impossible to mention every movie, song, band, fad, fashion, television show, and trend that might be a favorite with a given reader. I have tried to suggest the dominant ones but, no doubt, have omitted some that would have made interesting reading.

More specifically, as I mention in my note on sources, the passages on slang for each decade are meant to suggest only a tiny portion of the rich and lively language that teens invent and use to maintain the distance between themselves and others. I have tried to balance my selection between the familiar and the curious for each decade while avoiding salacious sexual and bathroom expressions (which of course make up a significant proportion of all slang). For the full flavor of teen slang throughout the century, I enthusiastically recommend Tom Dalzell's *Flappers 2 Rappers* (1996).

Finally, every effort has been made to check and double check facts, dates, and spellings. Any errors that remain are entirely my own.

Acknowledgments

Many people from many quarters have helped me with this book. Colleagues, friends, family members, and students have all shared information, memories, opinions, and photographs over the two and a half years spent on this work. They have seemed genuinely interested even when every conversation with me ended up on the topic of teenagers.

As always, librarians have been my mainstay. Pam Draper of Clemson University, Rita Smith of the University of Florida, Dee Jones of the University of Southern Mississippi, and Lucy Caswell of the Cartoon Research Library of Ohio State University have been invaluable. I also thank Barbara Rich and the staff at DC Comics, who lend dignity and efficiency as well as a sense of humor to the business of comics. The staff at the Museum of Modern Art Film Stills Archive provided expert help.

Among my student assistants, two deserve special mention. Rebecca Bridges gathered general statistical information as well as insights into fashion and into the phenomenon that is Madonna. Jessica Vaughan provided significant help with research on the Eighties. Both offered not only well-organized paperwork but charming and informative conversations about teens.

I have had expert help on statistics from Stacey Willocks of Clemson University, who organized an overload of information with unfailing good sense, efficiency, and thoroughness. I will be forever grateful.

Among my colleagues, I especially thank Tom Inge for sending this project my way, Ray Barfield for his information about radio and comic strips, Bart Palmer for lending me films and for reminding me of the MOMA Film

Stills Archive, Trent Hill for information about country music, Jim Hawdon for sending me Stacey Willocks and for offering sociological information and advice, and Tharon Howard for helping me understand the Internet—not an easy task. I also thank my friend and colleague Mark West for his fine work on censorship and for his steady encouragement during all my projects.

I also thank the following for their interest and support: Suzanne Richard, Laura Gerren, Richard Plate, Scott Hazle, Alice Ray, Jean Ann Holder, Lew Waddey, Mary Sue Deters, Amy Deters, Andrea McMurray, Albert Doumar, Mary Lou Kaub, Megan Clough, Karen Paisley, Birma Gainor, Autumn Sam, Louise Jenkins, Lauren Grubb, and Hilda Terry.

I thank the following school principals for their cooperation in obtaining photographs: Irvin Cunningham, Pendleton High School, Pendleton, South Carolina; George Frakes, Highlands High School, Fort Thomas, Kentucky; Dennis Goldberg, Greencastle High School, Greencastle, Indiana; Sheila Hilton, T. L. Hanna High School, Anderson, South Carolina; David C. Hinson, Spruce Creek High School, Port Orange, Florida; Pamela Mc-Queen, Villa Madonna Academy, Covington, Kentucky; Jackie Menser, Sedgefield Middle School, Charlotte, North Carolina; and Les Morse, Dzan-tik'i Heeni Middle School, Juneau, Alaska. The photographs from South Hills High School in Pittsburgh, Pennsylvania, were obtained from Roger Rollin; the school no longer exists.

I thank Barbara Rader of Greenwood Press for her editorial guidance and understanding. I thank Bruce Rollin for solving my computer problems. As always, I thank Roger Rollin for his love, patience, and encouragement, and for putting up with my monomania for these two and a half years.

Finally, very special thanks go to Jonathan Waddey, my research assistant on post-Fifties music and television. Without him, those chapters would have taken twice as long to write and been half as informed. His expertise and good sense about that most crucial element of teen culture, rock music—and his ability to explain it to this aging listener—were invaluable.

· 1 ·

The Early Decades, 1900–1920

The teen of the Nineties, or even of the Fifties, did not exist in America in 1900. Adolescence in the early decades was a brief time between childhood and adult responsibilities. The large majority of teens did not attend high school but entered the workforce as soon as they could find jobs. If they lived on farms, they took on major tasks even during childhood. They married young and had children of their own by the time they were in their late teens or early twenties. The blue jean–rock and roll culture was four and a half decades away.

POLITICS AND NATIONAL EVENTS

Politically, the century began in unrest. President William McKinley, a Republican who had been elected in 1896 largely because of his support of high tariffs to protect American markets, was beginning to see the importance of world trade and instituted a campaign to persuade the Senate to adopt a more open posture toward trade with other countries. At the same time, as his second term began in 1900, rumors of a plot by European anarchists to assassinate several heads of state prompted fears for McKinley's safety. On September 6, 1901, on a speaking tour in Buffalo, New York, the president was shot by Leon Czolgosz, who had concealed a revolver under a handkerchief. McKinley died eight days later, and Vice President Theodore Roosevelt took office. A century which began with a political assassination would see several more before its close.

Teddy Roosevelt, who had first served as McKinley's secretary of the navy, had distinguished himself by his often unauthorized moves to strengthen that arm of the U.S. military. He resigned the post to lead a volunteer cavalry regiment, known as the Rough Riders, in the Spanish-American War and became a national hero when he charged up Kettle Hill near Santiago, Cuba. Images of Roosevelt astride a rearing horse, wearing a jaunty hat and waving a sword, captured the popular imagination, and when he became president, his unorthodox ideas and energetic use of presidential power often endeared him to the people while frustrating the political machine that manipulated vast economic power in the country. Roosevelt took on the nation's richest men—J. P. Morgan and John D. Rockefeller among them—by enforcing the Sherman Anti-Trust Act and insisting that big business needed to benefit all citizens, not just the privileged few. He was the first president to recognize the need to conserve our forests, water, and minerals, and he took various actions to prevent private money interests from taking over public land. He visited the construction site of the Panama Canal where he was photographed running a steam shovel. He invited the American educator Booker T. Washington to lunch at the White House. He was the first American to win the Nobel Prize for mediating in peace talks with representatives from Russia and Japan in 1905, which led to the Treaty of Portsmouth. He constantly advocated physical exercise, a vigorous respect for nature in all its forms, and the priority of the people over big business.

Political unrest, on a smaller scale but with global implications, permeated many homes between 1900 and 1919. The campaign to give women the right to vote, which simmered throughout the second half of the nineteenth century under the leadership of Elizabeth Cady Stanton and Susan B. Anthony, was kept in the public eye by annual meetings of the National Woman Suffrage Association and by efforts made to pressure individual states to enfranchise women. Many women donned banners and marched in parades. Some embarrassed their husbands and children but others won the support of their families. The part taken by women during World War I changed many minds about woman suffrage, and, in 1917, voters in New York amended their state constitution to permit women full suffrage in state affairs—a major victory in the movement. By the next year, fifteen more states had followed suit. Other countries had given women the vote earlier, but this was the first time the franchise came from the voters themselves. Congress delayed submitting an amendment to the U.S. Constitution until 1919, but in August 1920, the Nineteenth Amendment was passed and women took their place as fully enfranchised members of the American electorate, just in time to vote in the national elections.

Racial Tensions

With the passage of the Fourteenth Amendment in 1868, which gave Negro men the right to vote, many Americans heralded the successful completion of the struggle to free the slaves. However, although racial prejudice might be expected to subside after 1900, the reverse was true. Laws that protected segregation, known as "Jim Crow" laws, gained momentum. In 1915 the Knights of the Ku Klux Klan was founded in Georgia, taking its cue from an earlier organization active in the immediate post–Civil War days; cross burnings and lynchings increased in many parts of the country. Native Americans tried to create pride in their heritage by establishing in 1911 the Society of American Indians, which advocated reservation schools and the preservation of American Indian history. They were still not considered U.S. citizens. A deep hatred of Germans was voiced after the sinking of the *Lusitania* in 1915 and in 1917 America entered World War I. Although many whites were prejudiced against blacks and immigrants, young white Americans adopted the music and dance styles of blacks and immigrants as their own, effectively creating cultural mergers with the very people many of their parents feared, ignored, or hated.

The Airplane and the Car

Two events in the early years of the century changed the lives of all Americans completely. Wilbur and Orville Wright made the first powered airplane flight, and Henry Ford built the first automobile that members of the general public could afford.

With Orville lying face down on the lower wing and Wilbur running alongside holding one wing tip, the Wright brothers' twelve-horsepower motorized craft rolled down a monorail on the cold, windy beach at Kill Devil Hill near Kitty Hawk, North Carolina, and lifted smoothly into the air, flying about ten feet off the ground for twelve seconds. The date was December 17, 1903. By the end of the century, safe and affordable air travel would dominate the travel industry, flying would be a popular sport—and career—for many young men and women, the Air Force would have changed the way wars were fought, Americans would have walked on the moon, and an exploratory unmanned ship would head for Mars.

Henry Ford's Model T, introduced in 1908 for $850, had an even bigger impact on the daily life of Americans and especially on the lives of teens. Aiming to make a good car that was inexpensive to produce and run, Ford predicted that "about everybody would have one" eventually, making him probably one of the few successful prophets of modern life. The public loved his Tin Lizzie, or flivver, especially as the price gradually dropped to $290 in 1923. Americans had bought more than fifteen million model Ts before 1927. The automobile changed American work and leisure, especially in rural areas where it gave farm wives the option of driving to the nearest store for canned goods and teens the opportunity to meet other teens away from their homes and families. Of course, it also increased parents' fears that the lure of towns and unsupervised teen leisure would destroy the family's

When the barn-storming pilots came to town to demonstrate their flying skills, these daring 1919 teen girls purchased airplane rides for fun. Reproduced courtesy of Roger Rollin.

unity, and they were right to be fearful. The popularity of the automobile, and the freedom this machine gave the young, was the first dramatic and irrevocable instance of twentieth-century American teenagers' separation from their parents' influence, beginning gradually but increasing sharply throughout the coming decades.

Birth Control

Yet another kind of freedom, beginning in the early years of the twentieth century, was to have as much impact, especially on teen girls, as the airplane and automobile: the freedom, for women, from bearing unplanned children. The movement to make birth control available to all began with Margaret Sanger's efforts in 1912. Trained as a nurse, Sanger became increasingly outraged as she watched women from New York's Lower East Side die from self-inflicted abortions because physicians refused to give them sensible birth control advice when they requested it. Her own mother had died young after bearing eleven children. Sanger was convinced that the link between poverty and large families could be broken only if information about contraception was free and provided to all who wanted it. Women could then reach beyond home, marriage, and children, she believed, toward lives in the larger world. After a trip to France with her husband, where she discovered that French women were taught birth control by their mothers, she began publishing newsletters and pamphlets to inspire women to "think for themselves" and to give them the information they needed to prevent pregnancy. She was arrested on charges of sending obscene material through the mail (she thought self-inflicted abortions were obscene) and fled to England where she continued to study and gather information about contraception.

On October 16, 1916, America's first birth control clinic opened in Brooklyn, run by Sanger and her sister. A crowd of women waited in lines that grew increasingly long on that first day, proof that Sanger was right in her sense of women's need for information. A few days later, Sanger was again arrested and this time jailed, but she had made a start. Although her views were controversial and even repugnant to many, her efforts dramatically changed the social and sexual lives of all women, especially of teenagers during the last half of the century. Until her death in 1966, she continued to maintain women's right to a sexual relationship without fear of pregnancy, and she witnessed the sexual revolution that characterized the Sixties in America, which represented the triumph of her campaign: free or affordable birth control available to all.

World War I

The second decade of the twentieth century was overshadowed by war—the "Great War," with its staggering loss of life and its proof that a war really could engulf the whole world. When Theodore Roosevelt split the Republican party in 1912, after announcing he would not seek the nomination, Democrat Woodrow Wilson won the election with a large electoral majority but a small popular vote. Soon it became clear that, despite his attempts to focus on issues at home, the unrest in other parts of the world would claim his attention. When Archduke Ferdinand, the heir to the throne of Austria-Hungary, and his wife were assassinated by a Serbian terrorist in 1914 and Austria-Hungary declared war on Serbia, other European countries entered the conflict. Germany, Bulgaria, and the Ottoman Empire, who called themselves the Central Powers and supported Austria-Hungary, wanted to maintain the trade routes to the Adriatic Sea controlled by Austria-Hungary, which the Serbs wanted released to them. France, Belgium, Japan, the British Empire, Liberia, Montenegro, and Russia, known as the Allied Powers, who weighed in on the side of Serbia, saw an opportunity to increase their trade routes. Wilson declared the United States a neutral power, and for a while, America benefited from the increased trade in goods necessary to conduct the war.

However, remaining neutral and continuing to trade with countries embroiled in such a conflict became difficult; it was impossible not to take sides at some point. In 1915 the Germans, later claiming the ship was armed, bombed the British liner *Lusitania*, and 128 Americans on board were killed. Stating that there were times when a country was "too proud to fight," Wilson continued to maintain his neutral stance in spite of increasing pro-war sentiment in the country. When, in early 1917, the Germans announced that they would resume submarine warfare against the United States, Wilson issued a declaration of war "to make the world safe for democracy," and the United States joined the Allied Powers. Young men were drafted as soon as a draft law was passed in May, and Americans threw themselves into the war effort with voluntary rationing through victory gardens, "gasless Sundays," and "heatless Mondays." Hatred of the Germans so permeated the society that German measles became known as "liberty measles" and the ground meat known as hamburger was called "liberty steak."

By summer 1918, the German forces were weakening. With the collapse of Bulgaria, the Germans appealed for an armistice. By the end of October, Austria also asked for an armistice. By November 11 the war was over and the Allied Powers were victorious. In the months following the Great War, Wilson took the lead with his Fourteen Points for Peace, which included the model of the League of Nations, a world organization devoted to peace. So great was the hatred of the Allies for the Germans that the peace treaty, the Treaty of Versailles, made Germany completely responsible for the conflict and obligated Germany to pay enormous war reparations. Wilson continued to push forward his concept of the League of Nations; however, the compromises and amendments he encountered, especially in his own country, so changed his original concept that he finally advised the Senate to vote against the treaty. Ironically, then, the United States was not part of the League of Nations, even though its president had created it. Some historians believe that Wilson's stubborn refusal to compromise sowed the seeds of World War II; by 1923, Adolf Hitler was beginning to fashion Germany's Nazi party.

Disasters

The twentieth century has had perhaps more than its share of disasters. The San Francisco earthquake of 1906 resulted in many thousands dead and homeless. The unsinkable *Titanic* struck an iceberg and sank in 1912, killing approximately 1,500 passengers and crew members. The flu epidemic of 1918–1919 wiped out whole families and killed millions worldwide. The saddest and most immediate disaster for the young, however, was the loss in war of so many lives, mostly young men in their teens. Some of them died from exposure to the new and frightening chemical weapon, mustard gas, which was used for the first time by the Germans at Ypres. For young American men in particular, during and after World War I, being drafted into military service and facing the possibility of violent death on foreign soil became a fact of life until the draft law was repealed in 1973.

TEENS AT HOME

When the century began, fewer Americans lived in cities than in small towns and on farms, but by 1920, the balance had shifted. Many of those who did live in the cities were immigrants, mostly from Eastern and Southern Europe. They thronged into New York City's Lower East Side, where they lived in squalid tenements while they sought the freedom of opportunity they believed America offered. For these fledgling Americans, the idea of a teenager having his or her own room would have been regarded with amazed disbelief, by adults and teens alike. Some families moved frequently, usually to other cities like Boston and Philadelphia, where they sought out relatives, friends, a little more space, and a chance to work at their trades. The U.S. Census Bureau placed the number of immigrants per 1,000 residents at 10.4 for the years from 1900 to 1910, the highest rate by far during the entire century.

At the other extreme, many families moved westward, to the Great Plains and the open spaces, where, like the New York immigrants, they sought the individuality and freedom that America represented. While the outdoor space around them may have been greater, they too lived in cramped places—in sod houses, log cabins, covered wagons, and caves. Rural Southerners fared little better. Teens in these parts of the country worked just as hard, and had just as little privacy, as those in the crowded cities.

But the less crowded, separate dwelling—the bungalow-style house—was growing in popularity and affordability, thanks to the demands of the increasing number of middle-class families and the new availability of prefabricated houses from such mail-order companies as Sears, Roebuck, and Company. These houses might have three or four bedrooms and a spacious lawn. On the other hand, as the century began, many of them did not have plumbing or electricity, but by 1920 that too was beginning to change. The popular image of the teenager with his or her own room, and later own telephone, radio, and record player, was slow to emerge, but had its roots in this Sears mail-order bungalow.

New inventions gave other kinds of freedom. Refrigerated railroad cars and trucks made fresh food available throughout the country. Radio, which began as a communication device to transmit Morse Code, began to evolve into a home entertainment center, bringing shared cultural experiences to Americans nationwide. The portable vacuum cleaner gave housewives clean carpets with a minimum of effort (although early models weighed over ninety pounds). Soap flakes, safety razors, cellophane, milk cartons, and zipper fasteners all made their appearance during this period. In 1900 Kodak introduced the Brownie camera, which made taking good photographs possible and affordable even for children; it sold for one dollar.

TEENS AT SCHOOL

School was considered a form of work, although it cost families money through lost wages if their children attended regularly—and in these early years few did. In 1900 only 11.4% of teens between the ages of 14 and 17 were in high school; the number inched up to 15.4% by 1910. Wealthier teens, whose families did not need their income, stayed in school longer. Less well-off teens left school to help their families at home or on the farm, or to learn some craft or trade. Teens who stayed in school before 1910 attended a six-year high school and studied literature, history, and some math. By 1905 teachers had begun to complain that some students were too immature for high school subjects, created discipline problems, and often dropped out of school. Schools were becoming overcrowded, too, as students entered high school in increasing numbers. In 1909 the first junior high school was established in Columbus, Ohio, followed by one in Berkeley, California, in 1910. By 1920 there were 400 junior high schools around the country (Wiles and Bondi 1993, 5) and the pattern of the four-year high school was well established.

The setting for H. Irving Hancock's 1910 teen novel *The High School Freshmen* was a fantasy world to most teen readers, though perhaps there was a grain of reality in the details. Gridley, an "average American city of thirty thousand" in some unspecified part of the American Midwest, supports a school of 240 students, 100 of whom are girls. The school employs sixteen teachers, four of whom are men; classes meet from 8 A.M. until 1 P.M. In assemblies, girls and boys sit on opposite sides of the auditorium, and boys always wait until after the girls have left the classroom—the "recitation room"—to make their own exit. After school most of the boys can be found on the football fields (in actuality, football was a sport mostly confined to college campuses). What the girls do is seldom mentioned, unless the plot calls for them to help the boys catch a thief, solve a mystery, or cheer on their favorite players. Hancock even tells proudly how much the building—the latest and best in schools—cost: $200,000. The plot centers around the principal's threat to cancel the athletic program if grades drop.

By 1920 the number of teens in school had doubled and the literacy rate had increased dramatically. As school became more fact than fantasy, it disappeared from the novels teens enjoyed, replaced by fantasies of crooks, gunmen, stolen money and jewels, fast cars, independence from all authority, and instant media fame.

TEENS AT WORK

One of the reasons for the increase in school attendance was the work of the National Child Labor Committee, established in 1904 to publicize and correct the exploitation of children in the wage labor force. After failing to induce the states to regulate themselves on this issue, the committee turned to the federal government, and in 1916, after much opposition, got the Keating-Owen Act through Congress. The provisions regulating child labor were attached to interstate commerce, which Congress controlled, and established the minimum working age as fourteen, sixteen for workers in mines and quarries. No one under sixteen could be employed at night, and the workweek was established at forty-eight hours, with an eight-hour workday. Ironically, in 1918, the Supreme Court declared the Keating-Owen Act unconstitutional, and it would be several more years before lasting laws were put in place. The reformers, however, had succeeded in exposing the abuses of child labor to the public, and some industries began to police themselves. On the other hand, according to Elliott West, by preventing these children from working, the system was "making poor families even poorer" (West 1996, 71). Of course, at the same time, factory work was increasingly unsuitable for children as the processes became more complicated.

In 1900 one out of every five children aged ten to fifteen was gainfully employed, a huge increase over the figures for 1870, and the numbers continued to grow through 1910. Obviously the working life was more important than the school life in these early years, especially on farms. Teen children in the family were essential to farming. Boys learned early to do the heavy work of preparing the fields, and girls learned to plant, hoe, and weed. All helped with the harvest or in emergencies when crops were threatened by frost, wind, or torrential rains. Teen girls could do all the work around the house: laundry, cleaning, canning, cooking, and minding the younger children. Boys and girls fished and hunted for food. Families who headed west needed every pair of hands to establish homesteads and manage livestock. Sharecropper families in the South depended on the labor of every family member just to acquire basic food and shelter.

In urban areas, most adult men could not earn enough money to support their families, so children and young teenagers had to earn wages to contribute to the household—not only or even mostly so they could have spending money. By age seventeen or eighteen, they had households of their own to support, but in their early teen years, they worked wherever they could find employment and brought most of their earnings home.

John Spargo's 1906 exposé of child labor, *The Bitter Cry of the Children*, describes the working conditions in glass factories, textile factories, and mines, all industries that routinely employed children. He met one thirteen-year-old girl whose frail appearance made her look more like a child of ten or younger. She worked in a flax mill in New Jersey, barefoot, in pools of water, twisting coils of wet hemp in a room filled with steam. In the glass trade, boys of fourteen and younger worked carrying the bottles on asbestos shovels from one manufacturing process to another, going back and forth with their hot loads hundreds of times during an eight-hour day for a wage of from sixty cents to one dollar for the day. Since these factories worked round the clock, many younger boys and girls worked at night, and evidently preferred it since they could then play during the day. However, they got little rest and those who tried to go to school were too sleepy to learn much. Rheumatism, pneumonia, and stomach ailments were common among these children and teens, as well as injuries and amputations caused by machinery and lung disease resulting from textile lint and coal dust.

Some city children worked closer to home, sewing, making cigars, or running errands for neighborhood shops. By the time they reached their teens, however, they tended to move away from their immediate neighborhood to places where they could feel more autonomous. Some made money by carrying messages for businessmen, some became bootblacks, and some became junkers and scavengers, picking through trash for whatever they could sell or use at home. Some became street peddlers, selling candy, gum, suspenders, and their own talents as entertainers—singing, dancing, or spinning out a line of patter for a few cents.

The Newsies

Early in the century, one of the most visible and active trades for enterprising city boys (and a very small number of girls) was selling newspapers. In his book *Children of the City* (1985), David Nasaw tells in detail the fascinating story of these working youth, most of whom were between eleven and fourteen years old. The big publishers of newspapers, William Randolph Hearst and Joseph Pulitzer, engaged in an intense rivalry for readers. Their greed, coupled with the need of thousands of boys for paying jobs, produced a street trade of surprising proportions and power.

Newsies quickly rose to a unique status in the world of the street. They set their own schedules, manipulated their own territories, answered to no bosses, and enjoyed their work. Despite their intense competitiveness, they respected each other's territory and engaged in little violence. Their numbers were so great that truant officers, and reformers who wanted to enforce the ordinances controlling street trade, had little influence over them. At one point, in 1899 when they formed a union, they managed to shut down newspaper distribution in the New York area, all the way to Providence, Rhode Island, for about two weeks, forcing the Hearst and Pulitzer corporations to compromise with them. In several cities they formed associations or "republics," through which they governed themselves with remarkable wisdom. In Boston and Milwaukee, the boys elected their own judges and congressmen and established their own court system, choosing their leaders without regard to race or ethnic background. By 1920, however, the automobile had speeded up city life and put fewer people on the sidewalks and into public transportation. The need for newsies faded, but they had proved that, given the chance, young workers could operate a trade without the degree of supervision most adults wanted to impose on them.

Girls at Work

Girls during this time did not fare as well. While their brothers moved out onto the streets to find work, they were expected to stay at home to care for the younger children and to help with cooking, laundry, and cleaning. Reformers cautioned against letting girls into street trades, considering the streets too dangerous for them. As they reached their mid-teens, some sought employment in secretarial positions or sewing factories, places that could also be dangerous. The poor working conditions in such factories made headlines when the Triangle Shirtwaist Company in Manhattan, which employed about 600 young women, mostly immigrants, caught fire on Saturday, March 25, 1911, just at closing time. The ten-story building had been cited in the past for fire safety violations; this time the worst happened. As hundreds of young women surged onto the elevators and down the stairs, they found exits blocked, fire escapes collapsed, elevator cables burned and snapped, a rotted hose falling apart. Many jumped from windows to their deaths; others burned alive in the stairwells. In all 146 women died. Their charred bodies were laid out on a pier so that family members could crowd around to identify their loved ones. The horror of the disaster reached beyond families. Many thousands marched in the funeral parade for the young women; fire safety standards were reformed in New York and other parts of the country; and the International Ladies Garment Workers Union was formed as a direct result of the fire.

Spending Money

Few teens had any money of their own except what they contrived to save from their wages, usually by lying to their parents since asking for money to spend on their own amusements would appear too greedy and perhaps jeopardize the family's security. Nasaw quotes a working girl from Manhattan who was asked how she got money for herself.

Oh sure, there's a lot of girls that "knock down." You take this week in our place,— we all made good overtime. I know I got two forty-nine. Well, I guess there wasn't a single girl but me that didn't change her [pay] envelope, on our floor. Whatever you make is written outside in pencil, you know. That's easy to fix—you only have to rub it out, put on whatever it usually is, and pocket the change. (Nasaw 1985, 136)

Newsies who loved the arcades and nickelodeons had an easier time: when they earned a few extra cents, they just took time from their work and enjoyed the games and movies until they needed more extra cash, then went back to work. But then, as now, money was one of the chief areas of frustration for teens. They were old enough to earn it but not old enough to keep it and spend it on their own amusements.

FASHION

At the turn of the century, the Gibson girl look was still the most coveted fashion for girls. The Gibson girl, whose name came from the glamorous ladies in 1890s magazine illustrations by Charles Dana Gibson, wore her long hair drawn away from her face, full and loose on the sides and piled high on top and in back. She wore a high, tight collar on her shirtwaist, with large "leg of mutton" sleeves, a cinched-in waist, and a long, slightly hobbled skirt. Her large, wide-brimmed hat was decorated with lace, silk flowers, and feathers. Her full-bosomed, tiny-waisted figure was usually the product of a boned, laced corset, with heavy petticoats, bloomers, and stockings underneath her skirt, and low-heeled pumps. For evening, dresses were cut very low to show lots of bosom and shoulder. The look was queenly, mature, rounded; it could be worn by women from their teens well into middle age.

Daily wear for teen girls around 1918 was much simpler. Especially popular was the sailor-style dress: white, with a full skirt stopping just above the ankles, a wide collar, and a dark tie in front. For party wear, the style might be adapted in sheer, floating fabrics edged with lace. Teen girls took pride in very long hair, usually pulled back into a coil at the neck, or, for the traditional "sweet sixteen" portrait, coaxed into long "tube curls" over the shoulder and adorned with a large black bow in back. When girls graduated from childhood to early adulthood, they donned corsets, lengthened their skirts, wore elaborate hats for day and a lower neckline for evening, and abandoned long, flowing hair tied back with ribbons for an upswept hairdo with pins to hold it in place.

Boys wore knickers—loose pants that stopped just below the knee—with long socks and sometimes a close-fitting jacket and cloth cap. Shoes were probably hightopped with buttons. It was an important day in a boy's life when he got his first long pants, usually around the age of fourteen. Older boys wore slim, buttoned jackets and trousers for day with shirts with high, detachable shirt collars and narrow ties. They cut their hair short and wore fewer beards and mustaches than they had in the mid-nineteenth century. Their hats were generally flat-crowned straw boaters, a style adopted by girls.

During these decades, children apparently looked forward to dressing like mature women and men, and their parents made little effort to adopt the

Teen girls showing off their fashionable clothing. Reproduced courtesy of Jean Ann Holder.

styles of the young—one of the most visible differences between the culture of 1910 and that of the last half of the century.

SLANG

Teens have always separated themselves from both children and adults by using slang—a kind of secret language that constantly changes to maintain its value as a currency, as a way to identify those who are "in" or "out" of one's social group, and as a protector of privacy. Some of the slang terms in use in these early decades have found their way into the casual language of the late twentieth century. To have a "crush" on someone still means to be infatuated. To "kid" a person still means to deceive, "dough" still means money, "to flunk" a course still means to fail it, to "swipe" means to steal, and to "cram" for a test still means to study intensively, especially memorizing a lot of facts, immediately before the test.

Other terms now seem quaint or mysterious, or they mean something different today, such as these 1900 college students' words and phrases:

jump—to be absent from a lecture

play horse with—to ridicule

A fashionable "Sweet Sixteen" portrait of a Pennsylvania girl. Reproduced courtesy of Jean Ann Holder.

dead—perfect, complete

fluke—an utter failure

plunker—a dollar

beef—a mistake

tacky—untidy

yap—a contemptible person (Eble 1996, 150–153)

In Hancock's 1910 novel for teens, *The High School Freshmen*, fourteen-year-old hero Dick Prescott catches a "footpad," or thief, and his friends say admiringly, "That kid's the mustard!" while his archenemy, class bully Fred Ripley, calls him contemptuously, and several times, "a mucker"—a nobody.

LEISURE ACTIVITIES AND ENTERTAINMENT

Baseball, the favorite spectator sport, was a consuming pastime for adults and teens alike who experienced vicarious thrills by following the careers of their favorite players—especially Ty Cobb. Between 1907 and 1915, Cobb,

An Ephrata, Pennsylvania, boy in knickers at age twelve. Reproduced courtesy of Jean Ann Holder.

who played for the Detroit Tigers, won nine American League batting titles in a row and became one of the first five players elected to the National Baseball Hall of Fame. Despite his reputation as a brawler, he was one of the most popular players of these decades. In rural areas, older boys and some girls played the game with rubber balls and boards as bats, with stones or just imagination to mark the bases.

After the turn of the century, except in the most rural areas, the traveling carnival was eclipsed by the amusement park, with its bright lights, shooting galleries, tests of strength, freak shows, exotic dancers, and rides. Whole families could enjoy these parks, but teens especially enjoyed the roller coasters and the dark Tunnel of Love, where young couples could enjoy some brief physical contact otherwise forbidden. The magician and escape artist Harry Houdini traveled around the country thrilling audiences with his incredible tricks. As they had since before the Civil War, minstrel shows brought audiences ragtime music, jokes, and jazz dancing, usually performed by white men in blackface, but gradually they were eclipsed in cities and larger towns by vaudeville shows. These variety shows combined singing, dancing, jokes, comedy routines, and female impersonators in a lively mix of talent and races—blacks performed alongside whites, Gentiles alongside Jews: "on the vaudeville stage all men and women were created equal" (Slide 1994, xiv). To be on the vaudeville stage, especially the Palace Theatre in New York, like Eddie Cantor, George Jessel, or Ethel Waters, was the dream of many a talented teen during these decades.

Rural Teen Leisure

For rural teens, church activities afforded social opportunities to meet others away from home. Solomon Loewen, who grew up in a Mennonite community in Kansas in the early years of the century, remembered the difficulties of teen life in that environment; having quit school at age fourteen, most teens worked on the farms without much opportunity for play. To help fill this need, his church organized the Christian Endeavor, which met once a month for music, Bible study, and informational programs about missions. Church choirs and annual songfests also provided places to meet other teens, and at large church meetings, the young people waited on tables and washed the dishes, "to which the boys and girls looked forward. Here they would fraternize, and the guys would pick the girl they thought would make a good cook and homemaker. It was work, but also good, wholesome entertainment" (Loewen 1989, 38). Loewen also remembered caroling parties:

Before the age of the automobile, the young people would go by wagon and team of horses. They drove from farmyard to farmyard and sang the joyous songs of the season. When it was very cold, they would sit on the floor of the double box of the wagon and cover up well in order to keep warm. At times they would use hot bricks to keep their feet warm. Occasionally they would be invited into a home where they could warm up and enjoy some refreshments and hot coffee. (1989, 38)

When Loewen's father bought a Model T Ford in 1908, he and his friends could go to the nearby college, seven miles away, for programs of music, literary readings, or a "chalk-talk"—a lecture accompanied by drawing in chalk. "It was an easy drive for an enjoyable evening and had parental approval" (38). He comments later that girls had fewer opportunities to get together with their friends than did the boys; they had to entertain themselves at home with playing the organ or piano, or sewing costumes for a dress-up party.

Movies

City life provided quite a different set of pleasures, which were, on the whole, more accessible, to boys than to girls. These entertainments are described vividly in several books and articles written by Nasaw. Between 1900 and 1905, the penny arcade was the major attraction for leisure hours on the street; in the larger cities, they were housed in long rooms packed with machines called "Kinetoscopes," each of which had a crank and a peephole.

A boy put in a penny to view a speeding train, a robbery, or a sexy dancer; the crude films lasted only a minute, but their novelty and escapism provided maximum value for the time and money invested, and thousands of boys spent their after-school and after-work hours crowded around these machines. "No adults stood in their way, censored their choices, or told them how to behave" (Nasaw 1985, 120).

As moving pictures grew in length, arcade owners added projectors and chairs so that patrons could enjoy a longer show. The price went up to a nickel for these "Nickelodeons," and the attendance increased as well. Nasaw says that by 1908 there were as many as ten thousand nationwide; in New York City alone, between 75,000 and 100,000 children daily attended these shows (1985, 121). In these early days, the movies were regarded as amusement for the lower classes—they were crowded, dirty, and distasteful to refined folk. Audiences, especially the young who were there without supervision, shouted, booed, cheered, ate, and drank their way through the shows. A few enterprising theater owners tried to appeal to a more genteel audience by choosing better locations and adding comfortable chairs, better ventilation, and fancy exteriors to what they now called movie "palaces" and advertised them as being appropriate for ladies. Since they showed the same pictures as the cheaper storefront theaters, the young continued to patronize the "nickel dumps" where they could be free to behave as they wanted. In segregated America, of course, such freedom did not extend to blacks, who were prohibited from attending the picture shows or "flickers" with whites. In some Southern cities, theater entrepreneurs who tried to open theaters for blacks met with resistance and the destruction of their property (Nasaw 1993, 172–73).

Many adults—parents, educators, and reformers—were appalled by the popularity of these crude entertainments, claiming they would surely destroy the moral training the young people received at home. Chicago's Jane Addams, the famous social worker who established Hull House, a settlement house, called the nickelodeons "houses of dreams." She believed that the burglaries and pilferings taking place at Hull House were due in large measure to the boys' desire to get tickets to the moving picture show.

Eleven- to fifteen-year-olds were too influenced, too affected, too attracted, even addicted, to the pleasures of paid entertainment. . . . Adolescents were prone to dreaming, even without the stimulus of the big screen. What the movies did, the reformers feared, was exaggerate this tendency to dangerous levels. At an age where the boys and girls should have been anchored more firmly to the real world, they were indulging in daily flights of fantasy in darkened movie theatres and nickelodeons. (Nasaw 1985, 126)

The young movie-house patrons knew what they wanted. When Addams tried opening her own theater at Hull House and showing "clean" pictures, audiences were lukewarm. One twelve-year-old-boy commented, "I don't

Douglas Fairbanks as *His Majesty the American* (1919), a role which allowed him to show off his youthful energy and athleticism to their fullest. Reproduced courtesy of The Museum of Modern Art.

say it's right, but people likes to see fights, 'n' fellows getting hurt, 'n' love makin', 'n' robbers, 'n' all that stuff. . . . This here show ain't even funny" (quoted in Nasaw 1993, 184).

Of course, the two most popular film stars of the second decade made youth and leisure fashionable, even essential, for health. Douglas Fairbanks with his California tan, dazzling teeth, and muscular torso, preached the "glory of play" over a life driven by the desire for success in work. He enjoyed competitiveness in sports with other men; he radiated optimism and joy (May 1980, 114). Yet author Booth Tarkington, at the time, commented that Fairbanks' mind was "reliably furnished with a full set of morals" and that he would be a "sympathetic companion for anybody's aunt. Certainly he will never be older—unless quicksilver can get old" (quoted in May 1980, 115).

By far the most popular film actress of the day was Mary Pickford. She too embraced youthful looks and spirits, playing the role of a teenager many times, well after she was in her thirties and forties. Like Fairbanks, she revealed more of her body than any public person ever had, projecting an eroticism combined with sexual innocence that many later stars aimed for but few achieved. She once explained that "passion and unkind thoughts" show on our faces, but that the young "seldom have these vices until they

Mary Pickford as the *Poor Little Rich Girl* (1917). The twenty-four-year-old silent film star, known as "America's sweetheart," was playing an eleven-year-old in this scene. Reproduced courtesy of The Museum of Modern Art.

start getting old, so I love to be with them. The impulses of youth are natural and good" (quoted in May 1980, 125). In daily life, Pickford was a canny and hardworking businesswoman, but the image projected in film and advertising made her the icon of the new twentieth-century woman: pure, happy, healthy, and above all, young.

Music and Dancing

Another form of leisure activity "inflamed the desires" of the young just as much as the films: dancing. The romantic swayings of the waltz, and lively folk dances like the schottische and the polka, might have entertained adults in the early years of the century, but young people—especially girls—began to move to entirely different music. If boys found their entertainment in arcades and nickelodeons, working girls found theirs in dance halls where all social strata and all ethnic groups mixed and danced to the new jazz and ragtime music. The popular "animal" dances were, to the pure-minded, aggressively primitive in name and action: in the Grizzly Bear, partners embraced each other closely, the man's legs enclosing the girl's and her arms not on his shoulders but around his neck; and ragtime music encouraged rhythms and movement seldom seen in public before, at least in polite society (Nasaw 1993, 113). The steps to the Turkey Trot varied from place to place but were uniformly fast, including pumping and flapping arms (Stearns 1994, 96). Girls were fired from their jobs or even arrested for doing this dance; in 1914, the Vatican issued an official disapproval (1994, 96). Vice commissioners employed investigators to visit dance halls and sniff out transgressions, but they seldom found actionable offenses (Nasaw 1993, 110–12).

Ironically, though blacks were excluded from most dance halls as dancers, they generally provided the music in them. The most popular dance band of the day was that of James Reese Europe, who played for the society balls of the very rich as well as for Vernon and Irene Castle, popular white exhibition dancers and dance teachers. Dances with African folk roots became popularized into Ballin' the Jack and the Eagle Rock in African American communities and were eventually diluted into the Turkey Trot, Grizzly Bear, Bunny Hug, Monkey Glide, and Possum Trot for white dancers who tried to imitate the hip and knee movements of black dancers. Ragtime music, firmly associated with black culture, was wildly popular with the young. Their parents might be at home around the piano singing "Sweet Adeline" and "Down by the Old Mill Stream," but teens in cities and towns, especially working girls, were at afternoon tea dances in hotels doing the Turkey Trot, or staying out until one or two in the morning at a dance hall, where they had probably gone with a group of friends and where a girl might meet a boy the family did not know.

Dating and Sex

During these early decades, dating was an unknown phenomenon, although courtship was sanctioned by adults as long as it stayed within certain rules. In the ideal arrangement, a boy chose a girl who would probably make a good wife; if both families approved, the boy called on the girl and most of their social engagements were enjoyed at home or in groups where adults were present. After a time, they could go out unchaperoned, but by the time things reached this stage, marriage would follow soon. Ideally, of course, both bride and groom were virgins. Meanwhile, social and sexual exploration was difficult to achieve. Unmarried and uncommitted teens had no social structure to support their leisure hours except that provided by home, church, and, very occasionally, school—all areas controlled by adults.

However, teen relationships did not always—or perhaps even often—happen that way, and girls did get pregnant or turn to prostitution. Nasaw emphasizes the sexually charged atmosphere of the city—its houses of ill repute on every block, its suggestive posters, its men lounging on street-corners eyeing the passing girls, its bars and vaudeville theaters—but even rural life had its fallen girls and experimenting boys. In 1913 a famous article trumpeted, "It has struck Sex O'Clock in America: a wave of sex hysteria and sex discussion seems to have invaded this country" (quoted in Nasaw 1985, 140), but true to form, most of the article blamed girls for the new sexual freedoms; these young women danced the Turkey Trot, smoked, drank, used makeup, went to vaudeville shows, and, worst of all, used birth control. Boys, evidently, were able to fend for themselves on the street and to sow their wild oats without permanent damage, but girls easily fell into sin and degradation, taking society down with them.

Girls in Reformatories

Although most teen girls negotiated the dangers and temptations of work outside the home in America's growing cities, a few were sent to reformatories, committed by exasperated and desperate families who wanted to be free of the shame such girls brought them. Their story, as told by Ruth Alexander, resembles that of some teen girls in the nineties. Alexander examined the records of twenty-two girls who were committed to New York reformatories in the early decades—girls such as sixteen-year-old Ella Waldstein (not her real name), who had worked in a factory since age fourteen.

In the summer of 1916, [Ella] started "going around with a bad crowd of girls," often staying away from her Brooklyn home until one or two o'clock in the morning. . . . "When [her parents] asked her where she had been she would say she had been with a girlfriend or simply would not answer. No matter how they scolded her she never talked back." . . . Throughout the following year, tension within the Waldstein home mounted, peaking in the summer of 1917 when Ella's relatives learned that she was spending her evenings on Coney Island, usually in the company of a handsome married Irishman who . . . gave Ella expensive gifts. (Alexander 1992, 277)

Growing up in lower middle-class or immigrant homes where they experienced strict parental values and constant suspicion, or in worse cases violence, incest, parental illness, or the death of a parent, such girls escaped to the streets, amusement parks, or dance halls where they found some autonomy. They also met men who were willing to pay for sexual favors. Most of the girls were sexually naive, despite their parents' fears, and were easily taken advantage of—sometimes raped, beaten, thrown out of promised hotel rooms, and infected with venereal diseases. If they became pregnant, they were forced to return to their families and bear their parents' anger as well as their unwanted children. If they were committed to reformatories, such as Bedford Hills in New York, they usually served three years, part of the time on parole. Sometimes the reformatory experience tamed them and they emerged vowing to become the deferential young women that society wanted and rewarded. Others defied authority, behaving violently or insolently within the institution, then violating parole and disappearing, often to be committed once again to the reformatory. These were likely to be girls whose families did not want them back during or after their parole, and they were the most likely to become prostitutes. Alexander concedes that these reformatory girls are atypical, but she sees them as representative of many adolescent girls who were struggling "in the contest between modernity and tradition" (278).

Boys in Gangs

Rural boys rebelled by escaping from farm and family life in automobiles, traveling to nearby towns to socialize with girls whom their parents did not know and who perhaps were just as sexually curious as the boys. City boys, many of whom already spent most of their days on the street, often rebelled by becoming part of a gang. In the streets where space was at a premium, a gang occupied its turf and defended it against all comers. Kids were expected to stay in their own territory—usually a city block—and risked beatings and cuts if they ventured away. According to Nasaw, gang wars might appear to be related to hostility between ethnic groups, but actually were about territory: "It was, indeed, the only thing they could call their own" (1985, 33). He quotes comedian Harpo Marx who grew up on the street and remembered the danger when he had to venture off his turf: Marx "made sure to carry 'some kind of boodle in my pocket—a dead tennis ball, an empty spool, a penny, anything. It didn't cost much to buy your freedom; the gesture was the important thing'" (33).

Attempts to Control Teens

Adults then as now continually sought ways to contain or combat teen rebellion. Churches and settlement houses offered organized recreation and safe places to meet friends. Worried parents instituted curfews. City ordinances tried to control rowdy or lewd behavior in public places. Reformers in the legislatures fought for "wayward minor" laws to give parents legal means to discipline their teen children.

One solution, welcomed by adults and teens alike, was the scouting movement. When Robert Baden-Powell, an Englishman and a soldier, observed how valuable outdoor survival skills were in time of war, he founded the Boy Scouts in England. Some Americans already had similar organizations. In 1910 American businessman William Boyce joined Baden-Powell and others to create the official Boy Scouts of America. By 1916 there were more than a quarter of a million Boy Scouts throughout America (Oursler 1955, 46). The girls were not far behind. At a Boy Scout rally held in 1909 in England, a number of girls appeared and asked to join. Baden-Powell felt a separate organization would be preferable, and he asked his sister to organize it. Juliette Low of Savannah, Georgia, observed the success of the English Girl Guides firsthand and when she returned to the United States in 1912, ten girls inspired by her experience formed their own troop. Low wrote the first Girl Scout handbook.

Camping and the outdoor life have been the primary focus of the scouting movement for both boys and girls, with the aim of making young teens independent and helpful to each other and to others. This goal has expanded and shifted to fit the changing times. During both world wars, the Boy Scouts were placed at the service of the U.S. government. Both Boy and Girl Scouts are encouraged to be active in their communities, whether rural or inner city. Scouting broadened the experiences of girls in ways not otherwise available to them. It provided inexpensive camp attendance and regular opportunities to talk to a nonparental adult about teen concerns. During the 1920s, for example, a time when young teen girls often had little information about menstruation, the Girl Scouts offered enlightened discussions and informational material about it (Brumberg 1997, 46).

Books and Reading

Literature written for and read by teens became a battleground early in the century, with authors, publishers, and marketers lined up on one side, and parents, teachers, ministers, and legislators on the other—the teens themselves, as usual, were caught in the middle but managed to survive and read what they wanted to in any event. As with the arcades, nickelodeons, movies, and dance halls, a teen's own dollar hard-earned in the street or factory, or wheedled from reluctant parents, became a powerful incentive to those who produced the popular culture of these early decades.

Until the Civil War, little fiction was written specifically for teens. The Sunday School literature so characteristic of the early and mid-nineteenth century, exhorting virtue, duty, and abstinence from strong drink and other fleshly pleasures, seemed to regard its audience as either children or adults, and gave them pretty much the same lessons with only slight variations in plot and character. The war made boys into men very quickly; the girls too shouldered adult responsibilities, as nurses or as homemakers in the absence of their men. Following the war, when the boys stayed at home longer and the girls returned to more domestic routines, a market developed for books more sophisticated than those for children, featuring plots full of action and excitement, often with heroic teens in the leading roles. This market also made a clear distinction between girls' books and boys' books. These trends set the pattern for the twentieth-century teen book market.

Postwar novels for girls still centered around the home, such as the popular series about Elsie Dinsmore, created in 1867 by Martha Finley writing under the penname of Martha Farquharson. Elsie, a virtuous girl worthy of any Sunday School book, must constantly put her arrogant and erring father to rights while she weeps for his soul. In subsequent books Finley took Elsie through adulthood, motherhood, and grandmotherhood, but the demand for more books about Elsie and her family kept the series in print through thirty volumes, until Finley's death in 1909. Louisa May Alcott's *Little Women* (1868) was written directly for the market of teen girl readers; its gentle excitements and sense of real life have kept it popular with many readers throughout the twentieth century.

In the 1870s and 1880s girls sought heightened romance and danger in much of their leisure reading. They liked books in which home became a gloomy manor house governed by a handsome, mysterious man, where a girl without family or dowry might find employment as a governess or nurse and where, eventually, the lord of the house sees her beauty and virtue and falls in love with her. The most popular variation on this Cinderella archetype was *St. Elmo* (1867), written by Augusta Jane Evans Wilson, although there were dozens of others, not so literary but more breathless of pace and full of teary scenes of reconciliation. Ironically, Louisa May Alcott wrote such novels as well but in a form that has only recently been discovered. Even while she was writing her more famous books for "our pure-minded lads and lasses," as she called them, as "M. Barnard" Alcott produced a number of steamy tales of romance, danger, and pursuit, featuring languishing females desired and menaced by unsavory men. Just as her character Jo in *Little Women* did, Alcott knew how to crank out thrills for the masses, and for money. There is a direct line of descent from these books to books popular with teen girls at the end of the century—books by Judith Krantz and Danielle Steel and the "Flowers in the Attic" series by V. C. Andrews.

Dime Novels and Censorship

During the last part of the nineteenth century and into the early twentieth century, while the girls read domestic romances, teen boys devoured dime novels. Small paperbound books often written by anonymous hacks who wanted money more than literary fame, dime novels were printed on cheap paper and had plots set mostly in the American West. They told of strong, violent men in barrooms and shacks, battling the evil in other men and in the environment. Although not originally aimed at teen readers, when the price went from ten cents to five cents boys read them even more eagerly than before and publishers recognized their potential. Mysteries, detective stories, and even a little science fiction soon joined the Westerns and set a standard for exciting leisure reading that continues today in books by such authors as Tony Hillerman and Stephen King.

The late nineteenth century and the early twentieth century also had its censor, and one of his targets was the dime novels and romances so popular with teens. Between 1870 and his death in 1915, Anthony Comstock, through his Society for the Suppression of Vice, battled what he regarded as the obscenity and degradation that infected American Society: alcohol, contraception, pool halls, chewing tobacco, and leisure reading were among the vices excoriated in his 1883 book *Traps for the Young*. All were the work of the devil, in Comstock's view, and he succeeded in confiscating much of the offending literature and destroying it, with the blessing of many ministers and legislators, as well as parents who were convinced that their sons were headed for a life of crime because they read dime novels. According to Nilsen and Donelson, Comstock was responsible for thousands of arrests and convictions and even fifteen suicides (1993, 497–98).

Oliver Optic and Horatio Alger

Two writers produced books for boys which, although they had their roots in the dime-novel adventures, showed more literary skill and inventiveness. William Taylor Adams, writing as "Oliver Optic," and Horatio Alger, Jr., each wrote well over a hundred books and became the most popular boys' authors in the late nineteenth and early twentieth centuries.

Adams' most popular series was his "Blue and Gray" series about the Civil War, twelve volumes of adventure and information which eventually sold an estimated two million copies. With these and other tales of boys rising above adversity, Adams virtually supported his publisher Lee and Shepard well into the twentieth century, even though he died in 1897. Several of his books were published posthumously after appearing in the late nineteenth century as magazine serials and continued to sell a phenomenal number of copies. One of these was *Honest Kit Dunstable* (1911). At fifteen, on the eve of his high school graduation in the "first rank," Kit discovers that he is not his father's natural son. When this kindly but troubled man dies, Kit is turned out onto the street by his vengeful uncle. Because of his natural honesty, his determination, and his generosity of spirit, Kit discovers his uncle's plot to swindle the public, and his real father, the bank president, welcomes him with open arms. At the first meeting of the American Library Association in Philadelphia in 1876, Adams's novels were attacked for their shallow style, their unrealistic plots, and their pandering to what some saw as teens' dangerous desires for outlandish adventures. Whatever the librarians said, boys continued to buy and read Adams's tales in huge numbers.

Horatio Alger, Jr., had his first great success with *Ragged Dick* (1868), the story of an enterprising young bootblack who, through a series of lucky accidents coupled with hard work, native good sense, and honesty, rises to respectability. The book was written in desperation; Alger had failed in scandal as a Unitarian minister and had fled to New York City to begin again, hoping to make a living by writing. The story of Ragged Dick was first published in Oliver Optic's magazine *Student and Schoolmate*. As a hardcover book, it was the first of a long series of successful books for Alger, all of which had similar plots. Although librarians and parents deplored Alger's books just as they did Adams's—and even though both writers' work was unfailingly moral even by nineteenth-century standards—teens got the excitement and action they craved, as well as a sense of their own dignity and potential, from his novels. Alger wanted his books to have a believable tone, so he continued to live in the city, where many homeless boys visited or stayed with him while he observed their way of life and listened to their slangy talk. He was not a celebrity as a person, but, like Adams, the popularity of his books continued and even soared after his death in 1899. Many of his books were reissued and reached sales of one million by 1910. Gary Scharnhorst, in his thorough study *The Lost Life of Horatio Alger Jr.* (1985), speculates that Alger's books were popular because they idealized an earlier, preindustrial America, when going from "rags to riches" seemed possible for those with virtue and industry (149–50). This may explain why some adults loved them, but teens loved them for their nonstop action, their exciting coincidences which suggested that good luck was just around the corner, and their courageous—even tough—teen heroes. After 1910, when the world began to change dramatically, Alger's sales plummeted, but his name remains synonymous with the success story—both the ones he created and the one he lived.

Edward Stratemeyer and the Popular Series Book

Alger also indirectly aided the transformation of American teen books in the twentieth century. When his health declined in the mid-1890s, he needed a ghostwriter to complete some of the projects he had begun. He hired young Edward Stratemeyer, who became the most powerful force in books for teens in the early twentieth century and who created a phenomenon that continues into the 1990s: mass-produced teen series fiction.

Surprisingly little is known about the personal life of Stratemeyer, but by the late nineteenth century, he had already published a number of boys' books and was editing a weekly magazine for boys. He showed his ability not only to gauge what boys liked to read but also to produce it quickly, and in amazing quantities. In fact, he soon realized that he could produce ideas faster than he could write the books, and he began to supply outlines to hired writers who would then finish the books for him. These writers remained anonymous behind the various pseudonyms Stratemeyer created, such as "Arthur M. Winfield," "Victor Appleton," and "Franklin W. Dixon." One of his earliest and most popular series, the Rover Boys, signed by "Arthur M. Winfield," was published for more than twenty-five years. The Rover boys were Dick, aged 16; Tom, aged 15; and Sam, aged 14. Their mother is dead, their father is lost in Africa, and their uncle supports them, giving them a great deal of freedom. They are resourceful, "sturdy-hearted," and willing to fight when they have to. They love sports, playing tricks, teasing, and pretty girls—although the girls rarely have much to do in the plots except cheer the boys on and "blush prettily" on occasion. Each book (there were thirty volumes) takes them to a new place where they find adventure and fun.

Stratemeyer's series about Tom Swift was his most successful, selling millions of copies and resurrected in 1954 in a new series, Tom Swift, Jr. Published under the pseudonym "Victor Appleton," the Tom Swift series specializes in speed. Tom is a "lad of action" who uses the full range of vehicles in his adventures: motorcycle, air balloon, motor boat, submarine, and an "electric runabout" car. He fights bullies, thieves, liars, and cowards; the same ones return in book after book for a breathless series of chases and narrow escapes. In the second decade of the century, Stratemeyer made use of the newest form of popular entertainment, the movies. Under the name "Victor Appleton," he created the Motion Picture Boys series and even sent these adventurous chums to the French battlefields in 1919.

Stratemeyer's syndicate-produced books sold for fifty cents each, and teens bought them by the millions, both in the United States and, after they were translated, in other countries. Stratemeyer, who paid his hired writers between fifty and a hundred dollars per job, transformed his system into huge profits for himself. Predictably, a number of librarians, teachers, parents, and other concerned adults felt that these books were corrupting their teenage children and attempted, through publicity and countermoves, to stem the flow of money into the Stratemeyer Syndicate, but they were rarely successful for long against Stratemeyer's ability to give teens what they wanted to read, at a price they could afford to pay. Besides, it was difficult to find any overt immorality in Stratemeyer Syndicate books. Stratemeyer saw to it that they advocated honesty, health, diligence at study and work, and good manners, even while the young heroes were chasing thieves.

Between 1900 and 1910, there was less leisure reading available for teen girls. Stratemeyer, probably aware of the gap, in 1904 invented the Bobbsey Twins, authored by the fictitious "Laura Lee Hope." This series, which had a remarkably long life, is aimed at the preteen audience. It soon became clear that girls were tired of domesticity and wanted adventure just as much as boys did; Stratemeyer and others found the formula. Between 1910 and 1920, approximately eighty-five girls' series were published; some—like those for boys—lasted only one or two years, others much longer. Some heralded a girl who could do more than blush prettily:

The Motor Girls	1910–1917
Girl Aviator	1911–1912
College Girls	1914–1917
Girls of Central High	1914–1921
Moving Picture Girls	1914–1916 (from *Girls Series Books* 1992)

These girls, like their male counterparts, led the "strenuous life" advocated by Teddy Roosevelt. With their groups of chums they competed at basketball or

One of the first in the Ruth Fielding
series, 1913. Reproduced courtesy
of the Baldwin Collection, George
A. Smathers Libraries, University
of Florida.

tennis, rode horses, drove their own cars, aided the poor and afflicted, and
faced danger intrepidly. During the war, they went to the overseas front and
survived shellings and plane crashes. They also went to college in remarkable
numbers. Jane S. Smith notes that, although less than 4 percent of American
girls attended college in 1910, almost all the heroines of series fiction did:

A few girls might openly view higher education as an escape from the marriage market
or a way to cultivate a well-defined special interest, but most seemed to pack their
trunks with the vague assumption that it was simply the thing to do. . . . Their appeal
lay in the fact that they were ordinary girls, a bit wealthier and more pampered than
most, perhaps, but not so remote as to discourage the audience's identification with
them. Any of their readers could hope and expect that she, too, might be such a
heroine if her life presented such opportunities to shine. (Smith 1978, 166)

Through these books, says Smith, girls saw that college might be a "natural
and acceptable part of the process of growing up," not only an intellectual
pursuit.

One of the most popular girls' series from Stratemeyer was the Ruth

Fielding books, which, written under the name of Alice B. Emerson, ran from 1913 until 1934. An intelligent, ambitious girl from a modest background, Ruth combines her good nature and her powers of shrewd observation to make a success of her life. She goes with the Red Cross to the front in 1918 where she rescues her boyfriend, Tom Cameron, by dressing as a boy and crossing No Man's Land. In college, she wins a contest writing film scenarios, and by 1930, still reaching for success, Ruth has her own film company with Tom as its treasurer.

Although girls' series novels were more thoughtful and gently paced than the series novels for boys, librarians and concerned parents worried that their shallowness and fantasy elements might entice girls away from domestic goals. To the multitude of teen girls who bought and read them, however, they were as engaging and inspiring as their brothers' dime novels, and just as available. The world was changing; old Victorian values were no longer relevant. In these books, girls saw other girls seizing new freedom and opportunity, just as they saw some of their mothers, aunts, and teachers marching for women's suffrage, and they did not want to be left behind.

Booth Tarkington's Seventeen

Some influential popular culture still offered an image of teen life that seems regressive by comparison. The best-selling book in the entire country in 1916 was Booth Tarkington's *Seventeen*. Between 1910 and 1921, Tarkington was a literary phenomenon, having returned from alcoholism to win two Pulitzer prizes with a series of remarkably popular novels detailing American middle-class life. He enjoyed writing about young people. In 1914 he had written *Penrod*, a gentle novel about a preteen boy and his escapades, rather in the vein of Mark Twain's *The Adventures of Tom Sawyer* but without Twain's literary complexity. In 1915 he serialized *Seventeen* in *Metropolitan Magazine*, and when it reached bookstores in hardcover it was a triumph.

Seventeen is subtitled "A Tale of Youth and Summertime." It tells of the seventeenth summer of William Sylvanus Baxter, who is tolerated by his father, gently understood by his mother, and tormented by his little sister Jane. William spends the novel suffering a series of humiliations, some of which he shares with Genesis, a black servant (Tarkington's treatment of him reveals much about racial attitudes among the middle class in 1915). William's clumsiness causes him to fall downstairs or sit in Jane's paintbox. He must carry washtubs down the street in full view of his friends, he has no evening clothes for parties, Jane tattles on him, he has no money of his own. Most of all, he falls in love with Miss Pratt, who is visiting from another town. Miss Pratt, a vision in drifting white dresses, goes about with her tiny dog Flopit in her arms, charming every boy in town, speaking what to William is the most endearing baby-talk he has ever heard:

"Oh cute-ums! . . . Ickle boy Baxter goin' make imitations of darlin' Flopit again. See! Ickle boy Baxter puts head one side, then other side, just like darlin' Flopit. Then barks just like darlin' Flopit! Ladies and 'entlemen, imitations of darlin' Flopit by Ickle boy Baxter."

"Berp-werp! Berp-werp!" came the voice of William Sylvanus Baxter. (65)

William endures raptures when Miss Pratt pays attention to him, and utter despair when she pays attention to other boys. He dramatizes himself as a poet, an actor, as the noble Sydney Carton from Charles Dickens' *A Tale of Two Cities*. When Miss Pratt departs at the end of the novel, he is still holding the candy he wanted to give her, and he is devastated—but, Tarkington lets us know, not for long.

Throughout the novel, Tarkington frequently comments as a wise adult on the perils of being seventeen years old:

It is the time of life when one finds it unendurable not to seem perfect in all outward matters: in worldly position, in the equipments of wealth, in family, and in the grace, elegance, and dignity of all appearances in public. And yet the youth is still continually betrayed by the child still intermittently insistent within him, and by the child which undiplomatic people too often assume him to be. (26)

While these observations have plenty of truth in them, and while Tarkington strove to write a realistic novel, his amused and tolerant adult point of view while describing what to adolescents are real difficulties makes the novel poke fun at the adolescents with whom he is sympathetic. Tarkington's teens are sweet, silly, ineffectual people, totally immersed in their tiny emotional worlds and insignificant troubles; we must love them and be patient with them, Tarkington seems to say, while they grow out of it.

No doubt many teens read *Seventeen* with some pleasure; it is clever and funny, and in it they probably recognized themselves as well as Tarkington's basic good will. Nevertheless, the tremendous popularity of this novel among adults, balanced with the thousands of series books teens were buying for themselves—books depicting teens with power, intelligence, and freedom—suggests quite a discrepancy between how adults wanted to see teens and how teens wanted to see themselves. *Seventeen* looks backward to a gentle, small-town life of summer parties and walks in the moonlight, where love and the right clothes were a teen's biggest concerns—a life that probably never really existed except in literature and film, but one that simplified the problems parents faced. Series fiction, with its emphasis on new technology and new freedoms, also simplified the world, remaking it as teens wanted it to be.

REFERENCES

Alexander, Ruth. " 'The Only Thing I Wanted Was Freedom': Wayward Girls in New York, 1900–1930." In *Small Worlds: Children and Adolescents in Amer-*

ica, 1850–1950, ed. Elliott West and Paula Petrik. Lawrence: University Press of Kansas, 1992.

Angel, Ann. *America in the Twentieth Century*. Vols. 1 (1900–1909) and 2 (1910–1919). New York: Marshall Cavendish, 1995.

Berger, Michael. *The Devil Wagon in God's Country: The Automobile and Social Change in Rural America, 1893–1929*. Hamden, Conn: Archon Books, 1979.

Brumberg, Joan Jacobs. *The Body Project: An Intimate History of American Girls*. New York: Random House, 1997.

Eble, Connie. *Slang and Sociability*. Chapel Hill: University of North Carolina Press, 1996.

Fennimore, Keith J. *Booth Tarkington*. New York: Twayne Publishers, 1974.

Fuller, Kathryn H. *At the Picture Show: Small-Town Audiences and the Creation of Movie Fan Culture*. Washington, D.C.: Smithsonian Institution Press, 1996.

Girls Series Books. Children's Literature Research Collection. Minneapolis: University of Minnesota Press, 1992.

Hancock, H. Irving. *The High School Freshmen*. Philadelphia: Altemus, 1910.

Jones, Dolores B. *An "Oliver Optic" Checklist*. Westport, Conn.: Greenwood Press, 1985.

Loewen, Solomon L. "Games and Entertainment in the Early Part of This Century." *Journal of the American Historical Society of Germans from Russia* 12, no. 1 (1989):33–38.

May, Lary. *Screening Out the Past: The Birth of Mass Culture and the Motion Picture Industry*. New York: Oxford University Press, 1980.

Nasaw, David. "Children and Commercial Culture: Moving Pictures in the Early Twentieth Century." In *Small Worlds: Children and Adolescents in America, 1850–1950*, ed. Elliott West and Paula Petrik. Lawrence: University Press of Kansas, 1992.

——. *Children of the City*. Garden City, N.J.: Anchor Press/Doubleday, 1985.

——. *Going Out: The Rise and Fall of Public Amusements*. New York: Basic Books, 1993.

Nilsen, Alleen Pace, and Ken Donelson, eds. *Literature for Today's Young Adults*. 4th ed. New York: HarperCollins, 1993.

Oursler, Will. *The Boy Scout Story*. Garden City, N.Y.: Doubleday, 1955.

Scharnhorst, Gary, with Jack Bates. *The Lost Life of Horatio Alger Jr.* Bloomington: Indiana University Press, 1985.

Slide, Anthony. *The Encyclopedia of Vaudeville*. Westport, Conn.: Greenwood Press, 1994.

Smith, E. A. *American Youth Culture*. New York: Free Press of Glencoe, 1962.

Smith, Jane. "Plucky Little Ladies and Stout-Hearted Chums: Serial Novels for Girls, 1900–1920." In *Prospects: An Annual of American Cultural Studies*, vol. 3, ed. Jack Saltzman, 155–174. New York: Burt Franklin and Co., 1978.

Spargo, John. *The Bitter Cry of the Children* (1906). New York: Quadrangle Books, 1968.

Stearns, Marshall, and Jean Stearns. *Jazz Dance*. New York: Da Capo Press, 1994.

Tarkington, Booth. *Seventeen*. New York: Harper Bros., 1915.

Wallechinsky, David, ed. *The People's Almanac Presents the Twentieth Century*. Boston: Little, Brown, 1995.

West, Elliott. *Growing Up in Twentieth Century America*. Westport, Conn.: Greenwood Press, 1996.

West, Mark I. *Children, Culture, and Controversy*. Hamden, Conn: Archon, 1988.

Wiles, Jon, and Joseph Bondi. *The Essential Middle School*. 2d ed. New York: Macmillan, 1993.

• 2 •

The 1920s

The Twenties . . . the Jazz Age . . . Flaming Youth . . . these labels evoke excitement and change, fabulous wealth and wild parties, the romance of F. Scott Fitzgerald's *The Great Gatsby*. They conjure up images of fashionable young men and women dancing the Charleston and drinking bathtub gin, living in the careless leisure of the moment. This was the decade when the young came into their own—when everyone wanted to be young.

But it was a decade of dramatic contrasts too. The liberal ideas of psychoanalyst Sigmund Freud disturbed the moral and religious conservatism of many citizens; the peace after World War I was marred by racial prejudice; the "noble experiment" of Prohibition against the sale of alcoholic beverages, which began as a triumph for the reformers, led countless Americans to defy the law openly; and the economic boom turned into bust. Teens were both participants in and symbols of these struggles.

POLITICS AND NATIONAL EVENTS

Although the peace following World War I was welcome, it was an uneasy one at best. America's hostile encounter with other nations had made many Americans even more leery of foreigners than before. At first they feared sabotage, especially by the Russian Bolsheviks, whose philosophy of revolution and abolition of private ownership ran exactly counter to American ideals. With V. I. Lenin's triumph in Russia, his party firmly in power, and his efforts to create economic stability and greater prosperity for Russia's peasants gaining international attention, the voices of communism and anarchy spoke out more clearly in the West, and many Americans believed that the goal of the Communists was to take over the government in Washington, D.C., and install Communist rule.

Sacco and Vanzetti

Fears of Bolshevik sabotage set the stage for the famous trial of two Italian immigrants and admitted anarchists who were arrested for the April 15, 1920, murder of a paymaster and guard in Massachusetts. Nicola Sacco worked in a shoe factory and Bartolomeo Vanzetti peddled fish; both had alibis for the time of the murder, but their status as foreigners and their anarchist leanings prompted the prosecution to produce trumped-up and doctored evidence of their guilt and to suppress evidence of their innocence. Found guilty in 1921, Sacco and Vanzetti continued to attract attention as many prominent writers, attorneys, and public figures spoke out in their behalf, pleading for justice and deploring the conduct of the trial and its judge. Judge Webster Thayer was adamant, however, and he sentenced the two to be executed by electrocution, a sentence that was carried out in August 1927. The case continues to be a well-known example of how the American judicial system can be swayed by prejudice and fear.

Racial Fear and Pride

Some Americans were looking closer to home for trouble. The revived Ku Klux Klan had an estimated 4 million members by 1924, although membership in a secret organization is probably always greater than the estimate. Most members apparently lived in the North Central states—Illinois, Indiana, and Ohio—rather than in the South. They continued to carry out cross burnings, lynchings, and other acts of violence against any perceived immorality, not only racial trespassing.

One black man, however, rallied his people with a message of pride and hope. In 1916 Marcus Garvey had founded the United Negro Improvement Association (UNIA), calling for racial separation and urging "Africa for the Africans"; by the early Twenties, he had attracted many thousands of members in many countries. The National Association for the Advancement of Colored People (NAACP), an organization devoted to integration, felt threatened by Garvey's message and his appeal. When the Klan threatened Garvey's followers around the country, Garvey, believing he could deal with these threats by negotiation, met with a Klan leader in Atlanta in 1922 to explain their similar aims of racial separation. This meeting dismayed members of Garvey's UNIA as well as outsiders, and soon his movement was in serious trouble. In 1923 Garvey was found guilty of mail fraud and sentenced to five years in jail; President Calvin Coolidge released him after two years, but the damage to his organization was irreparable and he died almost unknown in 1940.

Business and Politics

Republican President Warren Harding, who in 1920 had won a popular vote of landslide proportions, faced a scandal in his administration early in the decade when his secretary of the interior arranged the private lease of some U.S. Naval oil reserves in Wyoming in an area known as "Teapot Dome," and then privately profited from the deal. Harding remained a very popular president, however, and when he died unexpectedly in office in 1923, the nation mourned. His vice president, the famously taciturn Calvin Coolidge, rode this crest of popular approval, won election for himself in 1924, and with his motto of "The business of America is business" presided over unprecedented American prosperity. Auto manufacturing and owner-ship soared, business mergers guaranteed greater profits to shareholders, factories became ever more efficient and flooded the market with goods, and advertising created an ever greater desire for all manner of comforts and luxuries. The best-selling nonfiction book of 1926 literally glorified the role of the advertiser and businessman; *The Man Nobody Knows*, by Bruce Barton, which retells the story of Christ in business terms, avows that Jesus Christ's real mission was selling. Americans, more of whom lived in cities than on farms for the first time in our history, began buying goods on credit and investing their savings in the stock market; the number of professional brokers multiplied to meet the demand. French pharmacist and self-help guru Emile Coué toured the country to popular acclaim, advising people to say to themselves twenty times each morning and evening, "Day by day, in every way, I am getting better and better," words which seemed magically to come true for many in the rising middle and upper classes.

Those who remained on farms, and those who toiled in the factories to create the goods other Americans could pay for, fared less well. Farmers, whose prices had been supported by government subsidy during the war, watched their profits plummet when the subsidies were withdrawn and bumper crops saturated the market. The year 1919 saw an unusual number of strikes by trade unions as unemployment rose to 10%, but the association of the unions with communism created a distrust that caused membership to fall throughout the decade, weakening the power of the unions to effect good working conditions for all.

Two Sensational Trials

Leopold and Loeb

Three of the decade's most famous teens were involved in one of its most sensational trials. Nathan Leopold, age nineteen, and his friend Richard

Loeb, age eighteen, were arrested in 1924 for the brutal murder of fourteen-year-old Bobby Franks, son of a wealthy Chicago businessman. Leopold and Loeb, who were also wealthy and privileged, as well as phenomenally intelligent, had graduated from prestigious universities, and Leopold, who was in law school, was already a recognized ornithologist. At first the police and the public could not believe in their guilt, much less understand their motivation, but when the evidence against them mounted, they both confessed. Their motivation was to commit the perfect crime and they had chosen Bobby at random to be their victim. Persuaded by their reading of Friedrich Nietzsche's theories about "supermen," they planned and executed their crime believing the body would never be discovered and that they would never be caught. They were, in fact, caught within ten days of the murder.

Into the scene of the public outcry over the "thrill killers" stepped America's most famous defense attorney, Clarence Darrow, who was determined to see to it that the boys received a fair trial but who also wished to test the death penalty in Illinois. He mounted an eloquent defense of Leopold and Loeb, pleading them guilty and emotionally handicapped but not insane. Using the theories of Sigmund Freud, Darrow asserted that, despite their wealth, the boys had not been happy children and that their fantasy lives had blurred their grasp of reality. He raised the issues of their homosexual attachment to each other (women were barred from the courtroom during this phase of the trial) and their earlier minor criminal acts. The trial lasted a month, during which it dominated the public media with the spectacle of two thrill-seeking teens, or two guilty but pathetic teens, depending on one's viewpoint. In his summation, Darrow stated that executing them would be a barbaric act, not fit for a civilized nation. The judge (Darrow's guilty plea had avoided a jury trial) sentenced each of the boys to life imprisonment for murder, plus ninety-nine years for kidnapping. The boys' youth was a deciding factor in the judge's decision. Richard Loeb died in prison a few years later when he was stabbed by an inmate. Nathan Leopold lived many years in prison, but he was eventually paroled; he died at the age of sixty-six.

Scopes Trial

Clarence Darrow also defended the most famous high school teacher of the decade, perhaps of the century. The year was 1925. Tennessee had just passed the Butler Act, which forbade the teaching of evolution in the public schools, and the American Civil Liberties Union (ACLU), which Darrow helped found, was eager to test the law's constitutionality. In Dayton, Tennessee, a small town near Chattanooga known for its Fundamentalist Christian citizens, John Scopes agreed to help the ACLU. A quiet young teacher at Central High, Scopes did not teach biology—he coached sports and taught other subjects—but he was interested in science and arranged to tutor three high school students in biology, making sure that the subject of evolution was broached. He was duly arrested for violating Tennessee law. In the heat of a Tennessee July, a jury was selected and the famous Monkey Trial began.

Clarence Darrow, a religious agnostic who deplored Fundamentalism, appeared for the defense, taking no fee for his services. The prosecution was conducted by the famous orator and public figure William Jennings Bryan, a devout Christian. These two giants of oratory, using every tactic in their verbal arsenal, attracted hoards of reporters and observers to the little town and its sweltering courtroom. A Chicago radio station broadcast the trial to a huge listening audience—something never before possible, or even imaginable. Scopes himself sat quietly by; the law, not he, was on trial.

After several days, Darrow surprised the spectators by calling Bryan to the stand to question him on the literal interpretation of the Bible. Bryan held to his belief that the Bible was to be taken as the literal truth, but Darrow questioned him closely about certain Biblical truths such as the six-day creation of the earth: how long was a day then? Under such scrutiny, Bryan appeared increasingly foolish; finally both sides retired exhausted and turned the case over to the jury. The jury deliberated only a few minutes before bringing back a guilty verdict, which meant that the case could be appealed. Scopes's conviction was overturned a short time later in an appeals court; he left Dayton and lived a quiet life thereafter. The law remained on the Tennessee books until 1967 but underwent no further tests. William Jennings Bryan, stunned and ultimately defeated, died of a heart attack a few days after the trial ended.

Prohibition

The decade of the Twenties in America is famous the world over for its unique venture into the Eighteenth Constitutional amendment, which prohibited the "manufacture, sale, or transportation of intoxicating liquors" within the United States as well as from without. No other country except Finland has tried to legislate against alcohol on a national level. Finland's experiment, carried out during the same decade, was also a failure.

In the United States, a complex blend of political and social forces, with their roots deep in the nineteenth century, led to Prohibition. One of these forces was the Protestant religions. Evangelical and missionary fervor, fanned by revivals that denounced strong drink as evil and degrading to body and soul, urged first temperance—the limited and responsible use of alcohol— and then complete abstinence. Another element was the fear and distrust of immigrant populations. The Irish and Italians, stereotyped as enjoyers of alcohol, seemed especially threatening; efforts to "Americanize" them often took the form of preaching to them about the evils of strong drink and intoxication. The cities, too, were in themselves threatening to those who stayed in towns and villages; they believed increasingly that city life with its crowding, materialism, and multiple temptations to shallow thrills and sin would, if unchecked, be the ruin of America, especially of its unprotected young.

The Eighteenth Amendment, which went into effect on January 16, 1920, was immediately under fire from opponents, violated by the general population, and seldom enforced with any consistency or efficiency. Although whether the actual amount of alcohol consumed in the United States went up during Prohibition is an open question, drinking certainly appeared to increase because of the attention focused on it. Bootlegging became a lucrative occupation for many, especially for the infamous Al Capone, the Chicago racketeer who is said to have made over $100 million in profits from his illegal businesses.

As illegal liquor became more expensive, those who could not afford it tried making their own gin and whiskey (sometimes called "bathtub gin," although it was not really made in bathtubs) occasionally with deadly results. Those who could afford it went to speakeasies, hidden bars and lounges where a whispered word at the door was required for admittance. The spectacle of widespread lawbreaking by average citizens, not to mention the gang wars and rackets resulting from bootlegging, persuaded many Americans that the "noble experiment" should be abandoned. When a full-fledged economic depression arrived in 1933, both houses of Congress proposed the Twenty-first Amendment, which repealed the Eighteenth. It was ratified in December of that year—a remarkable example of government efficiency— and a strange, complicated era in American history came to an end.

Two Flyers: Mitchell and Lindbergh

The excitement and daring of flight focused public attention on the men and women who flew the planes; their exotic expertise, their freedom from earth, their casual acceptance of the daily risk of death made them romantic and heroic figures especially to teen boys. During the Twenties, one famous flyer was humiliated by his peers yet became a prophet for American airpower. The other became the greatest symbol of American bravery and know-how in the decade, capturing the popular imagination as no twentieth-century hero had before.

At age nineteen Billy Mitchell left college and enlisted as a private in the U.S. Army. He was assigned to the aviation section of the Signal Corps in 1915 and took flying lessons on his own time. By 1918 he was commanding hundreds of U.S. and French planes during World War I in Europe, bombing enemy targets aggressively and winning a promotion to brigadier general for his military success. Afterward, in Washington, D.C., as assistant chief of the Air Service, he began to advocate an independent U.S. Air Force. His superiors in the Army and Navy found him insubordinate and, sending him off to San Antonio demoted to colonel, hoped to silence his criticism of the military hierarchy.

They did not reckon with his determination; he continued to write and speak his views. After a Navy dirigible crashed in September 1925, Mitchell publicly accused the Navy and the War Department of incompetency, negligence, and "official stupidity." The military response was a court-martial in which Mitchell was tried by thirteen officers, none of whom had ever flown. Despite defense testimony by famous aviators, Mitchell was found guilty of conduct that "brought discredit on the military service" and suspended from rank and duty for five years. He resigned from the service early in 1926.

In the Twenties, Mitchell predicted that the airplane would surpass the battleship as an instrument of war; he predicted that Alaska would become strategically important; and he predicted that the Pacific Fleet at Pearl Harbor was vulnerable to enemy attack. Most significant of all, he predicted the importance of an independent Air Force. All these predictions came true, but Mitchell did not live to see them. He died in 1936, before World War II proved him right.

Charles Lindbergh, in contrast, was showered with an outpouring of love and admiration by the American public. Like many teens who fell in love with airplanes, Lindbergh left college to learn to fly and soon bought his own Curtiss *Jenny*. He tried barnstorming and wing-walking and became an air-mail pilot in 1926. The shy twenty-five-year-old, nicknamed "Lucky Lindy" after surviving a parachute accident, began seeking financial backers to make a run at the $25,000 Orteig prize offered to the aviator making the first nonstop flight from New York to Paris. Several other, more experienced pilots had died trying, but Lindbergh persisted and finally persuaded the Saint Louis *Globe-Democrat* newspaper, along with some businessmen, to fund his flight. Moreover, he volunteered to fly solo.

Lindbergh chose a modified monoplane built by the Ryan Aircraft Company; his backers named it *The Spirit of St. Louis*. The wings were lengthened, and a huge fuel tank was installed, leaving no room for a windscreen. To save weight, Lindbergh had a wicker chair installed instead of a regular pilot's seat, and he refused to carry a radio. He took off in the rain from New York's Roosevelt field on May 29, 1927, a little before 8 A.M.; at 10:22 P.M. on May 21, at Le Bourget Airport outside Paris, his little plane landed safely, after thirty-three and a half hours of continuous flying and a constant struggle to stay awake.

Paris went wild. More than 100,000 people, who had waited into the night at the airport with alternating optimism and despair, rushed his plane and carried Lindbergh out of the cockpit onto their shoulders. Many more thousands, hearing of his success, headed for the airport, creating the largest traffic jam in French history. When they arrived, they surrounded the small building where the exhausted Lindbergh was recovering. When he returned to America, he was unprepared for the even greater public excitement that surrounded him. Letters, telegrams, parades, pleas from the press for interviews and films—all the trappings of sudden and incredible fame—invaded his private life. He had gone literally overnight from an obscure Minnesota mail pilot to an international hero, a symbol of hope and success for millions. With crime, speakeasies, wild flappers, and dissolute college boys dominating the media, America's image needed a lift, and Lindbergh provided it. He seemed, with his Midwestern modesty, his shy youthfulness, and his famously tousled hair, to represent all that was innocent and good about America.

Stock Market Crash of 1929

Since the middle years of the decade, some business analysts had predicted that stock prices, having reached an incredible high, could not hold steady. The mood of optimism continued, as the promise of easy wealth lured more and more investors to the market, driving prices to new highs. However, by 1929, the analysts' warnings had apparently persuaded some speculators that it was time to cash in. On a windy, cool October 24, 1929, which later came to be called Black Thursday, the market opened down a little; by 11:00 A.M., it was obvious something was seriously wrong. Brokers were selling; no one was buying. As prices dropped and still no one bought, brokers and market watchers began to panic. The ticker-tape machines which announced prices of individual stocks and their activity could not keep pace with the speed at which prices were falling. The increasing delay caused further panic since the brokers could not tell what was happening. By noon the worst had happened. Outside on Wall Street, reporters began to gather, watching as stunned investors tried to assess their losses. Many discovered that they were not only broke but in debt as well. One group of bankers met quickly to try to supply a cushion of money to prop up the market with their buying power, but it was too little too late. On Tuesday, October 29, a few optimistic brokers again tried selling, but again there were no buyers. According to Janet McDonnell, the speculators had finally run out of luck. Sales of household goods and cars had already declined, the construction industry was experiencing trouble, unemployment was rising, and people were saving rather than spending. If Wall Street investors had heeded these warning signs, a recession rather than a crash might have been the result. Unfortunately, they behaved as if the boom could last (McDonnell 1995, 415–417). Although the popular notion of many failed businessmen jumping out of Wall Street windows to their deaths is an exaggeration, the emotional consequences were almost as severe as the financial ones. Fortunes were lost in a few days, and the nation's optimism went with them.

TEENS AT HOME

One of the most visible results of the economic boom of the early Twenties was emergence of the suburbs. As automobiles became more affordable and building materials cheaper, the number of single-family dwellings outside the central urban areas increased dramatically. One estimate suggests that more than twice as many new houses were begun every year between 1922 and 1929 than at any other comparable previous time (West 1996, 101).

A new standard of living was now possible for middle- and working-class families. Vacuum cleaners, good quality plumbing, and Frigidaire refrigerators, which now could make ice cubes, all became accepted parts of middle-class family life, along with fresh fruits and vegetables at local markets, provided by train and by truck on the rapidly improving road system. Even more desirable for many were the new processed foods: bread already baked and sliced (at about 12 cents a loaf), milk in bottles (17 cents), canned soups, frozen vegetables, peanut butter and breakfast cereals—Kellogg's Corn Flakes, Kellogg's Rice Krispies, and Post Grape-Nuts. Life expectancy increased with these healthful foods, and the women who entered the workforce appreciated their convenience. Not all foods were healthful, however; teens could enjoy some of the junk food they still eat today: Butterfinger candy bars, Milky Way bars, and Wrigley's gum.

Radio

The new home appliance that affected the way in which Americans lived in the Twenties most was the radio. Experimenters had for years been developing the technology of radio, but most historians place the beginning of the radio age in America in November of 1920, when Pittsburgh entrepreneur Frank Conrad broadcast the election returns from his new radio station KDKA. By 1924 there were five million radios in American homes (West 1996, 89) with the number growing yearly; it had become a national obsession. Those who could afford them bought elegant, wood-encased radios, but many tuned in on homemade crystal sets with headphones, which could be afforded even by poor families in isolated regions of the country. Teens in Oregon could make their own radios and listen to the same music and sports events as those in New York. Alone, with friends, or with their whole families gathered around their sets in the evenings, they cheered on their favorite boxer and heard the latest tunes. Among farm families in Wisconsin and Illinois, individual radio ownership lagged behind that of city dwellers, but listening to the national broadcasts was a pleasurable and unifying community activity.

Radio homogenized American popular culture as had no phenomenon before, but the racial stereotyping that seems to permeate American life dominated early radio as well. In 1929 NBC began airing a fifteen-minute comedy show about two Chicago black men who were always in some kind of trouble; soon *Amos 'n' Andy* was a national phenomenon that was heard throughout the country and in rural communities by adults, teens, and children alike, even in department stores and restaurants. Well into the thirties and forties, despite protests by black Americans, 7 P.M. was *Amos 'n' Andy* time in millions of homes.

Comic Strips

Like the radio, the daily comic pages were a remarkable unifying force in American life in the Twenties, shared by all family members at all socioeconomic levels throughout the country. Begun around the turn of the century and carried—thanks to syndication—by all the popular newpapers, several strips reflected even more than radio the remarkable social changes that marked the decade. Some, the gag strips, focused on a single joke in the last of four panels; others offered more serious narrative lines that continued for days or weeks.

A typical late 1920s comic page in, for example, the *New York American* or the *San Francisco Examiner* carried several of the most popular gag strips and story strips. "Barney Google," with his "googly" eyes, was the poor little guy everyone picked on; he invented the term "heebie-jeebies" and later teamed up with his hillbilly buddy, Snuffy Smith. "Mutt and Jeff," the tall guy and the short guy, often appeared with recognizable people from the news. "Bringing Up Father" followed the bumbling Jiggs, a newly minted millionaire who just wanted to enjoy his humble Irish roots, while his domineering wife, Maggie, a stylish flapper, tried to make him more genteel. "Krazy Kat," hopelessly in love with Ignatz the Mouse, every day got beaned with a brick for his troubles, even when Offissa Pup put Ignatz in jail. This strip, drawn by George Herriman until his death in 1944, was a remarkable comic strip, fascinating and highly respected even today for its word play and surreal settings.

Just as the radio soon had its soap operas—daily fifteen-minute family dramas sponsored by soap companies—the comic strips had their more serious side. "Little Orphan Annie" first appeared in 1924, with her pouf of red hair, her blank eyes, and her dog, Sandy; she took up residence with her millionaire friend Daddy Warbucks (who had gotten rich by selling arms) and met slumlords and crooks head on in her street-tough optimism. "Gasoline Alley" reflected the craze for cars in small-town life and the problems they brought. When the publisher complained that the strip might not appeal to women as much as men, artist Frank King commanded, in 1921, to "Get a baby in there fast!" The bachelor character Walt Wallet soon found a baby on his doorstep (Harvey 1995, 49). The baby was named

Skeezix, and as he grew, the other characters aged—an innovative touch that is still unusual in the comic-strip world. Both "Little Orphan Annie" and "Gasoline Alley" achieved phenomenal popularity and continued into the last decade of the century.

The strips also recognized women's new freedom to vote, smoke in public, abandon their corsets and stays, shorten their skirts, and go to work. "Tillie the Toiler," which first appeared in 1921, was about a lovely flapper who longed for a handsome escort but was constantly courted by the homely Mac; "Winnie Winkle," with her bobbed hair and fashionable outfits, frequently had to cope with her pesky little brother, Perry. "Betty Boop" began life in the movie cartoons but quickly moved to the comic-strip page where she played a sweet, silly, sexy movie star.

The first of the few comic strips in the century to recognize teens as a separate group was "Harold Teen," first drawn in 1919 by Carl Ed (pronounced "Eed" according to Goulart in the *Encyclopedia of American Comics* 1990, 172). Although teen life—in the Twenties as in the Fifties—seemed impertinent, dissolute, or wild in the reality of the front page, in the fantasy of the comic page it was sweet and innocent. Harold and his friends may have dressed and talked in the latest jazz-age fashion, but they hung out at the soda fountain instead of the speakeasy and worried mostly about dates and money, very much as "Archie" and his pals did in the Fifties and still do today.

Family Dynamics

The configuration of families and the expectations Americans had of them were changing. Whereas, at least in the popular notion of the family, the father had been the undisputed head of the family and his authority unchallenged, popular magazine articles and books were now beginning to extol the virtues of a loving family, in which the father shared his power with others. Sociologists Robert and Helen Lynd confirmed such changes in their classic study of Muncie, Indiana, *Middletown* (1929). In one of their surveys, they asked teens to rank the most desirable traits in a father and in a mother. By far the most desirable trait in a father was "Spending time with his children, reading, talking, playing with them, etc." (Lynd and Lynd 1929, 524). Second was "Respecting his children's opinions." In contrast, a mother's most desirable trait, by a considerable margin, was "Being a good cook and housekeeper," and second was "Always having time to read, talk, go on picnics or play with her children."

In another survey, the Lynds asked teens to rank sources of disagreement with their parents. Both girls and boys ranked "the hour you get in at night" and the "number of times you go out on school nights" as the two most troublesome family issues. "The use of the automobile" was ranked fifth by boys and fourth by girls. "Your spending money" also ranked high for both genders. Items that were not on the Lynds' list but were added by the teens were even more revealing: smoking, drinking, dancing, riding in cars to other towns, and, for girls, "petting parties." Obviously, the new freedom was making itself felt in family tensions for many middle- and working-class teens. At the same time that families were seeking to become more intimate, loving, and accepting of each other, teens were finding opportunities and incentives to move away from their parents and family and affirm their independence with their peers.

TEENS AT WORK

This decade saw a major change in the number of teens in the workplace. In earlier decades, work was clearly valued more than school, in both rural and urban environments; teens were encouraged to work first and go to school later, if at all. Families needed the income their older (and sometimes their younger) children could provide. Urban children sought the validation and excitement, as well as the spending money, that work offered; rural teens as part of family economy did not earn wages but had the economic possibilities of land ownership and management when they grew older.

During the Twenties, however, the situation changed. In 1920, according to Elliott West, more than 51% of males aged between fourteen and nineteen and more than 8% of the children aged between ten and fifteen were employed. By the end of the decade, these numbers had fallen dramatically, and the number of young people attending school rose just as dramatically. As West points out, such figures may not be reliable, since the employment of the young is difficult to document (1996, 119), but the trend is clear.

The causes for the shift are multiple and complex. The economic boom in the cities caused by technological and manufacturing advances put a number of young people out of work. Young boys who once carried messages, for example, were replaced by the cheaper, more efficient telephone. As crop prices fell, rural teens sensed economic opportunity slipping away from them and migrated in larger numbers to the cities. In the Southern states, where employment of the young was always high relative to the rest of the country, young people still worked hard in the textile, tobacco, and farming industries, but in the Western states, a flood of immigrants, especially from Mexico and the Philippines, worked the large fruit and vegetable farms, where they accepted extremely low wages for their back-breaking labor. Many second-generation Mexican-American teen women in California found employment in canneries and clothing factories, or as seasonal farm laborers or domestic workers. Although many aspired to clerical positions, their ethnic appearance and background usually denied them those opportunities (Ruiz 1992, 65). African-American youths suffered from discrimination as well, finding all but the most menial jobs closed to them and good schooling often completely unavailable. In contrast, America's middle- and working-class white American teens were entering school in rapidly accelerating numbers. In "Middletown," the Lynds found that employment in factories for young men in their late teens was high relative to their proportion in the population; management preferred the quicker reflexes of the young to run the increasingly complicated machinery. A few teens took part-time jobs, and a small number left school at the legal age of fourteen for a variety of reasons, only a few of which concerned work. The importance of work, nevertheless, had been eclipsed by the importance of school in the lives of teens in "Middletown" as well as in most other parts of the country.

TEENS AT SCHOOL

Some of the most dramatic and long-lasting changes of the decade were made in the schools. Reforms in the politics of child labor, in sociological theories of the family, and in the concept of adolescence coalesced around reform of school, especially the secondary, or high, school. At this crucial time, while young people were still theoretically under the control of their parents and other adult figures but were also beginning to take part in some aspects of adulthood, such as working and driving a car, serious preparation for American life became the concern of states and local communities. Ironically, one of the results of these attempts to guide youth carefully into adulthood was the increasing involvement of teens in their own social sphere, where adults were neither invited nor welcome. This isolation was felt even more in college, where teens' isolation from their homes and families became not only social but physical, and where the peer culture dominated choices and values almost completely.

High School

Changes in the high school curriculum and social structure came with remarkable swiftness. By 1925 most of the courses and most of the structure of the high school day, as it has come to be most familiar, were in place in most schools. This was, however, still segregated America; black students in both North and South were mostly taught in poorly equipped schools with inferior equipment and old textbooks, despite the amenities available in white schools because of the economic boom.

Students' days were spent going from class to class, sitting in bolted-down seats in neat rows, being quiet and listening to the teacher, and giving back textbook information—snatching, as today, a few minutes of social chaos in the hallways during the change of classes. They took English, math, foreign languages, history, geography, and sciences in newly equipped laboratories. Teachers tended to rely on textbooks for information and expected students, by and large, to give back the text on tests. Most students took several achievement tests during their four years; the new emphasis on testing was part of the effort being made to standardize schooling and provide a basic education for all (although it raised more questions than it answered; see West 1996, 128–32).

However, students were also offered a range of options never before available in high schools. Vocational training for boys became an important addition to the curriculum during this decade; shop classes for metal work, auto mechanics, drafting, and office skills were edging aside more academic subjects in the competition for public dollars and support. It was important to prepare boys for jobs rather than college, especially among the middle classes where high school attendance was at an all-time high. Girls now took courses in home economics, where they learned about balanced meals, well-made clothing, and child care. They learned to be intelligent consumers; boys learned to make the goods consumed. In Middletown, the Lynds found that many parents worried that vocational courses were robbing their children of their college preparation, but the trend was nationwide.

Another national trend that characterized the decade was the teaching of American history and civics. History heretofore in the schools had been a broader subject, including European and ancient history as well as American. As more immigrant families spread across the nation, the need to assert the character of America as a unifying force made many believe the need for America-focused courses was urgent, especially courses that extolled citizenship and democracy. Americanization became the duty of both primary and high schools, especially when immigrant children lived in their communities, a situation especially acute in Western border states during the wave of immigration from Mexico during the 1920s. Many such students were forbidden to speak their native language in school; they were simply "immersed" in English and expected to learn it, and then learn their subjects in it, without any bilingual or English-as-a-second-language training. Immigrant teens sometimes found themselves assigned to a first-grade classroom with six- and seven-year-olds. Textbooks embedded messages about American hygiene, food, housing, clothing, and family structure into the language lessons, and teachers Americanized the names of their immigrant students. In an effort to acculturate Native Americans more quickly, teens and children were sometimes taken from their reservation schools and sent to boarding schools to learn American language, culture, and the religion of Christianity (West 1996, 134–40). Many of these attempts were well-intended. Reformers wished to open up more economic opportunities to such minorities, and occasionally they were successful. Just as often, however, the youth who underwent forcible acculturation felt more different, more isolated than before, and they turned inward to their own people and folkways for comfort and support.

During the Twenties, for the first time, school became the center of teen social life. The number of curriculum-related clubs began to decline as the number of social organizations and activities increased. Athletics, especially football, became the dominant unifying force for high school students; boosting the team was the duty of all students in all grades, and the athletes themselves were the stars of school life. The school mascot—whether Green Dragons, Bearcats, or something else—was the rallying symbol for all extracurricular activities, and athletic events took precedence over all other activities. The school year was designed primarily around games and practice times. The Lynds found that, in "Middletown," even the tradition of "chapel," the term for school convocations left over from a more religious structure, became on occasion "Pep chapel" (1929, 217). Segregation was still a force against the apparent unity, however. In the Lynds' "Middletown," Negro students were allowed "under protest" in the schools, but any school with a Negro on its basketball team could not play in the YMCA building where tournaments were held (479).

Such purely social clubs as there were took the form of fraternities and sororities, which schools often tried to outlaw because of their exclusive membership policies, their secrecy, and rumors of hazing. In any event, school itself had become the center of life for most teens, especially white middle- and upper-class teens. In previous generations, school was a place to go when teens were not working. In the Twenties, as the Lynds found, home became the place to go when a teen was not at high school (211).

College

College attendance shot up during the Twenties. By the end of the decade, according to the U.S. Bureau of Education, 12% of young people aged nineteen, twenty, twenty-one, and twenty-two were in school full-time (Fass 1977, 407). Many different kinds of colleges were available, from the elite Eastern single-gender schools, to Midwestern coeducational residential colleges, to junior colleges and Negro colleges. The dynamic African American Mary McLeod Bethune worked especially hard on behalf of Negro girls in Daytona, Florida; she was able to raise many dollars for her efforts, which culminated in the establishment of Bethune-Cookman College in 1925, a coeducational four-year college still active in Daytona Beach. The Lynds noticed that students from "Middletown" tended to choose colleges close to home, but the opportunities, especially for women, to experience new environments were opening up rapidly. No longer were they available only to the privileged few.

Once there, students experienced the freedom—and the difficulty—of an environment controlled largely by their peers rather than by adult authorities. Those who had gone to study and achieve academic success fell into the minority; most students, according to Paula Fass, spent less than half their time on studies or intellectual pursuits (1977, 173). Instead they enjoyed athletic and social activities and studied only when absolutely necessary to pass—and they encouraged others, especially freshmen, to do the same.

A group of sorority girls, State College, Pennsylvania, around 1920, wearing the latest fashions in bobbed hair. Reproduced courtesy of Jean Ann Holder.

Football became a national craze, and huge stadiums came to dominate many campuses; game weekends topped the student's social calendar.

Much campus social life, at large and small schools, was controlled by fraternities and sororities. Being chosen by a good fraternity (one with the most socially adept, wealthy boys, for example) was a formidable hurdle for many freshmen; to get in was to find a ready-made group of friends and comrades. Their rituals and symbols allied the new student with long-standing traditions, giving him an immediate identity in the chaos of college life. Getting in was easier if one had good looks, an easy-going personality, stylish clothes, and a car. It was also easier if one was white and a Gentile, although several national Jewish fraternities were already in place and black fraternities were beginning to be established on the nation's campuses. Black fraternities, however, were often prevented from joining a college's interfraternity organization (Fass 1977, 152–53).

For girls, the sorority provided the same haven along with the same rites of passage, as well as an informal but rigorous education in becoming a woman by Twenties standards. One researcher estimated there were between fifteen and twenty sororities on the campus of every coeducational college during the decade; at Indiana University, 220 girls lived in dormitories, while 600 girls lived in seventeen sorority houses (Rothman 1978, 181). Sororities were also restricted in their membership; they sought out girls with good families, manners, and style. Once chosen, a girl was taught by her comrades how to wear her hair, dress, play bridge, smoke, and dance—all of which aimed to make her a good companion for a fraternity boy and, ultimately, a good wife. "The college age is the mating age and many fine friendships ripen into love and marriage follows," said one woman dean (1978, 182). Another commented that the spirit of the sorority was "more important than any other influence in determining the moral character of our colleges" (183). Indeed, this was true, in that girls in sororities usually learned how to encourage a boy's sexual advances just so far and no farther.

The image of the college student in the Twenties was created in large measure by F. Scott Fitzgerald's best-selling first novel, published in 1920: *This Side of Paradise*. Popular with young readers throughout the decade, the semiautobiographical account of Fitzgerald's first years in college describes cutting classes, shoplifting, joyriding in cars, sleeping on the beach, petting, and getting drunk, as well as falling exquisitely and painfully in love, learning poetry, talking about life with friends, and experiencing the deepest loyalties and betrayals. Its portrayals of languishing students and wild flappers shocked many adults, as Fitzgerald probably wanted, but if they were an exaggeration, they also had a degree of truth that appealed to many teens of the decade, who were experiencing freedoms never before available to the young and reveling in the excitement of the Jazz Age.

FASHION

The "Flapper" or "Sheba"

The sweeping skirts, elaborate hats, and tight-waisted blouses of the fashionable ladies of the first two decades disappeared quickly early in the Twenties. As they entered the workplace, smoked and drank in public, and danced the Charleston to jazz music, women refused to be bound any longer by any tight underwear or binding dresses. The popular press called them "flappers," a word some said came from their fashion of wearing unfastened galoshes which "flapped" when they walked, or from the idea of young birds flapping their wings. The origin of the term is still mysterious, but it certainly referred to a fashionable teenage girl with a certain look; if she was an especially beautiful and sexy flapper, she was a "sheba."

Her clothes revealed her new freedom and sexuality. Necklines were lowered and softened even on daytime dresses and blouses, sleeves disappeared for evening, waistlines dropped to an easy slimness around the hips, skirts shortened even for evening to reveal the ankles and calves, and stockings were rolled down to reveal bare knees. Favored fabrics for the popular short, loose dresses were floating and sheer, occasionally with heavy beading on evening dresses, which were sometimes completely backless and softly draped. Tight cloche (or bell-shaped) hats, ropes of long beads, and low-heeled pumps with a shaped Cuban heel completed the look. Many women and girls dieted to achieve the boyish, flat-chested, slim-hipped body required by the clothes. Winter coats also lost their waists, their length and bulky fabrics creating a kind of "tubular" look. According to fashion scholar Alison Lurie, "Thousands of women entered the second decade of the twentieth century shaped like hourglasses, and came out of it shaped like rolls of carpet" (Lurie 1981, 73). On the other hand, the one-piece bathing suit, a very revealing garment, appeared for the first time. Only the daring wore it at first, but it promised more freedom for women in physical sports. Daring, active women also tried bloomers or knickers for sporting occasions.

An even more dramatic change took place in hairstyles. Instead of long hair, worn down for day or piled high in the evening, girls began to "bob" their hair, cutting it short and straight across the back and sometimes plastering it into curls very close to the head or with a single curl in the middle of the forehead. Bobbed hair became a symbol of rebellion for many girls of the day, who deliberately shocked their parents by going to the beauty parlor to get the new style. Some girls even cut their hair in the more exaggerated Eton style, very much like a boy's with a shaved neckline in back and hair falling over the face in front. The new styles required more trips to the hairdresser, and the number of beauty parlors skyrocketed; in New York City between 1922 and 1927, the number grew from 750 to 3,500 (Rothman 1978, 186).

Women and girls also wore more cosmetics than ever before. In earlier decades, a "painted" woman was automatically an immoral one. During the Twenties, mascaraed lashes, face powder, rouge, and red lipstick appeared on most women and girls who wanted to appear fashionable. They often plucked their eyebrows into a high arch, like the film stars of the decade, and used lipstick to shape their lips into a "beestung" look—tiny and pouting.

Such artifice, like bobbed hair, caused many arguments between teens and their parents, and how girls appeared at high school became a source of contention. Paula Fass quotes a seventeen-year-old girl who complained that just a little rouge and a slightly shorter skirt made her parents think she was "indecent" when she was really "a nice girl" and wearing the same things her friends wore (Fass 1977, 284). One "Middletown" teen boy warned his mother that if his younger sister did not wear silk stockings to high school instead of the unfashionable lisle ones she had been made to wear, none of the boys would pay any attention to her (Lynd and Lynd 1929, 163). For their part, parents worried about the expense of the new emphasis on fashion, and some schools tried to enforce dress codes. In one Ohio high school, a girls' social club instituted their own regulations: no sheer fabrics, silk stockings, makeup, or "transparent sweaters worn without waists" (i.e., without a camisole under them) (Fass 1977, 216). Obviously, some girls were indeed wearing those things to school.

Many have commented on the combination of boyishness and sex appeal in the flapper style. Certainly it did flaunt the combination of youth and sex in a way never before seen in girls and women. Lurie, however, asserts that the style was less boyish than childlike; the dropped-waist blouses and Mary Jane shoes with their round toes and straps over the arch that were stylish in the Twenties had been worn by children in earlier decades. Was the young flapper displaying her sexuality and at the same time keeping real sexual activity at bay by looking like a child? This same question would be raised about the model Twiggy in the Sixties and again in the Nineties about model Kate Moss.

The "Sheik"

Rudolph Valentino's exotic appearance and manner in the 1921 movie *The Sheik* became the ideal for fashionable young men in the Twenties, and, like young women, men adopted styles that enhanced their youth. Beards and mustaches disappeared; shoulders and waists became slimmer and clothes were tightened through the middle; and collars softened and were worn open. Boys still wore knickers into their early teens, but when they chose their long pants, the fit was looser. The new popularity of golf and tennis caused many young men to adopt the distinctive styles of sport clothing whether they played the sports or not. Loose white flannel trousers, very wide in the leg (it would be a few years before men played tennis in shorts), sleeveless V-necked sweaters worn over open-collared shirts with cuffs turned up, and wing-tip shoes were a kind of uniform for the elegant young men of the day, who might also wear golfing knickers with a striped sweater on other days. Hair was trimmed short and often parted in the middle. The raccoon fur coat, big and bulky, was fashionable wear for college boys who could afford it.

The image of the sheik with his flapper was popularized in drawings by John Held, Jr. His amusing caricatures, some of which appeared on the cover of *Life* magazine, caught the flavor of the fashion that distinguished the Jazz Age. A 1925 cartoon of young people at a fraternity party captured exactly what was so appealing, and so disturbing, to many about the new style of dress and the behavior that went with it (see Mizener 1972, 51). In it, several stylish young couples in evening dress are sitting on the stairs of a fraternity house, openly kissing and embracing while the girls' short skirts creep well above their open knees and the tops of their stockings become clearly visible, yet the girls and boys look completely relaxed and innocent. The cartoon is titled, perhaps ironically, "The Dance-Mad Younger Set." Though none of the young people are dancing, the energy of the drawing lets us imagine the uninhibited jazz that provided the accompaniment to their easygoing embraces.

SLANG

The Twenties, with its explosion of youth culture, saw an accompanying explosion of slang. As in every decade, it identified those who were part of that culture and excluded those who were not. The sheer number of slang expressions associated with American teen life, and their originality and exuberance, would not be matched again until the Fifties and Sixties. One of the charms of the "Harold Teen" comic strip was its dialogue; it provided an easy lesson in the teen vernacular. The decade even saw the publication of slang dictionaries to translate the latest wordplay for the uninitiated.

A good-looking, regular guy was a sheik or a jazzbo; if he dressed especially well, he was Brooksey (from Brooks Brothers clothes). If he especially liked women, he was a lounge lizard, and he probably liked to pet or neck. He would never be a four-flusher (cheat) or leave a girl to hoof it (walk) home. A good looking girl was a sheba. She might also be the berries, your sweet patootie, the cat's pajamas, or the bee's knees. If a sheik tried to flirt with her when she was not interested, she might say, "Applesauce!" or "So's your anchovie."

One of the worst insults was to call someone "wet"; it meant completely dull, unfashionable, boring. Hooch was only one of a multitude of words for alcohol, and as always, there were many words for getting drunk: pie-eyed, ossified, oiled, crocked, polluted, and so on. An unattractive girl was a dumdora, oil can, flat tire, or pickle; an unattractive man was a grummy ostrich, parlor hound, or porcupine. Money might be jack or shekels. Something really good was swell, and something really funny was a hoot.

LEISURE ACTIVITIES AND ENTERTAINMENT

With economic good times came more money available for having fun, especially for teens in towns and cities; rural teens, dependent on the family farm income, had a harder time, but by the end of the decade they too found ways to enjoy movies and dancing. For younger teens in places like "Middletown," traditional forms of leisure were still part of their lives. They enjoyed school sports, community events, church activities, and reading books and magazines. Older teens, with access to automobiles and perhaps the independence available on a college campus, savored their new freedom and privacy by abandoning the kinds of group socializing that characterized teen life in earlier decades for the date and the possibility of sexual experimentation it offered.

The Car

The rapid growth of the automobile industry and the phenomenal rise in automobile ownership during the Twenties offered visible proof of the economic boom being enjoyed by the country. It revolutionized the family budget and the family time. In the Lynds' famous *Middletown* study, some residents said they preferred a car to indoor plumbing; others said they would give up food and new clothes before they would give up their automobiles (1929, 255–56). Weekends and free time were spent driving, instead of walking or visiting nearby neighbors or relatives. Real vacations became possible as families piled into the car to visit towns that had been inaccessible to them. In rural areas, the car did not so much change the basic pattern of life as expand it. Maintaining a network of friends and relatives was still the most important element of social interaction; the automobile made it possible to visit those farther away.

The freedom experienced by teens in their cars was unprecedented, and it frightened adults. Families learned that their teen children would rather go driving or do something else with their friends than join the family in the car, and no longer did parents become as easily or quickly acquainted with their children's friends, which raised a whole new set of moral problems. Courtship moved from the front parlor to the automobile; in "Middletown" in 1924, the "sex crimes" committed by nineteen girls in juvenile court took place in automobiles (Lynd and Lynd 1929, 258). The Lynds offer a revealing anecdote about a Sunday School teacher who was giving a lesson on temptation to a group of working-class boys and girls in their late teens: "Can you think of any temptation we have today that Jesus didn't have?" A boy's quick response was, "Speed!" Speeding and car stealing were on the increase in "Middletown," a manifestation of the "motor insanity" that dominated the Twenties (1929, 258).

Teens who went to college found that having or not having a car made a considerable difference in one's social life. Fraternities especially sought young men who had cars; sorority girls listed a car as among the most desirable traits in a date. Fass's important sociological study of college students in the Twenties, *The Damned and the Beautiful*, explores the issues on campuses through student newspapers; one of the most pervasive from Princeton to UCLA was conflict over cars. Students either had cars or wanted them, and in assertions of their personal liberty they often used them to escape the controlled environment of the campus. Administrators tried various prohibitions and bans on them, partly because of traffic jams and parking problems but mostly because in their eyes cars encouraged immorality (Fass 1977, 485). To many, the automobile represented all the changes in teen moral values—smoking, drinking, sexual experimentation, rejection of the family in favor of peers—that emerged in the Twenties.

Dating and Sex

The decade of the Twenties marked the first time the term "date" was used in its popular sense: an occasion where a boy asked a girl to join him for an afternoon's or evening's outing, for which he generally paid. It was not group activity, and it was not courtship, but something different from both. More important, it was created and maintained by teens themselves, especially middle-class girls, who viewed it as important to popularity and ultimately to marriage but who, by the Twenties, needed more than holding hands in the parental sitting room. The date was, by its very nature, away from home, away from chaperonage, yet the girl was also protected to some degree by the rituals surrounding it.

The automobile and the telephone made the system possible, not to mention spending money. The boy was to initiate the encounter and to provide the funds and the transportation, to dress appropriately, and to be courteous and considerate. He was not to offer sexual advances too quickly, although he should give the girl the sense that he finds her attractive. The girl was to dress as attractively as possible, to be pleasant and amenable to the boy and his friends, to make conversation, to dance well, and to take responsibility for limiting sexual behavior. "The date, as a bargain, was unromantic but affectionate. In dating, *style* mattered a great deal. Performance was far more important than the unmediated expression of feelings" (Modell 1989, 96).

For high school teens, dating behavior was somewhat constrained by the proximity to home; college teens had the freedom of the fraternity house, where they could drink, smoke, talk freely, and engage in sexual behavior with fewer constraints. The "petting party" was the most notorious arena for testing sexual feelings and responses. During the decade necking came to refer to ardent and prolonged kissing, while petting described many kinds of erotic activity, but usually referred to caresses and fondling below the neck. At petting parties, where couples engaged in these activities with other couples nearby, the group nature of the event provided automatic limits on how far to go. Although girls and boys might feel pressure to engage in petting, the parties allowed them to experiment in relative safety. Data on sexual behavior among teens in the decade is almost nonexistent, since taboos on adults speaking frankly to the young about such matters were still largely operative, but popular evidence suggests that most teens petted to some degree. The old notion of "nice girls don't" had apparently disappeared. Rosalind, the perfect flapper in Fitzgerald's *This Side of Paradise*, responds to a suitor who thought she was "won" because he kissed her:

Those days are over. I have to be won all over again every time you see me . . . There used to be two kinds of kisses: First when girls were kissed and deserted; second, when they were engaged. Now there's a third kind, where the man is kissed and deserted. If Mr. Jones of the nineties bragged he'd kissed a girl, every one knew he was through with her. If Mr. Jones of 1919 brags the same every one knows it's because he can't kiss her any more. Given a decent start any girl can beat a man nowadays. (1920, 181)

Fass comments that there were still "two kinds of women" in college in the Twenties, but the difference was no longer between "sexual and non-sexual" women but between "sexual women who lived by the rules and those who did not" (1977, 264). According to John Modell, the same was true for high school teens (1989, 87). The "rules" apparently meant that beyond petting, or perhaps even before petting, one should feel some serious affection for one's partner. If sexual intercourse took place, it was nearly always between engaged couples. Evidently, despite the new freedoms and the openly sexy behavior and frank talk among Jazz Age teens, the incidence of premarital sex did not increase and remained mostly a preparation for marriage. In fact, dating and physical intimacy of any degree were still, for both sexes, aimed at finding a marriage partner. Amory Blaine, Fitzgerald's alter ego in *This Side of Paradise*, experiences many sexual thrills in the course of the novel, most of which involve kissing, but when he meets Rosalind, they fall deeply in love and within weeks are discussing marriage, although his lack of money and position soon causes her to send him away.

Many parents were disturbed by their teens' apparently lax and openly sexual behaviors, calling them dangerous and immoral. Indeed they were by parental standards, but teens themselves denied that they were promiscuous. For young immigrant or second-generation teens, the changing patterns of dating and sexual behavior caused an especially high degree of friction at home. In cultures where chaperones were essential, the freedom of young men and women to date and to find time alone was severely restricted. When a Mexican-American girl, aged sixteen or seventeen, walked home from school with a boy, her mother slapped her for such openly rebellious behavior (Ruiz 1992, 73). In cities, it was easier for these teens to escape such supervision and still live at home, but in small towns, some took more drastic steps and moved away from home or married at age fifteen or sixteen (1992, 74). The screen images of sexy Latin men and women were moneymakers in Hollywood but very disturbing to the parents of such teens, who worried that their girls would become flappers in appearance and behavior.

For many during the decade, the implications of the term "flaming youth" were summed up in the sexual escapades of a woman like Fitzgerald's Rosalind, who, as Fitzgerald describes her, is "quite unprincipled; her philosophy is carpe diem for herself and laissez faire for others. She loves shocking stories." She has an "eternally kissable mouth, small, slightly sensual, and utterly disturbing" (1920, 171). John Held's cartoons kept this image in the public eye; his cover for a 1926 issue of *Life* shows a young flapper sprawled fetchingly on a couch, legs askew, reading Sigmund Freud and Havelock Ellis. The title is "Sweet Sexteen." On the other hand, popular journalist Samuel Crowther in 1926 stated that the most important characteristic of the flapper was her independence: "She is no clinging vine . . . [she has] awakened to the fact that the 'superior sex' stuff is all bunk. . . . The flapper is to-day our most important national institution" (quoted in Colbert, 1997, 352).

Sports

During the Twenties, the spectator sports of baseball and boxing remained popular with Americans across the country. Thanks to radio, their excitement could be shared by adults, teens, and children alike, providing rallying points of national identity and larger-than-life heroes to cheer to victory.

Football was still a sport played only in wealthier high schools and colleges, but it was becoming popular across the country as fans followed their college teams to victory. Being a teen football star was becoming a ticket to national fame. The big Eastern colleges built huge stadiums to hold the thousands who attended their games, and smaller schools tried to do the same, sometimes with disastrous financial consequences if they did not produce winning teams. The need to recruit winning players grew from this period in the history of the sport.

Sports in which more young Americans themselves could participate, such as tennis and golf, rose dramatically in popularity during the decade. Americans demanded and got more golf courses, tennis courts, and swimming pools than ever before, and they used them to remain slim, fit, and tanned— a look that was becoming more fashionable as participatory sports became more available. In this decade, cosmetics that promoted rather than prevented a tan were introduced.

The most famous teen of the decade in sports was Gertrude Ederle. At seventeen she won three medals in swimming in the 1924 Olympic Games. Her goal, however, was to swim the English Channel in record time and to be the first woman to do so. In August 1926, she entered the water at Cap Gris-Nez, France, and began the thirty-five-mile crossing in cold wind and rough seas. After twelve hours her trainer tried to persuade her to stop but she continued. When she arrived at the beach in Kingsdown, England, she had made the swim in fourteen hours and thirty-one minutes, the best time a man or woman had ever achieved in a Channel swim. She had, in fact, surpassed the best time for men by two hours, a feat many had said could never be accomplished. America welcomed her with a huge parade and the demand for many public appearances. Although she lost her hearing as a result of her difficult swim, her feat inspired young men and women everywhere. She spent much of her later life encouraging people to learn to swim and donating her time and money to charitable causes connected with swimming.

Ederle's superb physical strength and attractiveness, as well as her determination, offered an alternative to the image of idle teens smoking and dancing the Charleston in speakeasies. Sport has always been connected with youthfulness and beauty, but in the Twenties the connection became even more important as an antidote to the media's attention to flaming youth. Health resorts, which had previously been places to rest and "take the waters," became places to play active sports and get a tan. The Scout movements encouraged young people to be outdoors; communities erected centers for teens to play various sports. Physical health, with its implication of accompanying moral health, became an ideal for many, and the image of the teenager glowing with robust, wholesome strength appealed to many who rejected the flapper lifestyle.

Music and Dancing

This was the Jazz Age, when jazz music and dance steps swept the country. The distinctive rhythms and harmonies of jazz had roots in black slave culture, but as it found its way into white culture—or as white culture took it over—styles of orchestration, the use of blues notes and harmonies, and the emergence of skilled solo performers created a complex range of jazz music. "Jelly Roll" Morton and his Red Hot Peppers band popularized the New Orleans style of jazz in the late Twenties, while Louis Armstrong thrilled listeners with his trumpet solos and his original ideas about melody and improvisation. Many regard Armstrong as the finest jazz musician of them all. The great Negro singer Bessie Smith sang the blues in the late Twenties like no one else during her short career, which peaked in the late Twenties. New York, which glowed with musicals featuring jazz during this period, offered George Gershwin's *Lady Be Good* in 1924 and in 1926 the famous all-Negro musical *Shuffle Along*, which played to such packed houses, of black and white fans alike, that at one point the street outside the theater had to be made one way. It toured successfully coast to coast. One of its featured performers was a sixteen-year-old chorus girl, Josephine Baker, who often stole the show by doing "crazy things"—"just mugging, crossing her eyes, tripping, getting out of step and catching up, doing all the steps the rest were doing, but funnier" (Stearns and Stearns 1994, 134). She was so popular that she made $125 a week, an amazing salary for a Twenties chorus girl.

Most middle-America teens listened to the songs that came from Tin Pan Alley, the New York City district where white popular music was published. The comic strip "Barney Google" inspired a little ditty: "Who's the most important man the country ever knew? Barney Google, with his goo- goo-

googly eyes!" Rudolph Valentino's famous movie inspired "I'm the Sheik of Araby . . . your love belongs to me." "Sweet Georgia Brown" and "Bye Bye Blackbird" were popular tunes, and teens and adults did the Charleston to "Ain't She Sweet?" The mood of the decade was summed up by "Ain't We Got Fun!" and, ironically, one of the most popular songs of mid-1929 was "Happy Days Are Here Again." Hoagy Carmichael's famous love ballad "Star Dust," which was composed in 1929, became one of the most recorded songs in popular music history.

Late in 1923, twenty-five-year-old George Gershwin, already famous as a Broadway composer, was asked by orchestra leader Paul Whiteman, who called himself the King of Jazz, to create a new piece of music for his band. He wanted an experiment, something that could be performed like a symphony but which was rooted in jazz sounds. The composer said later that he was inspired by the rhythm of train wheels clicking on a track and by the whole sweep of American life of the Twenties—its pace and love of city life. In a single month he composed *Rhapsody in Blue*, which was first performed on February 12, 1924. From its opening bars with the famous clarinet solo, to its romantic theme, it was a spectacular hit—a remarkable blend of symphonic form with jazz and blues which has become the signature of American music.

Popular Dances

The dance craze that began before 1920 intensified during the Jazz Age. From the "animal dances" of the previous decade, teens turned to the shimmy, the toddle, the black bottom, or the varsity drag when they went dancing—all of them more athletic than earlier dances, and all accompanied by the rhythms of jazz. Adults were often appalled at the wild grappling and groping that characterized many of them, especially when dances like the tango required close body contact between the dancers, but the young refused the disciplined ballroom style of their parents.

The Charleston is the dance most associated with the Twenties. Supposedly originating in Charleston, South Carolina, with its tradition of slave culture and free-wheeling dock and trade areas, it seems the epitome of Jazz Age freedom. A difficult dance to perform, it requires that both partners stay on the balls of their feet, twisting their feet at the ankles, kicking high in back from the knees, and constantly "toddling" or bouncing with their upper bodies to the beat. It could not be done by a girl in a long skirt; the short Charleston "flare dress" characteristic of flapper styles was almost a requirement (it sold for under $2 in department stores), as were sheer stockings and low-heeled pumps which showed off the legs as they kicked out. A flapper's bare knees were emphasized by the Charleston's move of bending the knees and opening and closing them in time to the music. Its suggestion of sexual license probably accounted for some of its popularity, but the Charleston's sense of fun and freedom invited anyone with enough energy to try it. Charleston contests were held weekly in many parts of the country.

In high schools, dancing was the favorite activity of many teen girls, and dances were the dominant social activity for girls and boys together. Formal dresses for girls became a significant part of their clothing budget, even in families with little money to spare. On college campuses, jazz ruled, and uninhibited dancing marked every fraternity party, often to the despair of the administration. The famous American choreographer Agnes de Mille remembers a friend of her father's describing a dance at a Cornell fraternity house: "the guests, growing impatient of chaperonage, broke all the light bulbs on the floor and danced for the rest of the evening in the dark on crushed glass and the rolling bodies of their brothers and their dates" (de Mille 1980, 19). Fass emphasizes that dancing itself was not what distinguished the young from their elders, but the particular kind of dancing. She quotes a poem from a school paper:

Jazz and the bunch jazz with you
Dance and you're by yourself,
The mob thinks it's jake
To shimmy and shake,
For the old-fashioned stuff's on the shelf. (Fass 1977, 303)

Even rural youths were not immune to or protected from the dance craze of the Twenties. They still attended barn dances but now in some communities jazz was played and the Charleston was danced, along with the traditional polkas and square dances. Public dance halls with Negro bands also began to appear in rural areas; they often served liquor and had no chaperones. Teens went there to dance the latest dances and to meet other teens separated from them by their farm life, even those from other ethnic groups. Going there was a way for rural teens to rebel but also a new way to find a potential marriage partner.

Movies

By 1920 those who were teens had grown up with nickelodeons, and movies were already part of their lives. In the Twenties, however, movies took over the popular imagination in ways that thrilled young and old alike, but worried some as well. Movie attendance rose dramatically across America; most people across all socioeconomic groups saw at least one movie a week. One national study of teens in 1922 showed that 40% went at least twice a week and 45% more than once each week (Fuller 1996, 184–85). "Middletown," population 35,000 in 1920, had nine theaters, all of which operated year round seven days a week. High school students attended frequently, sometimes with their families but increasingly with peers and on dates.

The great silent screen stars Douglas Fairbanks and Mary Pickford were at the height of their popularity when the decade began, making as much as a million dollars a year, but soon other stars equaled or eclipsed them. In 1921 Rudolph Valentino played in *The Sheik*, a film treatment of a popular novel by Edith M. Hull in which the dark and dangerous sheik carries off the heroine, who escapes him only to be recaptured and to succumb finally and enthusiastically to his irresistible charms. Valentino's flashing eyes and flaring nostrils, his bare chest and pomaded hair made him the screen's sexiest leading man for the next few years. At his public appearances women would scream and faint, or beg for kisses. When he died unexpectedly in 1926, the line of people waiting outside his funeral service stretched for many blocks and women wept openly. His legend as a screen lover continued for many years, bolstered by the periodic visits of a mysterious woman in black to his grave.

Charlie Chaplin had already established his popularity by the Twenties, especially with his character of the "little tramp," the little man with the tight jacket, baggy pants, and derby hat. Chaplin's physical clowning and his expressive face made him a great favorite with all moviegoers. In 1925 he made one of his greatest films, *The Gold Rush*; its scene of the tramp eating his shoes with great finesse and grace, is one of the classic moments in all of film.

In 1922 a seventeen-year-old beauty named Clara Bow won a magazine contest to be named "the most beautiful girl in the world." By 1927 her film career was at its height when she starred in *It*, a film adaptation of Elinor Glyn's novel exploring sex appeal—does a girl have "it" or does she not? Bow's portrayal of a flapper who cuts the neckline of her dress away to make herself attractive to her boss caused her to be known as the "It Girl" for years afterward, although her popularity faded with the coming of talking pictures.

The screen's quintessential flapper was Joan Crawford. An expert at dancing the Charleston, she made movie history by dancing on tables in the wild party scene in the 1928 silent film *Our Dancing Daughters*, a film still considered a perfect evocation of the age despite its melodramatic plot. Unlike Clara Bow, Crawford enjoyed a long film career even after talking pictures eliminated the silents.

The new sexual frankness of movies was an important part of their appeal for teens. For the first time, teens were sitting in darkened theaters, perhaps with dates, while the screens filled with flirtation, touching, and intense kisses and embraces between beautiful and sophisticated people. Girls watched the women closely and learned to imitate their way of moving, of gazing at a man, of closing their eyes when they kissed, of fending off unwanted caresses. Boys wondered if they could learn to kiss like that, to be

Joan Crawford's famous scene in *Our Dancing Daughters*, a 1928 Jazz Age classic film. Reproduced courtesy of The Museum of Modern Art.

as virile, brave, attractive, and handsome as Valentino or Fairbanks. A teacher in "Middletown" feared that movies were making teens too aware of sex, too sophisticated; a judge opined that movies were a major cause of delinquency among teens (Lynd and Lynd 1929, 267–68).

Fashion and appearance were as important as behavior when teens looked to the movies as models. They plastered their walls at home and their lockers at school with pictures of the stars they loved so they could see them all the time. Girls examined themselves in the mirror for the flaws they could never see in their screen favorites; they mimicked the hairdos, dress, makeup, and ways of walking and sitting that they saw in films. Boys too used the movies to learn about the right table manners, clothes, and style of behavior in nightclubs, even though most of them would never enter the kind of nightclub they saw in the movies. A new kind of consumerism was the result; teens used their money to buy cosmetics and clothes in unprecedented numbers. The fan magazine *Photoplay* deliberately targeted young people aged from eighteen to thirty as the most avid moviegoers and fans and created its advertising to appeal to that group; knowing that they had only small amounts of spending money, the magazine concentrated its ads on small-ticket items, especially cosmetics (Fuller 1996, 162–64). Mexican-American girls in the barrios wanted to "Follow the Stars" and use Max Factor cosmetics (Ruiz 1992, 71–72). Farm youths too saw on the screen, although less often than their urban counterparts, standards of consumption they could only hope for.

In 1927–1928, film took two enormous leaps forward. Al Jolson had made a film called *The Jazz Singer* as a silent movie. It concerns a Jewish boy whose father expects him to be a cantor but who wants more than anything to sing jazz. His father rejects him but his mother loves and supports him while he becomes a big star in New York, often performing in the black-face minstrel style that had been popular for years in traveling shows throughout the country. The director of the film wanted to add sound to the musical numbers only, but Jolson, already a popular personality and singer, wanted to try adding some dialogue. He ad-libbed some lines before he began to sing in one scene and again in a later scene in a short, teasing conversation with his mother in the film. The director kept the scenes, and when the film opened, audiences were thrilled. For the first time, they heard an actor's voice coming from the screen at the same time he spoke.

Some predicted talking pictures, or "talkies," would never last. Even Charlie Chaplin is supposed to have said, "The movies need talking like Beethoven's music needs lyrics" (Wallechinsky, 1995, 414). Within a year, however, hundreds of theaters had converted to sound, despite the initial expense, and audiences were eager to attend. Film stars like Clara Bow who turned out to have unattractive voices found their careers at an end; acting styles adjusted to accommodate more dialogue and more realism. Chaplin was eventually able to revive his career with a different kind of film. The era of the silent film had ended.

The other major development in American film, which coincided with talkies, was the advent of the movie cartoon and the success of Walt Disney. During the mid-Twenties, silent cartoons were popular, and Disney had made various kinds of cartoon shorts, even combining cartoons with live actors in his Alice in Cartoonland series. In 1928 his studio needed a financial boost. He had already created the appealing character of an energetic mouse (first naming him Mortimer and then, as the story goes, at his wife's suggestion, renaming him Mickey) and put him into two silent cartoons. Disney needed more, and unlike some producers, he was sure that talking pictures were here to stay. He decided to set a Mickey cartoon to music and began work on *Steamboat Willie*, in which the mouse plays wild music on various instruments, even on the animals around him. After some false tries and a huge investment of money, Disney, always a perfectionist, had the cartoon he wanted, in which the sound perfectly coordinated with the screen action. It premiered in New York City on November 18, 1928, with great success (Jackson 1993, 16), and Mickey Mouse was on his way to becoming an American icon, a figure popular throughout the world and the centerpiece of the twentieth-century phenomenon that has become Walt Disney.

Books and Reading

The term "flaming youth" came from a 1923 novel of that title by Warner Fabian (Fass 1977, 453), but the writer most associated with the Jazz Age, for intellectual and popular readers alike, was F. Scott Fitzgerald. Fitzgerald had virtually created the popular image of flaming youth with *This Side of Paradise* in 1920, a book which now seems mannered but still captures the extreme emotions and confusion felt by many in their late teens as they confront the world's inadequacies and hypocrisies, as well as their own. In 1925 Fitzgerald wrote what was to be his finest novel: *The Great Gatsby*. He captured in Daisy Buchanan the wealth, leisure, and carelessness of the upper classes in the mid-Twenties, and in Gatsby himself the bewilderment of a man who wants to be part of that life and cannot—a feeling Fitzgerald knew only too well, and one which was probably familiar to many who saw the economic boom but could experience it only in the movies.

In Harlem, a quiet revolution in literature was occurring. While whites ventured north occasionally to the Cotton Club for its jazz music and dancing, many blacks were moving into Harlem permanently—it was nearly all black by 1925—and experiencing a new sense of pride in African-American culture which has come to be called the Harlem Renaissance. Among them was the young Langston Hughes, who went to Columbia to study in 1921, at age nineteen, partly to be near the excitement of Harlem. He left school two years later and went on an extended personal voyage to Africa and Europe; a famous story about him says that he threw all his books into the sea when he set out, so that he would not be influenced by anything except what he saw and heard. When he returned, he became one of America's foremost poets, essayists, and critics.

Most middle-class Americans preferred other kinds of books. Sinclair Lewis produced two best-sellers during the decade; in 1921, readers loved *Main Street*, the story of small-town American life. His second best-selling novel, which focused on religious revivalism in the Midwest, was based on the phenomenal career of Aimee Semple McPherson. The stylish McPherson had attracted thousands of followers since 1921 to her spectacular revivals in Los Angeles, but in 1925 she disappeared under mysterious circumstances. She later claimed dramatically that she had been kidnapped, but evidently she had been engaging in a tryst with a lover. Lewis's 1928 fictionalization of these events, *Elmer Gantry*, shocked and fascinated many with its frank revelations of the business side of religion.

Magazines

Books, at this time, were taking a back seat to magazines for most middle-class Americans. The *Saturday Evening Post* was read by millions of men, women, and youth, and the *Ladies' Home Journal* and *McCall's* were read by women and girls nationwide. College students were also reading the same magazines, including *Life*, which was a humor magazine then, but also tried to adopt H. L. Mencken's sophisticated cynicism by reading his *American Mercury* magazine, which aimed sarcastic barbs at the American "boo-boisie."

When the Lynds investigated magazine reading in "Middletown," they got a surprise. Between 3,500 and 4,000 issues per month of various "sex adventure" magazines circulated through this small Midwestern town (1929, 241–42). Despite the apparent religious, political, and moral conservatism of the population, readers across age and socioeconomic groups were evidently finding some salacious thrills in "sex adventure" magazines like *True Story* or *Telling Tales*. The stories, usually written in the first person, describe events such as a mother's advice to her daughter on her wedding night or a woman's struggle with a rival for her man's affections. The endings were invariably moral, but they aimed to represent "life" to young people who might have no other way of finding out about it (1929, 241). Movie magazines, also very popular, described to girl readers how the stars worked and played, and fed their desire for glamour and adventure. Boys were more likely to turn to *Whiz Bang* for sexual thrills and various pulp magazines for excitement and adventure.

School reading for high school students was not nearly as exciting. Despite some appeals from researchers to include more modern literature—such as *The Virginian* or *Ramona*—in classrooms to attract young people to read more, teachers tended to remain with the old standbys that they knew well from their own school days. George Eliot's *Silas Marner*, Charles Dickens's *A Tale of Two Cities*, William Shakespeare's *Julius Caesar*, and Alfred, Lord Tennyson's *The Idylls of the King* were standard fare and were taught "intensively"—many weeks given over to the laborious discussion of a single book (Nilsen and Donelson 1993, 558).

Left to themselves, however, boys and girls preferred other books. Both continued to enjoy series books in great numbers, many of them published by Edward Stratemeyer and his syndicate. The Rover Boys remained popular well into the Twenties, while girls' series books still tended to lag behind boys' in numbers produced. In 1927 Stratemeyer began his most popular series yet—which became probably the most popular boys' series in the world—the Hardy Boys. Frank and Joe Hardy began their adventures in *The Tower Treasure*, written by an anonymous author under Stratemeyer's invented name "Franklin W. Dixon," and continued rapidly with two more books in the same year, *The House on the Cliff* and *The Secret of the Old Mill*. Stratemeyer had the formula for success, and when he died in 1930, the books were continued without a break. They have been transformed into comic books, detective handbooks, two television series, and even coloring books for younger teens.

Librarians continued their periodic assaults on this kind of "junk reading" for teens. Mary E. S. Root in early 1929 published a list of books which she thought ought not to circulate in a public library; it included series books like the Bobbsey Twins and Tom Swift and novels by Horatio Alger and Oliver Optic—all great favorites of teen readers across the country (West 1988, 28–29). Her list prompted some to defend this reading, but many librarians supported Root's elitist viewpoint—a situation that suggests that some adult readers were completely out of touch with the young, despite their desire to encourage more reading among teens.

REFERENCES

Barfield, Ray. *Listening to Radio, 1920–1950.* Westport, Conn.: Praeger, 1996.

Colbert, David, ed. *Eyewitness to America.* New York: Pantheon, 1997.

Dalzell, Tom. *Flappers 2 Rappers: American Youth Slang.* Springfield, Mass.: Merriam Webster, 1996.

de Mille, Agnes. *America Dances.* New York: Macmillan, 1980.

Encyclopedia Britannica Vol. 22. Chicago: William Benton, 1967.

Fass, Paula. *The Damned and the Beautiful: American Youth in the 1920s.* New York: Oxford University Press, 1977.

Fitzgerald, F. Scott. *This Side of Paradise.* New York: Charles Scribner's Sons, 1920.

Fuller, Kathryn H. *At the Picture Show: Small-Town Audiences and the Creation of Movie Fan Culture.* Washington, D.C.: Smithsonian Institution Press, 1996.

Goulart, Ron, ed. *Encyclopedia of American Comics.* New York: Promised Land Productions from Facts on File, 1990.

Harvey, Robert C. "The Captain and the Comics." *INKS: Cartoon and Comic Art Studies* 2, no. 3 (November 1995): 39–56.

Jackson, Kathy Merlock. *Walt Disney: A Biobibliography.* Westport, Conn.: Greenwood Press, 1993.

Lewis, Guy. "Sport, Youth Culture and Conventionality 1920–1970." *Journal of Sport History* 4, no. 2 (Summer 1977): 129–150.

Lurie, Alison. *The Language of Clothes.* New York: Random House, 1981.

Lynd, Robert S., and Helen Merrell Lynd. *Middletown: A Study in Contemporary American Culture.* New York: Harcourt, Brace, 1929.

McDonnell, Janet. *America in the Twentieth Century: 1920–1929.* New York: Marshall Cavendish, 1995.

Mirel, Jeffrey E. "Adolescence in Twentieth Century America." In *Encyclopedia of Adolescence*, 1153–61. New York: Garland, 1991.

Mizener, Arthur. *Scott Fitzgerald and His World.* London: Thames and Hudson, 1972.

Modell, John. *Into One's Own: From Youth to Adulthood in the United States 1920–1975.* Berkeley: University of California Press, 1989.

Neth, Mary. "Leisure and Generational Change: Farm Youths in the Midwest, 1910–1940." *Agricultural History* 67, no. 2 (Spring 1993): 163–184.

Nilsen, Alleen Pace, and Ken Donelson, eds. *Literature for Today's Young Adults.* 4th ed. New York: HarperCollins, 1993.

Perry, George, and Alan Aldridge. *The Penguin Book of Comics.* London: Penguin Books, 1971.

Petersen, James R. "Playboy's History of the Sexual Revolution, Part III: The Jazz Age (1920–1929)." *Playboy* 44, no. 4 (April 1997): 80+.

Rothman, Sheila M. *Women's Proper Place.* New York: Basic Books, 1978.

Ruiz, Vicki L. " 'Star Struck': Acculturation, Adolescence, and Mexican American Women, 1920–1950." In *Small Worlds,* ed. Elliott West and Paula Petrik, 61–80. Lawrence: University Press of Kansas 1992.

Stearns, Marshall, and Jean Stearns. *Jazz Dance.* New York: Da Capo Press, 1994.

Wallechinsky, David. *The People's Almanac Presents the Twentieth Century.* Boston: Little, Brown, 1995.

West, Elliott. *Growing Up in Twentieth Century America.* Westport, Conn.: Greenwood Press, 1996.

West, Mark I. *Children, Culture, and Controversy.* Hamden, Conn.: Archon, 1988.

· 3 ·

The 1930s

During the early Thirties, teens experienced the Great Depression through their families and schools. Many saw their fathers out of work for the first time, perhaps even standing in a bread line for food to feed their families. Many men had to find new careers for themselves in low-paying work, just to keep their families together, while mothers, because of the need for low-paid clerical or social service work, could find employment more easily than fathers. In extreme cases, mortgages on houses were foreclosed, and families had to move in with relatives or live in shelters. Many teens sought jobs themselves rather than stay in school where they could not help their families financially. In particularly depressed areas of the country, schools shut down for lack of funds, making teens even more idle. Some teens left home so they would not be a burden, or they left out of boredom or frustration and rode boxcars around the country looking for handouts or temporary work. The result was a much more serious, more psychologically independent teen than the sheik or flapper of the Twenties. By the end of the decade, teens had begun to establish a genuinely separate culture in which they looked to each other rather than to adults for authority and support.

POLITICS AND NATIONAL EVENTS

Stock Market Crash of 1929

The booming economy of the Twenties laid the groundwork for disaster. As the wealthy invested more in the stock market, often receiving quick, substantial profits, the gap between the classes widened. When the market collapsed in October 1929, Herbert Hoover had the misfortune of being president during the worst financial crisis in America's history, and he may have worsened the crisis by his reluctance to use federal funds and power to offer relief. He persisted in believing that recovery needed to be largely an independent effort, with only indirect government support. When he did finally establish a federal loan agency, the damage to his political image had been done. By the election of 1932, the worst year of the Depression, his name had become synonymous with poverty, evictions, foreclosures, debt, cold, and hunger. A "Hoover blanket" was a newspaper used to provide warmth to a person on the sidewalk or park bench; "Hoovervilles" were collections of shanties thrown up as makeshift shelters for those who no longer had homes.

His campaign was completely devastated when the Bonus Army, thousands of veterans and their supporters, marched into Washington, D.C., and camped there, waiting for the passage of a bill that would give them an immediate bonus. When the bill was defeated, many of the marchers straggled out of the city, but others delayed until Hoover ordered the city cleared. A few arrests were made, and Hoover reluctantly agreed to use force but only if necessary. His Army chief of staff, General Douglas MacArthur (assisted by a young Dwight Eisenhower), thought force was necessary, and he ordered saber-wielding cavalry officers and six tanks into the crowd of milling protesters. Hoover himself was evidently shocked by what had happened, but the damage was done. He lost the election conclusively to the elegant and energetic young Democratic candidate, Franklin Delano Roosevelt.

Roosevelt and the New Deal

When Franklin Roosevelt was inaugurated on March 4, 1933, unemployment had risen to more than 12 million—almost 25% of the population—and banks were failing everywhere as panicked investors continued to withdraw all their funds. In his inauguration speech, Roosevelt offered Americans a "new deal": "This great Nation will endure as it has endured, will revive and will prosper . . . the only thing we have to fear is fear itself."

He was as good as his word. Within a week he had taken steps to reopen America's banks, and within a month he had legalized the sale of low-alcohol beer to increase tax revenues, even though Prohibition was still in effect. During his first hundred days in office, he proposed, and Congress passed, the initial legislation he needed to bring direct relief to Depression-weary Americans. By the beginning of his second term, Roosevelt had established several government agencies which together reshaped the relationship between government and people. In 1933 the minimum wage was established—at 40 cents an hour.

As usual, minorities suffered most from the Depression. Southern blacks, who already had a high unemployment rate, generally found themselves shut out of even more jobs, victims of employers who refused to hire a black man or woman, or would even fire one, in favor of a white employee. Before Roosevelt's New Deal legislation, state and local relief agencies were not penalized for turning blacks away. Mexican Americans, legal immigrants who came over the border to find work and even some who were U.S. citizens, were occasionally sent back to Mexico in order to protect American jobs. Native Americans drew some unfortunate attention from the New Deal with the 1934 Indian Recovery Act which allowed the U.S. government to appoint the chairs of tribal corporations, a move calculated to protect white interests in Indian land even while they appropriated more of it.

Farmers in the Midwest, already struggling to keep their land profitable, resented the intrusion of the Agricultural Adjustment Administration (AAA) into their affairs, but they suffered a worse blow from Mother Nature. During 1933 and 1934, as the drought of 1930 moved west, the worst dust storms in history plagued the land—land already weakened by the overproduction of the booming Twenties. Winds in Oklahoma blew the soil away in huge, choking clouds, some of it as far away as Chicago, where, during a single storm, four pounds of dust per person fell on the city between May 9 and May 11, 1934 (Watkins 1993, 192). Government intervention could achieve little in the face of this natural disaster. Many farmers simply left their land to the winds and headed west in search of employment, a fruitless migration depicted poignantly by John Steinbeck in his 1939 novel *The Grapes of Wrath*.

When Roosevelt campaigned for reelection in 1935 and asked the people if they were better off than they had been in 1932, most of them believed they were and chose him for a second term by a landslide, the biggest victory in American election history. In his inaugural address, he expressed his pride in all America had accomplished but said, "Here is the challenge to our democracy. . . . I see one third of a nation ill-housed, ill-clad, ill-nourished." He proposed to help this one-third. Some began to wonder about Roosevelt's aims, however, when in 1937 he suggested reorganizing the Supreme Court to allow him to appoint a new justice for every justice over seventy years of age, up to six new justices in all. Since the Court had struck down some of his New Deal agencies, it appeared that Roosevelt was trying to "pack" the Court to increase his own ability to use federal power. His plan was soundly defeated. An economic recession occupied him in 1937, as did labor troubles, and by 1939 foreign policy and the possibility of America's involvement in World War II eclipsed the New Deal.

Two Notorious Trials

In addition to the economic woes that united the country, all Americans young and old were fascinated by two courtroom dramas during this decade. Teenagers were at the center of the first; the second concerned one of the country's favorite symbols of youth, Charles Lindbergh. Although the country may have been united in their interest, the trials revealed the deep racial and ethnic divisions that still plagued America.

On March 25, 1931, during a train ride through Alabama, a group of white teens got into a fight with a group of black teens—all of whom evidently, as was so common during these severe Depression years, were hoboing on freight trains. When the white teens lost and were thrown off the train, they enlisted the help of local law enforcers, who rounded up the nine black youths and jailed them in the town of Scottsboro, Alabama. The oldest was twenty; the rest ranged in age from nineteen to thirteen. The sheriff also found on the train two white girls, aged nineteen and seventeen, also transients, who claimed they had been raped by the black youths. In the South, the penalty all too often for such an alleged crime was lynching, but some in Scottsboro favored a speedy trial instead. Within weeks, eight of the "Scottsboro boys" were found guilty of rape and sentenced to death. The youngest was spared.

Outraged citizens from other parts of the country believed this Southern "justice" was a travesty—a legal lynching. Letters poured into Scottsboro pleading for the boys' pardon, ministers preached sermons about their plight, and celebrities and writers such as scientist Albert Einstein and writer Thomas Mann spoke out in the boys' defense. Benefits, starring jazz artists like Duke Ellington and Cab Calloway, were held to raise defense funds. Poet Langston Hughes wrote eloquently of visiting them in the penitentiary in 1932, where he saw "Brown America" locked up. In November 1931 the Supreme Court overturned the initial convictions. After a series of subsequent trials lasting until 1937, only five of the nine Scottsboro boys (some now grown to men during their long jail terms) were convicted. Clarence Norris, the only Scottsboro boy alive by the mid-Seventies, was officially pardoned in 1976 by Governor George Wallace and died in 1989.

The South, of course, had no monopoly on distrust of anyone "different." In 1932 famous flyer Charles A. Lindbergh was still America's darling. To ease the pressure of the constant publicity, he and his wife and young son Charles Jr. spent weekends at their large home in an isolated area of New Jersey. On the evening of February 29, the baby's nurse found Charles Jr.'s crib empty and a window open; in the room was a ransom note requesting $50,000. After two months of frantic, media-saturated investigation and an attempt to pay the ransom, the baby's body was found in a grave not far from the house. In September, a German immigrant attempted to purchase gasoline using money from the ransom; he was arrested and charged with the crime. The trial was labeled the trial of the century not only because of the celebrity of Lindbergh himself, but because of the public's fascination with and hatred of the accused kidnapper, Bruno Richard Hauptmann.

From the first, the case attracted public attention, but when the trial began, the courtroom became a circus. Newspapers vied with each other to get their reporters into the courtroom and to print the latest stories. Crowds of spectators camped outside the courthouse, where they ate picnic lunches and yelled encouragement to "Lindy" or jeered those they disliked when they came and went. Tickets to get in sold for up to $100. Even high school students took advantage of the excitement. Some, who were excused from school to work for the reporters as copyboys, discovered how to finance their yearbook: on a large sheet, they collected autographs from the various reporters and others involved, copied the sheet, and sold the copies, headed "The Trial of the Century," for 25 cents each (Walker in Colbert 1997, 386). Hauptmann was convicted of kidnapping and executed in the electric chair in 1936. Since then, some investigators have suggested that Hauptmann was as innocent as he claimed to be, that his defense was a travesty, and that he may have been framed in order to appease the public's need to see someone punished for the crime. Others find the evidence against him still compelling. The case remains something of a mystery.

Gangsters and Heroes

During the Thirties, the distinction between gangsters and heroes was often blurred, to the dismay of many parents and authorities who worried that young people were worshiping the wrong idols. Dramatic newspaper coverage of real events, and fantasy movie versions such as the 1931 *Public Enemy*, starring James Cagney who appeared in gleaming cars with gorgeous women, attracted all the population, not just the impressionable young. The gangsters themselves were eager to contribute to their mystique.

John Dillinger, who began his life of crime as a teenager, was finally jailed in 1924, in his early twenties, for attempted robbery. Jail only increased his appetite for crime, and when he was paroled in 1933, he went on a year's crime spree that amazed lawmen and enthralled the public and the press. The availability of automobiles made it easy to hold up a bank and drive into the next state to avoid prosecution, and Dillinger led his pursuers on chase after chase, stealing thousands of dollars, killing, being jailed, and escaping. He once supposedly held a homemade wooden gun on a guard. Although the story was untrue, Dillinger himself enjoyed perpetuating it. By November 1933 he had been designated Public Enemy No. 1. In the end, it seems, he was too trusting of women. His girlfriend notified federal agents when she and Dillinger were going to attend a movie at the Biograph Theatre in Chicago in April 1934. She wore red so that the agents could identify her. When Dillinger emerged with the "woman in red," as she has come to be known, the agents gunned him down.

One of Dillinger's gang, a young man whose appearance gave him the nickname Baby Face Nelson, began his life as a criminal at age fourteen with car theft. He loved to kill, and any job he took on invariably became bloody. He admired Dillinger, but he wanted to be "bigger." After Dillinger was killed, Baby Face became Public Enemy No. 1 and organized his own gang, intending to elipse Dillinger with his own crimes. He died in a shootout with the Federal Bureau of Investigation (FBI) a few months later, in November 1934. Nelson, trapped, simply came at the agents with his submachine gun firing. One witness said, "It was just like Jimmy Cagney" (Sifakis 1982, 522). He killed the agents, returned to his car, and ordered his companion to drive. He had taken seventeen bullets. The next day his body was found a few miles away. The press called the story "thrilling" and created sympathy for his "pretty widow" and her broken heart (522).

The criminals who courted publicity the most, however, were Bonnie Parker and Clyde Barrow. Clyde was twenty-one and Bonnie nineteen when they met in 1930. Together they roamed around Texas and Oklahoma committing minor robberies, sometimes kidnapping and releasing their victims but sometimes killing for fun. Enjoying their notoriety, they posed for pictures which they sent to newspapers; the most famous shows Bonnie with a machine gun, smoking a cigar. Bonnie also sent her poetry to newspapers and was delighted when it was printed. Eventually their gang of five dissolved; their former cohorts informed on them to gain leniency. They were ambushed near the Texas-Louisiana border in May 1934 and died in a burst of gunfire that left twenty-five bullets in Clyde and twenty-three in Bonnie (87).

Americans in the Thirties had bona fide heroes too, men and women who represented honesty as well as strength and courage. In 1930, when Joseph Louis Barrow turned sixteen, he was only a few years away from his world heavyweight boxing title, which, now as Joe Louis, he won in 1934 and kept for twelve years, through twenty-five challenges. When he knocked out Max Baer, who was considered the best white fighter of the time, the press really began to take note, although not always in a flattering way, sometimes resorting to racist epithets like "darky" or worse. He became America's hero in 1938 when he knocked out the German Max Schmeling, who was a symbol of Adolf Hitler's arrogant racism, in the first round. During World War II Louis volunteered for the U.S. Army and fought charity bouts to help the American cause. When his career ended in 1951, after he was knocked out by Rocky Marciano, the crowd cheered Louis, who had helped combat racism in professional sports.

Black Americans had another champion during the Thirties. Jesse Owens, born in Alabama and raised in Ohio, electrified the sports world with his performance at the 1935 National Collegiate Track and Field events; he broke three world records and tied a fourth. As the 1936 Berlin Olympic Games approached, American hopes were pinned on Owens not only because of his outstanding athletic ability but also because, as a black man, he would give the lie to Hitler's increasingly public and fanatical notions of Aryan superiority. Owens won four gold medals. When he defeated the German favorite Lutz Long in the long jump, Long walked off the field with his arm draped around Owens in open defiance of the German leader, and the crowd cheered them both.

American women had their own hero in Amelia Earhart. Born in 1898, she learned to fly as a teenager, and by the age of twenty-four she owned her first plane. She set the women's altitude record a few months later. After Lindbergh's successful flight from New York to Paris, promoters looking for a "Lady Lindy" found her in Earhart. With her lanky body, cropped and touseled blond hair, and shy smile, she even looked like the famous flier. In 1932 she flew solo across the Atlantic, as he had done, in a grueling flight that almost ended in disaster and became a sensation. Her desire was not for fame (she filed gushy adoring letters under "Bunk"); she wanted to test herself to her limits because she loved to fly.

She was also an outspoken champion of women's abilities. She spent a season as women's career counselor at Purdue University in 1935, where she advised college women to trust their individuality and to seek careers for themselves. During the same year, on a touchdown in Oakland, California, sixteen-year-old Gene Shaffer, a reporter for the University High School paper, pushed forward among the older reporters and asked her what she would advise high school students.

The other reporters turned and looked at her aghast, but Earhart answered immediately. "Aviation is the career of the future," she said warmly. "You and your fellow students have the first chance in history to train yourselves and become a part of it." Gene stood looking at the slender, five-foot-eight, 118-pound woman, built exactly like her, who had flown herself across two oceans. At that moment Gene felt the personal impact of her mother's favorite expression: "Hitch your chariot to a star." (Keil 1990, 29)

At the age of thirty-eight, Earhart set out to circumnavigate the globe at its most difficult spot—near the equator—saying, "I want to do it because I must do it." With her navigator Fred Noonan she took off from Miami on June 1, 1937. After arriving in New Guinea in early July, they readied themselves for the most difficult part of the journey, a stretch of Pacific Ocean which had only a tiny island for a refueling stop. What happened after they left New Guinea is still a mystery. Static-plagued radio messages were received from her, but she evidently could not receive the messages sent to her from the ship tracking her progress. Her plane disappeared. Despite a massive search—the largest in naval history—no verifiable trace of Earhart and Noonan or the aircraft was ever found.

TEENS AT HOME

Since graduation from high school during the Thirties usually meant no job, or at best a temporary, part-time job, middle-class teens tended to stay at home longer, sharing the life of the family and contributing as much as they could to keep it afloat. John Modell, who studied the financial trends of such families, found that before 1930, any extra dollars in the budget often went for a teenage daughter's clothes. She was entering the marriage market, the family reasoned, and deserved special adornment (1989, 130). The Depression changed that. During the Thirties, teen daughters' clothing allowances were the lowest in the family, and teen sons were not much better. Now the preference went to the father, whose appearance was important to his finding and holding a job (131). Dating, which had emerged in the Twenties as an important ritual of teen life, was restricted; few teen boys could afford to entertain a girl, and not a few families gave up their cars during these difficult years. Young adults who might have married now postponed their official engagements indefinitely, often feeling constrained to stay within the family to help out all they could.

Food and Games

One of the most famous American foods appeared during these hard times. Spam, the budget-stretching canned mixture of shoulder pork and ham, helped many families economize since "real" meat was a luxury that could be enjoyed only occasionally. Spam became even more well known when it was widely distributed to soldiers during World War II. Other foods invented during the Thirties were destined to become teen favorites: cheeseburgers, soft ice cream, canned beer, and chocolate chip cookies all made their appearance during this decade (Wallechinsky 1995, 596).

Staying home became more interesting when in 1933 a laid-off salesman invented America's most famous board game: Monopoly. Charles Darrow, who based his game on Atlantic City, made the little houses and hotels out of scrap lumber. His friends loved the game, and soon he could not make enough games to satisfy the demand. Monopoly gave players the fantasy of easy money, of playing the real estate market for huge profits, wheeling and dealing with the big shots, even as the American economy stumbled along and few people had any available cash for a night on the town much less the money to buy a railroad. Parker Brothers bought the rights to Monopoly and by 1935 found themselves flooded with orders. Darrow eventually became a millionaire. According to the *People's Almanac*, the popularity of the game rises every time the economy falters (Wallechinsky 1995, 626).

Comics

The funny papers continued to be a source of family amusement. The perennial teenager, Harold Teen, continued to amuse readers with his hip teen slang. In 1930 Blondie appeared, to become with Dagwood one of the most famous of all comic-strip characters. In the first strips, Blondie was a

Harold Teen (in dark pants) and his buddies are "he-men" in this strip from December 12, 1933. © Tribune Media Services. All Rights Reserved. Reprinted with permission.

jazzy flapper engaged to Dagwood Bumstead, whose rich father disapproved of his son's choice of fiancées. They married anyway and moved to the suburbs, and Dagwood went to work for Mr. Dithers, where he remains today—angling for a raise, oversleeping and crashing into the hapless mailman every morning, squabbling with his neighbor over tools, coping with Daisy the dog, and always trying to get a nap on the couch or a soak in the tub. During the years, Blondie changed from a flapper to a suburban housewife and gave birth to their children Cookie and Alexander (who only in the Eighties became teenagers) and now runs a catering business—all still wearing her Thirties hairstyle.

From 1937 to 1940 (and again from 1950 to 1955), black newspapers carried a strip called "Torchy Brown, from Dixie to Harlem," about a beautiful black girl who rose from humble Southern beginnings to perform at the Apollo Theatre. Drawn by African-American Jackie Ormes, Torchy, although not a teenager, was a Cinderella figure for aspiring black girls. The interdependence of the black community formed a subplot to her adventures.

Little Orphan Annie became even more popular during the Thirties, ironically partly because of its anti-Roosevelt stance. It was "the first nationally syndicated comic strip to be unabashedly, unrelievedly, 'political' " (Harvey 1995, 50), anticipating such strips as "Li'l Abner" and "Pogo." The character of Daddy Warbucks, introduced early into the strip, believed in self-reliance and spunk, not government handouts, a philosophy practiced by his ward, Annie. Those who supported the New Deal believed the strip had become too critical of the government, but they continued to read it nonetheless.

Three adventure strips introduced during this decade represent the increasing variety of cheap family entertainment to be had on the comic pages. In 1931 Chester Gould took a cue from Prohibition crime and the popularity of "true crime" pulp magazines to create a detective he called "Plainclothes Tracy." An editor for the Chicago Tribune liked the idea but suggested that the character needed to be a policeman and that "Dick Tracy" would be a good name: "they call plainclothesmen 'dicks,' " he observed (Harvey 1995, 51). The immediately popular strip was the first to display gangsterism, gunfire, murder, and mayhem in the funny papers. Tracy's two-way wrist radio was a prophetic bit of gadgetry, and the "Crime-Stoppers" notebook gave readers a sense that they too could fight corruption. Gould's host of bizarre-looking characters—not the least Tracy himself with his razor-like jaw always in profile—and the dark, shoot-em-up plots continue to fascinate readers today.

The year 1934 saw the appearance of an exotic teenager. "Terry and Pirates," drawn by Milton Caniff, took a teenage boy, Terry Lee, on various adventures fighting the villains of the China Seas, who were led by the sexy Dragon Lady. When war broke out between Japan and China in 1937, the

Teenage Terry charms the Dragon Lady in this strip from May 21, 1939. © Tribune Media Services. All Rights Reserved. Reprinted with permission.

strip began to include those events and made the Japanese the villians, even though politically America was neutral in the conflict. Today its depiction of Orientals seems extremely biased, but evidently even the Japanese themselves read it (Perry and Aldridge 1971, 107–8). Although Harold Teen continued to represent the gently funny side of adolescence, Terry soon offered a more mature young man for teens to enjoy, especially when he entered the army in the Forties.

Equally virtuous and up to date was "Roy Powers, Eagle Scout," a strip which ran only five years beginning in 1937 and called itself the "official strip of the Boy Scouts of America" (Horn 1996, 332). Seventeen-year-old Roy led the Beaver Patrol troop in mild adventures around the neighborhood, then later around the globe to Africa and Egypt, but the "thrilling, clean-cut story" evidently did not appeal to American teen boys as much as did Dick Tracy and other less clean-cut heroes.

In 1937 another youthful hero appeared in the comics, but this one represented the past. Prince Valiant was six years old in the first strip (Perry and Aldridge 1971, 138) but soon became an adolescent. Set in Arthurian England and drawn by Hal Foster, the story recounted in quasi-medieval prose and carefully detailed drawings the life of a young prince as he wanders through Olde Englande, grapples with outlaws and evil wizards, and rescues lovely maids imprisoned in ancient fortresses and castles. He is always brave and stoic, always young and handsome. Although he sometimes disguises himself, the kindly peasants he befriends recognize his innate nobility—the perfect hero for teens and an intelligent story for literate adults. The strip remains unique among comics for its serious, thoughtful prose, expert drawing, and well-researched settings.

Radio

Of all the media, radio occupied the place of highest honor in the Thirties home. Families in all parts of the country, at all socioeconomic levels, even those who could afford little else in the way of entertainment, bought and listened to radios. Whether a large, heavy, elegant console or a small table model, the radio became the family gathering place in the evenings and on weekends. Probably at no other time in American history have families shared entertainment as they shared the radio during the Depression.

In the great majority of white middle-class families, the days came to be structured around their favorite programs: soap operas during the day; adventure shows in the late afternoons when the children were home; music, family comedy and variety shows in the early evening, and thrillers and horror shows in the late evening.

One of the perennial favorites was *Amos 'n' Andy*, which began as a fifteen-minute show and aired almost daily at 7 P.M. during the decade. It became, according to one commentator, "a national institution" (Barfield

1996, 138). This show, in which white men played black characters, was the descendent of minstrel shows, variety stage shows popular from the mid-nineteenth century until well into the twentieth century in much of the country. In these shows, white men blackened their faces, spoke in exaggerated Negro dialect, and pretended to be happy and ignorant "darkies," dancing and singing joyful or sentimental tunes about plantation life. Amos and Andy were two city men who were always scheming to get ahead and were always running afoul of the pretentious Kingfish; all the characters were buffoons. Even though it was genuinely funny, the show's popularity suggests the racism—albeit innocent and unconscious—that continued to afflict America.

Jack Benny was almost as popular, with his lineup of guest performers, his corny violin playing, and his famous stinginess. Probably one of the most famous moments in radio was his response to a holdup man who said to him, "Your money or your life!" Benny's response was a long silence, and then, "I'm thinking it over!" Audiences loved his trips to his "vault" to get a few cents; sound effects suggested stairs into a deep cavern, clanking chains, and ancient squeaking doors. Another show with popular sound effects was *Fibber McGee and Molly*; every week Fibber would head for the closet, Molly would say, "No, Fibber, don't open that . . ." and the sound of piles of junk falling out of the closet would drown her out, to the enjoyment of millions of listeners. Edgar Bergen and his famous puppet Charlie McCarthy, with his goofy sidekick Mortimer Snerd, were popular, and Blondie made the transition from comic page to radio (and eventually to movies), as did, for a brief time, "Terry and the Pirates" (Barfield 1996, 121). Henry Aldrich was a favorite teen character in stories about his various scrapes and escapades. The opening of the show usually featured his mother calling to him, "Henreee! Henry Aldrich!"

Crime occupied the airwaves in the form of *Gangbusters*, introduced by gunfire and sirens, and concluded by a description of a most-wanted criminal. *The Shadow*, the story of a man who could "cloud men's minds" until he was invisible and hence catch them in their criminal acts, sent chills around the family circle as the Shadow's distinctive voice intoned slowly, "Who knows—what evil—llllurks—in the hearts of men? The Shadow knows!" The ensuing, diabolical laugh became one of the most famous sounds in all radio. The show became a cult program for some college students in the Thirties, who scheduled their Sunday fraternity house dinner around it (Barfield 1996, 164).

Such shows, and others aimed for younger audiences but equally action-packed and gun-fire-riddled, faced organized opposition from parents in the mid-1930s. Sponsors such as Kellogg's, Ovaltine, and General Mills were gaining considerable revenue from targeting young audiences with *Buck Rogers* and *Jack Armstrong, All American Boy*; like their predecessors the dime novel and the series adventure tales from the Stratemeyer Syndicate, such shows traded on the kind of high adventure and fantasy that many believed was too stimulating to young minds. "Practically nothing is left to the imagination," wrote one critic, "Radio supplies the real cries of children, the laughter of men, the ratatat of the machine gun" (quoted in West 1988, 38). The networks responded by drawing up a code that required the shows to respect "adult authority, clean living, high morals, fair play and honorable behavior" (West 1988, 40) and by trying some educational programming. Predictably, the new shows attracted few listeners or sponsors, and young teens continued to enjoy their fantasies as they liked them, unalloyed by overt educational motives.

Radio supplied much more than fantasy and entertainment. One of the most famous and controversial figures of the decade was Father Charles Coughlin, a Catholic priest in Detroit who at one time received thousands of letters a week in praise of his Sunday sermons. With his distinctive and mellow voice, he had raised money to build a church, but when the Depression deepened in the early Thirties, he spoke out in favor of the New Deal. Soon, however, he became disenchanted with what he regarded as its halfway measures to control the national finances, and he began to speak of banks and banking with anti-Semitic overtones. As he ranted against Roosevelt, Jews, and communists, his sermons became increasingly disturbing to the church and to many citizens, although they continued to listen in great numbers and some were even attracted to his proposed Union party. Eventually he was banned from speaking on network radio; nonetheless, many still remember the power of his radio personality.

Radio also supplied the news, at times with a sense of drama that had seldom been possible before. The crash of the German zeppelin *Hindenburg* in Lakehurst, New Jersey, on May 6, 1937, brought into many homes an eyewitness account of the disaster as it was happening. Announcer Herbert Morrison was on the scene, just announcing a successful mooring, when he suddenly broadcast,

"It's burst into flames! Get out of my way, please, oh my, this is terrible, oh my get out of my way please! It's burning, bursting into flames and is falling on the mooring mast and all the folk, we—this is one of the worst catastrophes in the world! It's a terrific sight. Oh, the humanity and all the passengers!" And he burst into tears. (Wallechinsky 1995, 91)

Thirty-five people died. Morrison's own human and completely unplanned response expressed the shock and horror of listeners around the country.

"War of the Worlds"

On October 30, 1938, America experienced one of the most remarkable demonstrations of radio's power and of its ability to confuse fact with fiction in the minds of listeners. Actor and director Orson Welles and his Mercury

Theatre players offered a radio version of H. G. Wells's story "The War of the Worlds." Since it was airing on Sunday evening, opposite Edgar Bergen and Charlie McCarthy, Welles wanted to do his best to ensure a good audience. One of the actors, John Houseman, remembered Welles's use of pauses, believing at the time that no one would stay tuned if he made the story go any slower (Colbert 1997, 393), but the director's timing was perfect. After the slow beginning, Welles created an entirely believable scenario—the shocked voices of those witnessing the Martians' landing in New Jersey, leaving destruction in their wake. Some who had tuned into Edgar Bergen twirled the dial during a commercial and came upon what sounded like a news broadcast: "Ladies and gentlemen, this is the most terrifying thing I have ever witnessed! . . . Wait a minute! Someone's crawling out of the hollow top. Someone or . . . something . . ." (Wallechinsky 1995, 45).

Panic ensued. People flooded into the streets, or jammed the phone lines to their local police station or radio station, and so did not hear the station break, which announced this was only a play, or the second part of the story which took place well after the fictional landing. A fifteen-year-old girl, vacationing in New Jersey with friends, said, "I don't want to die here. I want to go home to my mother," but her hostess said, "How can I take you home? The roads are all full of those horrible things." Only when someone changed the station did the girls realize the events were fiction. Someone else recalled that a women's missionary group had accidentally heard it and fell on their knees to pray for deliverance (Barfield 1996, 152–53).

Welles closed the show with a comment that this was a way of saying "Boo" on Halloween, but almost no one heard him. Houseman remembered the few hours after the show as a "nightmare"; the actors were detained by the police and harassed by reporters who crashed into the studio and suggested that thousands of deaths had resulted from the broadcast (Colbert 1997, 194). In fact, little actual injury had taken place, and the lawsuits that were brought—almost three quarters of a million dollars' worth, according to Houseman—were dismissed. Perhaps radio was still a little new, and audiences had not yet learned to listen with a measure of disbelief; after all, some remember, in the early days, believing that tiny people were inside the box talking (Barfield 1996, 19). Perhaps the growing sense of danger from war made Americans anxious and edgy. Whatever the reason, the panic over the "War of the Worlds" is something that older Americans still remember with amazement, possibly with a shiver.

TEENS AT WORK

With up to a quarter of the population unemployed in the early Thirties, jobs for teens, always relatively scarce, became almost nonexistent. Those who did hire help were more likely to give a job to a man with a family to support than to a teen, and those teens who found jobs were generally the first fired when the business foundered. The part-time job of selling newspapers still attracted many young teens, boys and girls, and girls babysat or sewed to make a little extra cash. Middle-class boys could work in family businesses or get jobs at the local drugstores as soda jerks (so called because of the jerking movement of pulling the levers that controlled the syrups and fizzy water) mixing up sodas and cherry Cokes. This cash, instead of allowing the teens some freedom and spending money, usually went to help support the family. Sharecropping and migratory families, already at the lowest end of the financial spectrum, suffered the most hardships, but even middle-class families, when they had to economize, generally eliminated the things that had grown so important in teen culture: recreation, cars, and clothes (Modell 1989, 129). Teens in the South were still able to work in textile mills and on farms, and in the Midwest and West on family farms and large orchards, but the work was as grueling and underpaid as ever and usually meant schooling itself became a part-time occupation.

Although child labor laws, hard won in Congress during the first two decades, were still in effect, the necessity for the whole family to work usually meant they were also ignored. A fourteen-year-old girl employed as a piece worker in a knitting factory described her day: after getting up at 5:30 A.M. for the three-mile walk to the factory, she had to work fast because in piece work, "every minute counts." She made about 6 cents or less per piece. The machinery broke constantly, and she had to wait for it to be repaired, which meant that she would not make any money during those times.

When I come to the water fountain, no matter how tired and numb I may feel, I am always angry and disgusted. The water is lukewarm; the fountain is rusty and filthy. . . . As usual, half my lunch has been spoiled. I can either put it on the table where I keep my work and where it becomes squashed, or I can put it in a box under my bench and give the rats the first choice. (Quoted in Meltzer 1969, 47–48)

She was one of the lucky ones. Many thousands of teens looked for work and found nothing. Those who had graduated from high school often graduated into enforced idleness; after repeated discouragements, many simply chose to do nothing. John Modell comments that "until their early 20s for both young men and young women, *complete idleness was the modal experience* at any given moment" (Modell 1989, 122, Modell's italics).

One of the phenomena of the decade was the number of teens who, unable to find work and unwilling to burden their families any longer, took to the road. The sight of young people—as many as 300,000 of them and 10% of them girls—hopping freight cars, riding to the next town, sleeping where they could, eating at the Salvation Army, panhandling or stealing was a common one all over the country. They tended to travel in gangs for safety, and at times the girls dressed like males (as did the girls who accused the Scottsboro boys) to further protect themselves. Many headed for cities like Charleston, South Carolina, where at least they could stay warm; many dreamed of finally getting to California. They were sometimes targets of violence and distrust in the towns they visited, especially from the railroad guards. Ed Paulsen, interviewed by Studs Terkel for his book *Hard Times,* graduated from high school in 1930 and "walked out into this thing" of no job, no prospects. He became a teen hobo and told Terkel about some of his experiences:

Hal and I are ridin' on the top of the boxcar, it's a fairly nice night. All of a sudden, there's a railroad dick with a flashlight that reaches a thousand miles. Bam! Bam! He starts shooting. We hear the bullets hitting the card, bam! like that. I throw my hands up and start walking towards that light. Hal's behind me. The guy says, "Get off." I said, "Christ, I can't." This thing's rollin' fifty miles an hour or more. He says, "Jump." I says, "I can't." He says, "Turn around and march ahead." He marches us over the top. There's a gondola [an open, shallow freight car] about eight feet down. He says, "Jump." So I jumped and landed in wet sand, up to my knees. . . .

You stole, you cheated through. You were getting by, survival. . . . It wasn't a big thing, but it created a coyote mentality. . . . A coyote is nature's victim as well as man's. We were coyotes in the Thirties, the jobless. (Terkel 1970, 33–34)

Not surprisingly, statistics showed that youthful crime was on the rise. One government study from 1938 states flatly, "The frequency of youthful crime is appalling" and quotes J. Edgar Hoover on the "stark fact that our misguided boys and girls are thieving, robbing, holding up banks and stores, and shooting down employees, proprietors and the police who attempt to capture them" (Melvin and Smith 1938, 84). However, the trend was most noticeable during the early Depression years; in 1933, the number of youthful offenders declined slightly (1938, 85) perhaps because the Depression seemed to level off at that point, thanks in some measure to two of the New Deal's more successful programs: the Civilian Conservation Corps (CCC) and the National Youth Administration (NYA).

The CCC and the NYA

The Civilian Conservation Corps was one of the earlier New Deal efforts. Established in the spring of 1933, it provided a budget of $500 million to house 250,000 workers aged seventeen to twenty-seven in camps around the country, where they would work for no more than nine months grading roads, building fire towers, laying phone lines, cutting down diseased trees and planting new ones, fighting fires, conducting surveys, and so on. They worked for the National Park Service, for the Army Corps of Engineers, and for various flood control projects (Watkins 1993, 130–131). Although the program has come under fire for being racially segregated, it offered educational opportunities that would have been unavailable to the young men at home, and it awarded eighth grade diplomas as well as high school diplomas to those who earned them. And all was not work. A description of a North Dakota CCC camp mentions baseball, softball, basketball, track, volleyball, horseshoes, tennis, and pool. There were intercamp leagues, camp newspapers, and voluntary vocational training (Hendrickson 1981, 20). This state, one of the hardest hit by the Depression and the dust storms, still benefits from many of the structures built by the CCC (1981, 22), as do many state and national parks around the country. When Congress ended funding for the program in 1942, it was regarded as one of Roosevelt's successes, and many young men who had been through the program remembered it gratefully.

The CCC did not address the problem of younger teens, who still had trouble staying in school or finding work. In 1935 Congress established the National Youth Administration, the purpose of which was to keep students in school and to offer them a kind of apprenticeship which might increase their employability upon graduation. It operated a school work program in which high school and college students were paid small salaries to do various kinds of work around their buildings and campuses. The NYA also offered transient camps and a resident program where teens might live for two weeks at a time and learn various home-making and vocational skills, or, early in the program, perform various kinds of jobs around the community. Aubrey Williams, the director until the program ended in 1942, intended his agency to offer equal opportunity to black Americans and appointed the dynamic Mary McLeod Bethune to oversee the Division of Negro Affairs.

As with the CCC, some local agencies who administered the programs performed better than others, and like virtually all relief programs, it tended to impose American middle-class values where none were wanted or needed, especially in ethnic communities (Palladino 1996, 39–41). By 1940, according to the NAACP, in Georgia, a state where blacks still suffered from high unemployment, the NYA "managed to serve, in sheer numbers, more Negro young people than any other state" (quoted in Watkins 1993, 261). Throughout the country, teachers and financially strapped students who participated in the NYA were enthusiastic and grateful. Grace Palladino cites one eleventh grader's pride at using his first check to buy decent school lunches for himself and his brothers and sisters, then eventually buying shoes and getting his teeth fixed, all with his own money (1996, 44). Ed Paulsen, the teen hobo interviewed by Studs Terkel, was amazed when he was finally taken off a train and sent to one of the NYA's transient camps:

We ate a great meal. It was wonderful. We go upstairs to bed. Here's a double-decker, sheets, toothbrush, towels, everything. I sat down on this damn bed, I can't tell you, full of wonderment. I thought we'd gone to heaven. . . . The NYA was my salvation. I could just as easily have been in Sing Sing. (Terkel 1970, 33–34)

TEENS AT SCHOOL

One of the general patterns of teen life between 1900 and 1950 is the increase in the number of teens in school. At the beginning of the century, school was a relatively minor part of life for most teens; gradually more teens entered school, stayed, and graduated, until, at midcentury, school occupied most of teen life, sheltering and nourishing a separate teen culture. The Thirties were a fulcrum for this shift.

In the early days of the Depression, school was often expendable. Communities who witnessed their businesses closing up and their banks failing first cut back on the number of days the schools were open, then, all too often, closed them altogether, particularly in such hard-hit states as West Virginia and Arkansas. According to one estimate, by 1933, 2,600 schools had closed, and 10 million children in other schools suffered from periodic closings and abbreviated terms (Meltzer 1969, 46). Many teachers during these desperate times took salary cuts and continued to work, often bringing food to school or using their own funds to provide shoes and books to students who could not afford them. In Chicago in 1933, after two years of almost nonexistent pay, teachers threatened to strike; thousands of them invaded City Hall and local banks. Fifteen thousand students took to the streets in their support, but to little avail. The chief result was that "unpaid policemen were cracking their clubs against the heads of unpaid schoolteachers" (quoted in Meltzer 1969, 46).

If schools remained open, many of the programs established in the Twenties were cut, old textbooks were reused, and buildings were barely maintained. Attendance inched up, however, simply because many students would rather be there than looking for work where there was none, some because it was now compulsory; they stayed to graduate because there was little else to do.

Some high school students participated in a famous educational study calculated to determine whether a "progressive" education, such as that advocated by John Dewey, was better than a more traditional education which emphasized language, the classics, history, and fine arts. The Eight Year Study, as it was called, began in 1930 to track two groups of students, one taught by the progressive method and the other by the so-called essentialist method, from their first year in high school until their graduation from college (West 1996, 127), testing them periodically to determine whether one group or the other scored better. Since the study was administered by the Progressive Education Association, its results were predictable: the progressive students won. The argument continues to this day between these two basic approaches to education; probably the chief result of the study was the incorporation of periodic testing into the school year (West 1996, 128), along with the ever-renewed belief that such tests are important and meaningful.

FASHION

Fashion is always a sensitive mirror of a culture. In the Thirties, the wild flapper and relaxed sheik styles of the Twenties gave way to more sober clothes, reflecting the seriousness of the economic crisis. Men adopted a more rugged look, with dark, double-breasted suits, wide trousers, and thick-soled shoes, all giving an impression of solidity and strength. Women too wore longer skirts, dark colors, thick fabrics, and shoulder pads—suggesting that they, too, could shoulder the burdens of the Depression (Lurie 1981, 77–78). Coats were lengthened and, for those men and women who could afford it, featured large fur collars. Clothes for teens generally mirrored these trends: simple skirts and blouses for girls, dark trousers and sweaters for boys, with little ornament.

On the other hand, Hollywood and the movies offered the most glamorous fashion images of the century. Female stars like Jean Harlow sashayed across the screen in revealing gowns that looked more like lingerie: satin, completely backless, with deep decolletage, adorned with feathers and sequins, often with mink or ermine wraps draped over their shoulders. Men too wore full-length furs, often with their tuxedos, in the movies—and, occasionally, in real life, if they could afford them. Silver-blond hair in curls cut close to the head, thin eyebrows, small vivid lips, and sloping shoulders were the desired look among women who watched the movies; men who wanted to be fashionable imitated the looks of rugged Clark Gable. Such images provided the fantasy; hand-me-downs and home haircuts often were the reality.

In 1939 the DuPont Company changed the way in which women dressed with the introduction of nylon stockings. As skirts rose toward the popular knee length of the Forties, these sheer stockings, more affordable and durable than silk, were a touch of glamour and practicality for all American women.

SLANG

As in all other decades, Thirties teens had their own way of talking, a sign of their separateness. A particular patois was spoken by those who hoboed on the freight trains or who worked in soda shops; later in the decade, swing music brought its own speech as well (see Dalzell 1996, 28, 36, and 38). Other less distinct groups of teens smoked "coffin nails" purchased with "jack," disapproved of anything "cheesy," and laughed when they thought something was "a hoot" or "a scream." Like Harold Teen in the comics, and Rudy Vallee on the radio, when they really wanted to agree with something they said "Yowsah!" (yes, sir), and like the tough street kids in the movies, if an authority figure was about to catch them, they advised each other to "cheese it" (to run away). Tom Dalzell offers some less familiar and particularly inventive examples of vivid Thirties slang: You had "the eagers" for someone if you were really interested. If a "Joe" (guy) was conceited, he was "the Big It." If someone was talking nonsense, you said, "Booshwash!," and if someone just was not paying attention, they were simply "fog-bound." (1996, 29–35).

LEISURE ACTIVITIES AND ENTERTAINMENT

Without jobs, teens found themselves at leisure more often than they might have wanted. This increased, widespread idleness of the young was a constant source of worry to Depression adults, especially parents and those in authority such as teachers, community leaders, police, and social workers, who projected their own fears for the future onto those who would soon shape it.

In 1938 the American Youth Commission conducted a study of young people in Maryland between the ages of sixteen and twenty-four (Bell 1938). The whole purpose of the survey, apparently, was to offer statistical evidence to support the efforts being made to build "youth centers," places where teens could gather and participate in communal activities—but especially those sanctioned and probably controlled by adults. Everywhere in the report are the values of middle-class adult authorities; for example, a large amount of space in the report is given to library use, showing that many young people do not have access to a public library, or do not use the ones they have. The researchers stress that the higher the education and the financial position, the more acceptable were teens' leisure activities (1938, 166).

One of the most interesting parts of the Bell report is the verbatim responses of teens themselves about their use of leisure:

I play cards, loaf, eat, and sleep.

I don't read no magazines, I read True Stories . . . well, I guess that's a magazine too, ain't it?

Getting drunk.

Nothing to do, just do nothin'.

I think.

Ride on the beer truck, ride in a car, loaf.

I sit in the barber shop.

I sit in front of the door.

Gamble, shoot craps, read, and play pool.

See what devilment we can get into. We generally get a bottle of whiskey and all get canned.

The researchers add a "tsk tsk" comment: "So much for the 'purposeful and constructive activities' of large numbers of our youth" (166–68). In these voices, however, we get some insight into real teen life during the Thirties, as well as a suggestion of the irreverence with which teens themselves regarded efforts to control their leisure time.

A similar study done the same year by the Works Progress Administration (WPA) on rural youth bemoaned the fact that so few young people on farms and in villages belonged to any organizations; religious and community groups were failing their young by not providing places to go and things to do—"a wholesome social and recreational life" (Melvin and Smith 1938, 86). This study also noted the absence of libraries for many communities and the link between educational and financial status and idleness, as well as the increased power of movies and the automobile in young people's lives. In the South, "The majority of both races find nothing to do but to sit idly around, tramp off to their neighbors, or while away the time at the store. Their houses are unattractive and their minds unstimulated" (1938, 80). As with other studies, this one shows its bias toward white middle-class adult notions of leisure, even while the statistics and anecdotal data seem to suggest youth who preferred to manage their own time without regard to how it suited adults.

As Grace Palladino points out, the more teens stayed in high school, the more they learned to look to each other for their values (1996, 45). For example, teens on the Lower East Side of New York, an area particularly hard hit by the Depression, managed in a remarkable way to carve out their own places for leisure. Suzanne Wasserman describes the "cellar clubs" organized by older teens and youth in their early twenties and serving as many as 10,000 young people during 1934 (Wasserman 1991, 46). In the tenement areas of the city, teens had always made the streets their escape from crowded or oppressive family life, but the cellar clubs offered even more freedom and privacy. With names like the Hy-Hat Club, the Happy Nights Social Club, or the Royal 50 Club, they generally included youth from all ethnic groups in the neighborhood; girls also participated and were welcomed although they had no voting rights. Clubs would sponsor various social activities and thus raise the money to pay the rent on their cellar or storefront location. If a boy was out of work, his club was a safe and friendly haven in the crowded tenement life of the Lower East Side. On summer evenings, the boys might move their couches outside; one club boasted showers and hot water (1991, 47). As usual, some adults in authority characterized the clubs as dens of vice populated by juvenile delinquents and threatened to close them down (47). The clubs persisted, nevertheless, well into the postwar period, a tribute to teens' ability to find their own space, mentally and physically, even in the most unfriendly circumstances.

Sometimes an adult could make a considerable difference. Bishop Bernard

J. Sheil of Chicago founded the Catholic Youth Organization (CYO) in 1930. He offered boxing lessons and competition to tough, streetwise teens who were, as he once put it, not interested in checkers (Gems 1993, 237). His organization was open to all races and ethnic groups; it provided free medical care, all equipment and instruction, clothes, travel to tournaments, and the opportunity for a college education. In return, it expected the athletes to maintain passing grades, avoid vulgar language, behave like sportsmen, and, if Catholic, partake of the sacraments (1993, 236). The combination of toughness, discipline, and dignity was a winning combination; at one time in the early Thirties, the CYO tournament finals attracted 18,000 fans. A vigorous speaker against bigotry of all kinds, Sheil worked with the B'nai B'rith Youth Organization and became the first Gentile to win the B'nai B'rith humanitarian award. He founded community centers for blacks, Japanese, and Native Americans, among others. Many teen drop-outs found renewed self-respect in Sheil's organization.

Dating and Sex

Although dating activities for teens were curtailed by lack of funds during the Thirties, the dating rituals that had begun in the Twenties had become even more entrenched by the end of the decade. Boys selected: they asked girls to movies or parties, tried to dress well, called for them at their homes, and paid for the activity. Girls responded: they said yes or no, and if yes, had the responsibility on the date to be attractive, well-dressed, and amenable to the boys' choices. Desirability as a date no longer suggested desirability as a possible life mate; instead it meant social status, financial ability, pleasing looks, and sociable personality. One "rated" and then one dated. Courtship as it had been known—a clear statement of choice as a marriage partner—had generally disappeared. Dating was more fluid, commitments less binding.

Beyond these customs lay the more problematic area of sex. Whether or not to kiss or hold hands on the first date was often a question for both sexes, but the popularity of petting among college students had begun to filter down to the high schools, and a more crucial question became whether to pet or not to pet, and if a girl did, was she still desirable as a date? When a boy was fortunate enough to have access to a car, the privacy thus gained created even more pressure toward sexual experimentation; parking became one of the forbidden fruits of dating. Older girls were more likely to "go all the way." Out of a group of 383 girls in one 1938–1940 survey, by age eighteen, 23% of them had had intercourse (adapted from Chadwick and Heaton 1992, 140).

Women's magazines, such as *Ladies' Home Journal*, published advice columns for girls which always advised caution and restraint, and occasionally books and articles told boys how to control and sublimate their natural—

but dangerous—desires. Sex education in the high schools was rare, and even libraries were very wary of materials that might give teens more information than they ought to have. Instead, teen girls often found the information they really wanted in pulp magazines like *True Romance* or in "handbooks" like *Sex Facts for Women, How to Make Love,* and *The Art of Kissing.* These offered observations such as "Man was created strong. Woman was created weak. Therefore, it is up to a man to protect his woman" (Morris 1936, 6). On hand-holding in the theater, Morris observes, "There is a delicious little game that can be played in this fashion by entwining your fingers in hers time and time again or rubbing your fingers together" (1936, 17). Although they were ostensibly aimed mostly at men's initiating behaviors, their breathless tone seemed more like romantic fiction, such as this from *The Art of Kissing,* on the French kiss:

if she is all that she should be, she should project the tip of her tongue so that it meets with the tip of yours. Heaven will be in that union! Lava will run through your veins instead of blood. Your breath will come in short gasps. . . . If you are a man, you will clutch the shoulders of your loved one. . . . If you are a woman, and being kissed, you will feel a strange languor passing through your limbs, your entire body. A shudder will go through you. (Morris 1936, 26)

Boys probably found more titillation—and perhaps a measure of the education they wanted—in such magazines as *Spicy Detective, Esquire,* or the more explicit, forbidden eight-page *Tijuana Bibles,* parodies of comic strips like Blondie and Dick Tracy in which the characters indulged in all kinds of sexual activity (Petersen 1997, 155).

The financial difficulties experienced by most middle-class people during the Depression meant that older teens had to proceed very cautiously toward marriage. From this necessity was born the custom of going steady—a period between dating and engagement in which a couple can learn about each other in a more intimate way than dating allowed, but still without the full mutual commitment of an engagement. Going steady usually meant allowing a few more sexual intimacies, but engagement came increasingly to mean that the partners would at some point "go all the way," especially since engagements were being prolonged as much as a year, or even two. Researcher John Modell believes that, during the Depression, Americans came to realize that delaying intercourse during engagement was overly constraining, and that the "largest effect of the Depression on marriage" was the increasing importance of timing, self-reliance, and "cooperation within intimacy," cultural changes which had long-lasting effects (1989, 153).

Music and Dancing

The popular songs of the Depression era offered both a dose of reality and some light-hearted fantasy. "Brother, Can You Spare a Dime?" presented a disturbing image in a minor key of the Depression's Everyman: the worker who helped build America's railroads and skyscrapers, who fought in the war, who was always available, always hard-working, who cannot understand why his rich friends do not recognize him, or why he should have to stand in a bread line now. "I've Got Five Dollars," written by Richard Rodgers and Lorenz Hart, reflected the lighter side of Depression courtship. The lovers list their assets, which amount to good health, a few shirts and some underwear, a little life insurance, some coats loved by the moths, and two faithful hearts. "A Shine on Your Shoes" by Howard Dietz and Arthur Schwartz urges the out-of-work guy to get his shoes shined and walk as if he hadn't a care. The Gold Diggers' song "We're in the Money" from 1933 rejoiced in spending, something many still could not do but enjoyed singing about.

The teenager beginning high school in 1935 was about to enter what some still feel was America's great musical age: the Swing era. Band leaders Tommy Dorsey, Glenn Miller, Duke Ellington, and Woody Herman performed in the big cities; small towners could tune in on their radios and enjoy the music too. The theme song of Swing, "In the Mood" by the Glenn Miller orchestra, first released nationwide in 1939 but really a decade older, represented all that was new and free in music. Another teen tradition, the "Hit Parade," attracted young listeners all over the country and was another step toward creating a genuine national teen culture. The songs were played in random order, with the number-one song played last; teens listened eagerly to see if their favorites would win. One listener remembers that on February 15, 1936, "Alone" was the number-one song, with "Moon over Miami" second; "Red Sails in the Sunset," which had just tied the record for a long hit, was gone from the charts (Barfield 1996, 176–77).

The dance craze that hit the Twenties saw a brief decline at the peak of the Depression. Dance marathons, which had been a happy if somewhat quirky result of the craze, featured dancing couples vying with each other, sometimes with the sponsorship of a hotel or other agency, to see who could dance the longest. They danced for forty-five minutes at a time, took a fifteen-minute rest, and danced again. A particular marathon in 1928 in New York City lasted eighteen days and was finally closed by the Board of Health (Stearns and Stearns 1994, 315); the winners divided $5,000 in prize money. Marathons were held during the Thirties as well, but they took on a different significance. With many teens out of work, dancing was all they had to do, and their need for the money made their efforts to stay on their feet more desperate than courageous.

In the South, in the Appalachian Mountains, and in Texas, young people liked a different kind of music, and during the late Twenties and early Thirties they gathered around their radios to hear the first big star in hillbilly music: Jimmie Rodgers. Like many other boys from the mountains, Rodgers learned early to play guitar and banjo. He began his career in the mid-

Twenties, when he himself was in his late twenties, with his famous "blue yodel" sound. Although he suffered from tuberculosis, he traveled on the vaudeville and tent-show circuit throughout the South and had become by the early Thirties "a household name in thousands of rural and small-town American homes" (Malone 1985, 81). He acted the part of the "young man about town," relaxed and charming; teens who heard and saw him responded eagerly to his easy style, and those who played music themselves were profoundly influenced by him, including Bill Bruner who at age seventeen substituted for Rodgers and afterward began touring himself, singing Rodgers's songs. The young Hank Snow, who listened for hours to Rodgers's recordings, tried to emulate the technique. He eventually billed himself as the "Yodeling Ranger" before his voice deepened (1985, 89–90).

In the Harlem clubs and smaller Negro gathering places around the country, music had a different sound, rooted in the blues and inviting jazzy dance styles. The color line was still there, but, as far as popular music and dance were concerned, it was beginning to blur. In the late Twenties, a dance called the Lindy, a basic two-step accenting the offbeat, was popular in black clubs (Stearns and Stearns 1994, 323). As dancers began to speed it up and add their own variations—especially breaking away from their partners or tossing their partners into the air—it took on a new look. By 1939 white teens were discovering it for themselves. One of them was fifteen-year-old Ernie Smith of Pittsburgh. Ernie sneaked over to the Negro District, where the dance was called the jitterbug, and watched the black dancers perform their smooth routines. He tried it at his high school prom, where he both shocked and impressed his friends (1994, 330). Later he bummed around with some dropouts and discovered the "first white girls" he had seen who could dance in the "authentic, flowing style."

Because they had more opportunities to see Negro dancers, or because they were simply less inhibited—or both—these mill-town girls were the first white girls in that area to dance the Lindy. It was one stage in a process taking place here and there across the country. (330)

Soon teens were dancing in the aisles of a Benny Goodman concert, prompting the police to wonder about their safety and their parents to shake their heads at their children's audacity.

Movies

The Thirties were, by all accounts, the Golden Age of the movies. When the Depression first hit in 1930, movie attendance declined briefly, then it skyrocketed. There are many figures in various sources on the number of theaters and the number of people who went—it is difficult to sort out which might be the most accurate—but all indicate that moviegoing was a phenomenon of the decade. For a time, especially when admission prices dropped, virtually everyone went occasionally, many as often as several times a week, including teens. Wasserman comments that even among New York's Lower East Side youth, all boys aged from ten to fourteen attended the movies between three and six times a week. Sometimes they used their lunch money to buy a ticket; even the poorest theater was a respite from unsuccessful job hunting, as well as a place to meet friends and girls (Wasserman 1991, 45). Rural teens often had no theater close by, but thanks to the automobile, they could and did drive many miles to the movies (Melvin and Smith 1938, 72). The 1938 Bell survey of Maryland about young people between the ages of sixteen and twenty-four comments dismissively about the popularity of movies, in keeping with the apparently elitist (one might even say stodgy) attitude of the researchers, but more than three-fourths of the youth they interviewed enjoyed them very much (Bell 1938, 171).

Studios worked overtime to supply films to a public hungry for the inexpensive but glamorous fantasy they offered, but despite the rush, some of America's best-known and still best-loved films were made during this decade. Some of them have never been surpassed for excellence in production.

The most popular star of the decade was a child. Shirley Temple made thirteen films between 1934 and 1939, each time playing a charming tot who makes everything right for the grown-ups around her, often lifting their hearts with her singing and tap dancing. Her bouncing curls, twinkling eyes, and pouty mouth made her more photographed than FDR, some said, and her fan mail was said to top 60,000 letters a month in 1936 (Wallechinsky 1995, 427). Film scholar Kathy Jackson has speculated on Temple's phenomenal popularity during the Depression. Certainly she was cute and remarkably talented, but in a world full of hungry children and suffering parents who often could not take care of their children as they wanted, she "embodied Americans' hope in the power of youth to right wrongs and ensure a better world. . . . It was the good-hearted, responsible, active child—not money—that held the ultimate hope for the Future" (Jackson 1986, 64).

Cartoons too continued to increase in popularity. Walt Disney's studio expanded with more talented animators than ever and began using the Technicolor process. In 1933 he made the definitive cartoon of the Depression: *Three Little Pigs*. Its theme song, "Who's Afraid of the Big Bad Wolf?," became the studio's first hit song and America's jolly musical antidote to the Depression blues (Jackson 1993, 21). Toward the end of the decade, Disney took a chance on making a full-length cartoon feature. Determined that it should be as perfect as he could make it, he struggled to finance the film as costs rose. When it was released in 1937, *Snow White* was a tremendous hit, and it set the tone for all Disney products to come in the excellence of its animation and the quality of its music. In 1939 Shirley Temple presented Walt Disney with a special Academy Award—one large Oscar and seven little ones—which established Disney's studio and the art of film cartooning as "part of the creme de la creme of Hollywood" (1993, 28).

Not all movies were happy family entertainment. America's three classic horror films were produced during this decade: *Dracula* and *Frankenstein* in 1931 and *The Mummy* in 1932. The first established Bela Lugosi as a star, in a role he had created on stage, and the other two featured Boris Karloff, a cultured and elegant actor who had a long career in such films. In 1933 came the classic thriller *King Kong*, which featured the new Empire State Building in its exciting climax.

This was also the era of the great gangster films; their plots and characters were based on the lives of the criminals and racketeers of the day. Edward G. Robinson created his greatest role as Rico in the 1930 film *Little Caesar*, the tale of an ambitious, scheming man whose career is ended when he is shot down in the streets, gasping the famous line, "Mother of Mercy . . . is this the end of Rico?" In 1931 James Cagney became Tom Powers in *The Public Enemy*, a film with two of the most famous film sequences ever created. Over breakfast, angry at his girl for what he perceives as her prying and possessiveness, he picks up half a grapefruit and smashes it into her face. At the end of the film, other gangsters murder him and leave his bandaged and trussed body standing at his front door; it falls inside "face first like a beef carcass" (Karpf 1973, 85) when his brother opens the door, while sweet music plays in the background. These two films became the models for many others made during the decade, though few were as good, and Humphrey Bogart added his name to the actors associated with gangster roles.

Such movies were usually preceded by a statement from the producers. They "sought to present to the American people an exposé of a national problem and a reassertion of traditional tenets for human conduct" (Karpf 1973, 43). Even though this may have gotten the films past the censors, they were exciting adventures and their flawed heroes were fascinating to watch as they rose and fell.

As always parents were concerned that their children might be seeing too much violence on the screen. Then sexuality appeared in the person of Mae West, who arrived in Hollywood in 1932 and began writing her own scripts in which she became the acknowledged mistress of the double meaning. Although little that could be censored actually happened in her films, her carefully timed one-liners and sly looks suggested amused eroticism. After she appeared on Edgar Bergen's radio show joking with Charlie McCarthy, even her name was banned on 130 stations (Petersen 1994, 152). The Catholic Church mounted an organized campaign against films featuring sexuality and violence and urged its members to join the Legion of Decency. As a result of this pressure, the Motion Picture Production Code, first established in 1934, began to be enforced, especially when Joe Breen took charge. Breen's office made sure that married people occupied twin beds on screen, that breastfeeding and pregnancy should not be seen, that words like *hell* and *fanny*

Andy Hardy Gets Spring Fever (1939). Mickey Rooney as the famous boy, with his wise dad the judge, played by Lewis Stone. Reproduced courtesy of The Museum of Modern Art.

would not be spoken, and that nudity was completely banned (1994, 144–46).

Teens themselves were represented on film during this decade by such stars as Deanna Durbin and Jackie Cooper in *That Certain Age* in 1938, by Bonita Granville as the newly popular heroine Nancy Drew in four films from 1938 and 1939, but most often by Mickey Rooney, whose succession of Andy Hardy films—seventeen of them beginning in 1937—made him the highest paid teenager in the country. In these movies, Rooney played a middle-class teen in a small town, whose father, a dignified judge, had talks with him to keep him on track when he yearned too much for money to buy a jalopy or was too interested in kissing a girl. This was Hollywood's wholesome fantasy version of teen life. College life, too, was mostly depicted in happy fantasies of football, cheerleaders, dating, and dances, perhaps because for most Depression moviegoers, college was indeed a fantasy, a carefree and exotic life they could not personally enjoy. A few dealt with pregnancy, and some with the difficulties of being accepted, but most were happy. Such films were Hollywood's way of introducing a new young star to the public: Loretta Young, Betty Grable, Susan Hayward, and Lana Turner first appeared as fresh-faced teens in such pictures (Umphlett 1984,

79). Black teens were virtually invisible in such movies, with the exception of 1934's *Imitation of Life*, the story of a wealthy white woman, her black maid, and their teenage daughters.

The movies that have come to be most associated with the Thirties, overall, are the musical comedies. In the 1938 survey of older Maryland teens, these were the pictures preferred by most young people. They liked the elegantly dressed characters; the opulent nightclubs, mansions, and hotels in which they sang and danced; the lyrical tunes; the carefree plots; and, of course, the happy endings (Bell 1938, 172). Fred Astaire and Ginger Rogers were the epitome of style in these films; they were, as dance critic Arlene Croce says, the "ideal romantic team. No dancers ever reached a wider public, and the stunning fact is that Astaire and Rogers, whose love scenes were their dances, became the most popular team the movies have ever known" (Croce 1972, 5). Together they made eight films between 1933 and 1939; the studio was so pressured to produce scripts for them that their plots often seem alike, but audiences did not care. They came to see the dancing. Watching the Astaire and Rogers movies now "we are free to enjoy dancing unpressured by extraneousness, as audiences of the Thirties were free . . . those audiences who could take their dancing, as it were, neat" (1972, 7). In some of their musical numbers, the effectiveness of black-and-white film has never been surpassed, its expressiveness never more beautiful. *Follow the Fleet* (1936), *Swing Time* (1936), *Top Hat* (1935), and *Shall We Dance* (1937) still stand out as the high mark of musical comedy achievement on film.

As the decade closed, however, a new kind of film appeared. Four hours long, in glorious color, with sweeping scenes of wounded Civil War soldiers and of Atlanta burning, *Gone With the Wind* took audiences by storm in 1939. David O. Selznick, an independent producer, spent three years ensuring the highest quality in his production of the best-selling 1936 Margaret Mitchell novel of the same name. Rhett Butler was played by the most popular male star of the decade, Clark Gable, and after many rumors and many auditions of hopeful American women, a British actress, Vivien Leigh, played Scarlett O'Hara. Hattie McDaniel won the first Oscar ever awarded to a black for her role as Mammy. But the film's most famous line almost did not reach the screen because of the Motion Picture Production Code and Joe Breen's enthusiastic enforcement of it. Selznick appealed to Breen and his office to let the line stand, since the millions of readers who knew the novel well would remember and anticipate it. When the picture opened in theaters, Rhett's famous line to Scarlett as he leaves her, was intact: "Frankly, my dear, I don't give a damn" (Colbert 1997, 395–96).

The same year, 1939, a seventeen-year-old girl became America's sweetheart in *The Wizard of Oz*. With its inventive combination of black-and-white film with color, its beautiful musical score, and its clever revision of the famous children's classic, the film was a hit and Judy Garland its star.

The role was originally slated for Shirley Temple, whose age was more in keeping with the character of Dorothy, but her studio refused to let her play the part (Jackson 1986, 71). Although Garland was clearly too old and well-endowed for the part, her beautiful singing voice carried the role and the film. Her song "Somewhere Over the Rainbow" encapsulated the hopes and dreams of all Americans as the Depression came to a close.

Books and Reading

The 1938 studies—Bell's of older Maryland teens and Melvin and Smith's of rural youth—paid a good deal of attention to library use among teens. They found, not surprisingly, a strong correlation between educational level and library use and a higher rate among white middle-class teens than among blacks (some libraries were not open to blacks) or children of farm laborers. Generally, younger teens used it more than older teens. There were still many parts of the country that had no access to a library. Those who did used it only about half the time (Bell 1938, 173).

Teens, nevertheless, did read. Many read magazines such as *True Story, True Romance*, or the newly popular *Life* and *Reader's Digest*. These were easily available, cheap, and did not have to be returned to the library. Pulp magazines were popular among boys; *Fight Stories* and *Action Stories* offered detailed and sometimes bloody descriptions of boxing matches or criminal activities. George Orwell remembered that these "Yank mags" were popular with English boys as well. They sold for three pence each, were much more graphic than their British counterparts and displayed more "cynicism and corruption" (Orwell 1939, 300). He cites a story in one of these magazines, "When Hell Came to America," which makes "the frankest appeal to sadism, scenes in which the Nazis tie bombs to women's backs and fling them off heights to watch them blown to pieces in mid-air." The editors used as an excuse a plea for greater restrictions on immigrants. Another part of the magazine offered insights into the "Broadway Hotcha girls" and some 25-cent transfers for sale called "Naughty Nudies" (1939, 300). As Orwell saw it, the American he-man and tough guy were taking over English boys' leisure reading.

Book publication dropped off during the early years of the Depression, but the best-sellers reflected the desires of the reading public to find ways to cope with the crisis. Several best-selling books offered philosophies of stoicism and stressed the importance of spiritual matters rather than material ones. Pearl Buck's thoughtful story of a Chinese family, *The Good Earth*, topped the best-seller list for fiction in 1931 and 1932. James Hilton's *Lost Horizon* appealed to only a small readership at first, but those readers appreciated its gentle Buddhist mysticism and recommended it to others; eventually, it sold as many as 6,000 copies a week. It became a modern classic and the name of its paradise, Shangri-La, entered the American vocabulary

(Hart 1961, 253). The best-selling work of nonfiction for 1938 was *The Importance of Living*, by Lin Yutang. The popularity of religiously oriented books for Americans began with the works of Lloyd C. Douglas, a Congregational clergyman; he produced a series of best-sellers, beginning with *Magnificent Obsession* in 1932, which espoused the principles of the New Testament as the way to the good life (1961, 252) and set the tone for such books well into the next decade.

The Thirties also saw the publication of John Steinbeck's *Of Mice and Men* (1937) and his best-selling *The Grapes of Wrath* (1939), which revealed the human toll of the Depression and the devastation of the dust storms in more vivid terms than the news could. Readers identified with the characters, with their simple struggles and their realistic dialogue, and appreciated their strength in adversity. They would survive, one way or another.

Not all American reading was so serious. Americans also enjoyed Harvey Allen's *Anthony Adverse*, a historical romance, and Erle Stanley Gardner's Perry Mason crime novels. When Margaret Mitchell's *Gone With the Wind* appeared in 1936, readers embraced the feisty Scarlett O'Hara in phenomenal numbers. The publisher at one point shipped out 50,000 copies in a day. Thanks to a perfect combination of historical accuracy and romance, it eventually became America's largest-selling novel (Hart 1961, 263).

Younger teens in the white middle class were still reading series fiction from the Stratemeyer Syndicate. Tom Swift books and the adventures of the Hardy Boys still had tremendous appeal for boys as did many series featuring automobiles, airplanes, and swarthy criminals. After a lull in the Twenties in comparable girls' fiction, Stratemeyer rebounded with its most famous and durable series, this one designed for girls: the Nancy Drew series. Beginning in 1930 with *The Secret of the Old Clock*, blonde, blue-eyed Nancy embarked on a series of exciting adventures; at least sixteen of the books were published in the Thirties alone, and the series continues well into the Nineties. The authorship of the novels has been twice questioned. The name "Carolyn Keene" was the pseudonym given by the syndicate first, evidently to Harriet Stratemeyer Adams, the daughter of the publishing mogul, who claimed for years to have written most of the popular Nancy Drew books. In the 1980s, a Midwesterner named Mildred Wirt Benson came forward with proof that she had been the author of most of the early books. Nancy Drew mysteries continue to be written under the name Carolyn Keene, but the real authors are still kept secret by the publisher. The books have been translated into many languages, as well as revised and updated several times, and were shortened in the Forties. Nancy's adventures have been the center of films and television dramas, games, coloring books, clubs, diaries, and cookbooks.

What accounts for the tremendous appeal of the Nancy Drew books for young teen girls—a popularity that has spanned seven decades? Certainly the action-packed plots, the rapid pace, and the simple vocabulary make them impossible to put down. Too, Nancy has the freedom that many girls desire but cannot have. She has no mother to scold or control her. Her father, attorney Carson Drew, is kindly and indulgent and even helps her out in her mystery solving; the housekeeper, Hannah Gruen, is there to keep house and prepare meals whenever Nancy is around. Her little blue roadster takes her anywhere she wants to go, and she never seems to go to school. Nancy also has many natural assets. She is pretty and intelligent. She knows how to respond to any social situation, but she maintains a careful scrutiny of her situation which never allows her to be taken advantage of. She combines a feminine interest in clothes with an almost complete lack of interest in her long-suffering friend Ned Nickerson. She has strength and courage; locked in closets or trapped in cellars, she can always figure how to get out by using her own ingenuity. Despite the worries of some parents and librarians who think the books are insignificant or trashy, such a character is bound to appeal to girls who are just beginning to find their identity in the world.

The four Bonita Granville movies made from the novels in the late Thirties are quite different. This Nancy bats her eyes at "Ted" (not Ned) to get what she wants, often tricks people to gain a silly advantage, and seems overall less independent and naturally shrewd than the Nancy of the books. The early books do suffer from the racism that permeated the times; blacks and other ethnic groups are stereotyped, and the criminals Nancy brings to justice are frequently swarthy gypsies with shifty eyes. That aside, she offers an entirely appropriate and healthy role model for young teen girls, even if her adventures are not credible. As Anne Scott MacLeod says, Nancy's independence is "not a gift coaxed from fond or dim adults." It is never seriously questioned, and more importantly, it has dignity; autonomy is Nancy's right. In this, she is "the very embodiment of every girl's deepest yearning" (1994, 40, 47).

Other girls' detective series followed in quick succession to capitalize on the success of Nancy Drew, although none of them has ever reached Nancy's sales figures. Judy Bolton appeared in 1932 and lasted until 1961; the Dana Girls series ran from 1934 until 1979; Kay Tracey had a shorter span—1934 to 1942. Obviously many girls were hungry for the kind of adventure stories that boys had been enjoying since the turn of the century. Just when and why they apparently turned to reading *True Romance* as older teens is a question only now being addressed.

Comic Books

Although comic books became a controversial part of teen life in the Fifties, they were invented in the mid-1930s when reprints of comic strips in book form were first given away as premiums in grocery stores and then sold on newsstands for ten cents (Perry and Aldridge 1971, 165–66). Newspaper syndicates picked up the idea and began to capitalize on it. The first bona fide comic book hero is still the most popular: Superman. When Action Comics introduced him in 1938, in a story written by Jerry Siegel and drawn by Joe Schuster, they established the basic pattern of the comic book: a hero with super powers, usually disguised as an ordinary man, who fights an assortment of bizarre and evil villains for "Truth, Justice, and the American Way." Superman was quickly followed by Batman, Captain America, and Captain Marvel as syndicates vied for a space in this growing market.

The exaggerated muscles of the hero, the skimpy clothing of the women, the dramatic foreshortening bringing the action toward the reader, the speech balloons and the depiction of sounds—"Zap!" "Paka-Thanng!" "Wok!"—all set a style that had tremendous appeal to teen boys, who became the prime audience for comic books. Though they seemed simple-minded and excessively violent to many adults, the stories in comic books resembled the great myths and legends of Western culture, and their crowded pages and constant interplay of text and pictures required more than childish intelligence to read. They filled a need for affordable, exciting reading and for fantasies of power at a time when most middle-class teen boys had little of either; probably the disapproval of adults increased their appeal. They were in the vanguard of the separate teen culture that was beginning to emerge.

REFERENCES

Barfield, Ray. *Listening to Radio, 1920–1950*. Westport, Conn.: Praeger, 1996.

Bell, Howard M. *Youth Tell Their Story*. Washington, D.C.: American Council on Education, 1938.

Chadwick, Bruce A., and Jim B. Heaton. *Statistical Handbook on the American Family*. Phoenix, Ariz.: Oryx, 1992.

Colbert, David, ed. *Eyewitness to America*. New York: Pantheon, 1997.

Croce, Arlene. *The Fred Astaire and Ginger Rogers Book*. New York: Vintage, 1972.

Dalzell, Tom. *Flappers 2 Rappers: American Youth Slang*. Springfield, Mass.: Merriam Webster, 1996.

Gems, Gerald R. "Sport, Religion and Americanization: Bishop Sheil and the Catholic Youth Organization." *International Journal of the History of Sport* 10, no. 2 (August 1993):233–41.

Girls' Series Books. Children's Literature Research Collection. Minneapolis: University of Minnesota Press, 1992.

Hart, James D. *The Popular Book: A History of America's Literary Taste*. Berkeley: University of California Press, 1961.

Harvey, Robert C. "The Captain and the Comics." *INKS: Cartoon and Comic Art Studies* 2, no. 3 (November 1995):39–56.

Hendrickson, Kenneth E., Jr. "Relief for Youth: The Civilian Conservation Corps and the National Youth Administration in North Dakota." *North Dakota History*. Bismarck: State Historical Society of North Dakota 48, no. 4 (1981): 17–27.

Horn, Maurice. *100 Years of American Newspaper Comics*. New York: Random House, 1996.

Jackson, Kathy Merlock. *Images of Children in American Film*. Metuchen, N.J.: Scarecrow Press, 1986.

———. *Walt Disney: A Biobibliography*. Westport, Conn.: Greenwood Press, 1993.

Karpf, Stephen Louis. *The Gangster Film: Emergence, Variation, and Decay of a Genre 1930–1940*. New York: Arno Press, 1973.

Keil, Sally VanWagenen. *Those Wonderful Women in Their Flying Machines*. New York: Four Directions Press, 1990.

Lurie, Alison. *The Language of Clothes*. New York: Random House, 1981.

MacLeod, Anne Scott. "Nancy Drew and Her Rivals: No Contest." In *American Childhood*, 30–48. Athens: University of Georgia Press, 1994.

Malone, Bill C. *Country Music, USA*. Austin: University of Texas Press, 1985.

Meltzer, Milton. *Brother, Can You Spare a Dime?* New York: Alfred A. Knopf, 1969.

Melvin, Bruce L., and Elna N. Smith. *Rural Youth: Their Situation and Prospects*. Research Monograph XV. Washington, D.C.: U.S. Government Printing Office, 1938.

Modell, John. *Into One's Own: From Youth to Adulthood in the United States 1920–1975*. Berkeley: University of California Press, 1989.

Morris, Hugh. *The Art of Kissing and How to Make Love*. Printed in the United States in 1936, reprinted 1987 and 1988 (n. p).

Orwell, George. "Boys' Weeklies" (1939). *A Collection of Essays by George Orwell*, 279–309. New York: Harbrace Paperbound Library, 1946.

Palladino, Grace. *Teenagers: An American History*. New York: Basic Books, 1996.

Perry, George, and Alan Aldridge. *The Penguin Book of Comics*. London: Penguin Books, 1971.

Petersen, James R. "Hard Times: Playboy's History of the Sexual Revolution Part IV: 1930–1939." *Playboy* 44, no. 7 (July 1997):104+.

Sifakis, Carl. *The Encyclopedia of American Crime*. New York: Facts on File, 1982.

Stearns, Marshall, and Jean Stearns. *Jazz Dance*. New York: Da Capo Press, 1994.

Terkel, Studs. *Hard Times: An Oral History of the Great Depression*. New York: Pantheon, 1970.

Umphlett, Wiley Lee. *The Movies Go to College*. Rutherford, N.J.: Fairleigh Dickinson University Press, 1984.

Wallechinsky, David. *The People's Almanac Presents the Twentieth Century*. Boston: Little, Brown, 1995.

Washburn, Carolyn Kott. *America in the Twentieth Century: 1930–1939*. North Bellmore, N.Y.: Marshall Cavendish, 1995.

Wasserman, Suzanne. "Cafes, Clubs, Corners and Candy Stores: Youth Leisure-Culture in New York City's Lower East Side During the 1930s." *Journal of American Culture* 14, no. 4 (1991):43–48.

Watkins, T. H. *The Great Depression*. Boston: Little, Brown, 1993.

West, Elliott. *Growing Up in Twentieth Century America*. Westport, Conn.: Greenwood Press, 1996.

West, Mark I. *Children, Culture, and Controversy*. Hamden, Conn.: Archon, 1988.

· 4 ·

The 1940s

All discussions of the Forties in America, whether in books or conversations, tend to separate into two parts: "during the war" and "after the war." It is a decade that seems to split neatly down the middle, divided by the atomic blast at Hiroshima on August 6, 1945, which, for good or ill, ushered the United States into the nuclear age. American teens shared in the wartime patriotism and seriousness, and then in the postwar euphoria and economic boom, just as they shared family and community life with adults. Whereas William Graebner, in his study of the decade, called it the Age of Doubt, finding Americans tortured by uncertainty about the future, teens seemed to enjoy life with increasing confidence in themselves, especially during the postwar period. After 1944 the culture of the teenager, just like the term *teenager*, moved rapidly into the public spotlight, as if during the war it had only been waiting impatiently to become a star.

POLITICS AND NATIONAL EVENTS

By 1940 Norway, Finland, Denmark, Belgium, the Netherlands, and France had all been seized by Germany or the Soviets. Only Britain held out, but as news reached Americans about the daily bombing raids on England, the antiwar sentiment in the States began to shift. Japan also threatened America's power in the Pacific, and when Japan bombed Pearl Harbor on December 7, 1941, America declared war on Japan. Germany, Italy, and Japan then declared war on the United States. By March 1942, Japanese people living in the United States were being "interned"—taken from their

Students lounging outside Harlan High School, Harlan, Kentucky, 1947. Reproduced courtesy of Mary Sue Deters.

homes and communities and placed in primitive camps in isolated areas. They were victims of American fears of another attack, especially a submarine attack on the West Coast.

Like all Americans, teens followed the events of the war—Coral Sea, Midway, Okinawa, D-Day—through newspapers, radio, and conversation. It was especially close and personal when their graduating classmates, barely seventeen or eighteen years old, immediately went into the service; many never returned. Like their parents and teachers, they mourned when Franklin Delano Roosevelt died on April 12, 1945, and rejoiced when the Japanese surrendered on August 14, 1945. Awestruck by the power of the atomic bomb, they realized its potential to change their world forever. As the extent of Adolf Hitler's persecution of the European Jews was revealed, they struggled to absorb the news, or disbelieved it, or blotted it out—just as adults did. One Jewish teenager, however, eventually became part of their school culture: Anne Frank was almost fifteen on D-Day, June 6, 1944. Her diary, found after her death in a concentration camp, has become standard reading for American teens, and has been made into a play and a film. Its touching picture of a girl in hiding from the Nazis reaching physical maturity, experiencing shy first love, then dying, all in the shadow of the Nazi oppression, is a kind of metaphor for all coming-of-age stories, except that it is true.

In school, teens studied the tensions of the Cold War: the arms race with the Soviets, the testing of the hydrogen bomb, and the policy of "containment": aiding less powerful nations if they were threatened by Communist invasion. They witnessed the establishment of the United Nations as an arena for peaceful international problem solving; in some high schools, they took it as a model for the tolerance and rationality they hoped to achieve. They observed and probably absorbed some of the adults' keenly felt postwar fears of Communist infiltration. They watched some of their favorite film stars, including Humphrey Bogart and Lauren Bacall, go to Washington, D.C. in 1947, to protest the accusations of the House Un-American Activities Committee that some of their colleagues had been engaged in communist activity.

The postwar period also bestowed some favors on teens. The transistor, invented in 1948, provided teens with a way to carry their music with them, away from the family. The housing boom allowed more teens than ever to have rooms of their own. In 1946 a ten-foot-tall, thirty-ton giant computer at the University of Pennsylvania, ENIAC (Electronic Numerical Integrator and Computer), whirred into business. *Time* marveled:

Its nimble electrons can add two numbers of ten digits in one five-thousandth of a second. New data can be fed into it at any stage of the process. . . . In nearly every science and every branch of engineering, there are proved principles which have lain dormant for years because their use required too much calculation. . . . In future, they may rely on ENIAC. (*Time Capsule: 1946*, 47)

Although today's computers have a thousand times more computing power and many millions of times more memory space, ENIAC made their technology possible (Colbert 1997, 438).

STUDIES OF AMERICAN TEENS

In 1941 Yale University sociologist August B. Hollingshead proposed to study a Midwestern community, which he disguised as "Elmtown," particularly its teenage population and the effects the social structure of the community had on them. He and his wife traveled to the town, somewhere in the region of Bloomington, Indiana, many times during the succeeding nineteen months to live for brief periods and to observe and interview, as casually as possible, the teens living there. *Elmtown's Youth*, published in 1949, offers many statistical and anecdotal images of teen life in middle America in the early 1940s.

Hollingshead called adolescence, that period between childhood dependency and adult independence, a no-man's land because it seemed to have no definition. Even the laws governing teenagers in "Elmtown" and its state were contradictory. The voting age was twenty-one, but teens could hold jobs without parental consent at age fourteen. School attendance was compulsory until age sixteen, unless a teen was validly employed. A boy could not marry without parental consent until age twenty-one; a girl could marry without parental consent at age eighteen. Boys under seventeen and girls under eighteen who committed crimes were tried in juvenile court. Civil law regarded girls as mature at age eighteen and boys at twenty-one, but tort law regarded all teens over fourteen as being adults (Hollingshead 1949, 151). If the law was so confusing, it was no wonder parents were confused. Hollingshead cited the example of parents who refused to allow their daughter to walk alone to church on Sunday evening, even though the daughter worked until 10 P.M. at a local theater on weeknights and walked home alone after work. In the high schools, students were expected to take responsibility for their own homework, but they needed a written excuse to leave school during class hours. Such mixed messages from adult authority resulted in considerable frustration among "Elmtown" teens.

On the other hand, English anthropologist Geoffrey Gorer, in his observations about American life during the Forties, was amazed by the virtual worship of youth that he perceived here. Adolescence, he thought, was considered the "peak of life"; it seemed to be the responsibility of adults to make sure that their teens enjoyed it. He thought that many adults felt guilty about the Depression and World War II because it had deprived so many young people of those carefree years (Gorer 1948, 122). American popular culture was saturated with images of youth and its power. He believed that in the popular comic strip "Blondie," good-natured but blundering Dagwood represented the lack of authority of the mature male in American culture; his son Alexander was his successful rival (1948, 49). The young soldier, not the older officer, was regarded as the representative of America; "our boys overseas" was the phrase used to describe these soldiers, not "our men." "Americans wish to think of themselves, to be presented as they were when they were at the peak of their life," he commented. "They identify with their children rather than with their parents" (122).

TEENS AT HOME

With the onset of World War II, American homes became at once more independent of material goods and more communal in spirit. Gasoline and metal rationing meant careful monitoring of the use of cars. Cellophane replaced foil in gum wrappers. Food rationing—especially of meat, coffee, butter, cheese, and canned vegetables—encouraged families to try Victory Gardens, raising their own vegetables in the back yard. A five-and-dime store in the Kentucky mountains sold baby chicks with the suggestion that people raise them to provide their own meat (Forester 1990, 232). Clothing was also rationed; at one point, citizens were allowed only three pairs of shoes a year. Cigarettes were a luxury many did without because tobacco farmers were encouraged to grow food crops instead of tobacco.

Every member of the family was expected to contribute something. Adults and teens alike contributed their time to neighborhood civil defense training. For the first time in American history, women entered the workforce in significant numbers. "Rosie the Riveter" became their symbol; with her sleeves rolled up above her powerful biceps, she was pictured on posters and magazine covers doing heavy factory work with skill and enthusiasm, an image that had plenty of grounding in reality. When fathers went into the service and mothers went into factories, some teens found themselves in charge of the household and of their younger siblings. For many this was a serious responsibility and they welcomed the chance to grow up fast. Others resented this kind of sacrifice; boys especially longed to get real jobs in defense where they could feel they were doing their part for the war effort.

Boys who quit school and failed to find jobs became a national concern; often they found their way into street gangs, where adults feared their unruliness was a hindrance to the war effort. "Since battlefield victories depended on a well-ordered, well-integrated, and productive home front, the issue of juvenile delinquency would have to be confronted—and resolved—at once" (Palladino 1996, 81). By 1943 public hearings, forums, radio shows, and magazine articles focused on teenage vandalism, drinking, smoking "reefers" (cigarettes with some marijuana in them), and general unruliness and disrespect, in school and out. Some reformers blamed mothers for being unable to control their children, especially the mothers who worked; others blamed parents for being too easy on their teens, giving them too much money and freedom. As in every other decade, the media were apportioned their share of the responsibility. Swing music led young listeners and jitterbuggers inevitably into sin, and comic books gave them strange and violent ideas.

When the end of the war allowed mothers to return home in large numbers, and fathers to resume their authority and responsibility, they found that home had changed dramatically during the early forties. Teens had experienced too much freedom to relinquish it peacefully. Older teens had already stepped into adult roles, and younger ones had correspondingly stepped up also. They wanted to be full partners in the household now, helping to make decisions about their own responsibilities rather than passively accepting parental rules. In response to this new climate at home, which bewildered many parents and caused others to despair, the Jewish Board of Guardians in New York appointed a team to carry out a series of studies about what teens wanted and needed. The result was "A Teen-age Bill of Rights," which first appeared in the *New York Times Magazine* on January 7, 1945, and was reprinted several times in other magazines:

1. The right to let childhood be forgotten.
2. The right to a "say" about his own life.

3. The right to make mistakes, and find out for himself.

4. The right to have rules explained, not imposed.

5. The right to have fun and companions.

6. The right to question ideas.

7. The right to be at the Romantic Age.

8. The right to a fair chance and opportunity.

9. The right to struggle toward his own philosophy of life.

10. The right to professional help whenever necessary. (Cohen 1945, 54)

The board advised parents to be patient and vigilant but from a distance: in other words, be available but not intrusive. Remember that a child's rights and a child's needs are basically synonymous.

The publication of this document probably would not have been possible at any previous time in American history. Gradually, over forty years, political, economic, and artistic developments had combined to make teenagers a separate group—separate from children because they had the right to make their own decisions; separate from adults because they still had a right to parental protection. Of course, it also originated in a white upper-middle-class society that had the luxury of allowing its teens a measure of financial and emotional freedom. To parents in poor communities, especially those in ethnic neighborhoods, such "rights" for teenagers must have appeared ridiculous. Nevertheless, they heralded a sea change in the attitudes toward and among American teenagers.

Conflict between parents and teens was, of course, nothing new in itself, but the apparent acknowledgment of equality between the sides and the way in which the conflict was played out in the media, on a very large public screen, were new. The *New York Times Magazine* continued its exploration of these issues in a regular column, titled "Parent and Child" which clearly aimed for the parental audience. In December 1946, Catherine Mackenzie noted the reissue of *Guiding the Adolescent*, first published by the U.S. Children's Bureau in 1933. The most notable thing about it, according to Mackenzie, was its lack of revision. The only new suggestion she found was one that urged parents to give teens space at home to entertain friends (1947, 42). The following year, Mackenzie offered advice to parents whose children seemed to belittle and devalue them. Be patient and tolerant, she recommended; remember that the struggle between dependence and independence is occurring in parent as well as child, and that it too will pass (1947, 44).

On the other side, with the inauguration of *Seventeen* magazine in 1944, teens—at least a sizable segment of them—acquired an advisor of their own. The editors advised teen girls not only on fashion, makeup, and dating, but also on politics, reading, jobs, education, and family life. One of its regular features, titled "Why Don't Parents Grow Up?" addressed such issues as curfews, allowances, and household chores. In the case of curfews, the magazine advised teens to cool it; getting along with parents was worth the occasional early night, and teens who cooperated would get more freedom in the long run ("Why Don't Parents Grow Up?" 94). Within a year, the magazine reached a circulation of more than one million (Palladino 1996, 103); girls who wrote to the editors expressed appreciation for their understanding of their needs and interests. The advice given in *Seventeen* was conservative by Nineties standards, but it went farther than adults had in the past to acknowledge teen dignity and responsibility.

Radio and Television

Favorite radio shows from the Thirties continued to bring pleasure to families during the early and mid-Forties. Young teens enjoyed *Jack Armstrong*, *Tom Mix*, *Sky King*, *The Lone Ranger*, and *The Cisco Kid* in the afternoons after school, often lying on the floor or sitting on the porch while they listened. *Your Hit Parade* still appealed to older teens, and shows like *Meet Corliss Archer*, which first aired in 1943, offered middle-class teens a chance to hear amusing versions of their own lives. *Archie Andrews*, already popular from the comic book which had begun in 1941, enjoyed a brief career on radio with his friends Reggie, Jughead, Betty, and Veronica. *Our Miss Brooks*, which aired first in 1948, focused on the career of English teacher Connie Brooks as she coped with a shy biology teacher, a domineering principal, and a dizzy landlady; it also offered funny images of high school students themselves, especially through scratchy-voiced Walter Denton, whose clumsy plots always meant well. Played by Richard Crenna, Walter—with his wheezy jalopy, slow-witted athlete buddies, and sweet girlfriend—represented radio's version of teen high school life until 1957.

During the evening, families gathered round the radio set to listen to drama shows. One girl's enjoyment of spooky shows got her into trouble briefly when she was a sixteen-year-old college freshman. Trying to imitate *Inner Sanctum*'s creepy plots, she wrote an essay about eyes following her everywhere; it was so successful the teacher, thinking she needed help, sent her to the school psychiatrist (Barfield 1996, 160).

The war brought some significant changes to radio. News occupied the airwaves for a good portion of the day, and the announcers' ability to re-create the seriousness and tension of situations abroad made them radio's new stars. Gabriel Heatter, H. V. Kaltenborn, Lowell Thomas, and others riveted listeners to their sets when they delivered their stories. Bulletins interrupting quiz shows or musical programs brought all family conversation to a halt while each listened intently. Thirteen-year-old Jeanette Caler experienced the moment when Paris was liberated; as her local station played "The Last Time I Saw Paris," she wept, saying she was "old enough to truly feel joy for the people being freed" (Barfield 1996, 179). GIs at home and abroad appreciated their radios, especially shows like *Your Hit Parade,* which reminded them of more carefree times.

After the war, more cars had built-in radios, and families taking long drives no longer missed their favorite shows. More important, in a development that signals the definite beginnings of a separate teen culture, technology now made smaller sets possible. Suddenly teens could own their own sets and did not have to listen with their parents. They could take their portables to their rooms, to their friends' houses, out onto the porch, even—those who were lucky enough—into their own cars. One high school student proudly owned a radio "about the size of a businessman's large attache case, but in pink and gray leatherette (very modern!), with a metal carrying handle." It weighed over four pounds, however, so real portability was rather limited; nevertheless, it represented independence (Barfield 1996, 37).

As radio stations became aware of this new audience, they devoted more afternoon airtime to disk jockeys and popular music, especially swing. The lucky boy who had access to a car with a built-in radio was soon very attractive to his friends. One group of teens had a unique way of enjoying the music: "[We'd] tune in to these programs, set the throttle on low, get out of the car, and dance alongside the moving vehicle, listening to our favorite songs. Every once in a while, someone would have to reach in the window and straighten out the wheel. No—no one was drinking, either" (Barfield 1996, 36). Rural teens had less access to the radio, since it was especially important for weather reports and livestock and produce market programs. Radio tubes and batteries could be expensive for farm families, so only a few rural teens were able to listen to swing (West 1945, 16).

In the South and East, teens were beginning to hear more "race music," or black rhythm and blues, from black stations such as Atlanta's WERD which began broadcasting in 1949. Such programs as *Tan Town Jamboree,* the *Heebee Jeebee Show,* and the *Sepia Swing Club* introduced white and black teens to B. B. King, Ma Rainey, and Arthur (Big Boy) Crudup, opening the white teen market for such music (Palladino 1996, 114–15), which they listened to only with each other. Even though radio lost its dominance as family entertainment, when radio sets became portable radio became a symbol of the separation of teens from the family and from the adult culture in general.

By the end of the Forties, families congregated around their television rather than around the radio. Although the first official television broadcast took place in 1927, when Herbert Hoover, then secretary of the interior, spoke from Washington, D.C., to an audience in New York City, television did not make its way into homes in substantial numbers until the late Forties. By then, its entertainment potential was attracting sponsors and performers. Newspaperman Ed Sullivan became the host of a weekly variety show called *The Toast of the Town* in the summer of 1948, with a program featuring music, dancing, and guest artists; among his guests on the first broadcast were comedy team Dean Martin and Jerry Lewis. The program continued on the air as a favorite family show until 1971, making it the longest-running show in television history.

Comic Strips

Favorite comic strips like "Blondie," "Gasoline Alley," "Popeye," and "Donald Duck" continued to be family entertainment, and the number of teenagers featured in the strips grew during the Forties. "Freckles and his Friends," begun in 1915, kept up with the times by selling defense bonds as well as working in espionage occasionally (Horn 1996, 124). "Etta Kett," begun in 1925, continued to keep teen girls posted about fashion, and "Harold Teen" still spouted teen slang and visited the soda shop, although during the war his attempts at undercover work seemed more ludicrous than Freckles'. These representatives of the funny side of teen life were joined in the Forties by "Archie Andrews," "Teena," "Penny," and "Bobby Sox." Archie first appeared in comic books in 1941; by 1947, he had his own daily strip, still in the company of his friends Reggie, Veronica, Betty, and Jughead, still having his troubles with money, dates, cars, and teacher Mrs. Grundy. Even in the Nineties red-haired, freckled Archie represents wholesome teen life in the comics; he is the "leading nonsuperhero in the comics" (1996, 42). "Teena" debuted in 1941 as a typical teenage girl, or bobby-soxer, having teenage troubles with boys until 1964. "Penny" began in 1943; her breezy adventures continued until 1970. In 1944 a strip about teen girls called "Bobby Sox" began, which followed the simple woes and fun of Emmy Lou and her boyfriend Alvin until 1979. Like the bobby-soxer films, these teen girl strips offered a fantasy of comfortable upper-middle-class life among the young.

Many comic strips during the early Forties became serious. "Li'l Abner" turned to acid satire at times, and even "Tillie the Toiler" joined the army. Comic strips were among the earliest popular media to encourage Americans to take part in the war effort; some became effective propaganda for the Allied cause by centering their plots on air power, battles, spies, and saboteurs. Comic strip boxer Joe Palooka joined the army; Dick Tracy and his cronies sought out treason and punished it violently. Even Tarzan and Superman found themselves in parts of the world affected by the conflict. "Terry and the Pirates," created by Milton Caniff in the Thirties, became the most thoughtfully patriotic of the strips. In the strip that ran on Sunday, October 17, 1943, Terry, who was about to leave for combat, was listening to Colonel Corkin's advice to remember all the enlisted men, transport pilots, and good guys who were working hard and counting on him. This was the only comic strip ever to become part of the Congressional Record (Couperie and Horn 1968, 85).

A few strips were designed in 1942 especially for the enlisted man but became popular with those back home as well, suggesting to teen boys some of what they might expect if they were drafted or went into the service. "GI Joe" satirized military life with its countless rules and apparently pointless rituals; eventually its name was given to all ordinary American soldiers. "The Sad Sack" was a goofy little enlisted man who was constantly in trouble but always was good-natured. One strip shows him apparently propositioning a buxom lady on the streetcorner; he follows her to her room, she takes off his pants, and while he stands by looking pleased, she irons them (Perry and Aldridge 1971, 154). Caniff also produced "Male Call," a densely drawn strip featuring GIs in battle as well as in the company of "Miss Lace," whose voluptuous figure soon adorned the walls of many barracks.

TEENS AT WORK

In the early Forties, the school dropout rate increased as teens sought work in defense industries. Restlessly aware that the war effort needed manpower, boys especially gave up the relative freedom of home and school life for the adult discipline of the assembly line, and for a regular paycheck. Those who stayed in school, by choice or because they were unable to find work, chafed at times under what they thought was age discrimination: the assumption that they could not do important work. Girls who were unable to work outside the home often found themselves taking care of the house and younger siblings while both parents worked. In 1942 the Federal Security Agency founded the High School Victory Corps, an organization designed to recruit boys—and girls—for the armed forces by encouraging them to stay in school so they would have the necessary physical and intellectual skills for the service (Palladino 1996, 72), but the plan failed. Teens preferred the immediate rewards of community service.

The National Youth Administration (NYA), which had given job training to many teens during the Depression, also trained them for jobs in defense. Teens who passed the application could live away from home for weeks or months at a time, while they trained and got valuable work experience in a variety of jobs. To some, living away from home was more attractive than working; for their part, parents occasionally sent their adolescent problem children to the work camps in a desperate attempt to control their behavior (Palladino 1996, 67). The training was strict, like a boot camp's; the NYA tolerated no slackers, and those who broke the rules were summarily sent home. Those who stuck it out were rewarded with valuable skills in industry and offices. The NYA offered girls, especially, new opportunities to work with their hands. When the NYA was phased out in 1944 many teens missed

Table 4.1
Teens in the Labor Force, 1943–1950

Figures represent persons aged 14 to 19 and are annual estimates of monthly figures.

	Boys	Girls
1943	4700	2930
1944	4950	2900
1945	4530	2720
1946	3700	2160
1947	3641	2067
1948	3580	2083
1949	3480	2054
1950	3444	1982

Note: Statistics show the decline in the numbers of working teens as World War II ended, when soldiers returned to working civilian life and teens began staying in high school in increasing numbers. Adapted from Table D 13–25 (p. 71), *Historical Statistics of the United States Colonial Times to 1957* (1960).

its training opportunities; with the war's end and veterans receiving employment preference, returning to or staying in school became their only option. The early surge in teenage employment was balanced during the second part of the decade by a return to the earlier rates of teens in the workplace (see Table 4.1).

On the other hand, in the retail trades and small businesses of all types, the demand for part-time adolescent labor remained unchanged. Most high school students had afternoons and early evenings free as well as weekends, the same time that many businesses and service trades needed help. Part-time jobs in bowling alleys, movie theaters, grocery stores, garages, department stores, and restaurants—especially short-order cafes and soda shops—provided teens with the extra cash they needed for gas, snacks, clothes, and dates. As always, however, such employment was considerably more available for a white teen than for a black one.

One of the major changes in teen employment patterns in the Forties is that their salaries, which had previously gone primarily to help the families, now went primarily into their own pockets. Although this was more common in middle-class families, even poorer families allowed their teens to use their own money, although they appreciated occasional contributions to groceries. Martha Burke, daughter of a factory worker in "Elmtown," began making 10 cents an hour in the local dime store as soon as she was out of grade school; then she moved into the office doing bookkeeping, where she eventually earned five dollars a week during her last two years of high school. At night she babysat. Her parents never bought her any clothes or gave her any spending money during her high school years (Hollingshead 1949, 270).

For middle- and upper-class teens, work was less necessary. Usually their jobs were intended to enhance their futures, and they got them through their parents' contacts. Teens who worked in certain kinds of jobs, though, could encounter prejudice. Middle- and upper-class Elmtown teens snubbed girls and boys who worked at hamburger stands or in cheap restaurants, complaining that they smelled bad from the cooking and that they mixed with lower-class people. Such teens often sought companionship among high school dropouts, and a few even dropped out themselves in response to their exclusion from school clubs and social activities (Hollingshead 1949, 277–82).

Farm teens developed work skills early. Farm boys could do all the farm jobs necessary by the time they were in their mid-teens, as could girls: milking, chopping wood, gardening, plowing, and mowing. They could earn their own money from selling produce, animals, or the furs of animals they had trapped; they could do all kinds of repairs on machinery and in the house. Their parents tutored them in these skills and expected them to help out during the afternoons and on weekends. In farming communities, high schools tended to assign less homework, knowing that the teens would be needed at home.

After the war, however, rapid technological developments in farm equipment began to change this picture. The number of tractors in use rose dramatically by the end of World War II; the development of mechanical pickers had a major impact on the number of agricultural jobs available to all workers, not only teens (West 1996, 213–14). Farmers were able to increase their output tremendously, but prices dropped as a result. Poor families no longer able to find even low-wage farm work migrated into the cities seeking jobs in industry, or they moved from farm to farm following the crop seasons. Farm teens no longer wanted to inherit the family land; they preferred to head to the city to find work and a different sort of life.

Their minds were saturated, as were no previous minds in the community, with the material and social values of the outside world, which reached them daily through talk, trips, movies, radio, newspapers, weekly picture magazines, "comic books," and so forth. . . . Due more to the car and the radio than all other influences combined, the fifth generation had many new wants and needs. (West 1945, 214)

Farming was no longer likely to satisfy them.

TEENS AT SCHOOL

Between 1930 and 1940, high school enrollment experienced a gradual trend upward, as soon as it recovered from the depths of the Depression and schools regained their financial security. With the coming of war, high

A classroom at South Hills High School, Pittsburgh, Pennsylvania, 1949. Reproduced courtesy of Roger Rollin.

school students absorbed the patriotism and seriousness of the times, launching countless scrap metal drives and selling war bonds, an activity which reached far beyond the urban schools. In 1943 a group of students in the Hi-Y Club from the tiny coal-mining town of Harlan, Kentucky, sponsored the sale of $103,000 in bonds, more than enough to build a bomber, which they then named (Forester 1990, 106). Teens all over the country helped roll bandages at the Red Cross and helped serve enlisted men in the canteens. The war seemed nearest when their classmates of only a year or two before were killed in battle; some high school newspapers ran "Gold Star" columns to mark their deaths (Palladino 1996, 64). Raising and lowering the flag, singing the national anthem, pledging allegiance to the flag during assemblies—all these routines took on a greater symbolism during the war.

Many boys, especially, were frustrated by symbolic activity. Longing for "real" war work, they dropped out of school to find jobs in the defense industry. Almost half of Boston's sixteen-year-olds quit school between 1940 and 1941. For the first time in this century, between 1940 and 1944, high school enrollments all over the country dropped (Palladino 1996, 66). Those who stayed in school experienced one of the most significant educational shifts of the century: from high school as a privilege to high school

What Every Freshman Should Know

What To Do On The First Day Of School:
If you are in doubt about the first day of school, don't come—come on the second day.
What To Wear:
Wear anything—just so it doesn't look good.
Attitude Toward Seniors:
An attitude of reverence is desirable—if you wish to live.
How To Find Your Locker:
Wait until the third week of school, then look in all the lockers—when you find an empty one, that's yours.
Assemblies:
Be the life of the party! Eat, drink, and be merry for there are classes in a few minutes.
How To Identify Teachers:
Teachers look very much like pupils except that they have gray hair and a scowl on their faces.
How To Study For Semester Tests:
Take lots of books home to impress the teachers. Don't open your books, however. Wait until the next morning, then copy all of your work from the girl in the horn-rimmed spectacles.
What To Do In The Library:
Chew gum, talk, sing, and look at picture books. All very educational.
Where To Smoke:
There are two smoking rooms on each floor, one for boys and one for girls. Cigarette machine in office.
How To Get To The Lunchroom:
Buy a pass on the elevator and a ticket to a reserved table with waitress service.
How To Pass Latin:
Wait till one week of school has passed. Note the girl with the highest grade, then fall in love with her.
What To Do When Approached By A Beautiful Girl:
If you don't know go back to eighth grade.

A 1940s yearbook from South Hills High School in Pittsburgh, Pennsylvania, offered this helpful advice. Reproduced courtesy of Roger Rollin.

as a right—moreover, a right for all socioeconomic groups, although blacks still suffered from underfunded schools which were supposedly separate but equal. Access to higher education was still problematic for blacks as well, although, with the establishment in 1944 of the United Negro College Fund, black high school students had new hope that the black colleges might survive (Hornsby 1997, 149).

In the early Forties, signs of the shift from privilege to right appeared in the public's increasing interest in the personal as well as educational problems of high school students and a clear statement of the school's duty to solve them. The solution usually lay in two areas: revision of the curriculum, replacing traditional programs with increasingly student-centered, vocational, or commercial courses of study; and the institution of guidance counseling.

In the Thirties schools had begun to include various kinds of vocational training in their curricula as well as arts and sports activities which supplemented the basic curriculum. Some schools were also turning to a college preparatory track for their brightest students. Educational theorists encouraged such changes; if the school was to serve all equally, programs of study must be available to suit all, in a given community. But in their attempts to

Typing class, South Hills High School, Pittsburgh, Pennsylvania, 1949. Reproduced courtesy of Roger Rollin.

be "modern," schools—especially those in rural or poor areas—sometimes ran into trouble. The southern Midwestern town disguised as "Plainville," which was studied by James West in 1940, offered a high school curriculum that looked advanced: eight forty-minute periods a day which included courses in bookkeeping, sewing, and typing as well as music theory, orchestra, and citizenship. West noticed, however, that the teachers for the commercial courses had little training in their subjects and that class time in citizenship was often spent discussing last night's ballgame (West 1945, 78–79). On the other hand, the "Plainville" adults were proud of their school's contribution to community ritual and enjoyed its debates, concerts, and graduation exercises as symbols of community modernity (1945, 81).

The citizens of "Plainville" had, their superintendent thought, exactly the kind of school they wanted, a position that tallied with the opinion of English anthropologist Geoffrey Gorer. Offering his pungent observations on American society in 1948, he commented, "The American public school is justifiably one of the chief sources of American civic pride" since it is created and paid for largely by the community itself (Gorer 1948, 99). However, he also believed that the American public school was primarily a social institution, responsible for "stamping the American character on children"— that is, offering youth an enjoyable life and pushing them toward independence. Its interest in conveying knowledge was only secondary, given a curriculum that largely ignored Latin, Greek, and European history in favor

Boys' gym class, South Hills High school, Pittsburgh, Pennsylvania, 1949. Reproduced courtesy of Roger Rollin.

of a variety of vocational courses and civics classes which visited "factories, constructions, police courts, and the like" (1948, 100).

Like the increasing number of choices in the high school curriculum, the guidance counseling movement sprang from a genuine concern for young people, but it was underscored with considerable anxiety about the rapid changes in their lives and at their escalating separation from adult norms and institutions. In 1942 a "Problem Check List" was administered to 603 students at a high school in Asheville, North Carolina, in an effort to identify students with particular needs. It asked students simply to select from a long list the problems that bothered them. As might be expected in wartime, most concern was expressed over the future, with finances and adjustment to school work second. As indicated by Table 4.2 students also expressed worries over personal and psychological relations, health and social activities, and home, family, morals, religion, courtship, sex, and marriage (Mooney 1942, 64).

Those who administered the test noticed that girls at all grade levels mentioned personal and social problems more than boys did, and boys at all grade levels mentioned worries about the future and their school work more than girls did. Freshmen were markedly more concerned than other grades about health problems; sophomores mentioned social activities more than

Table 4.2
Items in the Remaining Areas Marked by Ten Percent or More

	Number Marking
Personal Psychological Relations:	
Forgetting things	176
Not taking some things seriously enough	174
Losing my temper	143
Afraid of making mistakes	132
Taking some things too seriously	131
Nervousness	104
Worrying	85
Sometimes wishing I had never been born	83
Cannot make up my mind about things	79
Daydreaming	73
Social and Recreational Activities:	
So often not allowed to go out at night	139
Taking care of clothes and other belongings	107
Wanting to learn how to dance	87
Wanting to learn how to entertain	80
Too little social life	68
Too little chance to go to shows	65
Too little chance to do what I want to do	65
In too few school activities	64
Courtship, Sex, and Marriage:	
Wondering if I'll ever find a suitable mate	104
Wondering if I'll ever get married	72
Not being allowed to have dates	70
Girl friend	69
Deciding whether I'm in love	68
Curriculum and Teaching Procedures:	
Too much work required in some subjects	128
So often feel restless in class	124
Lunch hour too short	105
Wanting subjects not offered	74
The Future: Vocational and Educational:	
Wondering what I'll be like ten years from now	312
Wondering if I'll be a success in life	192
Deciding whether or not to go to college	140
Wanting advice on what to do after high school	138
Choosing best courses to prepare for college	114
Not knowing what I really want	108
Needing information about occupations	76
Needing to know my vocational abilities	66

Table 4.2 (continued)

	Number Marking
Choosing best courses to prepare for a job	66
Needing to plan ahead for the future	62
Social-Psychological Relations:	
Wanting a more pleasing personality	113
Being disliked by certain persons	97
Disliking certain persons	84
Feelings too easily hurt	80
Lacking leadership ability	61
Morals and Religion:	
Can't forget some mistakes I've made	148
Wondering what becomes of people when they die	103
Being punished for something I didn't do	96
Trying to break off a bad habit	84
Home and Family:	
Father not living	63
Sickness in the family	60

Source: Ross L. Mooney, "Surveying High-School Students' Problems by Means of a Problem Check-List," *Educational Research Bulletin* 21, no. 3 (March 18, 1942): 57–69. Used with permission of the editors of *Theory Into Practice*, Columbus, Ohio.

other grades did; juniors named problems with school work and curriculum most; and seniors named their vocational and educational futures most, along with personal relationships. Most of the students said they enjoyed filling out the list; some added that they had no one to talk to. Many asked for conferences to talk further about their problems.

Such a response proved to the researchers the need for systematic guidance counseling in the schools. It is also the first indication of a pattern that might have resulted from the war, but also might have had deeper roots, one of which increased throughout the century: the apparently lessening impact of parental authority and guidance on teen decision making, and the increasing school time and funding spent on filling this perceived gap. Leslie Chisholm, professor of education at the University of Nebraska and an ardent spokesperson for modern curricula and guidance counseling, expressed this responsibility in no uncertain terms:

Under the democratic way of life, all individuals are assumed to be of equal worth so far as their rights, duties, and opportunity for development are concerned. One of the major responsibilities of the school, therefore, is to provide a type of development in harmony with the needs of each individual who attends school. The extent to which the school fails in this fundamental responsibility is the extent to which it fails in the responsibility our democratic society has assigned to it. (Chisholm 1945, 25)

Despite such lofty ideals, high schools still had to cope with immediate problems that often sprang from social and racial inequities. In the early Forties, in the Midwestern town disguised as Elmtown, high school students repeatedly ran afoul of the school's tardy rule: any student late to class must, on presenting a valid excuse, get an admission slip from the principal's office; without the excuse, he or she must spend an hour in after-school detention. Students who worked in the office sometimes gave slips to their friends and denied them to others; students whose parents had money got away with skipping detention, usually with the principal's knowledge and complicity (he did not want trouble with influential parents), while students from poor families were punished harshly for similar offenses. One "rich kid" had her hair done instead of going to detention and nothing happened to her; one "poor kid" and "known troublemaker" skipped detention and then quit school when the principal demanded he bring his father to school before returning to class (Hollingshead 1949, 185–92).

In smaller towns, especially in the South, schools remained racially segregated, but in larger urban areas, schools were becoming more racially mixed. By 1947, as a result of the large number of defense jobs in California during the war, Fremont High School in Los Angeles had experienced an increased enrollment of blacks and Southern whites. In March of that year, *Time* magazine reported, the white California students erupted in racial hatred; six hundred of them went on "strike," hanging two effigies and gathering across the street from the school with placards reading, "No nigger wanted." The principal, Herbert Wood, entered the crowd, took down the effigies the students had hung, suspended all the strikers, and insisted that they appear before him in his office, with their parents, and sign a pledge agreeing that all Fremont students had the same rights and privileges ("Same Rights, Same Privileges" 1947, 21–22).

During the decade, public protest often went underground, into secret societies. High school fraternities and sororities, with their secret codes and restricted membership, were often attacked in the media in the late Forties; their existence seemed to fly in the face of the raceless, classless society that postwar Americans said they wanted. Some states and towns prohibited interschool clubs and tried to discipline students who displayed their loyalty to such societies. The National Education Association issued a "Law of Loyalty," which was posted on school bulletin boards, asking students to affirm their loyalty to family, town, state, country, humanity, civilization, and school (Graebner 1991, 97). Such concerns reflected those of the larger society, where the House Un-American Activities Committee was questioning the "loyalty" of many Americans, and where the United Nations was being held up as a model of one world. Buffalo's Riverside High School yearbook, *The Skipper*, for 1947, commented that the failure of the United Nations would mean the failure of society (1991, 73). Like their adult counterparts, many students continued to join such societies and find some identity in them, perhaps in some measure because they were, in public anyway, forbidden.

FASHION

As much as any other area of teen life, fashions reflected the split between the early and late Forties. When America entered the war, clothes took on the sober, patriotic mood of sacrifice and hard work. School clothes for girls were generally simple sweaters and skirts, and loafers worn with socks. In cold weather, girls kept warm, and kept their hair in place, with a scarf folded into a triangle with the ends tied under the chin. Boys wore loose, cuffed trousers, open-neck shirts, jackets with broad lapels, and lace-up oxfords. Older teen girls working in offices adopted a businesslike look of competence: tailored suits with slim waists and broad padded shoulders, shoes with wedge soles or high thick heels, and hats, sometimes with wide brims, usually fitted on the back of the head. In 1944 *Seventeen* magazine emphasized the importance of a "smart hat" and explained how to make an unusual hat pin. Gloves, as important to a girl's finished look as hats, usually extended to well above the wrist. Purses were often large, slightly rectangular soft pouches, meant to be tucked under the arm. Suits for older boys were often double-breasted, with wide cuffed pants; four-in-hand ties were broad and often short, not meeting the trouser waistband.

During the war, many women wore a uniform look whether they were in the service or not. They wanted to look efficient and capable of independence and action. Waist-length jackets, called Eisenhower jackets after the well-known World War II general, were popular with men and women, and service women wore ties, hats, and increasingly often, pants similar to the men's. Shoes were laced up, with sensible small heels. Overcoats for men and women often had broad shoulders and lapels and tie belts. Overalls were a popular look for girls, although they were made of softer fabrics than denim. Pinafores, or apron-like dresses worn with blouses, were a practical summer look.

Hairstyles for women became particularly important as more women entered factory work. Most girls had medium to shoulder-length hair, which had to be carefully fastened away from machinery. Many women tied their hair up in a kerchief as the simplest and safest solution. As always, high style began to elaborate on necessity. Stylish girls wore their hair swept up on the sides into rolls on either side of the head, leaving the back to hang in fluffy end curls. For parties, the long back hair might be caught in a "snood," a decorative net. Bobby pins became an important beauty accessory. Probably named for the flapper's bobbed hair, the small, narrow metal clips were essential for the rolled and fastened styles, and for anchoring wet hair into round "pincurls" until it dried into fluffy ends. Film star Lauren Bacall popularized the long bob, parted on the side and swinging over the face or held back with a barette. Increasingly, teen girls seeking glamour visited salons for permanent waves; girls who could not afford this luxury gave each other Toni home permanents.

The makeup styles of the glamorous film stars of the early Forties also appeared among teens, gradually increasing in use after the war until most girls of eighteen invested a good portion of their earnings in cosmetics. Eyebrows were plucked to a thin line and enhanced with eyebrow pencil which extended to the outer corner of the eye; lashes were long and mascaraed. Lips were full and moist with red lipstick. Creams, lotions, and nail polish became part of a girl's beauty routine when more affordable beauty products appeared on the market after the war.

Fashions in underwear did not change, however. All women, no matter how slim, wore—or were expected to wear—girdles of some kind, either elastic panty girdles or the more constricting corsets, and girls in their early and mid-teens wore them as well. Brassieres were substantial; slips were worn with most clothes. Stockings were sheer, and affordable after the war, but they had to be held up with garters, which were attached either to the girdle or to a separate belt. Stockings had seams up the back of the leg, and dark heels and toes. Every girl had to "keep her seams straight" and her slip from showing when she was dressed up.

After 1945, American film stars, models, and teenagers came to define the "American look," and it was not the look previously dictated by Paris fashion houses. Instead of elegant evening wear and chic suits and dresses, American girls wore casual clothes: sweaters, plaid skirts with pleats, and tailored jackets, and for really casual occasions, jeans rolled up to the knees. As *Life* magazine saw it in 1945, the American look included a slim waist, long legs, and a friendly smile revealing well-cared-for white teeth. The American girl was healthy and well-nourished; she bathed often, her nails were well manicured, her posture was excellent. She had a natural poise and enthusiasm that did not require or enjoy constricting, artificial clothes. She enjoyed athletics more than evenings at expensive restaurants. Above all, she was young, white, and upper middle-class. The younger girls were identified by their fondness for bobby socks, or "sox," worn with saddle shoes or loafers. These bobby-soxers were celebrated in such films as *The Bachelor and the Bobby Soxer* (1947), which portrayed their youthful style, swingy skirts, and fresh complexions.

Boys' styles changed less than those of the girls. For school, blue jeans, white socks, and loafers were standard in many places; slacks and open-collar shirts constituted dress-up clothes. According to *Life*, boys in a high school in Des Moines, Iowa, enjoyed the fad of wearing big GI-issue shoes every Tuesday, calling them "my old lady's Army shoes" ("Teen-agers" 1948, 71). The white T-shirt introduced by the U.S. Navy (called "T" because of its shape) became, after the war, the standard casual wear for boys, especially with jeans.

Boys also experimented with hairstyles. Pennsylvania boys might part the hair on both sides and comb the center forward or backward; Texas

Bobby-soxers, Villa Madonna Academy, Covington, Kentucky, 1946. Reproduced courtesy of Mary Lou Kaub.

boys might wear a "boogie" cut (long on the sides and short on top), a "burr" (very short all over), an Apache (a ridge of hair on top), or a "Hollywood" (ducktails meeting in back) (Smith 1962, 13). Although there was no look for boys equivalent to the glamour look for teen girls, the most popular boy at a Denver high school, represented in *Life* magazine in 1948, sported loose trousers, a school "letter" jacket with a white scarf at the neck, and a small-brimmed hat tilted back on his head.

There was another side to American fashion, however. As workers migrated to California during the war to seek jobs in defense plants and the population of that state grew, more Americans were exposed to the ethnic cuture of Mexico with its vivid colors and decorative patterns. White American girls in the Southwest, and gradually in the East, began to imitate the sandals, full skirts, cinched waists, and off-the-shoulder ruffled blouses they saw increasingly in magazines and movies. The Mexican Americans themselves, "the would-be bobby soxers of a less prosperous community" and usually children of immigrants (Palladino 1996, 58), dressed in a much more aggressive style. These girls adopted tight skirts, sheer blouses, and heavy makeup. The boys, known as *pachucos*, wore their hair long and ducktailed, and they adopted suits with tapered and draped pants, long jackets with broad shoulders, and wide-brimmed hats. A long watch chain was the chief accessory. These suits, known as "zoot suits," were associated with jazz musicians and gangsters as well as *pachucos*. In California in 1943, when white soldiers and sailors believed that *pachucos* were trying to date white women, they provoked bloody riots which spread across the country (Cosgrove 1988). The *pachucos* and their *pachuquitas*, not part of the white American mainstream, expressed their alienation in their clothes and suffered further discrimination as a result.

SLANG

The word *teenager* came into public usage in the Forties, although Tom Dalzell calls it "a word waiting for a concept" (1996, 63). The decade of the Forties also produced some of the most lively slang spoken by teenagers during the century. Swing music and jitterbug culture set the tone in the late Thirties; when the Forties began, white middle-class teens could also hear black jive talk on the radio: "Hiya cat, wipe your feet on the mat, let's slap on the fat and dish out some scat" (Dalzell 1996, 42). After Dizzy Gillespie's recording in 1945 of "Be-Bop," *bop* and *be-bop* became popular slang words to describe the sounds and bounce of the new-style jazz. Jive's combination of esoteric meanings, rhythmic and rhyming sounds, clever puns, and vivid images offered teens a chance to create their own space in language to the greatest degree yet in this century. In 1949 *Time* magazine claimed to overhear this conversation between teens in Atlanta, Georgia:

"Ahhh, Rooshan!
  "Climb into my zoom buggy and come on down to Rusty's for a naked steak and a P.C." (a hamburger with no trimmings and a plain chocolate milk)
  "Sorry, I'm going to see my N.W.A.B." (a girl who necks with any boy)
  "Dear Gussie, we must fall flat on our faces five times. Have been." (That's too bad. I'll see you later.) (quoted in Smith 1962, 15)

Something good was smooth, snazzy, gone, neat, rare, a killer-diller. Groovy was borrowed directly from jazz musicians, who when they were playing well, especially listening to their own sounds at the same time as blending into the group, were "in the groove," like the smooth-resting needle in the grooves of a 78 rpm record. The really groovy cats added "-reeny," or "-rooney," or "o-rooney," to any word to make it swing. A good-looking girl was an angel cake, butterfly, slick chick, fly chick, or filly. A smooth guy was simply luscious, a bunny boy, Jackson, Pappy, Romeo, or swooney. No girl wanted to date a drip, jerk, schmo, square, or geek. Necking was also known as smooching, schmotzing, monking, or hacking. Hep and hip were used interchangeably until the Forties, when hip became

Eighteen-year-olds picnicking near Covington, Kentucky, 1949. Reproduced courtesy of Mary Sue Deters.

the word of choice and the "hardest working word in 20th century American youth slang" (Dalzell 1996, 57).

LEISURE ACTIVITIES AND ENTERTAINMENT

During the Thirties, drugstores had become a favored place for teens to meet. In a holdover from Prohibition days, when it was the only place that sold alcohol legally, the drugstore offered Coca-Cola and Dr. Pepper—pick-me-up drinks that took the place of alcohol—as well as ice cream drinks and concoctions: sodas, shakes, malted milks, and sundaes. The sundae was invented, so the story goes, in response to an 1890s craze for soda-sipping, especially on Sunday; righteous ministers in many areas of the country obtained a ban on the creamy drink. A Wisconsin soda-fountain owner found a substitute when he poured syrup over ice cream and left out the fizzy soda water; at first he sold it only on Sundays because it was so popular he was losing money. Later he changed the spelling to get around the ministers, and advertised the "Soda-less Soda" throughout the week (Witzel 1994, 20).

During the Forties, drugstores carried on the tradition, with the addition of lunch counters where diners could get sandwiches as well as Cokes and ice cream. The atmosphere of the Forties drugstore and its significance to teen leisure is well depicted in Maureen Daly's 1942 novel *Seventeenth Summer*. High school students in the most envied clique go there after school each day to talk, drink Cokes, and clown around. Angie, the heroine, is at first shy about going into the drugstore and encountering these smooth teens so comfortable with each other, but when she begins dating a member of the crowd, she enjoys the social times there and feels superior to girls who are not part of what is now her crowd too.

Teen Clubs

In response to the adult perception that teens needed places of their own, but places to stay out of trouble, many communities created teen canteens, modeled on the canteens that served the armed forces. Civic-minded adults, often in partnership with teens but not always, found space where teens could have a jukebox, dance floor, ping-pong table, and Coke bar, sometimes with the corporate support of Royal Crown Cola or Coca-Cola (Palladino 1996, 86). Such places kept teens off the street and out of the dangerous atmosphere of roadhouses and clubs where alcohol was sold and where teens might mix with unsavory adults. Usually, such canteens were open only to high school students and forbade bringing dates. Adults were usually present to check on adherence to these rules. The clubs tended to be racially and ethnically segregated.

In a very few places, however, teens themselves ran the show. One of the most exemplary such organizations was the Brownsville Boys Club, established in 1940 in a poor section of Brooklyn, New York, known for its high crime rate. The neighborhood also had a number of boys, mostly Jewish, who had a strong sense of community and mutual support. After their afternoon recreation space at the local school was closed to boys over fourteen, they created their own club. Led by sixteen-year-old Jacob Baroff, the boys gathered representatives of existing clubs together and petitioned for a space to play basketball and to hold meetings. They soon secured a schoolyard and a room in the local library for their activities. They named themselves the Brownsville Boys Club and nurtured many underprivileged boys without any adult help or supervision for more than seven years.

During the war, the Brownsville boys did their part to help the patriotic effort. They had seen some of their founders, including Baroff, head for service abroad, so their involvement was personal and important. They participated in drives for scrap metal and, at times, were required to buy war stamps. After the war, moved by pictures of children in concentration camps, they adopted a war orphan. They collected more than $350 by eliminating bubble gum and candy from their budgets and sent the money to a boy whose picture they had "kinda liked" (Sorin 1990, 98). Gradually, too, the club became racially integrated and by 1947 had several all-black teams as well as integrated ones.

Slumber Parties

When white middle-class girls of the Forties wanted to get together, they often held slumber parties. They would congregate at one girl's house, put on their pajamas, and try to stay up as late as possible while gossiping, rolling each other's hair in pin curls, experimenting with makeup, eating junk food, playing records, and talking on the phone to boys. Often the measure of a successful slumber party was a visit by a group of boys who would show up in their cars and hang around, talking to the girls through the window and clowning. (More daring girls would drop a hint to the boys at school that they would be having the party, so the visit was not usually a surprise.)

Church Groups

Many teens, especially in small towns and rural areas, regarded church primarily as a place to meet friends. While they might attend Sunday services with their families, they looked forward to church-sponsored parties or Sunday-night youth group meetings. The teens in "Elmtown," for example, regarded church as a "community facility like the school, the drug store, the city government, and the bowling alley" (Hollingshead 1949, 246). Religion itself, and the importance of faith, was, for the majority, something they took for granted and not particularly related to going to church. Even church youth groups, as much as ministers tried to make them democratic and tolerant, had cliques.

Dating and Sex

During the early Forties, the "rating and dating" system, which had begun in the Twenties and was beginning to recover from Depression economics, suffered another setback because of the war. Suddenly older teen boys were going into the service, and college girls dramatically outnumbered men on campuses nationwide. High school students found themselves crowded out of movie houses, soda fountains, roadhouses, and canteens by men in uniform; rationing meant no car and only the plainest food. Even if a teen had a part time job, there was little on which to spend any extra money.

On the other hand, sexual strictures began to loosen. In the early Forties, out of a group of 664 females, 7.1% of sixteen-year-old girls had had intercourse, and 22.6% of eighteen-year-old girls. By the late Forties, the percentage of sixteen-year-old girls who had had intercourse had crept to 10.1,

A school slumber party, with a watchful teacher nearby, Villa Madonna Academy, Covington, Kentucky, 1949. Reproduced courtesy of Mary Lou Kaub.

and among eighteen-year-old girls to 29.3. Boys who were enlisted or drafted felt some pressure to have a girlfriend, some link with home, that they could treasure during the years away. Girls too could become caught up in the tensions of the time, fearing that the boys they loved would never return. Teens grew up fast in these circumstances, and for many, having sex was a mark of maturity and commitment. For others, as their parents' attention shifted from trying to control suspicious teen behavior to making various wartime sacrifices, the early Forties offered new freedoms. They could stay away from school, stay out late, enjoy streetcorner socializing, and even—in the case of boys especially—engage in stealing or vandalism to assert their independence.

Girls as young as fourteen put on makeup and seductive clothing and visited places where servicemen might pick them up: bus stations, canteens, and hotels. Sometimes they invited the boys home, sometimes they went to bars and movies, exchanging their companionship and good spirits for a pair of nylon stockings (Palladino 1996, 74). The popular press called them "V-girls," or Victory girls (an obvious analogy to the term "B-girl," or "bar girl," one who worked a bar encouraging men to buy her expensive drinks) and while the girls may have thought they were being patriotic, many adult authorities warned servicemen that they were indeed prostitutes and probably infected with venereal disease (VD). Until the war, condoms had never been promoted as protection against sexually transmitted disease, but when the U.S. Army surveyed its soldiers about their level of sexual activity and found that boys were having their first sexual experiences as young as fifteen, films warning of the ravages of VD became part of every soldier's training, and vending machines dispensing condoms (three for ten cents) were installed on military bases (1996, 76).

In the little Midwestern town of "Plainville," however, studied during the early Forties by James West, things were different. Dating continued in the same patterns as before: it began between age fourteen and age seventeen, although the majority of high school students did not date (West 1945, 195). Fewer girls than boys had dates. Riding in a car and going to a movie were the chief activities, and a car was practically essential for a boy to get a date. The community frowned on dating between social classes; if a wealthy boy dated a poor girl, he was assumed to be after sex. Of course interracial dating was absolutely taboo in most places, although by 1948 the Supreme Court of California had ruled that the state law prohibiting interracial marriage was unconstitutional (Hornsby 1997, 157).

In general, teens did not discuss sex with adults at all; in "Plainville," boys were assumed to learn what they needed to know from watching farm animals or from listening to other boys. Although girls talked more to their mothers, the taboos against using words like *menstruation* and *intercourse* persisted. Although the community publicly endorsed chastity for boys and girls until marriage, boys were expected to get some sexual experience before marriage, usually by age seventeen or eighteen, preferably in another town; girls who engaged in sex were disgraced until they got married.

During the postwar euphoria and economic boom, teens took up the old patterns of dating with enthusiasm and at a much younger age than before the war. Catherine Mackenzie in the *New York Times Magazine*, in the mid-Forties, discussed the pattern of early dating among teens. Thirteen- and fourteen-year-old girls said their favorite activity was dating; boys of the same age preferred sports and reading; consequently, the girls went out with older boys. In many cases, teens were pairing off as early as twelve and thirteen, and parents were taking it in stride by providing transportation and opportunities for partying at home (1945, 29; 1946, 34).

In middle-class homes especially, one's "first date" became an important milestone, the time when the boy and girl broke away from the crowd or clique and enjoyed each other's company alone. The chief goal of dating for a boy was to entice a popular girl to go out with him; the chief goal for a girl was to amass as many invitations for dates as she could. Such a system obviously privileged boys over girls, since only the prettiest and most popular girls tended to be asked for dates. Boys, however, still bore the financial responsibility for the date, and for providing the transportation, and the flowers if the evening was formal. Girls were expected to be nicely dressed, pleasant and entertaining company, and generally amenable to the boy's suggestions. Both genders had their "line," as it was called: a special kind of conversation peculiar to the date in which the boy suggested in various direct or indirect ways that he found the girl attractive and perhaps even might "love" her, and the girl devised ways to respond positively, suggesting that she found him attractive too, yet without encouraging him too much. *Seventeen* magazine featured regular advice columns and quizzes on dating to help girls with these skills, such as "First-Date Quiz" (September 1944, 4), suggesting how they should behave on the first date or rating their performance after the date. Real emotional involvement was not the point in this system; it was a kind of competition in which, ideally, both sides won.

Englishman Geoffrey Gorer, looking at American customs from the viewpoint of an anthropologist comparing different cultures, marveled at the institution of dating. He found it "the most singular feature of American social life," a behavior "peculiar to the inhabitants of the United States; subjectively it is the most important and enjoyable occupation of the peak period of one's life." He even commented that for many Americans, the "pursuit of happiness," one of the unalienable rights set down in the Declaration of Independence, "is an elegant periphrasis for 'dating' " (Gorer 1948, 123).

If after dating for a time, the couple decided to "go steady," they signaled this decision by exchanging high school rings, wearing similar clothes, or peroxiding similar streaks in their hair (Palladino 1996, 112). They dated several times a week, and necked heavily, or petted.

Although sexual fulfillment was not the goal of the date, even casual dates often ended in petting if both partners were willing, and especially if they were going steady—although sometimes girls felt boys pressured them into petting (Smith 1962, 187). Notions of petting ranged from necking, to light body caresses, to more intense caressing of breasts and genitals, to orgasm without coitus. The privacy of the automobile encouraged petting, since it had to be done in secrecy. The adult "line" assumed that teens, both boys and girls, would remain chaste until marriage; the reality was that teens experienced sexual pressures and longings that needed some outlet. The only one sanctioned, and even that covertly, was petting. One researcher saw it as a circular conspiracy game:

In this game some adults aid and abet the adolescents, while others work against them and attempt to maintain the mores; one sex plots against the other, not infrequently males outwit males and females hoodwink females; adolescents defy adults, and children their parents. The churches try to uphold the mores; the taverns and public dance halls aid in their circumvention. Although the police are charged with the maintenance of the mores, they regularly compromise between their strict enforcement and their open violation. (Hollingshead 1949, 417)

In 1949 one study stated that girls admitted to petting with an average of ten boys and boys to petting with an average of fifteen girls (Smith 1962, 190), leading a sociologist to assert that petting was the "most significant of heterosexual relations" up to the late teens, and an important sexual outlet before marriage. He also believed it was predominantly a middle-class activity (1962, 190).

In 1948 the first Kinsey report appeared. This controversial document, which changed the way in which Americans thought about themselves as sexual beings, was a dramatic public and documented testimony to the sexual activity of teenagers. Alfred C. Kinsey, an entomologist at Indiana University in the late Thirties, who was a specialist in wasps, was asked to coordinate a course on marriage. He prepared for it scientifically by collecting as much data as he could on the sexual behavior of men and women. He interviewed his students and asked them directly about all aspects of their sexual lives: intercourse, orgasm, masturbation, and homosexual activities—topics that had hitherto been taboo even in scientific studies. Although he gave up teaching the course in 1940, he continued his pioneering research for the next fifteen years, interviewing more than 17,000 informants (Petersen 1997, 165).

His first book, *Sexual Behavior in the Human Male* (followed in 1953 by *Sexual Behavior in the Human Female*), an 804-page document filled with charts and statistics, sold more than 200,000 copies in two months and generated considerable comment both positive and negative. He found that 95% of males had experienced some form of sexual outlet, 92% had masturbated, and 69% had had experience with prostitutes (Petersen 1997, 165). One of Kinsey's most interesting findings was that 32% of high school boys had had homosexual contact (Smith 1962, 144). Earlier studies had shown patterns of homosexuality among girls as well. Though such behaviors tended to be dismissed as "crushes" in the sociological literature, this high number suggested something more serious. Sociologists still insisted that it was a learned behavior brought on by the "discontinuity" in American society, which expected young people to leap from chaste childhood into marital sex without any transitional phase (1962, 143). West in his "Plainville" study and Hollingshead in "Elmtown," who had completed their research before Kinsey published his, found plenty of anecdotal and statistical evidence to concur with Kinsey's own. Although Kinsey offered no judgment about the behavior he described (except to deny any harmful effect from masturbation), West and Hollingshead both deplored what Kinsey's study revealed: the continuing pattern of secrecy and hypocrisy about the sexuality of the young.

The Car

Probably nothing changed teen leisure as much as the car. The rationing of gasoline, metal, and rubber during the war limited new car production; except for the very rich, adults made do with their old cars. After the war, however, car production could hardly keep pace with the demand. When parents became able to afford new cars, teens generally inherited the old ones. Those old jalopies enabled teens to seek space of their own to date or be with friends and provided transportation to school or work. Those with built-in radios were even more popular; teens could enjoy their music with friends rather than share the radio with family. Learning to drive gradually became an accepted rite of passage rather than a privilege, although some farm families disapproved of this new custom (West 1945, 57). In Atlanta, according to a 1947 story in *Time*, driving had to have style. Teen boys showed off their skills by "scratching": they would start the car in reverse, go backward in a tight semicircle, then slam into low gear and roar off squealing the tires ("Reeny Season" 1947, 25).

By 1948, thanks to cheaper raw materials, some car manufacturers had found ways to appeal to the young, or to those who wanted to seem young. Running boards were a thing of the past. The 1948 Cadillac added tapered tailfins like fighter planes; more car makers installed overhead-valve, high-compression engines; and designers phased out fenders and added chrome. General Motors car radios had elliptical speakers and signal-seeking buttons by 1947; Chrysler soon had a "Jukebox Dashboard" with blinking lights and lots of buttons (Widmer 1990, 84). Customizing became part of a teen's relationship with his car; the automobile "allowed the postwar youth to express himself in ways that no machine had, at least in recent memory"

(1990, 85). According to one estimate, U.S. annual car production increased from 83,700 in 1945 to 2,156,000 in 1946 and was still climbing at the end of the decade (1990, 84).

Drive-in Movies and Restaurants

The drive-in-movie theater, which first appeared in New Jersey in 1933, gradually increased in popularity as automobiles increased in affordability and availability. In 1944 a trade magazine for theater owners predicted that, after the war, drive-in movies would boom as gas rationing disappeared, all-beef hot dogs became available, people needed fresh air, and the young experienced the "resumption of normal restrictions upon their amorous impulses" (Valentine 1990, 144). The car offered privacy and mobility to dating couples, and a drive-in movie offered the opportunity to enjoy that privacy and see friends at the same time. It "successfully combined public and private life during a period in American history that was trying to strengthen both" (1990, 145).

Drive-in restaurants did the same thing, especially for teens. Drive-ins had first opened in the Twenties and the term was probably invented in 1937 (Witzel 1994, 96), but with the postwar economic boom and improvements in the technology of food service, they became part of the American teenage scene in the Forties:

The drive-in itself was a youthful vision of paradise. Youth liked its food tasty, moderately priced, and quick—just the way the drive-in served it. Equally important, teens liked their restaurants to have a stimulating atmosphere, and successful operations rarely disappointed on that score. The continual comings and goings of an eclectic caravan of customers made the dining-room-on-a-parking-lot the ideal spot for people-watching, making new friends, confronting rivals, and sparking romance. (Langdon, quoted in Witzel 1994, 8)

Richard and Maurice McDonald began their career in drive-in restaurants in the Forties, when they moved their Airdrome roadside restaurant to San Bernardino, California, and employed carhops in short satin uniforms to serve burgers, malteds, and barbecue. By 1948 they had been successful enough to start another kind of business; during the Fifties, the Golden Arches would appear. Doumar's Cones and Barbecue is a legend in Norfolk, Virginia, a place for dates and families alike. Mel Weiss and Harold Dobbs started a drive-in legend in San Francisco in 1947; Mel's Drive-in on South Van Ness featured live radio broadcasting and fourteen carhops, as well as good food, and attracted thousands of diners day and night until franchises began to compete and eventually put the California group of Mel's Drive-ins out of business. After it was used as a set in the film *American Graffiti* in 1972, however, the original diner became an icon of a simpler America, and it reopened in 1985.

Music and Dancing

If Forties teens wanted to sample the latest record, they visited their local music store, chose what they wanted to hear from the large 78-rpm discs on display, and went into a soundproof, windowed booth, which was usually large enough to hold two or three teens comfortably. There they slipped the disc from its paper case and put it on the turntable; they could play the whole thing before buying—or not buying.

The popular music of the early Forties, fueled by patriotism and the early swing movement, bounced and swung even more to Glenn Miller's 1941 "Chattanooga Choo Choo" and his 1942 "String of Pearls." Miller and his band toured tirelessly during the war, offering concerts to tired soldiers and civilians who were working hard for the war effort. Americans were saddened by his death in a plane crash in 1944. The Andrews Sisters' lively vocal arrangements of "Don't Sit Under the Apple Tree, with Anyone Else but Me" and "Boogie Woogie Bugle Boy of Company B" got audiences jitterbugging and singing along. The biggest popular hit of the decade, however, was a quiet ballad: "White Christmas," written by Irving Berlin and sung in the movie *Holiday Inn* by Bing Crosby in 1942. Its nostalgic longing for peace, home, and family echoed the sentiments of American servicemen and those who waited for them, as well as those of the whole society which longed for relief from the uncertainties of war. It won the Academy Award for Best Song and, as of the Nineties, had sold approximately 5 million copies in sheet music and 180 million records (Wallechinsky 1995, 500).

The favorite singer of teen girls in the early and mid-Forties was slender crooner Frank Sinatra, whose smooth songs and good looks caused riots when he appeared in person. During the mid-Forties he had his own radio show; fans would stand in line for hours, eating sandwiches from brown bags and comparing their Sinatra scrapbooks, waiting to squeeze into the theater. "They were the bobbysox crowd, long rows of sweaters and skirts and white socks rolled down over saddle shoes. By 3 PM—still three hours before the show—the street was packed tight with them" (Dunning 1976, 216). Some without tickets found devious ways of getting in to see "Frankie," such as hiding in the theater when the previous audience left. When he finally sang, they shrieked, gasped, and screamed in excitement and pleasure; some wept and some fainted.

Such public hysteria shocked and disgusted some adult observers, who feared teens were really getting out of hand. Swing music was "a major culprit," they thought. One Indiana state legislator worried that such music put teens in "sinful situations," with blaring juke boxes and "wiggling around. . . . It's the music that gets 'em" (quoted in Palladino 1996, 83–84). Such adults, especially those in authority, sought curfews and controls on juke boxes, believing teens needed to be protected from such immoral influences. Other adults saw such behavior as natural, a kind of "neo-Dionysian revel" that has always been part of life (Palladino 1996, 85).

Teens could listen to Glenn Miller, Bing Crosby, Frank Sinatra, and, in the later Forties, Frankie Laine at home, on the family radio, or on their new portables; such singers might have inspired fan behavior but they were still white and restrained. An increasing number of teens were listening to music away from home that would have shocked their parents even more. Rhythm and blues was reaching a wide audience, thanks to powerful black radio stations and a growing number of white disc jockeys who played it. Its frank sexual content and heavy beat mixed gospel, blues, and jazz into a liberating dance music that was irresistible to teens. White and black teens alike jived to "Sixty Minute Man" and "I Want a Bow-Legged Woman." Malcolm Little, later known as Malcolm X, described the energy of the music and the dancing it inspired: "Black girls, brownskins . . . even a couple of white girls there . . . doing the 'flapping eagle,' the 'kangaroo' and the 'split' " (quoted in Palladino 1996, 117–18).

Teens could and did behave more sedately at proms than they did at roadhouses and jukebox hangouts. They could fox trot and even waltz on occasion, although the jitterbug was still their favorite dance. The fast version in which boys tossed girls from side to side and then overhead was usually reserved for contests; the smoother version in which the boy pulled the girl firmly into her turns and released her out again, showed off a girl's swingy skirt without requiring athletic ability. An excellent smooth jitterbug appears in the 1946 dramatic film *Til the End of Time*, starring Guy Madison as a returning soldier who jitterbugs with his young neighbor at a local hangout.

By the mid-Forties, country music was no longer localized in the South and West. As many Southerners migrated to Detroit and California during the war seeking jobs in defense plants, they looked for their favorite singers, especially Roy Acuff, on jukeboxes, and increasingly, began to find them (Malone 1993, 182). Teens who liked this music could now tune in to powerful radio stations from the mountain areas in Tennessee and Kentucky which beamed out country and hillbilly music far beyond its roots. The popularity of the Grand Old Opry, which went on network radio in 1939, increased each year until it dominated the industry in featuring popular performers and introducing new ones.

Young soldiers from the South who loved bluegrass and country music introduced their Army buddies to the sounds, which then traveled overseas to a new market. "Barn dance" radio shows proliferated, and many country music concerts featured square dancing after the show—an activity some white middle-class parents sought to encourage as an antidote to the evils of Sinatra, swing, and the jitterbug. Mainstream popular performers recorded country songs: in 1943, Bing Crosby recorded "Pistol Packin' Mama" with the Andrews Sisters, and in 1950, Patti Page recorded "Tennessee Waltz," two big crossover hits for both performers. By the end of the decade, Hank Williams was the dominant country performer; his style and songs and those of many like him were commercialized during this decade to appeal to a wider audience than ever before, making the late Forties and early Fifties the boom period in country music.

Movies

In the early Forties, Hollywood produced many patriotic films and added trailers to feature films that encouraged patrons to buy war bonds and stamps. Many stars joined the service or entertained troops at United Service Organizations dances. America's most popular adult stars were crooner Bing Crosby and shapely, blonde Betty Grable. Grable's famous bathing-suit photo, showing her from the back, glancing over her shoulder, with her hair piled high and wearing very high heels to show off her famous legs, was the favorite pinup of GIs. Crosby and Grable were known for their upbeat musicals, but darker films, borrowing their style from the French film noir, were also popular, and have become some of America's classics. Film noir, which means "dark film," refers to their film style—shot in black and white, with many scenes at night or in deep shadow—as well as subject: crime. Humphrey Bogart's films, such as *Casablanca* (1942) and *Key Largo* (1948), as well as many others in this period dealt with stylish but ruthless criminals, tough but lonely detectives, beautiful but cynical women, and violent death. Another favorite topic of postwar noir films, sometimes mixed with the crime theme, was the returning GI unable to find his place in a changed world.

Throughout the decade, teens went to the movies in huge numbers. In "Elmtown," the disguised Midwestern town studied by Yale Professor August Hollingshead in 1941 and 1942, movies were youth's most popular recreation: over 90% of boys and girls attended regularly, usually two or three times a week; admission to the most popular of the town's three theaters cost 40 cents; the second-run theater cost 25 cents (Hollingshead 1949, 301–2). By 1948 the Hollywood Reporter claimed that attendance among teen girls had risen to 8 million a year; they spent $170 million on movies (quoted in Palladino 1996, 106).

Hollywood responded to this consumer market by producing many teen films throughout the decade, films which have come to be called bobby-soxer films in reference to both their stars and their target audience. With their fresh-faced boy and girl stars, like Mickey Rooney and Judy Garland, whose film characters suffered little more serious than the pangs of first love, these films provided adult audiences with images of innocence and hope

Babes on Broadway (1941). Judy Garland and Mickey Rooney, America's ideal teens. Reproduced courtesy of The Museum of Modern Art.

during the war, and white teen audiences with characters and situations familiar to them, set in a fantasy upper-middle-class world of lovely suburban homes, kindly parents, and parties. A staple in such settings was the black maid, who always had an elegant breakfast on the table even though the teen children were too eager to ride to school with their friends to eat it. Blacks were seldom seen in any other role. Even the first Academy Award given to a black—Hattie McDaniel in 1940—was given for the portrayal of Scarlett O'Hara's Mammy in *Gone with the Wind*.

The Henry Aldrich films were among America's most popular teen movies. Based on the popular Thirties radio show, twelve films featuring "America's dumbest high schooler" (Maltin 1997, 581) were produced between 1939 and 1944. In each, Henry got into a hopeless and escalating mess, hilariously involving everyone around him, but he always got out of it in the end. Actor Jackie Cooper starred in two of the films, but when teen actor Jimmy Lydon won a 1939 contest as America's most typical boy, he became the image of Henry Aldrich: cowlicked, squeaky-voiced, and charming (Ward 1991, 54). Many of the boy characters in the bobby-soxer films were innocent bunglers, but they eventually won the girls because of their good-natured patience. Peter Lawford, Van Johnson, Robert Walker, Johnny Sands, Scotty Beckett, and Roddy McDowell—and, of course, Mickey Rooney as Andy Hardy—all played such roles in the Forties.

The teen girls in bobby-soxer films, however, were extremely pretty and often polished in spite of their youth; they yearned precociously after older men such as Cary Grant and Robert Stack:

"Falling in Love with Love" was a popular song of the modern era, which fit these dreamy, impractical "belles of the prom." Typically, they wore sweaters, skirts, and saddle shoes. They disdained "boys" but there was always a nice boy-next-door to take their put-downs, complaints, and to provide a happy ending in spite of everything. (Ward 1989, 30)

The classic film of this genre is *The Bachelor and the Bobby-Soxer* (1947), starring Shirley Temple, the Thirties child star grown into a sweet, pretty teenager. In the film, she has a crush on playboy Cary Grant but loses him eventually—and charmingly—to her big sister. The screenplay won an Oscar for writer Sidney Sheldon (Ward 1989, 32).

Temple also played Corliss Archer in a series of films based on the radio show *Meet Corliss Archer*, which first aired in 1943. In one of these films, *Kiss and Tell*, Corliss thought she could become pregnant if she kissed her boyfriend. In another Temple film from 1942, her character sighed, "It's hard to find a proper gown, what with the war and all" (Ward 1989, 30). Elizabeth Taylor, Jane Withers, Mona Freeman, and Jeanne Crain all played similar sweet, innocent teen girls in bobby-soxer films. Few films of this era showed any other side to teen life except for *A Tree Grows in Brook-*

Good girl Shirley Temple in *The Bachelor and the Bobby-Soxer* (1947), with older sister Myrna Loy. Reproduced courtesy of The Museum of Modern Art.

lyn (1945), made from the Betty Smith novel about a Brooklyn tenement girl in the early 1900s who longed to transcend her lower-middle-class environment. Peggy Ann Garner won a special juvenile Oscar for her performance. In *Mildred Pierce* (1945), Ann Blyth played a bad teen with more mature glamour; as Veda, Joan Crawford's greedy and cold-hearted daughter, she steals her mother's boyfriend and eventually murders him, allowing her mother to take the blame. The adult public preferred the bobby-soxer films, reveling in the images of sexless, safe teen activities. Teen girls themselves loved them for the fantasy life they showed: upper-middle-class suburban life, parties, pretty clothes, indulgent parents, faithful and adoring boys next door. Teen boys probably preferred movies of the late Forties, such as *City Across the River* (1949), with Tony Curtis as a street teen, or *Knock on Any Door* (1949), starring John Derek as a youth who turns to crime after being rejected by society (Ward 1991, 46).

Books and Reading

The decade opened with a book that continues to have a major impact on American life and thought. Richard Wright's *Native Son*, published on March 1, 1940, shocked most thoughtful, literate Americans into realizing

Bad girl Ann Blyth with mother Joan Crawford in *Mildred Pierce*, 1945. Reproduced courtesy of The Museum of Modern Art.

the price the country was paying for its racial prejudice. It sold more than 200,000 copies during the first three weeks and made Wright a public figure (Urban 1989, 68–69). The powerful story of teenaged Bigger Thomas, caught up in a cycle of humiliation and ultimately murder, was brought to the New York stage in 1941, directed by Orson Welles, who had just finished making his landmark film *Citizen Kane* (and produced by John Houseman, who had participated in Welles's radio production "War of the Worlds" in 1938). Adapted by Wright, the play starred Canada Lee as Bigger. (In 1952 Wright wrote a film version of the book and played Bigger himself.) In 1945 Wright further disturbed Americans with his autobiography to the age of seventeen, *Black Boy*.

Two other books still read by teens in high school were published during this decade: George Orwell's satiric *Animal Farm* and Robert Penn Warren's cynical look at Southern politics, *All the King's Men*, both in 1946. The fears engendered by war and the atomic bomb brought Americans in unprecedented numbers to novels with Christian themes, as if they were seeking some kind of faith that would work in the modern world. *The Keys to the Kingdom* by A. J. Cronin (1941), *The Song of Bernadette* by Franz Werfel (1942), *The Robe* by Lloyd C. Douglas (1943), *The Miracle of the Bells* by Russell Janey (1947), and *The Big Fisherman* by Lloyd C. Douglas

Teen John Derek comforted by Humphrey Bogart in *Knock on Any Door*, 1949. Reproduced courtesy of The Museum of Modern Art.

(1948) all topped the best-seller lists. Some quickly made their way to the Hollywood screen as well.

For their part, many teens continued to find inspiration in series books. Nancy Drew and the Hardy Boys still captured their imaginations. Although the Stratemeyer Syndicate tried to introduce other girls' mystery series, such as the Dana Girls, Kay Tracey, and Judy Bolton, Nancy still topped the market. Some authors approached books for teens differently. Margaret Sutton's Judy Bolton mysteries had a slower pace and some thoughtful musings along with the mystery to be solved. Vocational books were popular with some teens; Cherry Ames and Sue Barton were the heroines of series books about nursing; Vicki Barr's job as a flight stewardess took her on exciting adventures.

Boys' series often offered fantastic wartime adventures. John R. Tunis wrote exciting sports stories with serious overtones; his *All American* (1942) attacks racial and ethnic prejudice among athletes and suggests that winning was not the ultimate aim of sport. Betty Cavanna's *Going on Sixteen* (1946) follows a girl through the social problems of four years in high school. Maureen Daly concentrated the events of her 1942 novel *Seventeenth Summer* into the three months of summer between high school and college. Written when Daly was a college student, its leisurely pace explores first love with a thoughtfulness and seriousness that made teen girls return to the book many times. It remained popular on library survey lists well into the Sixties.

Teens also continued to read comic strips and magazines. *Hot Rod*, which began publication in 1948, helped boys keep their old jalopies running or, if their fathers were willing, soup up the family car. Girls, after years of reading their mothers' copies of *Ladies Home Journal* and *Parents' Magazine*, finally got a magazine they could really call their own. *Seventeen* began publication in 1944. Although it devoted a lot of space to clothes, hair, makeup, and dating, it also urged participation in politics, devotion to social equality, and advocacy of teenage rights and responsibilities. Teen girls purchased the magazine in huge numbers; the editors' gamble on the existence of a lucrative teen market paid off.

Comic Books

For their recreational reading, many teen boys turned to comic books, a new form of inexpensive, exciting literature which began in the Thirties with Superman, the first costumed super hero. After Batman appeared in his own comic book in 1940, these two super heroes soon dominated the comic book industry. A large number of new comic book characters were introduced in 1941 as publishers sought to capitalize on the super heroes' success. Captain America reflected the patriotic spirit of America during the war. *Police Comics* followed the adventures of criminals and introduced Plastic Man in 1944 as an unusual crime fighter who could stretch and re-form his body in all kinds of curious ways, often making wryly humorous remarks while he did so. Will Eisner, probably the most famous illustrator of comics, introduced The Spirit, and later, Blackhawks, "a flying, fighting crew who encircle the globe in the cause of justice and freedom!" Sheena of the Jungle dazzled teen boys with her gorgeous body and skimpy animal-skin outfits.

In a conscious attempt to attract girls to the comic book market, psychologist William Moulton Marston in 1942 invented Wonder Woman for DC Comics. With her magic lasso and powerful bullet-repelling bracelets, she leapt across the pages embodying "militant feminism on a scale unprecedented in any mass medium" (Daniels 1971, 13). In a 1942 episode, a woman who looks exactly like Wonder Woman pleads with her husband to let her get a job. When he refuses, she takes a job as a nurse, while Wonder Woman goes to her home and takes her place in order to investigate the husband, who is trying to sell his invention of an antiaircraft shell. When the job argument continues, he chains her to the cookstove—a clever visual metaphor for the feelings of women in similar circumstances. Cartoonist Jules Feiffer sneered at the character: "Wonder Woman seemed like too much of a put-up character. . . . It was obvious that a bunch of men got together in a smoke-filled room and brain-stormed themselves a Super Lady" (quoted in Perry and Aldridge 1971, 167). Nevertheless, she lasted

A page from the first Wonder Woman comic book. Wonder Woman is a trademark of DC Comics © 1998. All rights reserved. Used with permission.

longer than most of the male characters created during the same decade. Jenette Kahn, president of DC Comics as the century closed, describes the appeal this way: "What little girl or woman wouldn't like to be, as Wonder Woman is, admired most for her power, her values and her open heart?" (quoted in Daniels 1995, 12).

REFERENCES

Barfield, Ray. *Listening to Radio*. Westport, Conn.: Praeger, 1996.

Chisholm, Leslie. *Guiding Youth in the Secondary School*. New York: American Book Company, 1945.

Cohen, Eliot E. "A Teen-age Bill of Rights." *New York Times Magazine*, January 7, 1945. 16–17+.

Colbert, David, ed. *Eyewitness to America*. New York: Pantheon, 1997.

Cosgrove, Stuart. "The Zoot Suit and Style Warfare." In *Zoot Suits and Second Hand Dresses: An Anthology of Fashion and Music*, ed. Angela McRobbie. Boston: Unwin, 1988.

Couperie, Pierre, and Maurice Horn. *A History of the Comic Strip*. New York: Crown Publishers, 1968.

Dalzell, Tom. *Flappers 2 Rappers: American Youth Slang*. Springfield, Mass.: Merriam Webster, 1996.

Daniels, Les. *Comix: A History of the Comic Book in America*. New York: Outerbridge and Dienstfrey, 1971.

———. *DC Comics: A History of the World's Favorite Comic Book Heroes*. Boston: Little, Brown, 1995.

Dunning, John. *Tune in Yesterday*. Englewood Cliffs, N.J.: Prentice-Hall, 1976.

"First-Date Quiz." *Seventeen*, September 1944. 4.

Forester, William D. *Harlan County Goes to War*. Privately printed, 1990.

Gorer, Geoffrey. *The American People: A Study in National Character*. W. W. Norton, 1948.

Graebner, William. *The Age of Doubt: American Thought and Culture in the 1940s*. Boston: Twayne, 1991.

Hart, James D. *The Popular Book: A History of America's Literary Taste*. Berkeley: University of California Press, 1961.

Historical Statistics of the United States Colonial Times to 1957. Washington, D.C.: Bureau of the Census, 1960.

Hollingshead, August B. *Elmtown's Youth*. New York: John P. Wiley and Sons, 1949.

Horn, Maurice. *100 Years of American Newspaper Comics*. New York: Gramercy Books, 1996.

Hornsby, Alton. *Chronology of African-American History from 1942 to the Present*. 2nd ed. Detroit, Mich.: Gale Research, 1997.

Kinsey, Alfred C. *Sexual Behavior in the Human Male*. Philadelphia: W. B. Saunders, 1948.

MacKenzie, Catherine. "Boys, Girls, and Dates." *New York Times Magazine*, November 11, 1945: 29.

———. "Unchanging Teen-agers." *New York Times Magazine*, December 8, 1946: 42.

————. "Teen-age Social Life." *New York Times Magazine*, September 8, 1946: 34.

————. "Teen-age Critics." *New York Times Magazine*, December 7, 1947: 44.

Malone, Bill C. *Country Music, USA*. Austin: University of Texas Press, 1993.

Maltin, Leonard. *1998 Movie and Video Guide*. New York: Signet, 1997.

Mooney, Ross L. "Surveying High-School Students' Problems by Means of a Problem Check-List." *Educational Research Bulletin* 21:3 (March 18, 1942).

Nilsen, Alleen, and Ken Donelson, eds. *Literature for Today's Young Adults*. 4th ed. New York: HarperCollins, 1993.

Palladino, Grace. *Teenagers*. New York: Basic Books, 1996.

Perry, George, and Alan Aldridge. *The Penguin Book of Comics*. Baltimore: Penguin Books, 1971.

Petersen, James R. "Male Call: 1940–1949." *Playboy* 44, no. 11 (November 1997): 86+.

"Reeny Season," *Time*, March 31, 1947: 47.

"Same Rights, Same Privileges." *Time*, March 31, 1947: 21–22.

Smith, E. A. *American Youth Culture*. New York: Free Press of Glencoe, 1962.

Sorin, Gerald. *The Nurturing Neighborhood*. New York: New York University Press, 1990.

"Teen-agers." *Life* 25, December 20, 1948, 67–75.

Time Capsule: 1946: The Year in Review. Time, 1996.

Urban, Joan. *Richard Wright*. New York: Chelsea House, 1989.

Valentine, Maggie. "Of Motorcars and Movies: The Architecture of S. Charles Lee." In *Roadside America*, ed. Jan Jennings. Ames, Iowa: Iowa State University Press, 1990.

Wallechinsky, David, ed. *The People's Almanac Presents the Twentieth Century*. Boston: Little, Brown, 1995.

Ward, L. E. "The Bobby-Soxers." *Classic Images* 174 (December 1989): 30–32.

————. "The Boys Next Door." *Classic Images* 195 (September 1991): 54, and October 1991): 46–47.

West, Elliott. *Growing Up in Twentieth-Century America*. Westport, Conn.: Greenwood Press, 1996.

West, James. *Plainville, U.S.A*. New York: Columbia University Press, 1945.

"Why Don't Parents Grow Up?" *Seventeen*, December 1944: 94–95.

Widmer, E. L. "Crossroads: The Automobile, Rock and Roll, and Democracy." In *Roadside America*, ed. Jan Jennings. Ames: Iowa State University Press, 1990.

Witzel, Michael Karl. *The American Drive-In*. Osceola, Wisc.: Motorbooks International, 1994.

· 5 ·

The 1950s

During the Fifties, public attention was focused on teens to an unprecedented degree in American culture. Even more than in the Twenties, being
young was an enviable state. Even more than in the late Forties, when America looked benignly on its bobby-soxers and boys-next-door as embodiments
of postwar vitality, teens occupied the fantasies of adults. In the Fifties, those
fantasies were more polarized than ever before. Now America looked at its
youth with a new mixture of hope and fear, of intense fascination and even,
at times, terror.

POLITICS AND NATIONAL EVENTS

Throughout the decade, the national mood swung between the exuberance of the postwar economy and the lurking fears of Communist takeovers
and hydrogen bombs. Teens were the chief beneficiaries of the booming
economy, but they also felt the fears that divided the country.

The Soviet Union under Joseph Stalin was clearly marked out as the enemy, whose aim it was to dominate the world. The "Iron Curtain" that had
fallen between East and West when the Soviets captured Poland, East Germany, and Czechoslovakia symbolized the trenched battle between the cap-
italist and the communist systems. When China too fell to the Communists
and the Korean War erupted, Americans felt threatened as never before.

The year 1950 saw the crest of the wave of McCarthyism that had swept
over the country leaving scarred lives and a bewildered public in its wake.
In 1948 Whittaker Chambers, a confessed Communist with a shady past,
accused Alger Hiss, a Harvard lawyer and the head of the Carnegie Endow-

Teens outside Greencastle High School, Greencastle, Indiana, 1956. Reproduced courtesy of Greencastle High School.

ment, of being a fellow member of the Party. Even though the House Un-American Activities Committee did not entirely trust Chambers's allegations, it nonetheless heard the charges, and eventually, in 1950, after two trials based on conflicting and peculiar evidence which attracted national publicity, Hiss was convicted of perjury and sentenced to five years in jail. The young Richard Nixon was active in the effort to convict Hiss, whose case symbolized the confusions of the Cold War between communism and capitalism.

In a criminal case that fascinated and divided the public, Julius and Ethel Rosenberg were arrested in 1950 for passing the secrets of the atomic bomb to the Soviets. Although some of the legal procedure in the trial was questionable and many Americans believed the Rosenbergs innocent, they were convicted and sentenced to death. The only Americans ever to be executed for spying during peacetime, they were electrocuted in New York on June 19, 1953.

Joseph McCarthy

On February 9, 1950, the junior senator from Wisconsin, Joseph McCarthy, made a speech to a women's group in Wheeling, West Virginia, in which he said, almost casually, that he had proof that there were 205 Communists in the American government. Although he may not have fully intended to start the wave of fear, accusations, and publicity that ensued, he certainly tapped into the Cold War fears of many Americans. The press knew they had a good story, although many doubted McCarthy's methods and honesty; his inability to come up with names seemed less important than his theatrical ability to accuse by suggestion and innuendo as well as by outright lies. Other politicians supported and encouraged him, and FBI director J. Edgar Hoover probably provided him with material from FBI files. McCarthy captured the public imagination with his slightly rumpled appearance, his way of accusing and then laughing off the seriousness of the accusation only to accuse again, his manipulation of photo opportunities, and his own apparent thoroughgoing patriotism.

When, in 1952, he became chairman of the Senate Committee on Government Operations, he acquired even more power to subpoena and accuse in public, but Dwight Eisenhower, the popular World War II general, was elected to the presidency the same year and wanted to distance himself from McCarthy's random and unsupported charges. In the spring of 1954, McCarthy announced that the U.S. Army itself was infiltrated with Communists, and he refused to recant this charge even when the Army threatened to bring countercharges against him. As a result, the first major congressional hearing appeared on live television, and it fascinated the public, adults and teens alike. Attorney Joseph Welch spoke for the Army; his sensible eloquence contrasted with McCarthy's unpolished aggressive style, which did not come across well on national television. The Army uncovered irregularities in McCarthy's handling of his staff, and when McCarthy retaliated by accusing a young attorney on Welch's staff of a shady association in the past, Welch had had enough. Rebuking the senator for his cruelty, he asked, "Have you no decency, sir? Have you no decency?"

Suddenly Americans saw McCarthy in a different light—cruel, unattractive, even paranoid—and their fascination with him cooled quickly. Hoover had already withdrawn his sympathies, and Eisenhower was glad to be rid of McCarthy. He was censured by the Senate later that year and ignored by the press that had fed off him. An alcoholic, his drinking became worse and he died three years later, at age forty-eight, of liver failure. His name remains a symbol for hatred, for unsupported and damaging accusation, for the danger of political power, and for the vulnerability of the public.

Juvenile Delinquency

The facts and the myths of juvenile delinquency dominated the 1950s as they did in no other decade. Only a brief examination is possible here, but much has been written about delinquency and the related issues of gangs, teen sexuality, attitudes and behavior toward school, violent teens—and all the efforts by adult authorities to control such undesirable behavior—in the Fifties. Delinquency was the topic of countless magazine and newspaper articles, books, and films during the decade, spiking to an all-time high in 1953 (chart in Gilbert 1986, 65). It was investigated and discussed on the floor of the U.S. Senate. Since the Fifties, even more analyses have been devoted to understanding why it loomed so large when other social issues—nuclear proliferation, racial prejudice, abuse of political power—might have been equally important. No single reason would be enough, but film scholar Peter Biskind offers one important one: "The inflation of the problem into a national obsession . . . reflected more than a social reality; it reflected a mood—the first wave of conservative backlash against what William Whyte called the 'filiarchy' "—that is, the autonomous youth culture, not delinquency itself (Biskind 1983, 197). Young people had more economic power than ever before, and with it they were reshaping the way in which America dressed, the movies it saw, the music it listened to, and the way it perceived work, school, and home responsibilities.

Defining delinquency was a problem in itself. From its original meaning of failing to do what was required (e.g., paying a bill), it had evolved into a blanket description of any youthful behavior that might be perceived as rebellious, from stealing cars and getting into knife fights to skipping school for any reason, staying out past a parental curfew, or wearing certain fashions in hair or clothes. A "JD" might look different through the eyes of parents, police, school authorities, or peer groups. The term itself seemed to provoke almost irrational fears among many adults—fears that books such as Benjamin Fine's *1,000,000 Delinquents* (1955) played on. According to Fine, Attorney General Herbert Brownell predicted that this many young people would become delinquents by 1954—a veritable epidemic of delinquency. Fine added that, by 1960, if things continued at the same rate, we would have more than 2 million (Fine 1955, 26). That number may have been inflated by the number of victimless "crimes" perpetrated by young people (e.g., dropping out of school) whose despairing parents wanted some outside authority's help in disciplining them. Fine's book enumerates crime after crime, from vandalism to torture to murder, noting that many were done just for thrills (1955, 19–30).

Communities around the country tried various ways to contain this problem of delinquent youths on the streets and in the schools, from efforts begun in the Forties to give teens clubs and canteens where they could meet and dance with minimal adult supervision, to gentle controls such as dress codes and curfews, to more punitive measures such as policing street corners and sending offenders to reform school. There was apparently a distinct difference between the kinds of offenses committed by boys and by girls. The typical JD was male, and his crimes were stealing cars, getting into rumbles, hanging out with a gang, or more violent acts of rape and murder. Girls' offenses were usually running away from home and, more often, sexual misconduct, although the misconduct usually was "mutually acquiescent" (Miller and Nowak 1977, 285). Even girls who could not be proved to be sexually active could be labeled "promiscuous" if they seemed sexually mature or threatening (1977, 285). Although cars were often stolen and "mutually acquiescent" sex acts were also committed by white middle-class youth, the lower-class and minority teens were usually the ones labeled JD and punished by the law. According to William Graebner, a scholar who has studied the decade from several perspectives, drugs were not part of the problem. Although the drug culture had infiltrated inner-city black communities, Graebner states in his study of Buffalo teens, "Nothing like the drug culture of the 1960s existed anywhere in the United States in the 1950s; in fact, many Buffalo youth characterize that decade as a 'golden age' for youth in part because of the absence of drugs" (1990, 119). Harrison Salisbury's 1958 visit to New York's inner-city communities revealed otherwise: "There's not a teen-age street kid in New York who doesn't know another youngster who takes dope occasionally. And most of them know who sells the dope" (1958, 36). Although drug use was more typical in black communities, it existed in white communities as well. Alcohol was even more prevalent, however. "With few exceptions," Salisbury found, "boys and girls drink from the age of eleven or twelve. . . . They drink anything put before them. But since they have little money they concentrate on wine" (1958, 35). Such drinking habits, and other kinds of more destructive and violent delinquent behavior, were not confined to the slums; middle-class teens indulged as well. They just were not officially punished (1958, 104–117).

The public constantly looked for something or someone to blame for this perceived epidemic of juvenile delinquency. Parents themselves, especially upper-middle-class parents involved with their jobs and social status, took some of the heat in magazine articles and in sociologists' opinions; because such parents were emotionally unavailable to their teens, their children turned to the peer group for comfort. Lower-class parents were seen as victims themselves of a system that allowed poverty and slum life to continue by ignoring them. Sometimes the youth were regarded as "sick": "The youth of today is suffering from a severe, collective mental illness [resulting from] the psychopathic virus," intoned one psychiatrist (quoted in Miller and Nowak 1977, 283). Such confusion was parodied beautifully in the "Sergeant Krupke" number from *West Side Story*, the 1957 Broadway musical that offered a romanticized yet gritty image of gang wars in New York City set in a Romeo-and-Juliet plot. In this comic song, the delinquents themselves act out these various "diagnoses": lack of discipline, lack of parental love, lack of a job, and the need for psychiatric care, arriving at the final, gleeful, only reason for the problem: "We're no good!"

Whatever the cause, and whoever they actually were, the nation saw such "black leather barbarians," as one pulp fiction author called them (Linna

1992, n.p.), as a threat. Rejecting the conservatism and work ethic of the "man in the grey flannel suit," they seemed to embrace lawlessness, sexuality, and rebellion. Like McCarthy's purported spies in the government, they were a danger from within, entrusted with the future of the country and working against all it stood for. The media attention focused on them, and the various legal and communal methods that attempted to isolate or control them, aggravated the apparent division between "good kids" and "bad kids." The truth was much more complicated.

The Beats

Although authentic Beats were generally adults rather than teens, the Beat movement had nonetheless a powerful attraction for white middle-class teens in the late Fifties. It offered an intellectual form of rebellion and the possibility of a life different from that of one's parents, a life less trammeled by conservatism yet without the dangers of violence and illegality represented by the juvenile delinquent culture.

"Beat" meant exhausted, cheated, or robbed; it also called up images of jazz and the passion of Beat poets, who wanted to recreate the feel of jazz in words rather than in music. Jack Kerouac, author of *On the Road* and one of the most influential authors of Beat literature, also believed it meant "blessed," as in beatific (Dalzell 1996, 95). It drew heavily from black culture with its jazz and easygoing lifestyle, which white Beats believed represented freedom from middle-class corporate hang-ups, or patterns. Beats borrowed black slang wholesale, especially from jazz musicians: hip, cat, dig, square, gone, cool, groovy, wild.

By the late Fifties, "Beat" had come to mean a whole lifestyle of casual clothing, poetry readings to music, deep conversations about the work of Jean-Paul Sartre, poetry, painting, jug wine, espresso, and spaghetti dinners. It meant marijuana and loving but casual sex. It meant the rejection of the nine-to-five workday, of suburbia, of retirement plans and cookouts. Its milieu was Greenwich Village in New York City, or North Beach in San Francisco. The image was one of freedom to stay up all night, to do things and read things and think things that one's parents could never do or read or think. Across the country, teens who had to stay in school could still read Allen Ginsberg's poem *Howl* and Kerouac's *On the Road* and dress in black berets and black stockings on the weekends. They could still imagine themselves as Beats and look toward a future of the kind of freedom that the Village offered those who could get there.

It was also very much a male-dominated culture. Women existed to cook the spaghetti and stay out of the way while the men talked, or be there for sexual gratification. But Wini Breines speculates that Beats had a powerful and perhaps unconscious appeal for many white middle-class girls: "The expansiveness and male privilege of the Beats, their intensity, adventures, frenetic activity, interest in black culture, and rejection of conventional middle-class life attracted 1950s teenage girls, as did rock and roll stars . . . they were interested in them as models. They wanted to be them" (1992, 147). They too wanted the freedom from domesticity represented by the Beats, even while they might be filling a hope chest with linens and silver under their mothers' watchful eyes.

Beats and their style affected the entire spectrum of American elite and popular culture—literature, music, fashion, language—and they will be discussed in more detail in those sections of this chapter. Some influential literary and social critics of the day found the movement distasteful, juvenile, and even dangerous. Norman Podhoretz complained that the Beats were to literature what "juvenile delinquency is to life," and that they were out to replace civilization with "the world of adolescent street gangs" (quoted in Miller and Nowak 1977, 386). By the end of the decade, newspapers and magazines, popular television, comic strips, and movies had all embraced the Beat culture as a true counterculture, and even though in the popular mind it was often reduced to a set of slang words and a "cool" attitude toward life, it was a harbinger of the greater freedoms to come in the Sixties.

Emmett Till

In August 1955 fourteen-year-old Emmett Till became the center of, and the victim in, "the first great media event of the civil rights movement" (Halberstam 1993, 437). Till left his Chicago home with his cousin, Curtis Jones, to visit a relative in the Mississippi Delta. Even though his mother warned him that the attitude toward black people was different in the South and that he should behave himself, he and his cousin did not entirely believe that things could be that different, and they settled in to enjoy themselves with Curtis's great uncle, Moses Wright, a sharecropper near the poverty-stricken town of Money. Although some of the facts are not clear, evidently Till and Jones drove to a store run by a white woman, Carolyn Bryant, and played checkers with some friends outside. Probably on a dare, Emmett Till went into the store and spoke to Bryant, or whistled at her. In the deep South in 1955, Till had violated an entrenched code: black boys never flirt with white women, or they might be lynched.

What happened then was revealed only after the trial ended. The next night, Bryant's husband and his half brother, J. W. Milam, took Till from the Wright house. Finding him unrepentant and cocky, they knew they had to kill him. They shot him in the head and tied his body to an old piece of cotton gin equipment with barbed wire and threw it in the Tallahatchie River.

When the horribly mangled body was discovered three days later, it was shipped back to Chicago to Till's mother. She declared the coffin should remain open so that all could see what Southern hatred had done to her son. The funeral attracted thousands, and the media began to zero in on the story. Bryant and Milam were arrested and tried in a packed courtroom. Moses Wright, despite threats to his life, appeared in court and identified Bryant and Milam as those who had taken Emmett Till away. Nevertheless, when the jury retired, they took only sixty-seven minutes to reach a verdict of not guilty. The prejudice of the deep South and its violent codes were for the first time revealed to the entire country.

After the acquittal, maverick journalist William Bradford Huie persuaded Bryant and Milam to sell him their story, which they did for an advance libel settlement of $4,000 (Halberstam 1993, 435). Thanks to the press, even by the time Huie published the story, the nation was already shocked by the murder. Convicted in the newspapers and finally in public opinion in their own town of Money, Mississippi, Bryant and Milam were ostracized and eventually lost their business.

The Montgomery Bus Boycott

Later in 1955, Rosa Parks's refusal to relinquish her seat on the bus to a white man revealed a less violent but more insidious side to America's racism. Blacks in Montgomery, Alabama, were required to move to the back of the bus as the front filled up with whites, and to leave the bus by the back door. Rosa Parks was a well respected member of Montgomery's black community and a leader in the local National Association for the Advancement of Colored People (NAACP). She and others had tried quiet rebellion previously and been put off the bus; black leaders had already discussed the possibility of a complete boycott of Montgomery's buses. A few others had already been arrested for refusing to give up their seats, but none with Parks's standing and visibility in the community. When she was arrested, the black community was ready, and the boycott began the next day. A new member of the community, the Reverend Martin Luther King, Jr., was chosen to lead it (Kohl 1995, 45).

For more than a year, despite harassment by whites, Montgomery's black citizens carpooled or bicycled around the city. Since they were the most frequent bus riders, the bus companies soon felt the economic impact. By the end of 1956, after a federal lawsuit ruled it unconstitutional, segregation in public transportation was no longer legal. For the first time, a group of African Americans had publicly joined together to fight for their basic rights as human beings, and they had won. Parks herself, after losing her job as a seamstress during the fray, moved to Detroit and continued her work on behalf of civil rights.

Teens in the News

Maureen Connolly

Maureen Connolly was sixteen years old in 1951, when she won the U.S. National Tennis Tournament. Called "Little Mo" by the press, she became an even bigger celebrity when in 1953, at the age of eighteen, she won the Grand Slam of tennis: the U.S. Open, the French Open, Wimbledon, and the Australian Open tournaments. Sports fans who had regarded tennis as a genteel or effete sport, and those who had never cared much for any sports, loved her youth and her aggressive style of play. Her career ended in 1954 when a horseback riding accident rendered her unable to play competitively.

Bobby Fischer

When thirteen-year-old Bobby Fischer won the National Junior Chess championship in 1956, he was the youngest champion ever, and Americans were suddenly fascinated by chess and by its youthful new star. At fourteen he won the U.S. Open Chess tournament; at fifteen he was the youngest international Grand Master in the history of chess. At sixteen he quit school, saying it had nothing more to teach him. Always an eccentric, he openly criticized the world chess establishment, claiming that the 1962 world tournament was dishonest—he came in fifth of eight contestants, losing to four Soviet players. Since then he has chosen to play only a few publicized matches.

TEENS AT HOME

The combination of the postwar economic boom, an increased consumerism, and the tremendous growth of advertising in magazines and on television produced one of the dominant stereotypes of American life: the Fifties home. Images of it were everywhere in the media, and it still has a nostalgic power, for good or ill, that few other images can match. Located on a suburban street among homes just like it, it was a "ranch style" house—all on one floor—or perhaps a split-level house. It had a manicured front lawn and a sidewalk where Junior rode his bike and Sister skated or played with the latest fad, the hula hoop. It featured a back patio where Dad grilled burgers and a superbly equipped kitchen where Mom cooked with appliances, such as an electric skillet and a refrigerator, in colors that matched her decor. They all watched television together in the den and sometimes ate their meals there on so-called TV trays—small, folding metal tables. When Mom did the cleaning, made so much easier by the newest vacuum cleaners and cleaning solutions, she wore full-skirted dresses and high heels. When Dad drove his late-model sedan off to work in the city, he wore a grey flannel suit and a hat. They were all healthy. They were all white. They always smiled.

This image, although a stereotype, did reflect some reality. More of the white populace did live in the suburbs and could indeed afford many of the latest conveniences. Moreover, many families built bomb shelters in their homes, stocked with water and canned goods and, in some wealthier homes, bars and easy chairs, against the time when the Soviets would unleash a hydrogen bomb on America. Even these activities suggest the consumerism that characterized American life in the Fifties. Thomas Hine has coined the word "Populuxe" for this phenomenon: "The essence of Populuxe is not merely having things. It is having things in a way that they'd never been had before, and it is an expression of an outright, thoroughly vulgar joy in being able to live so well" (1987, 4). For Hine, the "symbolic queen of Populuxe" was Barbie, the famous doll who was introduced in 1959. She was important not because of what she was, but because of what one could buy to outfit her—the latest Dior fashions in miniature, a house, a beauty parlor, and a Corvette (6).

White teens enjoyed unprecedented spending power. *Life* magazine in 1959 featured a teen girl from California shrieking with delight at a set of matched luggage; it showed, in a huge double-page spread, all the clothing, bicycles, sports equipment, records, cars, and so on that teens bought in a given year, and it warned that there was no stopping this economic jugger-naut ("A New $10-Billion Power" 1959, 78–87). Such prosperity meant that teens not only could have things but also their own space in the home, away from the family. Middle-class teens had their own bedrooms and the space to play records or visit with friends without encountering other family members. They had closets of their own to hold their increasing amount of clothing and sports equipment. They had their own record players and their own radios, so parents never had to listen to rock-and-roll music and teens never had to listen to Eddie Fisher's "Oh My Papa," Patti Page's "How Much Is That Doggy in the Window?," or Rosemary Clooney's "This Old House." Ironically, although the stereotype always pictured the family doing things together, the affluent lifestyle finally encouraged a different pattern: "Children and parents, urged to be companions and fellow playmates, had never lived so separated from each other" (West 1996, 182).

Comic Strips

Teens throughout the country remained avid readers of comic strips in their home newspapers. They still read "Little Orphan Annie," "Terry and the Pirates," "Dick Tracy," "Teena," and "Archie." The Fifties saw two new strips that focused especially on teens: "Beetle Bailey" and "The Jackson Twins."

"Beetle Bailey" first appeared in September 1950, drawn by the twenty-

"Teena," popular comic strip by Hilda Terry, from October 1959. Reproduced courtesy of Hilda Terry.

seven-year-old Mort Walker who had been creating cartoons since his early teens (Horn 1996, 52). At first Beetle was a kid going off for his freshman year in college. He was lazy and manipulative, as he still is in the Nineties. The strip did not do well at first, but when the Korean War heated up, Walker enlisted Beetle in the army, and he has been at Camp Swampy ever since, evading Sarge's temper, doing KP, or kitchen patrol, and trying to sleep. He continues to represent the young person's generally passive rebellion against the pecking order—represented in the strip by the army but reflective of school principals, bosses, and others in authority.

In November 1950, teen girls found an idealized image of themselves in the identical Jackson Twins, Jan and Jill. Their adventures centered around school, home, and their small city of Gardentown; they usually maintained their good manners and good sense even when their exasperating little brother got in their way. Their mirror-image looks—dark hair cut in a bob and good figures—were the source of many jokes in the strip. After 1970 the conservatism of the strip seemed increasingly dated, and it ended in 1979 (Horn 1996, 151).

Radio and Television

The radio no longer occupied the center of family life, as it had in the Forties. Now the radio was usually a small portable one in the possession of the teen in the family, and rock and roll was usually its sound. Radio had transformed itself into a medium for teens almost exclusively, both black and white, with disc jockeys who played the Top Ten from the rock and roll or rhythm and blues charts from the early afternoon until late at night.

The most famous disc jockey, or DJ, of the decade, and probably one of the most influential pop figures of the century, was Cleveland, Ohio's Alan Freed. When "Moondog" Freed howled and banged on a Cleveland phone book shouting, "Go!" while he played a rock song during his late-night show, thousands of teens caught the fever. "He became one of them, the kids, on their side as opposed to that of their parents, the first grown-up who understood them and what they wanted" (Halberstam 1993, 466). A brash exhibitionist and savvy observer of the music business, Freed, who was white, knew both black and white teens were buying rhythm and blues records in increasing numbers. Beginning in 1951, he devoted his show to the heavy beat and suggestive lyrics of this "race" music, and soon he had a mass teenage audience who called in their requests in huge numbers.

He began a series of rock concerts around the country which played to packed houses of screaming teens (Palladino 1996, 122–23). His promotion of the music was responsible, to a large degree, for the popularity of such stars as Bo Diddley, Fats Domino, LaVerne Baker, and the Platters. He set the style for wild DJ antics, such as Guy King's 1955 broadcast from atop a downtown Buffalo billboard (Graebner 1990, 5). King yelled to the teens below to honk their car horns if they liked the song he was playing: Bill Haley's "Rock Around the Clock." The resultant noisy traffic jam was yet another sign of the tremendous change going on in American radio in the Fifties.

Television now occupied the place the radio once did in family life. Parents and children shared their enjoyment of this new medium of entertainment, gathering around the set in the evenings to watch *I Love Lucy* (the most popular show of the decade), variety shows like *The Ed Sullivan Show*, dramas like *Dragnet* and *Gunsmoke*, and musical shows like *The Perry Como Show*. *Leave It to Beaver* offered an image of perfect Fifties family life. Children enjoyed the puppet show *Howdy Doody* and wore coonskin caps to celebrate the craze for Disney's television popularization of Western hero Davy Crockett, which quickly turned into a $300 million industry for Disney (Jackson 1993, 90). Although they might not always admit it, younger teens enjoyed Disney's new *Mickey Mouse Club* which opened in 1955; they enjoyed the lively singing and dancing by the Mouseketeers, especially Annette Funicello, and the serials such as "Spin and Marty." White middle-class teens also enjoyed *Your Hit Parade*, which, although it confined itself to mainstream pop songs, offered enjoyable renditions complete with Broadway-style dancing and a certain suspense about which song would be number one, always played last on the show.

Among the most popular shows of the decade were two quiz shows: *The $64,000 Question* and *Twenty-One*. Both offered thousands of dollars in prize money for contestants who could recall obscure facts, and many people groomed themselves to be contestants. Dr. Joyce Brothers, an attractive blonde psychologist, became famous on *The $64,000 Question* for her knowledge of boxing; she deliberately studied the sport because she knew that it would make an unusual combination with her gender and appearance—good for the show business that such programs actually were. These programs suffered from bad publicity, however, when the most famous contestant of the decade, Columbia professor Charles Van Doren, who appeared on *Twenty-One* in late 1956 and early 1957, confessed to a Congressional committee in 1959 that he had been given the answers in advance. The attractive, patrician Van Doren had fascinated millions of Americans, young and old, when, in the show's "isolation booth" he would perspire and appear to be thinking hard to come up with the right answer. An instant celebrity, he was mobbed for his autograph and sought out as a true American intellectual. Just as quickly, he fell from popularity, a victim of the power and fascination, new to Americans, of television.

Reflecting the self-conscious morality of the decade, the popular media celebrated religion to a remarkable degree. Billy Graham came to prominence during the Fifties, as did Oral Roberts and Norman Vincent Peale, all of whom appeared regularly on radio and television. The religious star of television was the Roman Catholic Bishop Fulton J. Sheen, an intense and powerful personality. On his weekly 1952 show *Life Is Worth Living*, he appeared in full bishop's regalia, complete with red cape, and used a blackboard to make his points effectively, such as the "3 D's" to describe parents who created delinquent children: doting, drinking, and discordant (Miller and Nowak 1977, 280–81).

Rock and roll appeared on television, too, but in a sanitized format. Elvis Presley's first appearances on television caused some shock; in the intimacy of the medium, showing the "distilled essence of Elvishood," it was "as if a family friend had begun a series of bumps and grinds in front of the sofa" (Marling 1994, 179). In a deliberately ironic comment on all the fuss about Elvis's hips, Steve Allen's show presented him dressed in white tie and tails, standing perfectly still, serenading a hound dog. Finally, the king of television variety shows, Ed Sullivan, was persuaded to present Elvis on his show, but in January 1957, in response to critical distaste for his previous appearances on other shows, Sullivan instructed the camera to shoot Presley only from the waist up; 82.6% of viewing Americans saw him and drew their own conclusions (Marling 1994, 180).

The popular family show *The Adventures of Ozzie and Harriet* centered around gentle, slightly befuddled, kindly, upper-middle-class Ozzie Nelson and his wife, Harriet, and their two sons, David and Ricky. A real-life family, but one very different from their television image (see Halberstam 1993, 516–21). David was the older teen son, well-behaved and steady. Ricky, the younger, played the kid who got into trouble, although it was very gentle, upper-middle-class, respectable trouble. In 1957 real-life Ricky wanted to make a rock and roll record for his girlfriend; Ozzie, who wrote many of the scripts, arranged for Ricky to sing on the show. When the show aired, sixteen-year-old Ricky, who looked remarkably like Elvis, sang the Fats Domino song "I'm Walkin'" and was an immediate hit especially with young white teen girls—and with their parents, who were relieved he was not the gyrating and openly sexual Elvis. He later said he "went from singing in the bathroom to the recording studio, with nothing in between" (1993, 519), but he had a phenomenally successful career as a bona fide teen idol well into the Sixties, and later as a more serious rock musician. After having lived out his teen life on television, observed by millions of Americans and controlled by scriptwriters, he was less than happy as an adult. He died in a plane crash in rural Texas, on December 31, 1985, on his way to a concert date in Dallas.

Also in 1957, in the summer, twenty-seven-year-old Philadelphia DJ Dick Clark launched *American Bandstand*, the clean-cut alternative to rhythm and blues and the sexy dancing its songs inspired. Using the format of a neighborhood record hop, similar to a number of local shows appearing around the country, Clark brought the Bandstand Kids to national television: well groomed teens who enjoyed dancing and rock music but did not wear jeans or leather jackets or go wild when they heard a rock beat. He promoted mainstream rock with his guest performers, and eventually he promoted himself as a trusted advisor to the young (Palladino 1996, 134). Such a program was yet another way the adult-controlled media, in their attempts to attract the lucrative teen market, capitalized on the supposed split between "good" and "bad" teens, between those who belonged to the Hi Y club and those who cruised the drive-ins in hot rods. In fact, as far as their media choices went, most teens were a little of both; they could enjoy Patti Page, *American Bandstand*, and *Your Hit Parade*, as well as Bo Diddley and the Platters' sexy rhythm and blues sounds late at night.

TEENS AT WORK

Continuing the trend that had begun in the late Forties, many teens entered the working world through part-time jobs while they stayed in school, using their wages not to supplement the family income but to pay for their own leisure activities, clothing, and cars. According to one estimate, in the mid-Fifties about half of the high-school-age teens worked at some time during a given year, and the numbers seemed to be inching up (Gilbert 1986, 20). These were the consumer teens who wielded millions of dollars' worth of economic power and helped to brand teen culture in the Fifties as exclusively a leisure culture.

There was another side to the story. With the trend toward vocational education, many teens prepared for full-time employment upon high school graduation. Vocational courses, and vocational schools, were generally segregated by gender; girls received training in nursing, secretarial skills, and beauty services, and boys learned welding, carpentry, and auto mechanics. In the vocational schools that could afford them, boys and girls had separate guidance counselors and separate cafeterias as well (Graebner 1990, 103–6). Such schools were also racially segregated. In Buffalo, blacks were denied entrance to the vocational schools and eased into academic high schools, where they would generally end up in lower "tracks" (1990, 103). The result was a systematic denial of black access to certain trades.

Working-class boys of any ethnic group, especially those in the inner city, faced the severest difficulties. If they were labeled delinquent, they found themselves left out of good vocational training and were shunted into correctional situations, without hope of academic success and without the opportunity to get jobs because of child labor laws. Harrison Salisbury pointed out that, fine as it was to insist that a child should not work full-time until age sixteen, such laws made no sense for many boys. Prevented by law from working, "forced to sit at desks all day long. . . . No wonder these youngsters become problems to themselves, to the schools, to a city" (1958, 156). Sociologist Martin Haskell, interviewed by Salisbury, stated that he believed that the laws were designed to remove boys from competition with adult labor, something that might have been necessary in the past but no longer made sense (229). Even boys who just bided their time until they could join the army might not be accepted there either, given the army's strictures

Home economics class, Greencastle High School, Greencastle, Indiana, 1957. Reproduced courtesy of Greencastle High School.

against poor health, police records, and illiteracy. Some authorities advocated a return to the Civilian Conservation Corps, which worked well during the Depression years, or similar forestry camps where boys could do useful work and learn skills as well (229). The problem was not solved during this decade, nor indeed in succeeding ones.

TEENS AT SCHOOL

By the early Fifties, the American high school had evolved from an intellectual, privileged venue of learning to a social center where teens established their own values and were their own arbiters of success and failure. In its efforts to serve every student equally, the American high school had broadened its curriculum to include all kinds of vocational courses. The number of extracurricular activities had also increased, partly in an effort to provide teens with safe, supervised recreation and keep them from becoming the dreaded juvenile delinquents, or at least from mixing with dropouts and delinquents. Of course, teens found plenty of ways to circumvent such arrangements, and the curricula and activities varied depending on the size, location, and social and ethnic populations of the school. School was, in any event, where the great majority of teens spent most of their time.

Ninth graders at Sedgefield Junior High School, Charlotte, North Carolina, 1956. Reproduced courtesy of Sedgefield Middle School.

In 1957 Professor James Coleman, a researcher then at the University of Chicago, carried out a sociological study of American high schools. He chose ten diverse schools in the northern Illinois area, including elite suburban schools, parochial schools, schools in farming and industrial communities, and small city schools. Apparently, since he makes no mention of racial mixing or any racial issues, they were all racially segregated despite the beginnings of school integration. Coleman's study nevertheless does apply to a majority of similar schools around the country.

Athletics and Cheerleading

Coleman administered various questionnaires about popularity, leisure activities, and cliques to the students as well as to teachers and parents. What he found was a general pattern of student values that privileged the athlete over the scholar, the well-to-do over the poor, and the boy over the girl. If an athlete was also smart, so much the better for his popularity, but even an average nonstudious athlete and an average studious athlete ranked higher than a brilliant, studious athlete; brilliant, studious nonathletes were at the very bottom of the popularity ranking (Coleman 1961, 309–10).

Competition, Coleman found, was the bedrock of high school life—but

High school football at Greencastle High School, Greencastle, Indiana, 1958. Reproduced courtesy of Greencastle High School.

not competition for grades as much as, for boys, competition in sports and, for girls, competition in popularity with boys. Boys' tastes, and their daily lives, were structured around sports; outstanding athletes brought glory to the school and to the entire community. The successful scholar "can bring glory to no one but himself" (1961, 309). Successful athletes were the school leaders, the most admired, the most popular of all. Successful athletic programs generated the "internal cohesion" called school spirit, which sets the school apart from others in the surrounding communities. Football, especially, was the center of school life for most of the schools Coleman studied.

For girls, the equivalent to athletic success was being a cheerleader. Cheerleaders were usually chosen for their good looks, an important attribute to girls, but being a cheerleader raised a girl to the top of the popularity list. It gave her an "inside track" with the athletes, the most popular boys in the school, and it assured her of dates and good times in the competitive world of girls—competition not on the playing fields but at parties and in clothes closets and beauty salons.

By the 1950s, in fact, the whole field of cheerleading had changed from an exclusively masculine activity in college, to a coeducational activity beginning to filter down to the high schools, to an almost exclusively feminine, high school activity which had become competitive even at junior high and grade school levels. Such girls were then prepared for varsity activities as cheerleaders, majorettes, and drill squad—all considered part of the glory of the athletic life of the school, but increasingly separated by gender. "In the 1950s some secondary school educators defined gender-appropriate activities as sports for boys and cheerleading (and sewing) for girls" (Hanson 1995, 24). The image of the "perfect couple" in the high school had become the football star and the cheerleader, both usually blonde, blue-eyed, and affluent. In black schools, athletes and cheerleaders were apparently very popular as well; the major difference with the white schools was in cheerleading styles. Only in the late Sixties did cheerleading squads begin to be racially mixed and did black dance movements become part of cheering (1995, 33–35).

Fear of Communism

Fears that the Russians might drop the atom and then the hydrogen bomb, which followed Americans from the Forties into the Fifties, found their way into the schools. Some parents built bomb shelters at home; many schools had monthly bomb drills. At the sound of a siren, students were trained to crouch under their desks with their heads down and covered, or to go quickly to basement rooms and sit against the wall.

More insidious was the fear of Communist infiltration into the teaching profession. In his research, Coleman found a deterioration in the relationships between students and teachers; teachers seemed to have lost the respect of the teens and had little influence over their values. Some of this attitude may have been the result of the McCarthy probe. Schools were beginning to require loyalty oaths from their employees, and to scrutinize their backgrounds carefully. In 1951 eight New York City teachers were fired for having possible Communist ties. Although the charges were never proved and by 1957 five of them had been rehired, the case provided some impetus for increasingly close scrutiny of teachers, especially any who might be at all unorthodox. Harry Mazer, a popular writer of novels for teens since the late Sixties, found himself drawn in his early twenties to socialist causes, and he worked as a union organizer and welder in the mid-Fifties. By 1955 he was becoming disillusioned with socialist thought after reading about Stalin's atrocities. In 1957 he was hired to teach tenth grade English at Central Square High School in Syracuse, New York, which he did with pleasure and with the commendation of his principal. But someone, he still does not know who, went to the administration and accused Mazer of being a Communist, "which I wasn't," he says (Reed 1996, 18). He was fired. It was a sign of the times; the principal liked him, but "with the politics of the time his hands were tied—he had no choice" (1996, 18).

Fraternities and Sororities

The high school had apparently become a bewildering place for parents as well as teachers. Coleman found that parents were sending mixed messages to their children about school. Although they said they most wanted their teenage children to succeed academically, those same children believed their parents would rather they be popular than make good grades. The parents had evidently absorbed the students' own value code; the high school, Coleman speculated, had insulated the teen from adult values and perspectives. To many adults, the most disturbing evidence of this insulation was the power of the high school fraternities and sororities.

In 1953 the executive secretary of the National Association of Secondary-School Principals estimated that between 500 and 600 high schools nation-wide had such secret organizations even though they were prohibited or restricted by law in twenty-five states (Taves 1953, 49). Administrators tried to control the exclusionary tactics and the hazing that marked such groups, but often the fraternities and sororities wielded great social and emotional power over students and their parents, and through them over the school. A sorority or fraternity boycott of a scheduled school event could ruin it. Parents worried about early drinking and smoking which the societies seemed to encourage, and the distraction from studies that the hazing and the social life of the organizations demanded. A Flint, Michigan, mother told of her daughter's experience as an initiate: "The telephone rang all day and night. At midnight she would be sent way across town to deliver some silly package to an 'active.' . . . Once we counted. It rang thirty times in one night, all [sorority] calls" (1953, 108). More seriously, reports of suicides and emotional breakdowns resulting from a student's not being bid, as well as reports of sadistic hazing practices, crept into local gossip and into the news occasionally in communities that had such organizations.

Still, many girls and their mothers appreciated the social opportunities the societies gave their initiates and felt rather coldly philosophical about girls who did not get in: "You aren't going to get everything you want all your life. If you can't take it now, you never will be able to. It's just life," one sorority girl said (Taves, 1953, 110). When asked if the school was failing them in some way, sorority and fraternity members scoffed, saying they simply wanted something of their own, something that seemed modern and "with it." An administrator at White Plains (New York) High School commented that such societies were really archaic holdovers from nineteenth- and early twentieth-century college organizations dedicated to intellectual pursuits. To the small number of students who "made it," they represented acceptance and distinction, a way to stand apart from the crowd in a large high school. Even students who were not members fought for the right to keep them.

Racial Integration and Little Rock

With the Supreme Court's 1954 decision in the *Brown v. Board of Education* (of Topeka, Kansas) case, the American high school became the focus of national attention in a way it had never been before, and probably never will be again. The Court, setting aside its 1896 ruling of "separate but equal," stated that racial segregation in the public schools was unconstitutional; schools were required to make provisions to integrate. In a few states, the process happened with little fanfare, but in the South, where segregation was a long-entrenched way of life, integration was neither peaceful nor quick.

In Little Rock, Arkansas, the original plan was to begin integration in the elementary schools, but school officials quickly discovered that white parents were more frightened of their young children's sharing their school with blacks than they were of their teenagers' integration. Plans were made to integrate Little Rock's Central High School in 1957, and nine black students were chosen to make the move from the all-black Horace Mann High School. These nine students were ready and willing. They trusted their country and its laws, and they believed what they were doing was right and important for their future and for future black students (Halberstam 1993, 670).

They had not reckoned with Governor Orval Faubus, who began to sense that his political future lay not with the moderates but with those who completely opposed integration. Word began to leak to the media that Faubus was planning a drastic action. Reporters from around the country began to arrive in Little Rock, ready with equipment to broadcast events live. On September 3, 1957, Faubus made his dramatic move: he called out the National Guard, ostensibly to prevent violence in the streets, but in effect to keep the black students from enrolling. Eight of the students were telephoned by a local representative of the NAACP and advised that they needed protection; when they appeared and saw the mood of the mob that had gathered near the school, they quickly and safely retreated. The ninth student, fifteen-year-old Elizabeth Eckford, had no phone and did not know that she would not be allowed to enroll that day.

Approaching the school alone, in a crisp tailored dress she had made herself for the occasion, she met the screaming crowd with dignity, assuming that the soldiers were there to protect her (Halberstam 1993, 675). Instead, the soldiers blocked her with bayonets while the crowd yelled, "Lynch her!" Despite her terror, and with a remarkable calm that was recorded by news cameras for the world to see, along with the virulent hatred of many Little Rock teens and adults, she walked to a bus stop and sat down. A *New York Times* reporter, Benjamin Fine, and a white woman took charge of her and got her safely onto a bus. She had, in that short time when her very life was threatened, become symbolic of generations of suppression and abuse.

Within a few days, Faubus had to bow to the federal government. The U.S. 101st Airborne Division took over the school for several weeks and escorted the students each day ensuring their safety to and from the building. Within the building, however, as the year wore on, teachers and administrators had a hard time controlling many of the white students, who scrawled obscenities on the black students' lockers and harassed them—and any white students who were nice to them—at every opportunity. Even so, they welcomed the opportunity. As one put it, "For the first time in my life . . . I felt like an American citizen" (Palladino 1996, 182).

These students had allies, although sometimes they were not aware of it. One was sixteen-year-old Ira Lipman, whose family belonged to the Jewish country club where black student Ernest Green worked. Ira and Ernest had become friends, although both were aware of the social strictures on their friendship. Ira telephoned NBC reporter John Chancellor with inside news of the crisis, whispering into the telephone so no one would know of his activities. He realized the power of the news media to change the situation, and he wanted to help despite the danger he was in. His friend Ernest Green was the first black student to graduate from Central High School, in the spring of 1958.

Ultimately all but one of the nine graduated. Minniejean Brown, the most outspoken of the group and the least willing to take the insults of the white students, was finally expelled for dumping soup on the heads of some boys who had kicked chairs in her way and called her names (Palladino 1996, 184).

Orval Faubus closed the school in 1958–1959, but in 1959–1960, it reopened, integrated. Faubus's political career did not seem to be especially damaged, but, even more than in the Emmett Till case, the image of American racism had been broadcast worldwide. In 1960 schools in Alabama, Georgia, Louisiana, Mississippi, and South Carolina were still segregated (Layman 1994, 127).

Sputnik and James B. Conant

During that same turbulent autumn, the United States witnessed the Soviet Union take the lead in space exploration. The Soviets successfully test launched an intercontinental ballistic missile and put a satellite with two radio transmitters into orbit around the earth (Halberstam 1993, 624). The satellite was named "Sputnik," which in Russian means "fellow traveler." The word charmed the public, but the idea that the Soviets were ahead of America in technology alarmed educators and politicians. The attention that had been focused on the schools by delinquency and racial problems now shifted. Magazines and newspapers featured stories comparing young Soviet students with American high school students. While Soviet youth were studying science and math, Americans were playing football, taking shop and stenography, and reading love comics on the sly in English class. Even worse, teens were watching too much television and "studying" to rock and roll music. Our future was at stake if America did not crack down on its high school students with tougher academic standards.

Into this climate stepped Dr. James B. Conant, a chemist, a former president of Harvard University, and the outgoing U.S. ambassador to the Federal Republic of Germany. With grant money from the Carnegie Corporation, he launched a critical study of the American high school, one that he hoped would encourage change in the "comprehensive" high school, that particularly American kind of high school that educates every kind of student in a "democratic environment" (Gardner quoted in Conant 1959, x). Conant believed that average schools could become better, even excellent, schools, and to that end, in his report, he made twenty-one recommendations about everything from the teaching of writing to the organization of home rooms. The chief thrust of his reforms was a curriculum that stressed four years of English, mathematics, and foreign languages. He acknowledged the importance of vocational education, but he believed basically that the best education was due to the small percentage of bright students who wanted it, and that such education should be restored to importance in the high school.

Thanks to Sputnik, the federal government was already funneling more money into the schools for science, math, and language study. Conant's book, subtitled "A First Report to Interested Citizens," aimed to draw administrators, school boards, teachers, and parents into the battle for our best and brightest. As Grace Palladino points out, however, Conant's goals seemed to favor white middle-class males more than anyone else (1996, 170–72). Conant was hailed as a reformer and a harbinger of hope for the American high school, but his ideas worked to continue the race and class separations that marked the "democratic" American high school.

FASHION

With the bobby-soxer trend in the late Forties, teen fashion began to attract the attention of the public. In the Fifties, it attracted the designers themselves, who began to court this new, lucrative market for clothing. Teens' disposable income was estimated at $9 billion at mid-decade, and the first shopping malls had appeared; there were 1,600 of them in the country by 1956 (Layman 1994, 156).

Adult women were adopting Dior's "New Look": the cinched waist, peplum jacket, sweeping full skirt or pencil-slim skirt, calf-length, and very high-heeled pumps, all topped with the important hat and finished with gloves. Teen girls in the white-middle and upper classes had their own versions of the New Look. They wore wide elastic belts to cinch their waists over circle skirts or slim skirts. Sometimes the circle skirts were made of felt and featured appliques; the most common applique was a poodle, sometimes on a leash made from a real chain. With the skirts girls wore close-fitting sweaters, sometimes a sweater set, with a small scarf knotted at the neck, or a round-collared blouse with a circle-shaped pin at the collar. On dressed-up occasions, they might also wear a small hat with a turned-back brim, wrist-length

The latest prom wear modeled by teens at Ephrata High School, Pennsylvania, 1952. Reproduced courtesy of Jean Ann Holder.

white gloves, and high heels. At school, they wore penny loafers or dirty buckskin oxfords and ankle socks along with their approximation of the New Look, a signal that they were still teens and were going to keep their basic style elements despite adult fashion. For casual wear, they increasingly wore jeans, with the pants rolled up to midcalf, topped with a loose shirt not tucked in. Prom nights saw them in tight-waisted dresses with full skirts over several petticoats, with high heels and gloves. Hair was usually shorter than in the Forties, with short bangs curled by pin curls, or sometimes pulled up in a short pony tail. Underneath, they still wore bras, often in a pointed style, panty girdles or garter belts to hold in their stomachs and hold up their nylon stockings, and full slips in addition to their crinoline petticoats.

White middle-class boys wore loose, cuffed trousers with loose-fitting, wide-lapeled jackets, white shirts, and in the early Fifties, fairly wide ties. Toward the end of the decade, ties became very narrow, as did belts; a very thin belt, worn with pleated pants low on the hips, perhaps with the buckle slid around to the side, was cool. Suits developed natural shoulders, and three buttons were featured on the jacket. With the addition of button-down collars, by 1959 the look was lean, slim, and controlled. At school, boys wore cardigan or pullover V-neck sweaters, topping a button-down-collar white shirt, and penny loafers or dirty bucks, usually with white socks, as did the girls. A more middle-class look was jeans, with the bottoms turned up into wide cuffs, and plaid shirts. Boys who were better off liked the

Motorcycle boots and jeans: the cool guys at Greencastle High School, Green-castle, Indiana, 1956. Reproduced courtesy of Greencastle High School.

preppie look (named for boys who went to private high schools, or preparatory schools). In warm weather, this usually meant madras plaid shirts, Bermuda shorts, and penny loafers without socks. Hair was cropped short in a flat-top or crew cut, or worn a little longer and swept back on the sides. White sport coats were traditional prom wear.

Boys and girls who had less money to spend on clothes, and often felt excluded from the mainstream white middle-class teen culture for economic or ethnic reasons, expressed their disdain for the "clean teens" by wearing black leather jackets, tight-fitting jeans, and, for the boys, tight white or black T-shirts and lacedup shoes with pointed toes or motorcycle boots. Sometimes they stored their cigarette packs in their rolled-up T-shirt sleeves. Girls wore very tight sweaters and heavy makeup. The flamboyant styles of black rock singers also influenced these teens, who adopted the stars' extreme "drapes," or loose-fitting trousers with narrow bottoms, shirts with wide collars, and, in imitation of the famous song, blue suede shoes (Graebner 1990, 46). Boy and girl gang members sported jackets with their gang names on the back or the particular color combinations that identified them.

Color itself could have a rebellious meaning. The color pink seemed to be the color of the decade, across all social classes. First Lady Mamie Eisenhower loved it. Elvis wore pink pants and a pink suit, and he bought a pink Ford (Marling 1994, 40). Teen boys and girls wore pastel pink shirts. It seemed to represent a kind of freedom from rigid categories of male and female, of middle class and other class. The most popular color combination in the decade, especially for teens, was pink and black. Graebner sees this phenomenon as a class statement. Pink and black did not "belong together," they were not the colors of authority or of any athletic team. They "married" innocence and girlishness to "male malevolence" (1990, 74). In Buffalo, in 1953, the Jackie Wilson Fan Club adopted pink and black as their colors, making a conscious statement about their love of Wilson's rocking music, and perhaps an unconscious one about black music generally and black freedom from convention. To Graebner, the colors represented the working-class rebellion against the white middle-class dominance. Eventually, inevitably, the white middle class adopted the colors—in bathroom decor, cars, and advertising as well as in clothes—removing them from the black culture where they originated and making them fit for adult and clean-teen consumption.

Hair was a major symbol of teens' rejection of the middle class. Boys grew it long, combed it into a pompadour in front and in back into a "DA," or "duck's ass" style, and greased it. As Elvis Presley became popular, girls too wore DAs. But soon the predictable pattern asserted itself: the broad middle-class culture adopted its own watered-down version of this rebellious style. By the late Fifties, film star Doris Day cut her white-blond hair into a modified DA, the name of which was also modified to "ducktail," so "nice girls" could wear it too.

The rebellious style of some teens' clothes seemed a direct assault on authority, especially in high school, where dress became a battleground for control and Elvis was apparently the teens' general: "If a kid in a hot pink shirt and sideburns could earn enough to buy his Mom a new house in the Memphis suburbs just by twitching and looking strange, what use were all those moral lessons about hard work, grit, and pluck?" (Marling 1994, 174). In retaliation, across the nation, schools in the late Fifties adopted versions of Buffalo's "Dress Right" campaign, a voluntary program to bring homogeneity to school dress which received national publicity as being successful in combating juvenile delinquency (Graebner 1990, 99–103). For girls, jeans were out; only skirts and dresses were acceptable. Boys were required to wear ties or sweaters and jackets with their dress or sport shirts, and standard trousers, not the extreme "drapes" associated with zoot-suiters and rhythm and blues singers. Such codes only touched the surface of the delinquency problem; mostly they made school officials feel they were achieving some kind of order and democracy. In reality, the codes strengthened gender roles and class divisions, offered clothing designers and merchants an increased market for standard, middle-class, white teen styles, and gave teens who could afford them a reason to spend more money on clothes.

By 1957 Dior's New Look was being eclipsed by another style, a very different one aimed directly at teens. It was called the "sack," and it provoked a surprising amount of controversy. Rather than the cinched-waisted styles of the early Fifties, this dress style was loose from shoulder to knee, with a hemline just at the knee. It was also called a chemise, after the loose undergarment worn by women in the nineteenth century and early twentieth century. Chemise dresses freed girls from the tight girdles and bras that the narrow-waisted look required, as well as from the longer skirts that hobbled movement and the petticoats required by full skirts. Even Marilyn Monroe wore a sack dress to a press conference (Marling 1994, 43), though fashion commentators and outraged men said the style made women look like sacks of potatoes. Girls bought them and wore them, heralding a new fashion power. The stereotypical fashionable woman, age approximately thirty-five, was no longer the fashion arbiter for the nation. Now she was a teenager.

SLANG

Slang scholar Tom Dalzell believes that Fifties teen slang itself—at least, that used by the white middle class—was not particularly inventive or original (1996, 67). Nevertheless, as in every other decade, teens distinguished themselves from adults by their lively and descriptive language.

Cool was the word used most to approve of something. To cool it was to relax, take it easy. Girls who liked something might say it was neat; something a little offbeat might be kooky. Teens who enjoyed a really funny joke might say it fractured them; something that was easy was no sweat. Going to a drive-in movie and necking might be making out at the passion pit; teens who had entered a sexual relationship and might even be living together on occasion were shacking up. Oddballs and party poopers were people you did not want around.

The Beat movement injected many new expressions, most of them taken from black jazz musicians and the drug culture. Man, cat, and baby were terms of address for anyone, male or female. To dig it was to understand; a groovy scene at this cat's pad was a good time in his room or apartment, which one enjoyed before splitting (leaving). If someone went crazy or out of control, he had wigged out or gone off the deep end. Someone who was just boring was a square. Putting -ville on the end of a word brought all kinds of interesting constructions and marked the speaker as definitely not from squaresville (e.g., The party was dullsville, but I woke up in hangoversville). Coolness was the ultimate Beat state of mind, and the slang aimed to create coolness, a mood widely imitated among teens who aspired to the counterculture of the Beats. It was imitated by adults, too, for its originality and easy-going sound. It was a constant source of satire in the media; translating fairy tales or Shakespeare into Beat slang could produce hilarious results, as in Steve Allen's *Bop Fables* published in 1955.

City gangs of all ethnicities had their own slang, more often associated with violence, sex, and drugs. For them, to bop was to fight; to duke was to fight with fists; and a rumble was a gang fight. A traitor, who might let the cops know of a rumble, was cheesy; but you were tight (close) with your friends who did not squeal. Pot, pusher, and junkie came from this milieu. Sneaky pete was the kind of cheap wine that would sneak up on you and get you drunk fast (Salisbury 1958, 35). Jazz was worthless talk, as in "Don't gimme that jazz." To punk out was to be a coward.

LEISURE ACTIVITIES AND ENTERTAINMENT

The teen clubs and canteens which began in the Forties, especially in urban areas where efforts were made to control delinquency, continued to be fairly popular in the Fifties. Even if the centers were poorly equipped, inner-city teens frequented them because they were the only safe place to go. Journalist Harrison Salisbury visited one in the Bedford-Stuyvesant area of Brooklyn. There he saw fifty or sixty black boys, fifteen or twenty girls, and one white boy. They had decorated their "lounge" themselves with crepe paper, but it showed the effects of a break-in a few weeks before when walls had been torn down. The director commented that if the churches and synagogues of the area lived up to their responsibility, such teens would have better places for their leisure time (Salisbury 1958, 183).

In suburban neighborhoods, churches and synagogues, as well as town councils, did try to influence where teens spent their time away from school by providing places with juke boxes, pool tables, dance floors, and Coke machines. Schools sponsored sock hops, a dance where the teens left their shoes at the door and danced in their socks to records spun by a DJ.

But true to form, teens still found their own space. Middle-class white girls enjoyed the slumber party, where a group of girls stayed up all night in their pajamas, doing each other's hair and nails, eating snacks, listening to records, and talking on the phone to boys. The party was considered a real success if a group of boys showed up outside and hung around, holding conversations with the girls (who usually had covertly suggested that the boys visit) through the window. Drive-in restaurants got a reputation for being almost exclusively teen hangouts; in small towns, drugstores with booths and counters were popular after-school spots. On weekends, the balconies of movie theaters provided privacy for necking or a more public place to meet friends and act silly by throwing popcorn on those below. Drive-in movies were famous as "passion pits" as well as places for boys to show off a hot car or just see friends and hang out.

The Car

Middle-class boys enjoyed their leisure time more on the street than in their homes or those of their friends. Cruising was the favorite activity. Boys piled into cars and drove around the neighborhoods, down the main streets, and around the parking lots of drive-in restaurants, eyeing the girls, flirting,

Jalopies, Greencastle High School, Greencastle, Indiana, 1956. Reproduced courtesy of Greencastle High School.

and enjoying joking rivalries with each other, or sometimes engaging in more serious competition such as drag races. In a drag race, drivers in two cars accelerated from a standing start, and the winner was the first driver to get his car to cross the finish line. Drag racing was sometimes held on tracks under supervision, but most often it took place on back roads with only other teens to watch. Accidents were not uncommon. Drag racing had a fascination, a complexity of rules and codes, and a special vocabulary second only to medieval jousting (see Dalzell 1996, 74–81).

The teen boy's fascination with and increasing dependence on cars was one of the dominant features of the Fifties. A car ensured dates and friends; it represented freedom from home and parents as well as privacy to explore sex. It was also a venue for creativity. Customizing his car provided a boy with the opportunity to show off his talents and originality: he could add chrome, modify the engine to produce more speed and noise, remove hood ornaments for a tougher look, add "trumpets" (extensions to the tail pipe) or a "necker's nob"—a knob on the steering wheel to make driving easier with your left hand when your right arm was around your girl. He could practice all sorts of driving techniques like popping the clutch, snap shifting, and "laying a strip" (squealing the tires).

Boys' infatuation with cars echoed a shift not just in teen life but in the entire population: cars were becoming increasingly important to everyone. Cars themselves reflected the consumerist "populuxe" style of the Fifties as they grew larger, longer, lower, and gaudier. Tailfins and chrome accents increased, dashboards sported pushbuttons, and color combinations became more unusual—such as pink and grey. The result, says Thomas Hine, "was

Helping out a buddy, Greencastle High School, Greencastle, Indiana, 1955. Reproduced courtesy of Greencastle High School.

an automobile-buying frenzy. By the end of 1955, Americans had spent $65 billion on automobiles, an amount equal to 20 percent of the gross national product. That year, General Motors became the first company to earn $1 billion in a single year" (1987, 90). The most famous disaster in American automobile history occurred in 1958: the Edsel. Although it had been carefully designed and researched by Ford to appeal to young executives on their way to corporate success, it was a flop from the beginning. Its name seemed weird (it was named after Ford's father) and its front grille even weirder; some said it looked like "an Oldsmobile sucking a lemon" (1987, 92). It lost millions for Ford and for a time the entire industry seemed threatened by its failure.

Dating and Sex

The "rating and dating" system that had developed informally during the earlier decades continued throughout the Fifties. What had been an expression of private teen culture and teen freedom to choose became an increasingly complex, pressured system of social and sexual codes which—if myriad magazine articles, advice columns, and surveys are to be believed—caused teens more anxiety than pleasure.

Aside from the usual teen concerns about masturbation, wet dreams, and menstruation, both boys and girls in the Fifties worried to a remarkable degree about their physical appearance and whether they could get dates. These worries evidently began in the earliest teen years, when concern about pimples, weight, nails, teeth, and hair occupied teens' thoughts. Young teens also worried about whether to kiss on the first date, what to talk about to the opposite sex, and how to tell if one was really in love. Girls worried about how to keep a boy's respect and still let him "do what he wants to do" (Remmers and Radler 1957, 75).

Articles on grooming and clothes, as well as advice columns, encouraged teen girls—at increasingly young ages—to concentrate on their appearance

Enjoying the after school hangout, Greencastle, Indiana, 1957. Reproduced courtesy
of Greencastle High School.

as the key to popularity. Quizzes asked if girls knew the right hairstyle for
the right shape of face, when and where to wear gloves and hats, how to
lose those unwanted pounds, how to apply just the right shade of lipstick.
They also encouraged girls to buy beauty products: "To help you put on
your prettiest mouth a magnifying glass and a lipstick brush are invaluable"
(Glynne 1954, 172). If girls got it right, a date could be magic.

This is the moment to slip into your dress. . . . Pat your hair in place again, fasten
your necklace or bracelet, and step into your pumps. . . . And wheeee! Look now!
There really is another you in the mirror. A you that is practically exuding a subtle
new fascination, a wonderful femininity. Quickly, reach out for your flacon of per-
fume. . . . But be careful—don't overdo it.
    The heat of your beating pulse will warm the scent and give it life—sending it out
to greet all who come near you.
    You're off to a wonderful, wonderful time! (Glynne 1954, 172)

    The economy of the date was unchanged: the boy asked, the boy paid—
whether it was for Cokes or orchids. The boy provided the transportation.
The girl paid for her clothes and grooming since her chief economic responsibility was to look good. The date, according to Beth Bailey, was an
act of "consumption," a public act. Boys and girls alike wanted not so much

the company of a particular person, but to be seen in the company of a particular person. Dating began earlier, too; twelve- and thirteen-year-olds were engaging in the rituals, pairing off or double-dating, with parents providing needed transportation. For older teens, the prom remained the most public, most ritualized dating event—also often the most expensive: "In 1957, when median family income was $4,353, 42 percent of the boys and 72 per cent of the girls who went to proms spent over $15 on each prom they attended" (Bailey 1988, 62). As part of their symbolic entry into the adult world at graduation, teens dressed in more adult formal clothes at high school proms, listened to more adult music, wore orchids as symbols of sexual maturity, and generally behaved with adult decorum—at least publicly. The competition for a prom date was also more intense, and the lack of a date for one was a more visible failure.

In the Twenties, Thirties, and Forties, the mark of real teen success was lots of dates, with lots of different partners. In the Fifties, going steady was the mark of success. The choice of one person to date exclusively, even youngsters of twelve and thirteen, perhaps reflected the insecurities of postwar America. Going steady was not courtship leading to marriage, at least until eighteen or nineteen, but a kind of serial commitment, made visible by sharing class rings or jackets or matching madras shirts. *Seventeen* once suggested that a girl might sew a dress for herself, then make a boy a bow tie to match. When the teen found a new "steady," such symbols were easily transferred.

Going steady also signified increased sexual involvement. The longer a couple went steady, the more frequent and intense the sexual contact became. Although necking was widely accepted in casual dating, petting became a complicated set of maneuvers leading ever closer to intercourse. Boys were expected to pressure the girl gradually for more and more favors, while girls—at least, those who wanted to appear "nice" and continue to get dates and steadies—allowed only so much and no more, gradually increasing the contact until she reached what she regarded as the limit. The schedule usually went something like this: kissing, to necking, to above the waist outside the clothes, to above the waist underneath the clothes, to below the waist outside the clothes, to below the waist underneath the clothes. Statistics suggest that more teen girls were engaging in full, premarital sexual intercourse than in previous decades and doing it at a younger age. Out of 805 girls surveyed in the mid-Fifties, 14.5% said they had had premarital intercourse by age sixteen; 43.1%, by age eighteen (adapted from Chadwick and Heaton 1992, 140).

The double standard remained in place for the white middle-class teens. Boys were expected to "do it," and girls were expected to refrain from "doing it." The difference between boys and girls in their attitudes toward love and sex was never more pronounced: being in love for girls usually meant they were willing to engage in increased sexual activity, but boys, who were in love and who respected the girl, preferred less sexual activity with her (Breines 1992, 119). Such a system inevitably led to bewilderment and frustration for both. For boys who resisted the pressures of their buddies to "make out" with a girl and tell them about it in detail, the price was ridicule and a reputation as a "Percy" or nerd. When a girl gave in, the result might be a flurry of dates and phone calls for a time, then a reputation for being a slut, then loss of friends, and ultimately loss of dates. Sylvia Plath, author of *The Bell Jar*, who played by the "rules," probably spoke for many teen girls of the Fifties when she wrote in her high school journal: "I can only . . . hate, hate, hate, the boys who dispel sexual hunger freely . . . while I drag out from date to date in soggy desire, always unfulfilled" (quoted in Palladino 1996, 167).

The Kinsey Report 1953

The 1948 Kinsey report, *Sexual Behavior in the Human Male*, caused a stir, but 1953's *Sexual Behavior in the Human Female* brought biologist and researcher Alfred C. Kinsey even more vilification in the popular press. He was attacking, some believed, American girls, wives, and mothers—that is, the very moral fabric of society. The conformity on which American life was based was threatened when Kinsey lifted the veil of secrecy and repression. Nevertheless, as in 1948, Kinsey and his team offered facts—facts gleaned from interviews with almost 8,000 females from a wide range of ages and socioeconomic groups—and presented conclusions based solely on those facts. Like the first volume, the book is a massive, scientific document filled with statistical tables, and, like the first volume, it sold hundreds of thousands of copies within weeks (Petersen 1998, 142).

Kinsey's findings about teen girls centered mostly around masturbation and petting. Although boys still masturbated more frequently, girls certainly engaged in it; more than half of them had their first experience in their teens and more than half engaged in it several times a week (Kinsey 1953, 176, 179). Kinsey emphasized that he had found little evidence of damage from the activity itself. "We have, on the other hand, recognized a tremendous amount of damage which has been the result of worry over masturbation, and of attempts to abstain from such activity" (1953, 168).

Among the thousands of females interviewed about petting, he found that 39% had experienced it by age fifteen; 81%, by age eighteen. Thirty-five percent of girls had petted with more than ten partners. Kinsey saw it, as did the girls and women in his sample, as a socializing agent: "It is petting rather than the home, classroom or religious instruction, lectures or books, classes in biology, sociology, or philosophy, or actual coitus, that provides most females with their first real understanding of a heterosexual experience" (264). Kinsey's statistics showed that premarital petting, rather than inhibiting a girl's marital sexual response, actually facilitated it (266–67).

Kinsey had revealed that the stereotype of the virginal, innocent teen girl was a fantasy, and that even the stereotype of the home-loving, faithful wife might be suspect. To some congressmen, the country was beginning to resemble decadent Rome if Kinsey was to be believed. Although his research had been supported by Indiana University and the Rockefeller Foundation, many considered him a danger to American life. His Rockefeller funding was withdrawn shortly after the publication of the second study (Petersen 1998, 144). Exhausted by the work and the furor over his books, Kinsey's health failed, and he died in 1956.

Music and Dancing

In no other decade has music been of such paramount importance as an activity, an economy, and a symbol, and without doubt part of the reason was the new buying power of teens. The teen market emerged in the Fifties as the shaping force of popular music. With the change from fragile, expensive 78-rpm records to the handy 45s and then to the durable 33s, teens could easily spend more money for the music they loved on the radio or at record hops. The increasing power of the television and radio to reach all audiences and the remarkable phenomenon that was Elvis Presley also played major roles. Although the story of this decade is in large measure one of divisions along racial, gender, and generational lines, the story of the music is one of fusion. Black rhythm and blues artists adjusted some of their style to appeal to the market, while country performers softened their twangy, hillbilly styles into smoother vocals and instrumentals. By the end of the decade, some music marketers and chart makers as well as music producers abandoned labels like "country," "pop," and "R & B" and just lumped songs together by popularity (Malone 1993, 256).

Rock and Roll

An overview of the top records of 1955 (Layman 1994, 30) reveals the variety of music adults and teens enjoyed. The instrumental "Cherry Pink and Apple Blossom White" became a theme song for many proms that year; three versions of "The Ballad of Davy Crockett" reflected that craze; Roger Williams's florid piano solo "Autumn Leaves" was perfect for slow dancing, as were any of the three versions of "Unchained Melody" or "Only You," by the Platters. For fast dancing, Chuck Berry's hard-driving "Maybellene" was perfect. Pat Boone, a clean-cut singer who was marketed as an antidote to the sexual threat of Elvis, tried an upbeat sound with "Ain't That a Shame." This was a crossover record—a white pop performer recording a black R & B song, such as this one by Fats Domino. In the scramble to reach the powerful white teen market, many white artists did crossovers. Another, largely unsuccessful ploy to attract white teens to white performers was the marketing of the clean-teen image of bland singers like

Fabian, Tommy Sands, and movie star Tab Hunter (Doherty 1988, 207–10).

The dominant sound of the Fifties was rock and roll. Some believe the phrase itself was coined by DJ Alan Freed, but it had been part of the black vernacular for years as a slang expression for sex. The shortened form, "rock," acquired two meanings: sex and the quality of energy in the beat of a song (Dalzell 1996, 82–83). Freed introduced it to white audiences on his radio show and it soon became a kind of rallying cry for teens, a terse statement of their pleasures and their identity. Ironically, though, the song that came to symbolize the entire phenomenon was recorded in 1954 by a white man, former country singer Bill Haley, with his new band the Comets: "Rock Around the Clock." This song blasted across America in a wave of DJ hype—some DJs were said to have played it literally around the clock a few times—and teen euphoria. When it was used as background music for the film *The Blackboard Jungle*, it became more closely identified with teen rebellion.

Teens also enjoyed the music of Jerry Lee Lewis, whose uninhibited and sometimes violent piano playing caused riots in concert houses. His version of a black song, "Whole Lotta Shakin' Goin' On," was a masterful combination of rock, R & B, and country. Along with Elvis, he helped create the "rockabilly" sound. Country music scholar Bill Malone calls Lewis "one of the most superbly talented individuals in country music history" (1993, 250) even though his career suffered from his public marriage to his thirteen-year-old cousin. Johnny Cash and Marty Robbins were also highly marketed country performers who appealed to white urban teens as well as rural ones. The Everly Brothers, who sang in the rockabilly style, had a big hit with "Wake Up, Little Susie," a song about a couple who have fallen asleep at a drive-in movie and will have to face parents and friends who will think the worst.

Elvis Presley

The impact on the decade of Elvis Presley can hardly be overstated. His story, which has been told in countless books and articles, can be only suggested here. He was a true popular phenomenon, for which there can be no final explanation. He was nineteen, employed as a truck driver, when he wandered into a Memphis recording studio and cut a record for his mother. The producer, Sam Phillips, immediately recognized that this young man with the pomaded hair, as he said of himself, "didn't sound like nobody." He was a completely new talent, a blend of country and R & B that worked perfectly. His first official record, made in 1954, featured on one side "That's All Right, Mama," an R & B song, and on the other a jazzed-up version of "Blue Moon of Kentucky," a country standard. When it began to get airplay, teens requested it in a flood of phone calls. When Presley began to appear at country fairs, teen girls reacted with hysterical screams of joy: "They squealed themselves silly over this fellow in orange coat and sideburns. . . . He would give each a long, slow look with drooped eyelids. . . . They ate it up" (Yothers quoted in Colbert 1997, 456).

His sulky yet playful sexuality and exuberant hip moves terrified adults and thrilled teens; this was real liberation from Top-40 pop music. His clothes and hair announced disdain for the white middle class. Yet he could sing gospel as well as sexy R & B; he could croon a simple ballad like "Love Me Tender" with gentle sincerity and blast out "Jailhouse Rock" with total abandon. As a singer, he combined all the strains of American music: rock, hillbilly, country, blues. In his appearance and manner, he seemed to combine aggressive masculinity with a feminine softness, white Southern charm and innocence with the swagger and open sexuality of black performers. Few other performers, then or now, have so naturally embodied all these contradictions.

The Day the Music Died

Teens received a shock on February 3, 1959. Three of their favorite performers had been making a concert tour. Buddy Holly had thrilled them with "Peggy Sue" and "That'll Be the Day." Richie Valens's "La Bamba" had a Latino appeal. J. P. Richardson, calling himself the Big Bopper, recorded "Chantilly Lace." In a last-minute decision, all three boarded the same airplane, which crashed, and all three were killed.

Dancing Styles

The legacy of the Lindy was the jitterbug, a lively dance in which the boy and girl held hands and pulled each other through turns and jumps to the heavy beat of rocking songs. But the athleticism of the Forties eventually gave way in the Fifties to something more earthbound and openly sexy. In imitation of some of the moves they saw among black teens, white teens began doing something they nicknamed the "dirty bop," or "dirty boogie," with bent-knee and hip moves that perfectly matched the low-down beat and suggestive lyrics of the music. The teens on Dick Clark's *American Bandstand* television show, of course, did not do this dance; they stuck to the cleaner version of the jitterbug, at least while they were on camera.

A different form of jitterbug developed in the South. It was an easy, smooth combination of pulls, turns, and slides, feet close to the floor at all times, that came to be called the Shag. The Shag was a cool dance, but a different kind of cool from the dirty bop. At the other end of the spectrum, in another part of the country, was the Fish, which Harrison Salisbury watched when he visited teen clubs frequented by New York gangs: "a slow, quiet hip movement resembling a burlesque house grind . . . danced body to body with hardly any movement of the feet. Because it is nothing but a sexual exercise, some centers try to ban it. But when the director turns his

Elvis Presley, *Jailhouse Rock*, 1957. Reproduced courtesy of The Museum of Modern Art.

back the youngsters move together and grind away" (1958, 35). Latino teens enjoyed the merengue and the cha-cha, which made their way into white teen culture across the country.

Occasionally, teens enjoyed dancing as a group. The Stroll was a series of gliding steps done individually, in a square pattern. The Bunny Hop was done in a long line, moving forward gradually on the "Hop, hop, hop" command. Like many other dance fads, this one was soon regarded with amazement and disbelief that such a juvenile dance could ever have been popular.

Movies

Blondes, he-men, Bible epics, and experimental filming techniques dominated the box office in the Fifties. The stars who attracted the most theatergoers were Doris Day, Grace Kelly, Marilyn Monroe, Rock Hudson, John Wayne, Gary Cooper, and William Holden. Buxom bodies were generally the fashion for women, although slim, doe-eyed Audrey Hepburn offered a more innocent image that was popular with many teen girls. Reflecting the popular interest in religion, big films of the decade included *Quo Vadis* (1951), *The Robe* (1953), *The Ten Commandments* (1956), and *Ben Hur* (1959).

The wide-screen technique of Cinerama, which used three projectors, premiered at specially equipped theaters in 1952 to considerable success (Miller and Nowak 1977, 321), setting off a competition to bring viewers right into the action by surrounding them with the images. *The Robe* was the first film shot in CinemaScope; VistaVision, Panavision, and Todd-AO quickly followed. Large theaters added big screens and charged higher prices. Also during the Fifties, film producers flirted with "3-D," a film technique that made the images seem three dimensional rather than flat. Audiences had to wear special cardboard glasses with plastic lenses to see the effect. *Bwana Devil* was the first such film, although *House of Wax* was the most popular. Only a few such films were made because the fad quickly lost its appeal.

Censorship and The Moon Is Blue

In 1953 director Otto Preminger produced the film *The Moon Is Blue*, based on a popular stage comedy about a girl rather proud of her virginity and her encounter with an older man in his apartment. The Motion Picture Production Code instituted in 1934 denied the film its seal of approval because, although it contained no explicit sex scenes, the characters used the words *pregnant* and *virgin* on-screen and referred to aphrodisiacs. Preminger decided to release the film anyway; since the movie houses were no longer controlled by the studios, he was gambling that he did not need the seal for box-office success (Miller and Nowak 1977, 326).

He was right. All the furor over the film only increased public interest in it. In Kansas, however, it was the cause of a Supreme Court case. Kansas had long had a censorship law protecting its young people from obscene materials. Preminger offered to limit the film in that state to adults only, but the Kansas officials declined to show it at all, and the film company brought suit. By 1955 the case had made its way to the U.S. Supreme Court, which ruled that the state could not ban the film on charges of obscenity when the term was defined as vaguely as Kansas had defined it: as virtually anything that could threaten childhood innocence (West 1988, 60).

The case signaled the end of the power of the Motion Picture Production Code and the beginning of a trend toward frank films that dealt with serious social problems.

Teen Movies about Delinquency

The decade has become identified with teen movies, both those about teens—especially delinquent ones—and those made for the teen market. A young Marlon Brando perfectly represented one popular image of delinquency in *The Wild One* (1953), filmed in black and white. Brando's performance as the leader of a motorcycle gang which terrorizes a small town has become legendary for his delivery of Beat slang and his portrayal of the pain of being young and misunderstood. His black leather jacket and jeans became the uniform of rebellion.

In 1955 the film of Evan Hunter's novel *Blackboard Jungle* shocked many Americans with its images of wild and violent inner-city high school youth. The story centers around one teacher, played by Glenn Ford, who believes that the kids are not really bad, that they have the potential to be good citizens. His technique for reaching them involves getting one of their leaders, played by Sidney Poitier, on his side against the more recalcitrant kids. Eventually the strategy works, but not before some unforgettable scenes of violence and threat, especially one in which the boys smash a priceless record collection a teacher has brought to school in an effort to "reach" them. All of this is played out to the sounds of Bill Haley's "Rock Around the Clock," a song which teens across the country were listening to en masse. It was the first film to use rock music in this way, and it was filmed in black and white to suggest the stark reality it tried to depict. The movie was a commercial success, but it frightened many adults. Many organizations spoke out in disapproval of it, the American Legion declared it the film that hurt the image of America most in foreign countries in 1955, and the American ambassador to Italy had it withdrawn from the Venice Film Festival (Gilbert 1986, 184).

The same year brought an even more disturbing film: *Rebel Without a Cause*. Here, delinquency was a problem of the middle-class suburbs, not only of the inner city. James Dean, who was fast becoming a star after his appearance earlier that year in *East of Eden*, starred, along with Natalie Wood and Sal Mineo, as teens rejected by their families. In fact, the overall message of the film is the failure of the adult culture to be sensitive to the

Marlon Brando as *The Wild One*, with his gang, 1953. Reproduced courtesy of The Museum of Modern Art.

Natalie Wood and James Dean in *Rebel Without a Cause*, 1955. Reproduced courtesy of The Museum of Modern Art.

needs of teens for love, acceptance, and security. These teens live in a violent world; the film includes a disastrous game of "chicken," the murder of one teen by another, and the killing of one boy by the police. Audiences had to identify with the tortured teens themselves—"nice" kids gone wrong because the system failed them. The film made James Dean a genuine star. His life became a legend after he died violently in a car crash in 1956, just before the release of his last film, *Giant*. His name has become synonymous with the pain of being a teenager.

Such films were interesting to teens and disturbing to their parents. They were serious films that tried to face, even if ambiguously, the increasing separateness of teen and adult culture. When teens went to the drive-in movies or to the B-picture houses in their hometowns on a cheap date, however, they wanted other fare, and some movie producers, especially American International who specialized in the genre, capitalized on the market for quickly made, cheap, teen-focused movies. These films generally told lurid tales of gangs, hot rods, and sororities and featured actors who were seldom seen again on-screen. In 1958 *High School Confidential!*, filmed in CinemaScope, however, used several stars—Russ Tamblyn, Mamie Van Doren, and Jerry Lee Lewis, among others—to tell the story of a marijuana bust.

Science Fiction Films

The Fifties has also become known as the decade of cheap science-fiction films aimed at the teen market. The drive-in screens filled with science run amok: *Tarantula!*, *The Attack of the 50-Foot Woman*, *The Thing*, *Them!*, *The Blob*, and *The Fly*. Invaders from outer space took over in *The Day the Earth Stood Still* and *The Invasion of the Body Snatchers*, two films which are today regarded as classics despite their low-budget special effects. Often the ads promised more action than the pictures delivered, but they were still good scary fun for teens, who probably did not consciously associate the fears of communism and the bomb, which marked the decade, with the often hilarious monsters and aliens in such movies.

The most egregious of these films were *I Was a Teenage Frankenstein* and *I Was a Teenage Werewolf*, both released in 1957. The titles parodied the confessional pulp magazines as well as the public's fears of rampaging, primitive, monstrous juvenile delinquents taking over the streets and schools. In *Frankenstein*, a doctor rescues a young man (Gary Conway) from a car wreck and reassembles him. At one point, the doctor says in exasperation to his creation, "Answer me! You have a civil tongue in your head. I know—I sewed it in there!" (Maltin 1997, 674). Although teens probably did not care and just found the movie good for a funny scare, Peter Biskind calls *I Was a Teenage Werewolf* "Rebel Without a Cause in wolf's clothing, a film that pits conservative demonology against pluralist ideology, sorcery against therapy, Transylvania against Vienna" (1983, 217). Unlike *Blackboard Jungle* and *Rebel Without a Cause*, it takes a conservative stance toward delinquency: the kids are to blame. Tony, the teenage protagonist played by Michael Landon, is bad from the beginning, and therapy only brings out his badness in werewolf form. He can only die at the end of the movie. The cheaply made film grossed over two million dollars and supposedly got Landon his job on the popular television series *Bonanza* (1983, 223).

Biskind sees a sign of the times in these teen monster films. The teen culture, "fattened with hamburgers, movies, and rock-'n-roll, was, like Tony, about to become a monster. With its long hair and wild, unkempt beard, that monster was a hippy" (223).

Books and Reading

Popular reading for adults and teens during the Fifties, perhaps even more than popular music and movies, reflects the dramatic split between the generations which characterizes this decade more than any other. It also reflects the usual divisions—some would probably call it the hypocrisy—in everyone's tastes. The decade also saw a tremendous increase in the publication and sales of paperback books to both adults and teens. The market for them threatened to overwhelm the market for the hardback book trade.

As in other media, Christianity seemed especially popular, perhaps as one response to the postwar unrest centered on the Soviet (i.e., atheist) threat and the national fear of the bomb. In nonfiction, the Revised Standard Version of the Holy Bible topped the best-seller list for 1952, 1953, and 1954. In fiction, the Biblical tales *The Silver Chalice* by Thomas B. Costain and *The Robe* by Lloyd C. Douglas (which had also sold millions when it was published in 1943) led the best-seller lists in 1952 and 1953.

In 1955, however, Herman Wouk's lengthy novel *Marjorie Morningstar* topped the lists. The novel details a girl's efforts to keep her virginity while sampling life in Greenwich Village, an option that smart girls in their late teens liked to ponder. Even though the book was aimed at adults, it was read by many teen girls. Its theme revealed public fascination with the sexuality of teen girls, especially since the second Kinsey report was published in 1953.

Peyton Place, *Mickey Spillane, and the JD Novel*

Kinsey himself probably could not have foreseen the success of Grace Metalious's 1956 novel *Peyton Place*; by fall 1957, it had been published in paperback and was selling millions of copies. "It was not so much a book as an event, with a force all its own," a genuine popular phenomenon (Halberstam 1993, 579). Girls and women all over the country read avidly about the sexual frustrations and exploits of the men and women of the apparently peaceful New England town of Peyton Place. They evidently welcomed some direct representation of sexual feelings, since the majority of books written for them seemed merely vague and dreamy on the subject. This book offered more than titillation. Female readers especially liked its female characters, for Metalious was a feminist before her time. In Peyton Place, the women were just as interested in sex as the men; moreover, the independent women characters were rewarded, while those who relied on men to fulfill their lives seemed pathetic. Metalious herself was a plain, relatively uneducated woman who somehow touched directly on the unhappiness of masses of suburban American women as well as the sense among most teen girls that they had few choices in life except to become those unhappy suburban women.

While girls were devouring *Peyton Place*, boys discovered Mickey Spillane and his tough private-eye character Mike Hammer. With *I, the Jury* in 1947, Spillane tapped into what was apparently a male need for strength and dominance, especially of women, criminals, and, eventually, Communists in postwar America. He also tapped into the paperback market as no one before him had, anticipating Metalious's success. Spillane's work was pulp fiction; it sold for 25 cents a copy. As one editor put it, it was not "in the best of taste" (Halberstam 1993, 59), but its blunt violence and sexuality sold many millions of books. By 1950 teen boys who could not obtain copies for themselves read them on the sly beside the drugstore rack, where their sexy covers were easy to spot. *I, the Jury* was followed by *My Gun Is Quick* and *Ven-*

geance Is Mine in 1950, *Kiss Me Deadly* in 1952, and others in rapid succession. Critics deplored the books, but some thought Spillane was a sign of the times, "the ultimate cold warrior," a reflection of McCarthyism (1993, 61). Spillane himself was as brash and vulgar as his books. He scorned the intelligentsia of the literary market as "losers" and eventually played the part of Hammer on television, becoming his own creation and reveling in his success.

A similar kind of pulp fiction reveled in the image of the teenage hoodlum and the bad teen girl. The JD, or juvenile delinquent, paperback novel featured action-oriented stories of gang wars, teen crime, and drug abuse; but, most of all, they featured lurid covers: bosomy girls in tight sweaters and skirts, pressing against their black-leather-jacketed, cigarette-smoking boyfriends, or sexy girls terrorized by blue-jeaned tough guys. Writer and social worker Hal Ellison wrote many JD novels in the Fifties. The image of teen life in such books was every parent's nightmare as well as fuel for school principals and Senate committees. Teens may have read them on the sly for their sexual innuendo, but it is more likely that they enticed older readers with their guilty thrills.

Books Written for Teens

In the high schools, English classes still concentrated on the classics: William Shakespeare, Charles Dickens, Jane Austen. Some authors were writing for teen audiences, though, and their books were popular in libraries although not in classrooms. A survey conducted in 1959 showed that Maureen Daly's *Seventeenth Summer* (1942) was still popular with teen girls, as was Betty Cavanna's *Going on Sixteen*, Rosamond duJardin's *Double Date* and *Wait for Marcy*, and Sally Benson's *Junior Miss* (Nilsen and Donelson 1993, 566). Teen boys liked John Tunis's *All American* still, but, beginning in 1950, Henry Gregor Felsen's novels centering on cars were the main attractions: *Hot Rod* (1950), *Street Rod* (1953), and *Crash Club* (1958). All these books were relatively "safe"; even though teachers and parents might think they were a little trashy, they had clear moral messages aimed at young, white, middle-class teens. These same teens soon supplemented them with ventures into more lurid fiction such as *Peyton Place* and *I, the Jury*, probably without the knowledge of their parents.

In 1959 pop singer and movie star Pat Boone's *Twixt Twelve and Twenty* topped the nonfiction best-seller lists, perhaps purchased more by parents than by teens themselves. Boone was only in his mid-twenties, married to his high school sweetheart (with whom he had eloped at nineteen), and already the father of several children. His smooth baritone singing voice, preppie-style good looks, and openly clean and religious lifestyle made him extremely attractive to parents who wanted to guide their teens away from the evils of Elvis and his like. Many white, middle-class teens themselves, with their ability to enjoy all kinds of popular music and images, responded with mild although relatively short-lived enthusiasm. He seemed at times almost too good to be true.

A combination of autobiography and advice book for teens, Boone's book offered an image of teen life guided by Christian faith. In a casual, chatty style, he addressed issues of parents, going steady, friendship, grooming, and marriage, all in a context of Christian values and virtues. He admitted in the book that elopement was a big mistake because it was dishonest: "To avoid being sneaky I did a big sneak" (1958, 81), and he spoke frankly about the difficulties of teenage marriage: the "time-money problem" (82). To him "supreme faith" was "the commodity that no marriage should be without" (83) but the adjustments were difficult nonetheless. Boone's overall approach to the teen years emphasized a steady path toward maturity, accompanied by fun, acknowledging the great emotional ups and downs, but finding the pleasure in life primarily through faith.

The Catcher in the Rye

The Fifties saw the birth of the most famous teenage character in American literature: Holden Caulfield, the protagonist of J. D. Salinger's 1951 novel *The Catcher in the Rye*. Intelligent, nervous, sensitive, witty, and acutely disgusted with everything phony, Holden wanders around New York City for a winter weekend after he has been thrown out of yet another prep school. In his own voice, full of slang, profanity, and digressions, he tells his story. He visits bars, calls up girlfriends and ex-school-friends, tries to talk to cab drivers and nuns, and has an encounter with a prostitute and her pimp—all in an effort to assuage his deep loneliness. Only his little sister Phoebe offers him any real understanding and solace. In the book's most famous moment, he tries to wipe out the word *fuck* from the wall in Phoebe's school; he wants to protect all kids from the ugliness of the world he sees. He realizes soon that it is a hopeless task.

Catcher, Salinger's only novel, first published in *The New Yorker* magazine in the late Forties, was aimed at an adult audience. When it was published on its own, it still attracted adult audiences and was considered highbrow literature by some, although others thought it definitely a minor book by an author with promise. Soon, however, young adults in their twenties discovered it, then college professors were teaching it to their freshmen, and finally high school teens themselves were reading it, finding it—despite its urban and prep-school milieu—the first accurate representation of real teen pain and real teen language in American literature.

In the Sixties, *Catcher* gained even more popularity; its first-person, slangy style and its sense of disgust and anguish at the phony adult world were widely imitated in hundreds of novels written for teens, but none had its brilliance and impact. Moreover, none had its ability to cause censorship battles in schools across the country. Since the Fifties, it has been discussed in countless PTA and school board meetings and removed from countless library shelves and English class reading lists. Each year it still tops the list of challenged books in American high schools. Usually the reason given is the obvious one: the obscene word that Holden tries to erase. But the book's vivid, intelligent image of a teenager's pain, and even more, the bumbling, artificial, sometimes cold-hearted adult world it portrays, are an indictment of adult failure, and, although it springs directly from the post-war bewilderment of the late Forties and early Fifties, it still touches the basic sense of alienation from the world that seems to be part of teenage emotional life in every decade.

Magazines

Seventeen still led the field in white, middle-class girls' magazines, publishing articles on diet, makeup, fashion, and sewing as always. It also published fiction and articles by teen girls themselves. The January 1955 issue published several prize-winning stories, mostly about the topic of romance. One article written and illustrated by teen girls focused on movies, not only seeing them and enjoying them but discussing them intelligently. Other articles included boys as advisers on dating and in career profiles.

Working-class girls were reading other kinds of magazines. *True Romance, Modern Romance,* and *True Confessions* still had great appeal. Although they had steamy covers and their stories had suggestive titles, they were not particularly explicit. One popular joking description of their plots ran something like this: "He kissed me and then a cloud came over everything and then I was pregnant" (Miller and Nowak 1977, 166). Girls wanted romance as much as they wanted sexual information, and such magazines supplied it.

Boys still had hobby magazines and sports magazines, but in the Fifties a magazine appeared that would supply romantic fantasies to them for many years to come: Hugh Hefner's *Playboy*. In 1953 Hefner, who was only twenty-seven, was inspired by Kinsey's books on male and female sexuality and scornful of the sexual hypocrisy he saw around him. His first purchase for the magazine was the famous nude photo of Marilyn Monroe; it ensured the success of the first issue, which sold for fifty cents a copy (Halberstam 1993, 571). In it, Hefner offered a mix of pictures of seminude women and suggestions about sophisticated apartment living, with good music, good clothes, and good liquor. He was selling a lifestyle in which sex was openly celebrated as fun, along with other kinds of fun. His advice columns featured questions about sexual technique and sexual etiquette, as well as about stereo equipment, in a format considerably different from a "girlie" magazine. Although their parents might not approve, middle-class white boys could read this magazine with minimum guilt and maximum enjoyment and, at the same time, satisfy some of their curiosity about sex.

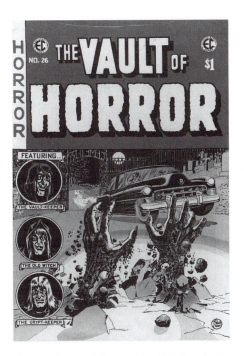

Cover, *Vault of Horror*, No. 26. A sample of a horror comic published by William Gaines and reviled by Frederic Wertham before a Senate Subcommittee on Juvenile Delinquency in the mid-Fifties. © William M. Gaines, Agent, Inc. 1952, renewed 1980. Used with permission.

Comic Books

Teen boys continued to be the chief readers and purchasers of comic books. Superman, Batman, Captain Marvel, and other super heroes still reigned; crime comics such as *Crime Does Not Pay* and *Crime Patrol* were still popular as well. EC Comics publisher William Gaines had ideas for a new kind of comic, and in 1950 he launched *Crypt of Terror*, *The Vault of Horror*, and then *The Haunt of Fear*. In these comics, stories did not depend on super heroes or happy endings. More like the tales of Edgar Allan Poe, these stories provided chills and occasionally black comedy, introduced by grotesque characters called the Crypt Keeper, the Vault Keeper, and the Old Witch, who often commented wryly on the action. The stories tended to be quite moral, ingenious, and witty at the same time they were horrific. According to comics scholar Les Daniels, they "took the public by storm" (1971, 65); their intelligence and wit appealed to more readers than ever before.

They also drew the attention of psychiatrist Fredric Wertham, who worked with delinquent boys in a Harlem, New York, clinic. When he noticed that many of his boy patients mentioned reading comic books, he asked to see their comics. He was shocked by the mayhem and violence in their pages, and he began a national crusade against the comics industry as a primary cause of teen delinquency. Although he had little support from his colleagues in the mental health industry—they, in fact, wanted to distance themselves from his extreme claims of causality—he got plenty from the public. He persuaded the New York legislature to form a committee to study comics, and he managed to get a bill through the state assembly and senate making it a misdemeanor "to publish or sell comic books dealing with fictional crime, bloodshed or lust that might incite minors to violence or immorality" (West 1988, 48). The bill was vetoed by the governor as bordering on unconstitutionality, but Wertham took his case to the people. In 1954 he published his book *Seduction of the Innocent*, which attracted many articles and reviews and incited a few boycotts of comics sellers (1988, 51).

Weeks after the book's appearance, Senator Estes Kefauver's Subcommittee on Juvenile Delinquency requested Wertham's testimony and then that of William Gaines himself. The senators held up copies of a comic and quizzed Gaines on the morality of such images (West 1996, 241). His answers, sensible though they were for a publisher of horror comics, did not satisfy the public, and the comics industry began to worry that Wertham's proposed legislation might soon pass. The industry's response was the Comics Code Authority, which spelled out ways in which the industry would police itself (Daniels 1971, 89–90). Comic books that met the requirements would carry a seal of authority; those that did not would be subject to banning. The words "terror" and "horror" could not appear on the cover, nor could the word "crime" appear in the comic book. For the next fifteen years, comics would be regulated by this code. Meanwhile, a large number of comics would go out of business. Teens "awoke in dismay to discover that what they looked on as an enjoyable pastime had become, for no apparent reason, a shocking sin" (1971, 89).

Mad *Magazine*

William Gaines and EC Comics had other options. The first issue of *Mad* appeared in 1952. The EC Comics staff had worked hard on it, and their work was repaid. It announced itself as "A comic book! Not a serious comic book . . . but a COMIC comic book! Not a floppity rabbit, giggily girl, anarchist teenage type comic book . . . but a short story mag" (Daniels 1971, 76). Within a few issues, *Mad* had established itself as one of the best and funniest satire magazines in the country. One of its targets was the comics themselves: Superduperman was a bumbling hero, Starchie was a juvenile delinquent, Poopeye fought characters from other strips, and so on. Other satires targeted current popular movies like *Julius Caesar* and literary classics like Poe's *The Raven*. *Mad*'s free-wheeling, uninhibited, manic wit continues to appeal to teens across the country. It is "an expression of youth culture that is consciously and defiantly different from that of grownups" (West 1996, 203).

REFERENCES

Bailey, Beth. *From Front Porch to Back Seat*. Baltimore: Johns Hopkins University Press, 1988.

Betrock, Alan. *The I Was a Teenage Juvenile Delinquent Rock 'n' Roll Horror Beach Party Movie Book: A Complete Guide to the Teen Exploitation Film. 1954–1969*. New York: St. Martin's Press, 1986.

Biskind, Peter. *Seeing Is Believing*. New York: Pantheon, 1983.

Boone, Pat. *Twixt Twelve and Twenty*. Englewood Cliffs, N.J.: Prentice-Hall, 1958.

Breines, Wini. *Young, White, and Miserable: Growing Up Female in the Fifties*. Boston: Beacon Press, 1992.

Chadwick, Bruce A., and Jim B. Heaton. *Statistical Handbook on the American Family*. Phoenix, Ariz.: Oryx, 1992.

Colbert, David, ed. *Eyewitness to America*. New York: Pantheon, 1997.

Coleman, James S. *The Adolescent Society*. New York: Free Press of Glencoe, 1961.

Conant, James B. *The American High School Today*. New York: McGraw-Hill, 1959.

Dalzell, Tom. *Flappers 2 Rappers: American Youth Slang*. Springfield, Mass.: Merriam-Webster, 1996.

Daniels, Les. *Comix: A History of Comic Books in America*. New York: Outerbridge and Dienstfrey, 1971.

Doherty, Thomas. *Teenagers and Teenpics: The Juvenilization of American Movies in the 1950s*. Boston: Unwin Hyman, 1988.

Fine, Benjamin. *1,000,000 Delinquents*. Cleveland: World Publishing, 1955.

Gilbert, James. *A Cycle of Outrage: America's Reaction to the Juvenile Delinquent in the 1950's*. New York: Oxford University Press, 1986.

Glynne, *The American Girl Beauty Book*. New York: Random House, 1954.

Graebner, William. *Coming of Age in Buffalo*. Philadelphia: Temple University Press, 1990.

Halberstam, David. *The Fifties*. New York: Villard Books, 1993.

Hanson, Mary Ellen. *Go! Fight! Win! Cheerleading in American Culture*. Bowling Green, Ohio: Bowling Green State University Popular Press, 1995.

Hine, Thomas. *Populuxe*. New York: Knopf, 1987.

Horn, Maurice. *100 Years of American Newspaper Comics*. New York: Gramercy Books, 1996.

Jackson, Kathy Merlock. *Walt Disney: A Biobibliography*. Westport, Conn.: Greenwood Press, 1993.

Kinsey, Alfred C. *Sexual Behavior in the Human Female*. Philadelphia: W. B. Saunders, 1953.

Kohl, Herbert. *Should We Burn Babar?* New York: The New Press, 1995.

Layman, Richard, ed. *American Decades: 1950–1959*. Detroit: Gale Research, 1994.

Linna, Miriam, comp. *Bad Seed: A Postcard Book*. Philadelphia: Running Press, 1992.

Malone, Bill C. *Country Music USA*. Austin: University of Texas Press, 1993.

Maltin, Leonard. *1998 Movie and Video Guide*. New York: Signet, 1997.

Marling, Karal Ann. *As Seen on TV: The Visual Culture of Everyday Life in the 1950s.* Cambridge, Mass.: Harvard University Press, 1994.

McGee, Mark Thomas. *The Rock and Roll Movie Encyclopedia of the 1950s.* Jefferson, N.C.: McFarland, 1990.

Miller, Douglas T., and Marion Nowak. *The Fifties: The Way We Really Were.* New York: Doubleday, 1977.

"A New $10-Billion Power: The U.S. Teen-age Consumer." *Life* 47, no. 9 (August 13, 1959): 78–87.

Nilsen, Alleen Pace, and Ken Donelson, eds. *Literature for Today's Young Adults.* 4th ed. New York: HarperCollins, 1993.

Nyberg, Amy Kiste. "William Gaines and the Battle over EC Comics." *INKS: Cartoon and Comic Art Studies* 3, no. 1 (February 1996): 3–15.

Palladino, Grace. *Teenagers: An American History.* New York: Basic Books, 1996.

Petersen, James R. "Something Cool: 1950–1959." *Playboy* 45, no. 2 (February 1998): 72+.

Petrus, Stephen. "Rumblings of Discontent: American Pop Culture and Its Response to the Beat Generation, 1957–1960." *Studies in Popular Culture* 20, no. 1 (October 1997):1–17.

Reed, Arthea. *Presenting Harry Mazer.* New York: Twayne, 1996.

Remmers, H. H., and D. H. Radler. *The American Teenager.* Indianapolis: Bobbs-Merrill, 1957.

Salinger, J. D. *The Catcher in the Rye.* New York: Little, Brown, 1951.

Salisbury, Harrison. *The Shook-Up Generation.* New York: Harper and Bros., 1958.

Sanders, Don, and Susan Sanders. *The American Drive-In Movie Theatre.* Osceola, Wisc.: Motorbooks International, 1997.

Taves, Isabella. "Report on High School Sororities." *McCall's*, April 1953: 49+.

Wallechinsky, David. *The People's Almanac Presents the Twentieth Century.* Boston: Little, Brown, 1995.

Wertham, Fredric. *Seduction of the Innocent.* New York: Rinehart, 1954.

West, Elliott. *Growing Up in Twentieth Century America.* Westport, Conn.: Greenwood Press, 1996.

West, Mark I. *Children, Culture, and Controversy.* Hamden, Conn.: Archon Books, 1988.

Wright, David, and Elly Petra. *America in the 20th Century, 1950–1959.* New York: Marshall Cavendish, 1995.

· 6 ·

The 1960s

With a youthful, enthusiastic John F. Kennedy as president, who was transforming Washington into what some considered a version of King Arthur's Camelot because of his administration's appearance of elegance and idealism, the decade began with high public hopes. Soon the Sixties were to become the most conflict ridden, turbulent decade in twentieth-century America, the one in which the gap between teens and adults widened to such proportions, on so many issues, that it seemed totally unbridgeable. It brought freedom and power previously unknown to young people—a combination that was both exhilarating and frightening.

POLITICS AND NATIONAL EVENTS

Vietnam

The conflict in Southeast Asia was not a war, nor does the term "event" capture it. It was an economic calculation, a bureaucratic maneuver, a gradually escalating threat, a violent entanglement, an irrational act, a nightmare, and a failure. It was the basis of the most divisive conflict in American history, and dozens of excellent studies have been devoted to it. Here we offer only the briefest outline and suggest its relevance to teens.

In the late Fifties, America replaced France as military advisor to the Republic of Vietnam, and very soon the Viet Cong, the Communist forces in North Vietnam, attacked American air bases and Americans were killed. In 1964 Congress granted President Lyndon Johnson authority to retaliate,

Students outside Highlands High School, Fort Thomas, Kentucky, 1965. Reproduced courtesy of Highlands High School.

but no war was declared. By 1965 ground combat troops were fighting as well and bombings increased, along with defoliation of the Vietnam jungle. Still no end was in sight, and President Johnson continued to draft teen boys, in unprecedented numbers, to fight in an undeclared war that America seemed to be bungling and losing. Massive protests among teens and young adults, especially on college campuses, shook the country throughout the late Sixties. Most of these demonstrations, inspired by the passive resistance of India's Mahatma Gandhi and the words of Martin Luther King, Jr., were nonviolent. Some young people in Washington, D.C., in 1967 approached the guards lined up to keep order and inserted daisies into the barrels of the rifles pointed at them. Many young men over eighteen openly refused induction and burned their draft cards; if they were able, some slipped away to Canada to avoid the draft.

When Johnson announced he would not run for another term as president, young people rejoiced, but President Richard Nixon, who took office in 1969, began bombing Cambodia even while he withdrew troops from Vietnam and while the country reeled from the shock of the My Lai massacre in which American soldiers, commanded by Lieutenant William Calley, murdered 400 women, children, and old men. In 1970 students at Kent State University in Ohio engaged in an antiwar demonstration, and some were shot by National Guardsmen. Four students were killed, igniting even more protests. As the draft was phased out in response to the clear message of the protest movement—that no young person should be forced to serve in an undeclared, unjust war against his will—the war dragged on, while American troops gradually came home, until 1973, when Nixon announced an agreement for "peace with honor" (McCloud 1989, 150).

The great majority of American soldiers in Vietnam were teenagers, aged, on the average, nineteen:

They were teenage warriors, statistically six years younger than those in World War II. Instead of a carefree adolescence, their first sexual encounters often were with prostitutes in Vietnam. Many had trouble relating to women when they returned. Youth often has fewer coping skills: death of friends hit them harder than if they had been older. There was no such thing as troop-ship decompression: in America's first jet-age war they were back "in the world" in hours. (MacPherson quoted in McCloud 1989, 91)

They were disproportionately poor and from ethnic minorities; they were boys who did not have the luxury of running to Canada or staying in school to graduate and then get a deferment for going abroad. Even worse, when they came home, they often met, not the appreciation and support the World War II veterans had received, but disgust, ostracism, and even cruelty from those who thought they should not have been there in the first place. It was the first time in our nation's history that veterans were regarded as poor citizens.

Junior high school teacher Bill McCloud, a veteran of Vietnam, prepared himself to teach the war to his students by soliciting letters from politicians, writers, journalists, and other veterans answering the question, "What should we tell our children about Vietnam?" In 1989 he collected the remarkable responses into a book, *What Should We Tell Our Children about Vietnam?* and added a list of books about Vietnam especially appropriate for young teens (153). In his summary of the responses, he notes that it was an unwinnable war, that America learned that it has limits to its power, and that all wars are "an enormous waste of life. All wars are failures because it means the leaders on both sides have failed to resolve their differences by peaceful and civilized means" (142).

Assassinations

Medgar Evers was assassinated in Jackson, Mississippi, in 1963, while he was working field security for the National Association for the Advancement of Colored People (NAACP). Evers had been the most visible black leader in the state. His accused killer, Byron de la Beckwith, was freed after a trial resulting in a hung jury, only to be convicted when the case was reopened in 1990. Evers's murder was the first in a series of killings that would mark the decade in blood. Four more times during the Sixties the nation witnessed the assassination of an important leader. President John F. Kennedy was assassinated when his motorcade passed through Dallas, Texas, on November 22, 1963. Schools, universities, and businesses across the country shut down when the announcement came over the intercoms that the president had been mortally wounded by gunfire. The subsequent arrest of Lee Harvey Oswald as the killer and then Oswald's murder by Jack Ruby, captured on television, kept the country reeling with shock and disbelief for days. Most Americans spent the Thanksgiving holiday that year watching the televised funeral proceedings interspersed with news reports about Oswald and Ruby. The murders continue to be investigated into the Nineties. Many believe that Kennedy was killed by conspirators rather than by Oswald alone.

On February 21, 1965, black leader Malcolm X, born Malcolm Little in Omaha, Nebraska, was murdered in a Harlem ballroom as he spoke to a crowd of followers. He had already suffered at least one attempt on his life, and he had commented in his autobiography that he would probably die young because he had alienated the Black Muslims, who believed in separation of the races, by organizing a separate Black Power movement which emphasized self-reliance. His autobiography, *The Autobiography of Malcolm X*, published the following year, has remained a best-seller; his message continues to inspire young black teens at the end of the century.

In 1968 two men were assassinated. Martin Luther King, Jr., had thrilled a massive audience in Washington, D.C., with his 1963 speech, "I Have a Dream," and he had established himself as the preeminent civil rights leader in the country. On April 4, 1968, he was killed in a motel parking lot in Memphis, Tennessee, where he had given a stirring speech the previous evening. Prison escapee James Earl Ray was arrested two months later, in London, for the killing. Although he was convicted as the sole murderer, conspiracy theories have centered around him as they did around Oswald and Ruby; he protested his innocence until his death in 1998. On June 5, 1968, Senator Robert F. Kennedy, younger brother of the slain president, was shot as he was leaving a hotel in Los Angeles. Kennedy was campaigning for the Democratic nomination for the presidency, and he was the front-runner at the time. Sirhan Bashira Sirhan, a Jordanian angered by Kennedy's pro-Israel stance, was arrested on the scene. As in the other assassinations, he was convicted as the single murderer, even though evidence to the contrary mounted.

King's nonviolent approach to racial unrest had inspired many young people, black and white, to participate in peace marches and to work for integration and voter registration. Some of them shed their own blood when they were beaten by police in Alabama and Mississippi, events journalist

David Halberstam witnessed and described vividly in *The Children* (1998). Robert Kennedy was able to speak to young blacks and whites together, to unify them in their hopes for a better world; his youth made him seem one of them. Young college students had worked eagerly for his campaign. His death alienated them further from American democracy.

The Great Society

Even in the midst of these events, Americans could take pride in some of the social legislation of the decade, some of it enacted as a result of President Lyndon Johnson's efforts to create what he called "the Great Society." The Civil Rights Act of 1964 prohibited discrimination on the basis of race; the Voting Rights Act of 1965 suspended the use of literacy tests for voter registration, which had been used to prevent blacks from registering to vote. Within three years, one million more blacks had registered to vote. John Kennedy established the Peace Corps and invited young people nationwide to serve those in other countries less privileged; college-age men and women responded eagerly. VISTA, Volunteers in Service to America, was organized to serve those at home who needed the help of volunteers who could build and teach. The Head Start program, with its goal of preparing underprivileged children to enter school on an equal footing with their middle-class peers, began during this decade. In 1962, with the help of federal troops, James Meredith became the first black man to enter the University of Mississippi. In 1966 the Supreme Court, in *Miranda v. Arizona*, held that arrested persons must be properly informed of their legal rights. In 1967 Thurgood Marshall became the first black member of the Supreme Court.

Science too made headlines. Telstar went into orbit on July 11, 1962, to begin transatlantic television broadcasting. On the night of July 20, 1969, Americans looked at the moon outside their windows, and inside, on television, watched Neil Armstrong take the first human steps on the moon and plant an American flag and a plaque which read, "We came in peace for all mankind."

The Hippies

During the Fifties, the Beats had shown Americans that there were other ways of living, ones that did not involve nine-to-five corporate success and a house in the suburbs. During the Sixties, the hippies—with Beat guru Allen Ginsberg as their icon—embraced this freedom with a passion and exuberance that affected the entire country. The black turtleneck shirts of the Beats were exchanged for brilliantly colored T-shirts with psychedelic designs; cool jazz turned into acid rock. Drugs, long hair, flowers, and the peace sign—the first two fingers raised in a V—became symbols of a gentle, passive rebellion.

The hippies were not an organized group; their only concrete beliefs were in the freedom to "do your own thing," or "if it feels good and doesn't hurt anybody, do it." They were largely white, middle-class, and well-educated, usually between the ages of seventeen and twenty-five (Brown 1967, 4). They "bloomed," as *Time* magazine put it, in every major city in the world, not just in the United States, and they came in many varieties depending on their tastes in music, clothing, and drugs. They preached love, acceptance, and peace for all. They sometimes gathered in communes or tribes where they enjoyed an open, relaxed sexuality; many became parents, some were married in unorthodox outdoor ceremonies. They enjoyed children and adopted child-like attitudes themselves. They opened their doors to their friends, offering food, drugs, or a place to sleep or "come down"—recover from a bad drug experience. Their views and life choices—natural childbirth, unprocessed food, social activism, Eastern spirituality, acceptance of homosexuality and ethnic differences—were often adopted by middle-class young adults, and older ones, who, while they stayed within the "straight" life of work and family, nonetheless valued the hippie way.

American hippies gravitated particularly to the Haight-Ashbury section of San Francisco, which they soon transformed into a colorful hippie colony that attracted tourists from across the country. In January 1967, they staged a "Be-In" in Golden Gate Park to which thousands of hippies came to enjoy flowers, drugs, and peace with each other. Observers—and countless parents—worried about the safety of the young dropouts from school and middle-class society who swarmed into "Hashbury," as it was called, or into the East Village in New York, either on weekends or for more permanent escapes. The hippie way of life, unfortunately, also attracted those less given to peace and acceptance, those who might regard the hippie as an easy target for sex, robbery, or violence. Many "weekend" hippies, and many of those who broke away for longer periods of time, returned home despite their differences with parents, seeking relief from depression, drug habits, and poverty. Hippie-dom did not always fulfill its promise.

Berkeley and Columbia

Many teens who went to college at seventeen or eighteen found themselves drawn to serious political activism because the colleges were the locus of the most intense rebellion against the "system," the bureaucracy of laws and customs which the young believed were senselessly oppressive. According to Grace Palladino, only a tiny percentage of college students in the mid-Sixties were willing to risk arrest by open, vigorous protest, but as many as a third to a half of the college students believed in what the radical students were doing (1996, 212). Some of the radicals joined Students for a Democratic Society, a radical group that included activists Tom Hayden and Todd Gitlin and attracted the most dissenting students on various campuses around the country. Many of the rest, who had worked hard to get into college and wanted the opportunity to study and receive a degree, resented the class disruptions and cancellations and the pressure to be politically involved. In the Sixties, college life was no longer the refuge it had been.

At the University of California at Berkeley, already known for attracting student rebels, massive protests erupted in 1964 when the administration banned political organizations from conducting fund-raising activities on campus. The Berkeley Free Speech movement spearheaded the demonstrations and the defense of those who participated, demanding that the protesters not be punished for disrupting the university. At one time, the state police were sent in to keep order. Students on campuses all over the country, with most of the rest of the population, witnessed the events on television, where they discovered that many college students believed themselves an oppressed class and were willing to risk a great deal to express that belief.

By 1968, as the war in Vietnam escalated, the number of demonstrations on campuses increased as well, and many of them were violent. The most dramatic one took place at Columbia University, where opponents of the draft, and of Columbia's involvement with the Institute for Defense Analysis, occupied the university president's office for ten days. Nineteen-year-old James Simon Kunen, who both participated in and observed the events of those days, kept a journal which became a book in 1969: *The Strawberry Statement*. The title refers to a professor's comment that the university was not a democratic institution, and that a student vote on an issue was the equivalent of "telling me they like strawberries" (Kunen 1969, 121). While students were being arrested, teargassed, and beaten—often on live television—to draw attention to an undeclared war where Americans were dying, such comments from university administrators seemed increasingly fatuous. Kunen closed his book with his own statement:

I do not want to fight in Vietnam, of course. But I also don't want to have to fight the draft, or fight the law, or fight anything. I'm a nineteen-year-old civilian, and I am tired of fighting.

One of these days I may fight in earnest and altogether so that I won't have to fight any more. (1969, 151)

The 1968 Democratic Convention

When the Democrats gathered in August in Chicago to choose their presidential candidate, the national unrest began to focus there. The Republicans had nominated Richard Nixon. Alabama's George Wallace, who had run an independent campaign, had attracted enough Democrats to worry party leaders. With the assassination of Robert Kennedy, Johnson's vice president Hubert Humphrey became the candidate of choice for many Democrats;

however, Senator Eugene McCarthy from Minnesota, who openly opposed the war in Vietnam, had become the favorite of the young adult voters. They campaigned hard for him nationwide, calling him "Clean Gene." The convention shaped up from the beginning as a clash between young and old, between culture and counterculture, between "hawks" (supporters of the war) and "doves" (those who opposed it). The lines were drawn even more clearly when activists Jerry Rubin and Abbie Hoffman collaborated to turn the convention into a media event to make this conflict dramatically visible. They, along with some others, declared themselves "Yippies"—a joke and a play on the word "hippies," but later they said it stood for Youth International Party—and began to "coax, goose, entice, and dazzle thousands of freaks to Chicago [to] create there a 'Festival of Life' against the 'Convention of Death,' a 'blending of pot and politics' " (Gitlin 1989, 235). Hundreds of college students converged on Chicago in the August heat.

Chicago mayor Richard Daley was ready with riot police, and the media were primed to cover it all. When the cameras cranked up and the convention began, America witnessed a spectacle such as it had never seen. Young adults gathered outside the convention center, shouting at police and at the cameras, then were handcuffed, beaten, arrested; the streets were a mass of confusion and violence. Inside, even on the convention floor while the business of the convention tried to continue, delegates and reporters engaged in insults and shoving.

Finally, eight people were arrested for inciting to riot, including Abbie Hoffman and Jerry Rubin, the "Yippies," and Bobby Seale of the Black Panther party. Although there were eight of them, they became known as the Chicago Seven. The ensuing trials, which continued well into the Seventies, were media events themselves, especially for Hoffman and Rubin, who mocked the procedures openly and often hilariously. Only Bobby Seale, who was eventually tried separately from the others on charges of contempt, ever served time.

Woodstock and Altamont

On August 15, 1969, in a field near Bethel, New York, 400,000 people gathered in a peaceful celebration of rock music and hippiedom. They ignored the mud and the inconveniences as the number of participants grew beyond all planning. It was called "Woodstock nation," and those who were there participated in an event the likes of which no one had ever seen. Drugs, especially marijuana, were used openly, but there was no violence, only an intense community of music and peace. One after another, rock performers—among them Janis Joplin, The Who, Jefferson Airplane, Joe Cocker, Joan Baez, Santana, and Arlo Guthrie—took the stage and looked out amazed at the crowd. Musician Richie Havens called it a "cosmic accident"

(Colbert 1997, 510). When Jimi Hendrix closed the two-day concert with "The Star-Spangled Banner," making his guitar imitate the sound of bombs, Woodstock had become the signal event of the Sixties. In 1970 director Michael Wadleigh released a three-hour film documenting Woodstock, which won the Academy Award for best documentary.

In November 1969, at the Altamont Raceway in California, a rock festival had different results. The Rolling Stones, the bad boys of rock, had scheduled a performance there, and for reasons still unclear, hired some Hell's Angels, the notorious motorcycle group, to maintain order. As the music began, the crowd pushed in closer and closer to the stage, which sagged under the weight of the equipment as well as people. The atmosphere already seemed threatening. Stones star Mick Jagger had to stop singing several times to plead for order. Ethan Russell, a photographer who specialized in photographing rock stars, watched as the concert became violent.

Suddenly, in the midst of that mass, where there is no space, absolutely no space at all, I see a circle of bodies open, crazily, like a sea urchin's mouth, quickly widening until there is an empty circle maybe thirty feet in diameter, and I stare aghast, knowing that the only way for that space to open is for people to swarm back over and on top of themselves and those behind them. . . . Then, in the circle, hulking, vague forms, the backs of Hell's Angels, can be seen, their arms pumping up and down. . . . This time sawed-off pool cues can be seen, their butt ends brought crashing down on collapsed forms, and it is clear that the Angels, for whatever reason, are trashing the crowd. (Russell 1985, 167)

When it was over, four people had died, one a young black man who had been stabbed on the stage when the Hell's Angels saw he had pulled a gun. Activist Todd Gitlin, who was also there, said that unlike Woodstock, this concert "felt like death . . . the effect was to burst the bubble of youth culture's illusions about itself. . . . Who could any longer harbor the illusion that these hundreds of thousands of spoiled star-hungry children of the Lonely Crowd were the harbingers of a good society?" (Gitlin 1989, 406–7).

Teens in the News

Linda Fitzpatrick

One personality became in 1967 a symbol of teen life first for readers of the *New York Times* and then for the nation: eighteen-year-old Linda Fitzpatrick. From a wealthy Greenwich, Connecticut, family, she went to good private schools, and her parents provided her with plenty of spending money and family vacations in Bermuda. Her parents remember her as an artistic, pleasant girl who participated in her family's life. They insist she could not have been involved with hippies in New York's East Village. Nevertheless, by the time Linda was a senior in high school, she was going regularly to the East Village. She had learned to smoke marijuana in Bermuda, on one of those family vacations, and she had embraced it completely. She was apparently leading a double life.

Soon, even while living most of the time at home, she began using LSD and methamphetamine and told her Village friends she was moving to San Francisco's Haight-Ashbury district. According to one, "She was a real Meth Monster, a real spaced-out speed freak. I told her she didn't need to go to California, that she'd get even more messed up in the meth scene out there" (Lukas 1969, 202). She left school and moved to New York's East Village, telling her parents she had a job designing posters, when in fact she stayed on drugs most of the time. In early October 1967, she and a friend of hers, known as Groovy, were found dead in the boiler room of a tenement, their heads bashed in with bricks. Although two men eventually confessed to the crime, no motive was ever discovered (1969, 204).

When *New York Times* reporter J. Anthony Lukas interviewed Linda's parents (at their request) and then published Linda's story, it provoked such an outpouring from worried parents that he was inspired to explore the lifestyles of other young people who had embraced, to one degree or another, the counterculture. The result was the book *Don't Shoot—We Are Your Children!* (1969), which contains profiles of nine other young adults including Linda's friend Groovy. Lukas had no final answers for worried parents, except that instead of focusing on the "generation gap," perhaps adults should focus on "the gap between what we say and what we do, the gap between the American dream and the American reality" (461). Although it was highly dramatic and ended tragically, Linda's story resembled that of thousands of other American teens in the Sixties, who longed for both freedom and security and were caught between the dream and the reality.

Rinker and Kern Buck

A different kind of Sixties teen gave Americans something to watch with pride. In the summer of 1966, two New Jersey boys flew alone across the country in a tiny plane, without lights or radio. The sons of a man who had left home in the Thirties to join a flying circus, Kern Buck, age seventeen, and his brother Rinker, age fifteen, had completely rebuilt the old plane. As they hopped from New Jersey south to Arkansas and on to Texas, the newspaper accounts followed their exploit with pleasure. They landed near San Diego after six days of flying, landing, staying in cheap motels, meeting the airport "geezers," and outwitting storms and mountains. Rinker has told the story of the boys' journey—and their accompanying telephone battles with their father—in *Flight of Passage* (1997).

TEENS AT HOME

The postwar affluence of middle-class suburbia continued into the Sixties, providing teens from such families with more privacy and freedom than ever before. The ranch-style house, spread behind a landscaped lawn, offered plenty of space for entertaining friends: a recreation room, a den, a finished basement—places where teens could turn the radio or record player up loud. Teens' own rooms became even more off-limits to adults and siblings. Those who were drawn to the hippie style decorated their rooms with posters of rock stars or psychedelic images, or black lights and Indian-print bedspreads (which could even be draped over windows). These spaces flaunted rebellion against the other parts of the house and what they stood for: parents entertaining country-club friends with cocktails and barbecues and making the small talk which could seem so irritating and phony.

The most radical hippies abandoned just this sort of well-bred suburban home in their search for peace and enlightenment. Those who became politicized in their freshman years at college—or those who wanted to be with people who were political—preferred living in walk-up apartments sparsely furnished with cast-off couches, where they could smoke pot, cook what they wanted, and sleep when they wanted with whom they wanted. "Weekend" or "plastic" hippies continued to enjoy their suburban homes during the school week and tasted the other life when they could, secure in the knowledge that they could go home again.

Even those suburban homes were changing in subtle but profound ways. In 1960 the number of seventeen-year-olds living in "Ozzie and Harriet families" was 17.5%, down from about 25% in 1950. By the end of the decade, the number of children of all ages living in such families had dropped to a little more than 14% (adapted from Chadwick and Heaton 1996, 27). Divorce was taking its toll. Perhaps in a search for the stability their parents failed to provide, teens themselves were marrying at eighteen and nineteen. The nostalgic popularity of television homes, such as those on the *Donna Reed Show, Leave It to Beaver*, and *Father Knows Best*—mother at home, father calmly authoritarian, kids rebelling in the mildest ways—suggests their disappearance in real life.

Minority Homes

For many American teens, life seldom resembled a suburban barbecue. Puerto Rican teen Juan Gonzalez described his world of gang wars, drugs, and violence in the New York City projects in 1965: the muggings and rapes in the stairwells, the noise, the smells, the racial prejudice and corruption among the police. He also said, "I guess in some ways the projects are better":

Like when we used to live here before the projects, there were rats and holes and the building was falling apart. It was condemned so many times and so many times the landlords fought and won. The building wasn't torn down until finally it was the last building standing. And you know what that is . . . there's no place for those rats to go, or those bugs, or no place for the bums to sleep at night except in the one building still standing. It was terrible . . . my mother was real scared. That was the same time she was out of work and it didn't look to us like anything was ever going to get better. (Mayerson 1971, 4)

Among American Indian youth, the suicide rate was high—over three times the national average (Henninger and Esposito 1971, 109). They were often taken from their homes and put into boarding schools where their morale declined even further. After realizing that the white culture held nothing for them, many of these teens became spokespersons for their culture. They returned to their elders, often angry, to become their elders' voices: "Rebellion of the youth, but with a difference. The temper, the mood, the philosophy, of the new Indians voiced no rebellion against their fathers, the tribal elders. Rather it was their guardian—the Great White Father—they were rebelling against" (Steiner 1971, 87).

In the Appalachian Mountains, teens were part of large, close families. A sociologist described the home of a family of eleven: "It is of wood and tarpaper, and stands on cement blocks. The wind blows right through it. There is no central heating, no plumbing . . . a fireplace provides heat, and eleven bodies leave their five beds to huddle near the burning coals" (Coles 1971, 127). Although hunger was a chronic problem, children were highly valued. Teen boys would "fuss over" babies "with an interest and tenderness which is almost unbelievable in the light of the usual male role" (Weller 1971, 132). As among many minority groups, teens in general were less valued than babies and children, and they were noticed only when they got into serious trouble. Teen boys were expected to protect their teen sisters, who tended to stay close to home doing routine chores and enjoying little social life outside home and church or outside an immediate group of friends. Their parents, even while maintaining the old ways, wanted better things for these young people—schooling, a job outside the strip mines— but breaking away was difficult. Usually they married early and settled into a pattern of life similar to that of their parents.

Radio, Television, and Comic Strips

Radio for teens had become a totally private affair, enjoyed in the car or on a portable radio in one's own room. The AM stations had become almost totally devoted to disc jockey shows which played the Top 40 hits day after day, just as black stations devoted their musical airtime to soul. New York had Murray the K, and Los Angeles had Bob Crane (who in 1965 left the airwaves to star in the television comedy *Hogan's Heroes*). Wolfman Jack's trademark howls became popular around the country, especially because for several years he would not let himself be photographed or seen in public. By the Seventies he was making plenty of public appearances and hosted his own television show. The power of such DJs to shape teen tastes and record-buying habits continued to be significant.

Television viewing was on the rise—up to more than five hours a day by 1965—and the Sixties saw an increase in shows that appealed to teens, while the family continued to enjoy *Bonanza, Gunsmoke,* and *The Lucy Show* (adapted from Schmittroth 1994, 868). In the early Sixties, *The Many Loves of Dobie Gillis* chronicled the troubles of Dobie, a hapless teenager who tried hard to avoid his father's middle-class life but could never acquire the girl of his dreams: "In revealing these dreams and anxieties, television made its first hesitant step toward recognizing the real world of postwar teenage America" (Grover 1997, 60). In *Mr. Novak*, James Franciscus played a youthful, handsome, serious high school teacher who worked hard to keep his students interested in school and doing the right thing. This show was the first to offer a thoughtful view of high school as a place where kids had to struggle against pointless authoritarianism, racial intolerance, lack of sex education, and frightened parents. More adventuresome was *Route 66* starring Martin Milner and George Maharis as two guys who drove their Corvette across the country having adventurous narrow escapes and helping people in trouble. In 1968 Aaron Spelling introduced *The Mod Squad*. This show dealt with campus unrest, the problems of the Vietnam veteran, and racial intolerance. Its three central characters represented a range of American teen-dom, even in their physical appearances: Link (Clarence Williams III), an African American who had been in a race riot; Julie (Peggy Lipton), the daughter of a prostitute and a flower child; and Pete (Michael Cole), the rich white kid rebelling against his family. Because the scripts combined current teen concerns with standard action situations, it reached a wide audience. As in the Fifties, many adults worried that teens were seeing too many violent television shows, and once again the Senate Subcommittee on Juvenile Delinquency deplored the situation, but their pronouncements had little effect on viewing habits.

Four television phenomena debuted during the Sixties: *The Andy Griffith Show, Laugh-In, Batman,* and *Star Trek,* all with continuing appeal to teens. In 1960 *The Andy Griffith Show* introduced America to Mayberry, an imaginary small town in North Carolina run by a genial sheriff the way an easygoing, affectionate, but firm father might run a large, slightly unruly, but congenial family. It ran for eight seasons but has maintained its popularity through reruns right through to the end of the century. It is still watched by a large proportion of teens who enjoy its gentle humor.

A different kind of comedy appeared in 1967 when the stand-up team of the Smothers Brothers began airing a variety show. Their frankly political humor, even though gently presented, made CBS nervous; after only a few months, the Smothers Brothers complained that the network was censoring their material, and the show was withdrawn. The door had been opened for something a bit more contemporary than Mayberry and *Bonanza*, and the stand-up comedy team of Dan Rowan and Dick Martin took the advantage with *Laugh-In*, the quintessential show of the late Sixties. It was truly "mod" with its wacky, rapid-fire, topical humor, its use of vaudeville-like quick comic sketches by the same performers each week, its miniskirted girls dancing the frug and the pony, and its use of current slang. Although the show lasted only briefly, its humor perfectly captured the hip spirit of mindless frivolity tempered with political and social savvy.

The comic book super hero Batman had enjoyed a run in film serials in the Forties. In January 1966, he took television by Bat-storm. Starring Adam West as Batman and Burt Ward as Robin, filmed in brilliant color, with an occasional "Zow!" or "Bam!" flashing across the screen like a speech balloon in a comic book, the show made fun of itself with clever and outlandish wit—the kind of humor that came to be called "campy." Big-name stars clamored to play famous villains like Joker, Catwoman, Penguin, or Riddler; others lined up for a few seconds of airtime on a guest shot. The show was wildly popular with teens and young adults across the country, who gathered around the television in groups and laughed uproariously at its silliness and its originality. Its closing lines asking viewers to tune in tomorrow, "same Bat-time, same Bat-channel," became a standard phrase for anything repeated. Although it was canceled in 1968, like Mayberry it has remained alive in reruns well into the Nineties.

Finally, between 1966 and 1968, *Star Trek* stumbled into television history. Created by writer Gene Roddenberry, the early episodes were a combination of space-cowboy science fiction and Sixties characters—multiethnic, well-educated, and desirous of living in peace with their fellow creatures, no matter how strange. The show attracted a following of adults and older teens, although by its third season the network had cut its budget so much that the show's quality suffered. When it was canceled in 1968, in an outpouring of support seldom seen for any popular entertainment, a few fans spearheaded a massive letter-writing campaign to NBC to bring the show back. It was obvious that the scripts—which included philosophic musings and literary quotations along with phaser battles—offered something deeply important to hundreds of thousands of viewers, a great many of them teenagers, who needed a sense of hope and possibility beyond the troubled years of the late twentieth century. *Star Trek* has continued in reruns ever since, and it has thus far spawned three spin-off series, hundreds of novels and books of facts about the series, and eight feature films, not to mention the yearly regional and national conventions around the country where fans of all ages dress as their favorite characters, visit with the stars of the show, and purchase millions of dollars worth of Trek-related merchandise.

Comic strips still provided casual reading at home for teens, but only one new strip that captured this audience was introduced during the decade. *Apartment 3-G* began publication in 1961. Written by a psychiatrist, it traces the adventures of three young women sharing a New York City apartment—a nurse, a secretary, and a teacher. As the decade continued, the girls' lives reflected the turmoil of the time; one girl married only to lose her husband in Vietnam. Although their friend Professor Papagoras acts as father figure for the girls, they live independent lives and deal intelligently with the kind of problems girls are likely to face on their own. The sophisticated artwork dignified the plotlines, offering attractive, mature images to teen girls contemplating a career before, or—daringly—instead of, marriage. The strip has continued well into the Nineties, adjusting itself to changing social climates.

TEENS AT WORK

In the Fifties, the number of teens working at part-time service jobs had gradually increased. During the Sixties, this trend gained momentum as suburbia opened shopping malls and fast-food restaurants. The need for unskilled work, especially in late afternoon and evening shopping times, opened the way to after-school and weekend jobs for millions of American teens. No particular prior training or experience was necessary in these jobs, and most teens used their wages for clothes, movies, and records. For such teens, work was fast becoming an adjunct to their leisure lives. They were not looking for career preparation.

Minority teens and those from less affluent families were excluded from this apparently idyllic situation. As mechanization decreased the opportunities for the young to enter farming or factory work, jobs that would earn a living wage were harder to get (West 1996, 294). Teens who needed to contribute to their family's income or who needed to pay for their own basic needs could not find jobs with a future. If they did not live in the suburbs, getting to a mall or a highway fast-food restaurant even to apply for a job was a problem. Dropping out of school, which had once meant entry into the kind of work one could do for many years, now brought the threat of serious long-term unemployment. As in every other decade, teens in the coal-mining communities of Appalachia or the seasonal farming areas of California or Florida often wound up performing the same back-breaking labor their parents had and living in the serious poverty in which they had been raised. Even if they did manage to get to a city, lured there by the prospect of a job, many were hampered by the lack of a high school diploma.

TEENS AT SCHOOL

The turbulence that had begun in America's high schools in the Fifties continued unabated into the Sixties, worsening, especially in the inner cities, by the end of the decade. In 1963 the Supreme Court ruled that prayer in

A freshman class, Highlands High School, Fort Thomas, Kentucky, 1965, apparently untouched by the turmoil of inner-city Sixties schools. Reproduced courtesy of Highlands High School.

the schools was unconstitutional, a controversial decision which continues to be tested well into the Nineties. Integration was still a struggle in the South; Mississippi schools were finally forced to comply with the law in 1969, although several Atlanta schools integrated quite peacefully. Growing enrollment created a teacher shortage, especially in schools where pay was low and discipline was a challenge.

In 1963 a Brooklyn College teacher of education, Edgar Z. Friedenberg, who was writing for the journal *Commentary*, complained about the tendency of high schools to be repressive and controlling. Citing two examples from Middle America, which he called Milgrim and Hartsburgh, where he had interviewed a number of students and visited several times, he described a rigid system of hall passes, detention for minor offenses, lack of free time or free space, dress codes, and social and ethnic prejudice. Both schools "move smoothly," but the "fundamental pattern is still one of control, distrust, and punishment" (Friedenberg 1963, 376). Students learn more than what is offered in the classroom. One boy, who was required to shave off his beard, "had played football for the school; he was told that, although the school had no legal authority to require him to shave, he would be barred from the banquet honoring the team unless he complied" (1963, 379). This, said Friedenberg, was a lesson in how "the high school is permitted to infantilize adolescence; in fact, it is encouraged to by the widespread hostility to 'teen-agers' and the anxiety about their conduct found throughout our society" (380). One thing a high school student learns most certainly is "that he can expect no provision for his need to give in to his feelings, or swing out in his own style, or creep off and pull himself together" (375). What worried him most was that the students seem to give in to this system of control.

Depending on one's point of view, author Bel Kaufman's semiautobiographical novel *Up the Down Staircase* (1964) offered an image of a school where teens did not give in to such control, or an image of control gone haywire. The best-selling book chronicles a young teacher's first year in an inner-city school, where she struggles with overcrowded classrooms, lack of administrative support, cynical senior teachers, violent or suicidal students, dropouts, and her own fatigue and disillusionment. Told through notes, letters, scribblings on the blackboard, bulletin board displays, administrative memos, and—most dramatically—her class's "suggestion box," where she encouraged them to put their complaints in writing, the novel creates a vivid picture of inner-city teens: a multiethnic mix of potential college students, kids marking time, and kids who just wanted to get out. Some of the notes from the "suggestion box":

> This school is run like a Army. The least little thing he (McHaber) get excited.
>
> He better watch his step, after all I pay his sallary with taxes!
>
> Linda Rosen—sex pot, Alice Blake—stuck up, and you like Joe Feroni, he's just asking for attention. (signed) Neglected
>
> You're lucky you're a women teacher, if it was a man he would of walked into something he didn't see coming his way, with a women my temper is controlled but a man doesn't last long. (This is the last time I am writting!) (Kaufman 1964, 111)

Teacher Harold Saltzman focused on the racial and legal struggles among teachers, administrators, and students in Franklin K. Lane High School in Brooklyn, New York. His book, *Race War in High School,* the story of the "10-year destruction" of the school, details the danger that teachers were in from violent students while administrators looked the other way or jockeyed for political position. He noted the dramatic increase in students of color in the school between 1958 and 1967: from 2.3% Puerto Rican and 21.5% Negro to 12.5% Puerto Rican and 47.4% Negro (Saltzman 1972, Appendix A).

Puerto Rican teen Juan Gonzalez offered the student's point of view of the inner-city school: drugs, drunkenness, fights and pushing in the hallway,

Cheerleaders, Highlands High School, Fort Thomas, Kentucky, 1965. Reproduced courtesy of Highlands High School.

the irrelevance of Shakespeare and algebra, teachers who could not control the class, a lunchroom clearly divided along racial lines: "This section, Puerto Rican. Up here, Negroes, and in the middle, whites . . . the white stay by themselves and they do it different" (Mayerson 1971, 15). Education, he observed, makes a boy dissatisfied with the neighborhood he can't escape.

In parts of the country where the standard of living was generally higher and the ethnic mix less intense, high school education responded more positively to the social changes in the Sixties. Television became part of classrooms in school systems that could afford it. Math and science study became more hands on and innovative; history courses began to address world and national events with an eye to minority contributions; and the decade saw the beginning of bilingual education. Other things changed less. Football and proms still occupied students' time and attention, as did cruising to and from school in their own cars and, for some seniors, getting off school property for lunch. Dress codes were generally observed without fuss. Basic classes still consisted of English, history, math, and science. Bright students still found ways to achieve. In 1967 eighteen-year-old Henry Friedman, having already earned his Ph.D., joined the faculty of Stanford University to teach math and science (Wright 1995, 124).

Showing off the football trophy, Highlands High School, Fort Thomas, Kentucky, 1965. Reproduced courtesy of Highlands High School.

On the other hand, bright minority students at predominantly white high schools felt keenly the discomfort of being different. Gretchen Sullivan Sorin was one of a handful of black students attending Colonia High School in New Jersey in 1965. Brought up in a middle-class home, she felt separated from the Black Power movement, even though she felt personal pride in being part of that heritage. She remembered acutely her embarrassment at being not the only black person in her homeroom, but being the only girl wearing knee socks—which she had chosen carefully to match her dress (Grover 1997, 44–45). To compensate for her differentness, she worked hard at achieving academic success and became president of her school's student council. William Quivers was the only black student at the conservative Palisades High School near Los Angeles in the early Sixties. He felt "numb for a while," then decided that he was a pioneer and would "hang on in there." He fit no stereotype, preferring classical music to soul and studying to athletics. Some of his classmates seemed quite unaware of him because he kept to himself so much.

I didn't want to stick out like a sore thumb. I remember when they said they were going to take the class picture, I was thinking about it and worrying about it, until one day they marched all the classrooms onto that central quad, and there I was right in the middle. I thought, there's no way to hide from this! (Medved and Wallechinsky 1976, 225)

Pep rally before the big game, Highlands High School, Fort Thomas, Kentucky, 1965. Reproduced courtesy of Highlands High School.

To the dismay of administrators and parents, open protest in the middle-class suburban high school had risen markedly by the late Sixties. Students banded together to express their dissatisfaction with smoking and dress regulations, curricular limits, sports management, textbook selection, and parking regulations. If their complaints were suppressed in the regular student newspapers, they created underground newspapers. They held strikes and sit-ins, demanding that the schools practice the democracy they preached. Even cheerleading felt such changes by the late Sixties. In an Illinois school in 1967, students boycotted classes for a week to protest the school's suspension of seventeen black football players, who had not attended practice to protest the racial imbalance in the cheering squad: only one of the six cheerleaders was black. North Carolina and New York experienced similar protests (Hanson 1995, 34). In a Texas school, which was 85% Hispanic, students stayed away from class for twenty-eight days to register their disapproval of a squad that had only a single Hispanic girl (1995, 35). Some of the protests made their way into the court system, and one found a sympathetic hearing from the Supreme Court when in 1969 it upheld a high school student's right of freedom of speech (Palladino 1996, 241).

Some schools could not afford the luxury of protest. In Appalachian school districts, such as Perry County, Kentucky, even new schools were poorly equipped for education. One student said that "his biology experiment consisted of 'looking through a microscope once.' . . . For many, the most elaborate equipment is the coke machine" (Schrag 1971, 120). Although vocational training was helpful, the overall dropout rate was high.

Because there were so few reservations that could support a school, the Bureau of Indian Affairs operated boarding schools throughout the country for Native American teens and younger children. The curriculum was the

Girls' basketball, Highlands High School, Fort Thomas, Kentucky, 1965. Reproduced courtesy of Highlands High School.

standard one, even down to training in Western music and art; classes were run strictly; history books contained little or nothing about their culture; the dormitory life offered little opportunity for socializing since the sexes were kept as separate as possible. Even speaking their tribal language became suspect, since it represented a secret from the authorities. In such an environment, alcoholism, glue sniffing, and suicide rates among teens were high, to say nothing of the dropout rate. Many Indian males had fewer than five years of schooling; even if they graduated, they left with the equivalent of a ninth grade education (Hennigan and Esposito 1971, 105–110). Without doubt, states one historian, the American Indian was the "most disadvantaged of all the country's many ethnic and racial minorities" (Wright 1995, 919–20).

The privileged youth who took over the Columbia and UC-Berkeley campuses in the Sixties seem a far cry from these minority teens in vocational or boarding schools, but protesters at Columbia and Berkeley believed that what they were doing would ultimately make school better for all Americans.

FASHION

Teen fashion in the Sixties—and adult fashion too—reflected the exuberance and the confusions of the decade. Little else can define this decade

Plaids were in fashion in Fort Thomas, Kentucky, 1965. Reproduced courtesy of Highlands High School.

so quickly as a fashion image, but there are several to choose from. For the majority of white teens in high school, the conservative clothes of the Fifties changed only a little: skirts were slightly shorter, hair was fluffed out a little more, and later in the decade, pants had a little flair at the bottom. Many high schools still enforced dress codes to keep the lid on the more extreme fashions, as did colleges. Freshmen girls entering the University of Kentucky in 1961 were expected to wear sweaters and skirts to class, wool dresses to church and to teas (with heels, hats, and gloves), and dresses or suits to football games. Bermuda shorts might be worn only in dormitories, never outside on campus and never downtown.

The preppie, or Ivy League, look was popular throughout the decade among middle- and upper-middle-class teens. This meant narrow ties and lapels on three-button suits for boys, or khaki pants worn with penny loafers. In warmer climates and seasons, Bermuda shorts were worn with madras shirts (which had button-down collars) and loafers with no socks. For school, girls wore plaid skirts, sweaters or tailored blouses, and flat-heeled shoes with stockings or saddle shoes and white socks. In summer girls, too, wore tailored Bermuda shorts, sometimes in pastel madras-like plaids, along with white blouses which had roll-up sleeves (always neatly folded above the elbow) and small round collars. Slim dresses with scoop necks and tiny straps ("spaghetti straps") usually in soft prints of tiny flowers, were popular on

Prom, Highlands High School, Fort Thomas, Kentucky, 1965. Reproduced courtesy of Highlands High School.

dressier summer occasions. The most popular hairstyle required teasing (also called backcombing or "ratting") the hair into a bouffant bubble-like shape and, for longer hair, flipping up the ends all around. All of this needed strong hairspray for staying power, and sometimes a tiny bow or hairband for accent. By the late Sixties, New York hairdresser Vidal Sassoon had introduced his geometric haircuts which showed off straight, un-teased or sprayed hair: very short at the nape of the neck, longer and falling forward around the face.

The high-fashion standard for the well-bred teen girl was set by First Lady Jacqueline Kennedy, whose bouffant hair, simple A-line dresses, and low-heeled pumps whispered tastefully that this was the way grown-up girls should look. Add a small purse on a chain and a string of pearls, and the look was perfect in its restraint—although sometimes girls wore pointed-toe stiletto-heeled pumps instead of the more conservative shoes. Girls seldom wore hats any more.

In the early Sixties, underwear still consisted of white bras, panty girdles or regular girdles, garter belts, hose, and slips. Strapless bras were essential for some sleeveless or spaghetti-strap dresses. By the close of the decade, panty hose had freed girls from much of this paraphernalia, and the bra-less hippie encouraged a more natural look in bosoms. The surfing craze helped loosen things up, too, with baggy shorts for boys and bikinis for girls. For the first time, those who lived inland could look like Californians: "Man

Tan" and Coppertone's "QT" (for "quick tan") were the first artificial tanning creams on the popular market.

Audrey Hepburn also became a fashion icon for thousands of American girls who longed for something a little different, a little less worldly. In slim black pants, just to mid-calf, and a tight black sweater, her boyish figure, large eyes, and cropped hair suggested fresh, innocent youth—a relief to late-blooming girls for whom the Marilyn Monroe–Jane Russell images of the Fifties seemed threatening. Susan J. Douglas remembers, "After the mammary mania of the 1950s, flat-chestedness was fashionable and soon came to signify intelligence and breeding. . . . Audrey Hepburn made me feel a lot better about not looking remotely like the 'after' picture in ads for Mark Eden Bust Developers" (1995, 104). Hepburn's Givenchy-designed clothes in *Funny Face* and *Breakfast at Tiffany's*, like Jackie Kennedy's understated dresses, coats, and shoes, enticed older teens into a world of elegance—which was sometimes available to them only via the sewing machine. Many girls still sewed for themselves, or encouraged their mothers to sew for them, although stylish off-the-rack clothes were becoming more affordable.

The wide-eyed, innocent look for girls found its perfect icon not in a grown woman but in a teenage girl: Twiggy, who wore simple little dresses even working-class girls could buy. Fifteen-year-old Leslie Hornby dropped out of school in England in the mid-Sixties to begin a modeling career. So thin and lanky that she was called "Sticks" by her friends, she acquired a new name and became, at age seventeen, the "Queen of Mod"—the style begun in England with Mary Quant's miniskirt and the boutiques of Carnaby Street in London. Her boyfriend and manager, Justin de Villeneuve (his real name was Nigel Davies), brought her to America in March 1967, and together they launched a fashion look that for many defined the decade. It was preadolescent, almost childlike—although the childlike image was partly created by a great deal of makeup: white eyeshadow, heavy black liner, false eyelashes on both upper and lower lids, and very pale, sometimes even white, lipstick. Daring girls sported this look right into the halls of their high schools.

Linda Benn DeLibero thinks the childlike-ness was Twiggy's basic appeal: "My friends and I were too young to have been in on the 'real' events of our time, too old not to have been changed by them. . . . As young, white suburban girls, both curious about and frightened by the changes occurring all around us, we were exceptionally susceptible . . . to anything that enticed without too much threat" (DeLibero 1994, 42). They bought all the Twiggy merchandise they could find: clothing, false eyelashes, pens, makeup, and lunchboxes. They also bought the attitude, to some degree, since it may have been a relief from the political intensity of the decade. Twiggy's ignorance soon became as famous as her innocent appearance. In one interview, a reporter baited her by asking, "Twiggy, do you know what happened at Hiroshima?" She answered, "Where's that?" (1994, 47). Most of all, American teen girls bought the "look": boy-cut hair, thin body, skinny legs askew in tiny miniskirt, white tights, and chunky shoes. Most girls could afford the clothes, but few except the thinnest could achieve the total look.

By the mid to late Sixties, the hippies and students in the movement proclaimed their liberation from high fashion and from the marketing enticements that kept it running. Jeans, tie-dyed shirts, sensible sandals, and natural hairstyles ushered in the "unisex" look; adults sometimes gazed wonderingly (or disgustedly) at a hippie trying to figure out whether it was a boy or a girl. The natural look for girls—folksinger Joan Baez was the icon—usually meant long unstyled hair, no makeup, and no bra—something else that was shocking to adults. Girls wore long print dresses—"granny dresses"—or jeans and loose, embroidered tops. Boys let their hair grow long, even if it was very curly; some who could grew beards. They wore loose shirts (or in hot weather no shirts), tattered jeans low on the hips, bare feet or sandals, and strings of beads sometimes called "love beads." Eyeglasses with tiny lenses—"granny glasses"—were popular for both sexes. Both boys and girls sported peace symbols on belts and jewelry; they liked fringe on sleeves and skirts; they preferred bell-bottom jeans. Both wore flowers in their hair. Indian prints, symbolic of passive resistance and exotic religions, were especially popular with those who experimented with meditation.

Some hippies enjoyed flamboyant dressing up. *Time* magazine described a typical scene in Haight-Ashbury:

Here, for instance is a sensible looking youth, hair cropped in approved undergraduate fashion. But he is wearing an open tan car coat with nothing underneath except Bermuda shorts. . . . A girl hurries past wearing wild tapered trousers striped in circles of blue, white, red and finally, polka dots. One regular promenader is a young man in an African looking conical hat with long colored streamers which almost hide his face. He also wears a floor-length cape of green silk lined with white iridescent material, blue jeans, and black leather boots. Every afternoon he strides up one side of Haight Street, then down the other, giving the gawkers a good look. (Brown 1967, 31)

At this level, hippie fashion came to imitate the extremes of high fashion, just as high fashion imitated the hippies—with designers charging huge prices for Indian-print dresses and patchwork skirts. As Ellen Melinkoff observes, "The hippie look started out as a political statement, an anti-fashion, and then became the fashion itself. It went from a gesture of protest by the disenchanted and disenfranchised to a cultivated look for those who wanted to be 'with it' " (1984, 129). Other ways to be "with it" in men's fashion were the Nehru jacket—a buttoned-up, single-breasted jacket with a high collar like that worn by the prime minister of India, with no tie but a strand or two of "love beads"—or brightly flowered, loose-fitting shirts not tucked in.

As always, ethnic groups excluded from full participation in American culture by law, prejudice, and custom embraced a different style, a visual symbol of their disenfranchisement. Mexican-American youth in Los Angeles liked a "continental" look: tight pants and jacket worn with pink socks and pointed-toe shoes. In many quarters, black leather jackets, tight blue jeans, and boots still represented rebelliousness—a Hell's Angels look that hinted of violence and flaunted respectability even among peace-loving hippies. African Americans, fighting publicly for their rights, showed pride in their heritage by letting their hair grow into Afro hairstyles and wearing ethnic prints, colors, and fabrics. Hippies, most of whom were white and had taken part in Freedom Marches, imitated these styles at times—yet another instance of white culture co-opting black although now perhaps it represented a more conscious effort to understand and accept.

SLANG

The youth culture of the Sixties—both mainstream and hippie—inherited the rich Beat slang of the Fifties, which had its own infusion of jive talk from the Forties. The resulting mix ultimately entered everyone's speech to some degree and remains vibrantly alive at the end of the century. Tom Dalzell's *Flappers 2 Rappers* (1996) amply covers the topic; we can only suggest here some of the dominant areas and words.

Mainstream teen slang was influenced by the disc jockey—that fast-talking presence on the teen's transistor radio who daily delivered up the Top 40 hits. Although that speech was a "slightly squared-down" version of Beat language (Dalzell 1996, 107), its rhymes and rhythms, its clever images, and its rapid delivery suggested a special language for teens only. If you were cool, you were a member of the in crowd; you hated drags and other uncool types. You dreaded getting zits worse than going to school—unless you were a bookbuster. Something you liked was groovy. On Saturdays you didn't care if you looked groady or scuzzy. You wore your shades and cut out for the beach or the strip in your wheels. Saturday night you wore your coolest rags, saw a flick, and made out with your babycakes. Sunday you caught some extra Z's.

As usual, school provided opportunities for originality, especially grades and test taking. A's were aces, C's were hooks, D's were dandies or dogs, F's were frongs or keepers. If you Christmas-treed it with flunkenstein on a multiple-choice test, you simply marked the answers without reading the questions, knowing you were going to fail ("The Slang Bag" 1965, 56–57).

Surfing added another layer to teen slang in the Sixties. Every dude wanted a bitchin' board, a bitchin' babe, or a bitchin' good time. "Surf's up" became a way for any teen to say, let's go, and the ability to hang ten and not wipe out was what you wanted most in any area of life.

Documentation of slang in other ethnic or cultural groups is difficult to find, but the *pachuco* argot of the Mexican-American teens offers an example of such slang. The language was generally used by delinquent youths, although all Mexican-American youths apparently understood it (Heller 1966, 60). It was made up partly of Spanish, partly of English words (for example, *ganga* for gang); *suave* meant fine or nice, *orale* meant okay. Occasionally English expressions would be translated directly into Spanish: *pintar el pizo en colorado*—to paint the town red. As with American youths, such slang marked teens as special, initiates into a world that excluded adults and certain other teens.

The hippie counterculture embraced drugs as a way to free one's mind from the humdrum world of the straights, and it brought a whole lexicon of drug-related slang into teen speech. Acid, pot or grass, crystals, smack, and speed were all ways to turn on if you were into drugs. You wanted to do your own thing, be laid back, stay mellow, make the scene, and not get spaced out or freaked, but you knew your friends would let you crash at their pad if you went on a bad trip. If you really liked something, you said it was far out or outta sight. You shopped at a local head shop and hoped you wouldn't get busted by the pigs. Much of this language was not only vivid and original but had the lure of the forbidden, making it all the more attractive to teens whether or not they used drugs.

LEISURE ACTIVITIES AND ENTERTAINMENT

For many American teens, leisure in the early Sixties meant cruising to the drive-in for burgers and fries, seeing a movie, playing sports like tennis or basketball, mall shopping, playing records and dancing at home or at parties, or just getting together with friends. For a large proportion, especially in rural areas, leisure often involved church activities—picnics and youth-group outings. Church summer camps and camps for Girl and Boy Scouts occupied the warm months for many teens. By the end of the decade, some new elements had been introduced.

Small shops selling the latest fashions, called boutiques, attracted trendy teen girls who wanted to sample miniskirts and new makeup. Boys who could not afford cars or who wanted a different kind of fun turned to small motorcycles; Honda and Suzuki led the way in this and had put 10 million of them on American roads by 1969 (Wright 1995, 982). Older teens enjoyed stand-up comedy routines on 33-rpm albums as well as music; Allan Sherman, Bob Newhart, Shelly Berman, and George Carlin were popular among the young. Those who lived near the beach embraced surfing as never before, cutting school whenever the weather was right. The surfing lifestyle was, by the end of the decade, more associated with drugs and hippies than with the more wholesome image of Beach Boys music and the film *Endless Summer*.

Drugs and Alcohol

The most dramatic change in teen leisure was the use of drugs. To varying degrees, alcohol and marijuana became virtual staples of teen social life. Teen drinking had always worried adults, hence the enactment of drinking age requirements. By the Sixties, many state laws required drinkers to be twenty-one; other states, eighteen. Younger teens could usually get alcohol if they wanted it by using illegal proofs of age or getting older friends to buy it for them. Driving across a state line to buy liquor where the drinking age was lower was common among teens in border towns.

In earlier decades, teen alcohol abuse was, in the popular mind at least, more associated with the lower economic and social class, but a new kind of alcohol problem surfaced in Connecticut in 1964—where the legal age was twenty-one—when investigation of a teen car accident revealed that adults had served alcohol to teens at a party in their homes. The judge in the case issued warrants against those adults, who included several executives of corporations ("Tragedy Stirs Furor" 1964, 18). The case highlighted how divided opinions on teen drinking were between teens and adults. A poll of 7,000 students nationwide revealed that they believed strongly that drinking was a serious danger to them, both at home and on dates, while only a few believed it was a slight danger or harmless. Some of those few were between the ages of twelve and sixteen (see Table 6.1) A number of adults believed that, since teens were going to drink anyway, they could at least drink at home where the dangers could be controlled and the notion of "forbidden fruit" mitigated.

Marijuana, or pot, had been a presence in the black community for decades. By the end of the Sixties, it became part of the lifestyle of white, middle-class and upper-middle-class teens—and adults too, who began increasingly to substitute it for alcohol. "Nice" or "clean" teens smoked routinely at parties, and when they got to college, it was most certainly the drug of choice. It was an interesting irony of the decade that when it began, possession of marijuana was a felony; by the end, it was a misdemeanor. The law ultimately had to admit that it could not police such a widespread habit. In another irony, California instituted the first advertising campaign directly aimed at teens against smoking cigarettes. Although teens had called them "cancer sticks" for decades, they smoked anyway; tobacco companies gave away small packs of cigarettes to teens even in the Fifties to encourage them to try it. Warning them in the mid-Sixties, when pot use was so casual, was an example of locking the barn door after the horse had escaped.

Table 6.1
How Teen-agers Looked at Drinking During the Sixties

	Would Not Harm Me in Any Way (%)	Might Be a Slight Danger, but Not Much (%)	Would Be of Serious Danger to Me (%)	No Response (%)
Drinking Alcoholic Beverages at Home	8.8	23.8	65.2	2.2
Boys	10.5	24.9	61.5	3.1
Girls	7.2	22.8	68.7	1.3
12 to 14	4.8	15.2	76.3	3.7
15 to 16	9.0	25.8	62.7	2.5
17 and over	16.6	31.7	50.2	1.5
12 to 14	2.6	13.6	82.0	1.8
15 to 16	6.7	25.3	67.1	.9
17 and over	12.8	29.5	56.3	1.4
Drinking Alcoholic Beverages on Dates or Out with Friends	3.2	13.5	81.1	2.2
Boys	4.7	17.6	74.7	3.0
Girls	1.7	9.7	87.3	1.3
12 to 14	3.3	10.6	83.2	2.9
15 to 16	4.0	15.7	77.8	2.5
17 and over	6.6	25.0	66.5	1.9
12 to 14	0.7	5.6	92.2	1.5
15 to 16	1.8	10.0	87.2	1.0
17 and over	2.7	13.8	82.1	1.4

Source: From *Senior Scholastic*, Dec. 1964 issue. Copyright © 1964 by Scholastic, Inc. Reprinted by permission of Scholastic, Inc.

Some teens, drawn to the hippie lifestyle, tried LSD; "dropping acid"—not illegal at the time—was daring and thrilling for many users, who claimed the visions they experienced changed their lives. A few were drawn more deeply into the drug lifestyle and experimented with amphetamines and tranquilizers. Drugs of all kinds were easily available and relatively cheap, as the famous San Francisco "Summer of Love" in 1967 proved. Thousands of teens and young adults made their way to California to experience peace, love, and drugs in an atmosphere of acceptance and community.

Dating and Sex

During the early Sixties, dating for most high-school-age teens remained the one-on-one "rating and dating" pattern that had begun during the earlier decades: boy asks girl to movie, dance, party, or prom; girl accepts, knowing her responsibility is to look pretty and be interested in the boy; boy pays for everything during the evening. Both engage in this process partly because they like each other, but also because they want to be seen with someone who confers status. Dates also offered opportunity for sexual experiment in the form of necking or petting. Younger teens were beginning to date more, even when parents provided transportation and the date involved being with a larger group of teens.

By the end of the decade, however, patterns were beginning to shift slightly, especially among white, middle-class teens. Leisure drug use, especially marijuana smoking, led teens to get together in groups more often than in pairs, partly for safety since it was an illegal activity, partly to tap into more sources for the drug, and partly for the enhancement of the experience. As the hippie style became the popular style of dress, teens paid less attention, or a different kind of attention—one that affected to be no attention—to what they wore to parties or on dates. Parties and even proms were becoming more casual, both in dress and in social acceptance of difference.

However, the most sweeping social change in teen life in many decades was brought about in 1960 by the Federal Drug Administration's approval of the birth control pill. Enovid, a tiny pill that fooled the female body into a state simulating pregnancy, was proven to prevent pregnancy when taken in correct cycles. Available in a small compact, it was safe and easy to use with few side effects. For the first time in history, girls themselves could control their vulnerability to pregnancy.

During the early Sixties, the birth control pill was prescribed mostly for young married women who wanted to delay childbearing. *Playboy* estimated that, in 1966, over half of the married women under twenty were taking oral contraceptives; by 1969, more than half of the college girls were using them as well (Petersen 1998, 148). Girls could engage in sex on a date, if they felt so inclined, with someone they merely liked—not necessarily loved or regarded as a potential mate. They no longer had to rely on the boy to provide condoms or on their own calculations of their menstrual cycle to be safe.

Girls who came into their teen years early in the decade still heard the echoes of "nice girls don't." The new sexual freedom, so hotly displayed or hotly discussed in all forms of media—music, movies, magazines, books, television—was simultaneously seductive and threatening. Rumors of "sex clubs" in the high schools surfaced, but these may have been more rumor than reality in most places. Even by the end of the decade, girls still got pregnant accidentally. Some doctors refused to prescribe the pill to single teen girls, and some girls did not know how to take the pills correctly. Still, the number of white girls who had sexual intercourse by age eighteen almost doubled from 23.4% in 1952, to 42.4% in 1968 (adapted from Chadwick and Heaton 1992, 140). Just as it was white teens who could afford dates, it was white teens who could afford birth control and the freedom it bought.

Black teens, however, especially those living in ghetto conditions, experienced dating and sex quite differently. Well over 65% of black teen girls age eighteen had experienced sexual intercourse in the late Sixties, and many had become pregnant, some several times. Poverty prevented the "date" ritual popular among white teens; ghetto-bound black teens generally socialized at each other's homes. Knowledge of the results of sex was often vague: "I didn't know anything about sex or where babies came from because didn't nobody tell me" (quoted in Gottleib and Hiensohn 1971, 178). One girl became pregnant for the second time at age fifteen, saying she could not remember how it happened: "I think maybe the reason I can't remember is because . . . I was so hurt and disappointed and everything else and I didn't know just what to do" (1971, 178). Abortion was considered out of the question; a girl's parents generally raised the child.

The same situation plagued poor teens in Appalachia. Dates involved going over to a girl's house and watching television with her family, or just walking along the roads together. Without jobs and without access to cars or even to entertainment should they have transportation, sex became a way to be with the opposite sex. Illegitimacy rates were high in this part of the country, too, and abortion or adoption were not options. The baby stayed in the family (137–38).

The Car

In the Sixties, even more than in the Fifties, a car was practically a necessity for teens. Many had part-time jobs in addition to their daily school and needed the transportation. It also provided privacy on dates and opportunities to be with a group of friends, and it was a symbol of the owner's identity.

For those few who could afford it, the ultimate teen status symbol, the Corvette, was restyled in 1963 as the sleek Stingray. The Sixties brought three major automotive developments that made some cars more affordable for teens, and some even more desirable as status symbols: the Mustang, the muscle car, and the Volkswagen.

In 1964 the sporty Ford Mustang was introduced. Available in a large variety of colors and styles, it proved an instant success. Also in 1964 the Pontiac GTO began a craze for the muscle car—the heavy car with a big chassis and powerful engine designed to appeal to drag racers or teens who wanted to look as if they had muscle themselves. Its chief appeal was less its look than its ability to accelerate and to hold the road at high speeds. The Chevrolet Camaro and the Pontiac Firebird appeared in 1966 to compete.

For those more conservative in their tastes and those who had less to spend, a number of foreign cars had begun to enter the American market, and smaller cars like the Ford Falcon were beginning to compete. A funny-looking car from Germany, first manufactured in 1947, was beginning to make major inroads in the American market. With its rear engine, its bug-like shape, and its good gas mileage, it was perfect for the teen who did not mind being a little different in order to have affordable wheels. As more of them appeared in the States, the price on used ones went down and even the hippies who shunned financial success could afford one. In San Francisco and many other cities, the VW Beetle, frequently decorated with flowers, peace symbols, and psychedelic shapes and colors, became part of the scene. Even more popular for hippies who moved in groups around the country was the Volkswagen bus, one of the first vans to achieve genuine popularity. The gaily painted and decorated VW bus, tooling along with its load of relaxed flower children who only wanted love and peace, has become the chief icon of the Sixties.

With gas prices still relatively low and the country still financially well off overall, an increasing number of middle-class parents provided cars for their sixteen-year-olds. Low-priced, gas-efficient imports such as the Volkswagen, and the Toyota which began marketing in the United States in 1960, made perfect second cars or teen cars. They became all the more attractive when consumer activist Ralph Nader exposed the safety problems in domestic cars like the small Chevy Corvair. By 1966 the National Traffic and Motor Vehicle Safety Act became law, requiring seat belts and other safety equipment that had been previously optional.

The dark side to America's love of the automobile was visible in the increasing number of teens committing auto theft. A study of Mexican-American youths in comparison with Anglo-American youths showed that this was overall the chief offense in both groups, although usually these teens claimed they did not want to steal but to "joyride." In 1956, in Los Angeles, more than 20% of Anglo-American juvenile crime and 17% of Mexican-American juvenile crime was auto theft, and the number apparently did not diminish by the Sixties (Heller 1966, 72–73). They often blamed girls for the need for a car, saying girls would go out only with boys who had one. They would risk a great deal for a car. As one nineteen-year-old Mexican American explained it, "A lot of guys I know have received stolen goods just to make the car payments. . . . When they get the car they don't think of this. . . . But when they find themselves in a bind, they say 'just once' " (1966, 73).

Music and Dancing

If the decade of the Fifties was the Golden Age of Rock and Roll, the decade of the Sixties was the Golden Age of Rock. Music became more than just a beat teens could dance to; its beat now underlay lyrics that had a message, making it both the accompaniment and impetus to many of the major events of the decade. The beat and the lyrics came in several different forms, all of which continue to be described and analyzed in detail in books and articles; here we can only suggest their chief characteristics and major figures.

Folk Rock and Surfing Music

Folk rock began in the late Fifties and achieved commercial success in the early Sixties with hits from the Kingston Trio and Peter, Paul and Mary. Less commercial but popular with teen girls, as well as with many others, was Joan Baez, whose accomplished guitar playing, pure soprano voice, serious demeanor, and long, straight hair attracted many girls to folksinging. The major figure to emerge from this movement was Bob Dylan, "often called our leading poet by adoring fans and aging establishment critics. . . . Dylan loves words, understands them, and uses them well" (Grossman, 1976, 65–66). His haunting rhymes and images transformed his minimal performance on guitar and harmonica, his raspy voice, and his small frame into an intense concert experience, and his deliberate avoidance of stardom and periodic changes of style fascinated audiences old and young. Other groups like The Byrds, Buffalo Springfield, and Crosby, Stills, Nash and Young moved folk rock farther from its Depression-era protest-song roots toward the Sixties California scene. The Mamas and the Papas had several popular hits in this tradition, as did the team of Paul Simon and Art Garfunkel, whose "Sound of Silence" (1965) expressed the disillusionment with American society than many young people felt during this decade.

California developed its own distinctive pop music based on its laid-back lifestyle. The Beach Boys released "Surfin' Safari" in 1962, followed by "Surfer Girl" and "Surfin' USA." Fueled by such disparate movies as *Gidget* and *Endless Summer*, surfer music made surfing the most popular teen sport in the country for a brief time, probably because, as Lloyd Grossman groused, "it offered a culture that was attractive and indolent based around a sport that no one who lived in an area without regular six-foot waves could be expected to try" (1976, 69). Jan and Dean ("Surf City") and the Surfaris ("Wipe-Out") rode this same wave of popularity. The Beach Boys eventually overcame their identification with surfing and hot rods when they recorded more complex songs such as "In My Room" and "Good Vibrations"—a song that in 1967 took twenty recording sessions to complete (Friedlander 1996, 75).

The British Invasion

On February 9, 1964, the Beatles appeared on American television, and rock music has never been the same. The four young men from Liverpool with their skinny "mod" suits and mop-like hairstyles were the vanguard and icon of the so-called British invasion in popular music. Deplored and feared by many adults because of the hysteria they induced in teen girls (at times the Beatles could not hear themselves play because of the screaming audience), and cynically dismissed early on by some critics as musically unimaginative, they nevertheless became not only one of the most popular rock groups ever but one of the most musically respected for their complex harmonies, interesting lyrics, and unusual orchestration. Their wit, too, endeared them to American teens. When John Lennon suggested that some of the royals in a concert audience "rattle your jewelry" instead of applauding, or when he said that the Beatles were "more popular than Jesus," he spoke for a whole generation who were trying to get free of the conservatism of the older generation.

The Beatles' biggest competition was the Rolling Stones, whose bad-boy image and raucous songs offered a daring contrast to the Beatles' musical complexities and fresh smiles. "The Stones are on a teen kick—period," said their manager, distinguishing them from the more general appeal of the Beatles, but American newspapers complained that they were "dirtier and streakier and more dishevelled than the Beatles" and they got a reputation for wreaking havoc wherever they went (du Noyer 1995, 67).

British groups the Kinks, the Animals, and the Dave Clark Five followed the Beatles and the Stones, trying to capitalize on America's obsession with swinging England and Carnaby Street styles. American television producers also tried to imitate the British groups by creating *The Monkees*, a show based on a rock group that vaguely resembled the Beatles. The four actors chosen for the roles had only a little musical talent and were coached into looking like a rock group. The show debuted in 1966 to a great deal of media hype and merchandise, and it had some success because of its improvisatory scripting and its attempts to look like the Beatles 1964 film *Hard Day's Night* (du Noyer 1995, 71). It was so obviously a calculated, profit-driven enterprise that it soon lost momentum, despite one hit single by the group, "Last Train to Clarksville."

Soul and Girl Groups

America's own music, whether it was called soul or "race music," reached during the Sixties an even wider audience than before, partly because of a new variety from Detroit called Motown—"elegant, danceable, more mainstream" than the Memphis rhythm and blues sound (Friedlander 1996, 160). "Shop Around" by the Miracles was the first big hit produced by the Motown Record Corporation. Founder Berry Gordy, Jr., went on to produce such hits as "Reet Petite," "You Got What It Takes," "Money," "Please Mr. Postman," and beginning in 1962, songs by Little Stevie Wonder who began recording for Motown at age eleven (du Noyer 1995, 54).

Classic soul was represented in popular music by Otis Redding, James Brown, Sam Cooke, and Aretha Franklin, all of whom incorporated strong gospel elements in their sounds. Ray Charles, who had begun his career at age seventeen in Seattle and had a string of hits in the late Fifties and early Sixties ("Georgia on My Mind," "Hit the Road, Jack," "What'd I Say," "I Can't Stop Loving You"), was known by the mid-Sixties as "the genius of soul" (Friedlander 1996, 161–62). White and black teens alike danced and sang along to Motown and soul, but there was an ironic difference in the way the music was produced. Motown was produced for white audiences by black producers, writers, and musicians. Soul, more popular than Motown in the black community, was controlled by white companies such as Atlantic and Stax (1996, 167).

During the Sixties, the teen girl finally got a voice of her own—through the popular girl groups, as they were called: the Ronettes, the Shirelles, the Dixie Cups, the Chiffons, Martha and the Vandellas, and the queen of them all, the Supremes. Although some may have considered these groups a fad, something on the fringe of the male-dominated rock business, teen girls rejoiced in these songs because they expressed, in rhythms, lyrics, and orchestration, the romantic longings as well as the rebellious pull of sexuality that have always marked girls' lives but have seldom had so frank an expression (Douglas 1995, 87–98). A song like "Will You Still Love Me Tomorrow" expressed exactly the dilemma that girls were feeling as they responded to both their mothers' warnings and the tantalizing freedom of the pill. "Dancing in the Streets" proclaimed a good time to be had by all, around the world. In "Be My Baby" and "Beechwood 4–5789" the girl did the asking, and in "My Boyfriend's Back" and "Don't Say Nothin' Bad About My Baby" girls were free to threaten, in a sassy sort of way.

Most of these groups were black, and they were glamorous. Their highly styled hair, elegant makeup, tight but tasteful dresses, and high heels represented self-confident womanhood even though many of them were teenagers themselves. The music of these groups, and their images, joined black and white teen girls together in admiration. As Gretchen Sullivan Sorin, one of only a few black teens in her New Jersey high school in the Sixties, noticed, the music bridged the gap between her and the white girls there. They all knew the lyrics, and they danced together in their basements. "In music, color did not matter" (Grover 1997, 45).

The man responsible for the commercial success of some of this music was Phil Spector, known as the "Tycoon of Teen" (du Noyer 1995, 65). Although he was a songwriter, it was his reputation as a producer that earned him the title. He created what he called his "little symphonies for kids," using large orchestras in small studios and multiple-echo techniques to create "a wall of sound" which gave a lush background to the singer and which sometimes was the most appealing and memorable part of the record.

Janis Joplin, Psychedelic Rock, and Bubblegum

One singer can hardly be categorized: Janis Joplin. With her wild hair and fluttering thriftshop clothes, she looked the perfect hippie. Although she was white, she sang low-down blues as well as some black blues singers, in a voice hoarse from overuse and with lyrics that seemed to understand all of the good and bad in life. She openly poured bourbon down her throat during her performances. She was a vision of someone living on the edge. Like many other rock stars of the Sixties, she sang hard and died young at the age of twenty-seven, in 1970, of drugs and alcohol.

The drug culture was responsible for psychedelic rock, mostly identified with San Francisco and the Haight-Ashbury. The Grateful Dead began here, as did the Jefferson Airplane. The Airplane's hit "White Rabbit" gave the title to one of the most controversial books of the 1970s, *Go Ask Alice* by Beatrice Sparks, the fictional diary of a teen girl hooked on drugs. Psychedelic concerts featured elaborate light shows designed to replicate the visual experience of LSD (Grossman 1976, 72).

Toward the end of the Sixties, "bubblegum rock" offered young teens an uncomplicated music; some of it was sung on a Saturday morning television show by a cartoon group based on the "Archie" comic characters. Some of the groups had names that deliberately conjured child culture— 1989 Musical Marching Zoo, 1910 Fruitgum Company—and whether they were real bands or just names for studio musicians was debatable (du Noyer 1995, 105). Bubblegum rock's most famous hit was "Yummy Yummy Yummy," sung by The Ohio Express. This phenomenon parallels the popularity of Twiggy among preteen and young teen girls; like her, it offered a mindless escape from the troubles the country experienced in the late Sixties, a return to childhood even more literal than that of the flower children. Of course, also like Twiggy, it was created with a cynical eye toward a quick buck.

Dancing

Dance styles changed dramatically during the Sixties, beginning with the Twist. Although the song had been recorded previously, Chubby Checker's version of "The Twist," complete with his special dance steps, galvanized American teens in 1960. It was all in the hips, which swiveled while the upper body twisted in the opposite direction, the weight shifting from one foot to the other. As Chubby said, "Imagine you've just stepped out of the shower and you're drying your back with a big towel. At the same time, you're stubbing out a cigarette with your foot" (du Noyer 1995, 88). Adults were at first amazed; although they worried when kids held each other too tight when slow dancing, the free-wheeling Twist bewildered them more.

Soon adults were doing the Twist too and enjoying the liberation of this new style. Joey Dee performed his version, the Peppermint Twist, at New York's Peppermint Lounge and in a movie called *Hey, Let's Twist*. Other versions were the soul twist, the Latin twist, and the joyous version you did to "Twist and Shout."

The Twist was the sensation of the early Sixties among white teens, and it ushered in a whole range of new dances such as the mashed potato, the frug, and the Watusi, none of which required partners or movement outside a tiny space on the dance floor. In the jerk dancers raised their arms one at a time, contracting their midsections in a sharp jerk. The pony featured prancing movements, and the swim, the same arm movements you used when swimming, even holding your nose. "Virtually all subsequent free-form rock'n'roll writhing is clearly descended from the Twist" (du Noyer 1995, 88). It was exuberant, the kind of dancing that did not require much skill and could be done at home by yourself if you felt like it, another liberation for white teen girls who enjoyed dancing more than the usual run of white teen boys. It was an attempt, in many ways, to approximate the freedom of black teens in their dancing, which white teens had long envied.

Public versions of this dancing were still performed on *American Bandstand* by Dick Clark's Philadelphia teens. Older teens who could afford them enjoyed going to discotheques, a French term for a dance club or bar where, instead of a band, a disc jockey played records from a wide selection (the word plays on the French for library, *bibliotheque*). There they would probably see a go-go girl. Suspended in a narrow cage, often raised above the dance floor, wearing hot pants (very short shorts) or a miniskirt and short white boots, she performed all the latest steps as if she were completely unaware of anyone around her. While the intent was probably to encourage other dancers to dance alone if they wanted (which many did), Susan Douglas finds the go-go girl "one of the sicker, yet more apt, metaphors for the teen female condition during this time" (1995, 98). The go-go girl was free to dance any way she liked, except outside her cage.

Movies

Early in the decade Hollywood aimed for the "blockbuster," the "epic," the big movie—big budget, big screen, big stars, big audiences. *My Fair Lady* (1964) and *The Sound of Music* (1965) had a fresh appeal for moviegoers of all ages. Joseph Mankiewiz's four-hour-long *Cleopatra* (1963) was touted for its expense and Egyptian spectacle, but it proved to be more interesting for those who were curious about the on- and off-screen romance between Elizabeth Taylor and Richard Burton. *West Side Story* came to the big screen in 1961, with a glossy rendition of the teen gang wars of the Broadway show.

As the decade wore on and the nation's troubles escalated, some popular

Teen idol Troy Donahue comforts Connie Stevens in *Parrish*, 1961. Reproduced courtesy of The Museum of Modern Art.

films concentrated less on size than on substance, and the result was often dark or violent. Arthur Penn's *Bonnie and Clyde* (1967) traced the careers of America's famous young Depression-era bank robbers to their bloody conclusion; although most of the film was witty and stylish, with a country-music background accompanying the getaway cars, the film's violent closing—a slow-motion sequence of the two being riddled with bullets in their car—was extremely controversial when it was released. The satiric film *Wild in the Streets*, produced in 1968, showed an America dominated by teenagers: a pop idol is elected president and lowers the voting age to fourteen, with chaos as the result. *Butch Cassidy and the Sundance Kid* (1969), on the surface a good-natured Western, depicted the lives of these outlaws with more than a hint of sadness and futility. *2001: A Space Odyssey*, released in 1968, used the big screen to its full potential to take audiences into deep space, and into the mysteries of the human mind. Its most famous character became HAL, a talking computer who almost wins a battle to take over the spaceship.

The tumultuous lives of teens still fascinated the film industry, although the juvenile delinquent film faded somewhat as America faced the real complexities of its social problems. Blonde teen heartthrob Troy Donahue romanced the girls on a tobacco plantation in *Parrish* (1961). *The Graduate* (1967) featured Dustin Hoffman as a middle-class college graduate who is naive and confused about what to do next with his life. After he is seduced by an older woman, he falls in love with her daughter and snatches her away in her wedding dress just as she is about to marry another man. The film, which approaches his confusions with wry humor and takes pleasure in his rejection of the middle-class recipe for success, made a star of Hoffman. *To Sir, With Love* (1967) is set in an inner-city London school, where a young teacher, played by Sidney Poitier, deals with his students' problems. The same year, Bel Kaufman's semifictional account of a New York City school, *Up the Down Staircase*, became a film. The Sixties versions of *Blackboard Jungle*, these films suggested that England and America shared many of the same challenges, although they did pretty up the reality of such high schools.

Hollywood still wanted to cash in quickly on teens as it had since the Forties and thus produced cheap biker movies and drug movies (*Maryjane* in 1968 is an example) to attract them as an audience, but Hollywood had more success with a run of "beach party" pictures, most of them starring teen singing star Frankie Avalon and ex-Mouseketeer Annette Funicello—two perfect examples of the clean-teen image. *Beach Party, Beach Blanket Bingo, How to Stuff a Wild Bikini*, and so on were musicals, with song-and-dance numbers interspersed with silly comic routines and slapstick situations. An excuse for parading pretty girls in bikinis, these films at times began with a provocative title, then developed the story around it (Jackson 1993, 127). The sexual suggestiveness coupled with the innocence of the actual goings-on offered the target audience of teenagers a vision of "paradise if there ever was one" (1993, 130). Although such movies tried, apparently, to persuade the public that teens were not all rioting in the streets and smoking pot, they did little to persuade the public that teen concerns could be serious.

The two films that most captured late Sixties teens as an audience were not standard Hollywood productions. *Endless Summer* (1966), directed by Bruce Brown, was a documentary about surfers traveling around the world in search of the perfect wave. Its gorgeous beach scenes—showing, finally, that perfect wave—coupled with witty narration depicted the surfing way of life with tremendous appeal. Posters from the film decorated many teen bedrooms during the late Sixties. In 1969 the quintessential Sixties film appeared. *Easy Rider*, a low-budget film written by actors Peter Fonda and Dennis Hopper along with counterculture novelist Terry Southern, traced the odyssey of two young men who motorcycle across the country searching for what might be the "real" America. Its scenes of spontaneous travel, of getting high on drugs, and of clashes with middle-class morality spoke to an entire generation of American teens and young adults who wanted, either literally or in their imaginations, to escape what they perceived as the hypocritical rat race of the working world. The film featured Jack Nicholson in an early role as a lawyer who joins the cyclists briefly.

By 1968 the movie rating system was in place. Administered by the Code and Rating Administration of the Motion Picture Association of America, it rated films G for general audiences, PG for suggesting parental guidance although all were admitted, R for admitting those under age seventeen only with an adult, and X for admitting no one under age seventeen.

Books and Reading

The best-selling books of the Sixties, fiction and nonfiction, represent in microcosm the intensities of the decade. Several have become standards in the Nineties high school classroom. Harper Lee's *To Kill a Mockingbird* (1960), *The Autobiography of Malcolm X* (1965), and Eldridge Cleaver's *Soul on Ice* (1968) made Americans face its racial inequities head-on. Joseph Heller's *Catch 22* (1961) made them see the inanities and horrors of military life, and Ken Kesey's *One Flew over the Cuckoo's Nest* (1962) represented through its scenes in a mental hospital the frustrations of ordinary people caught in a senseless bureaucratic situation. Truman Capote's *In Cold Blood* (1966), which he called a "nonfiction novel," took readers into the minds of two murderers who had killed an entire family for no particular reason, leaving us to wonder about the limits of human cruelty. Jacqueline Susann's *Valley of the Dolls* (1966) may have been the kind of "women's book" easily dismissed by serious readers and critics, but its depiction of nice, middle-class young women becoming addicted to drugs as they are drawn into a glittering media culture was both titillating to teen girl readers and chilling to older ones.

Betty Friedan expressed what thousands of American housewives had felt for years when she wrote *The Feminine Mystique* (1963), describing the "problem that had no name"—the vague, guilty dissatisfaction of financially secure wives and mothers who had college degrees and yet were either subtly or overtly excluded from positions of power. The book was a revelation as well to women who did not live in suburbia. Even the hippie movement and political groups such as Students for a Democratic Society, supposedly dedicated to equity for the masses, expected their women members to be cooks and secretaries. With Friedan and her book, the feminist movement took on new life and new political clout, and the National Organization for Women (NOW) was soon organized.

Teen girls were more interested in Helen Gurley Brown's *Sex and the Single Girl* (1962). The very title was iconoclastic, since hardly anyone in the media admitted that single girls had genuine sex lives. Like Brown's magazine *Cosmopolitan* and like *Glamour* and *Mademoiselle*, the book was filled with advice about decorating, cooking, mixing drinks, makeup and hairstyles, wearing sexy clothes, and attracting men. Brown further urged girls to think about a career, about having their own apartments, about having several partners, about being seductive and keeping their independence at the same time. It was a smash best-seller among girls in their late teens, and although it hardly seemed as socially conscious as Friedan's book, its message that girls could have many of the same freedoms as men probably enticed some of its readers into the women's movement in the coming decades.

Young Adult Literature

Until the Sixties, serious books written specifically for teens were relatively rare. Maureen Daly's *Seventeenth Summer* (1942) was a notable exception among the scores of junior-miss-style romances for girls, sports books for boys, and series such as Nancy Drew and the Hardy Boys. This decade's social and political upheavals focused to an unprecedented degree on the young. This media attention, coupled with the continually increasing, unsupervised spending power of teens, persuaded publishers that here was a new and viable market. They began to persuade some established writers to try their hand at this audience. One of the first to try it was Nat Hentoff, a music critic and columnist. His 1965 *Jazz Country* explores the Greenwich Village jazz scene through the eyes of a white teen boy who wants to play jazz with the black artists. In 1967 sports columnist Robert Lipsyte published *The Contender*, the powerful story of a black teen boy on the verge of delinquency who trains as a boxer.

The potential of the market was dramatically illustrated by the success of S. E. Hinton's 1967 novel *The Outsiders*. Because Hinton was a high school student when she wrote *The Outsiders*, she understood the teen world with a depth that adult writers could not approach. Set in Tulsa, where Hinton lived, the novel explores through the character of Ponyboy, whose voice Hinton assumed, the division between the delinquents and the "clean teens" and exposed the good kids as not so good after all. Hinton has often said that she wrote it because she did not want to read books about girls going to the prom and could not find anything else to satisfy her. Although its language seems tame in the Nineties, its violent scenes and its romantic sensitivity still bring teen joys and problems to vivid life.

Other writers found the doors open for books that took teens seriously. Ann Head addressed the consequences of teen sex in *Mr. and Mrs. Bo Jo Jones*, in which two middle-class teens are pressed into marriage by the girl's pregnancy. Paul Zindel tried a different style of narration for *The Pigman* (1969), telling his story in the voices of two different teens who have a touching encounter with an old man who collects ceramic pigs. John Donovan's *I'll Get There. It Better Be Worth the Trip* (1969) describes the painful experiences of a boy whose parents are divorcing; in his need for friendship and closeness, he engages in a brief homosexual experience with a friend.

Magazines and Comic Books

Seventeen continued to dominate the teen girl market in magazines; college-bound girls enjoyed *Glamour* and *Mademoiselle* as well. Although their dominant role was selling fashionable clothes, makeup, and hairstyles, these magazines always included articles about other aspects of Sixties life. Boys still had fewer general magazines devoted to them, but *Mad's* satiric humor kept them laughing and *Playboy* offered, along with its nearly-nude girls, advice about cars and sexual matters. In 1967 twenty-year-old Jann Werner began publishing *Rolling Stone*, the first magazine devoted to rock music and its performers; it sold well from the outset and attracted a following among older teens and young adults.

Comic books, still the staple reading of thousands of boys from age twelve to the early twenties, entered their "silver age." The super heroes from DC Comics—Batman, Superman, Green Lantern, and the Flash—continued strong, but Marvel Comics introduced their Fantastic Four, Spiderman, and the Incredible Hulk, a different kind of super hero who might sometimes appear a villain as well. In 1966 DC's Teen Titans series debuted, focusing on the "sidekicks" of the super heroes—the teen members of the crime-fighting teams. DC also appealed directly to the teen market by producing the *Legion of Super Heroes*, a series of comics about a teenage gang of boys and girls from other planets who had superpowers and banded together to fight greed and crime. The comics industry has always paid attention to its readers, but in 1967 DC went even further and hired thirteen-year-old Jim Shooter of Pittsburgh as a writer for the *Legion of Super Heroes* after he sent in an illustrated story (Daniels 1995, 122).

Older teen boys might seek out the new "underground comics" published by small presses, which offered very different images and humor from mainstream comics. Robert Crumb was the artist most identified with them, especially his creations *Fritz the Cat* and *Zap!* Often labeled "adults only" for their ribald sexual humor, their exuberant, grotesque artwork poked fun at the counterculture while they thrived on the new freedom that made possible the market for such work.

REFERENCES

Betrock, Alan. *The I Was a Teenage Juvenile Delinquent Rock 'n' Roll Horror Beach Party Movie Book: A Complete Guide to the Teen Exploitation Film, 1954–1969.* New York: St. Martin's Press, 1986.

Brown, Joe David, ed. *The Hippies.* New York: Time Incorporated, 1967.

Buck, Rinker. *Flight of Passage.* New York: Hyperion, 1997.

Chadwick, Bruce A., and Jim B. Heaton. *Statistical Handbook on the American Family.* Phoenix, Ariz.: Oryx, 1992.

———. *Statistical Handbook on Adolescents in America.* Phoenix, Ariz.: Oryx, 1996.

Colbert, David, ed. *Eyewitness to America.* New York: Pantheon, 1997.

Coles, Robert. "Appalachia: Hunger in the Hollows." *America's Other Youth: Growing Up Poor*. David Gottlieb and Anne L. Heinsohn, Editors. Englewood Cliffs, N.J.: Prentice-Hall, Inc., 1971, 123–28.

Dalzell, Tom. *Flappers 2 Rappers: American Youth Slang*. Springfield, Mass.: Merriam Webster, 1996.

Daniels, Les. *DC Comics: Sixty Years of the World's Favorite Comic Book Heroes*. Boston: Little, Brown, 1995.

DeLibero, Linda Benn. "This Year's Girl: A Personal/Critical History of Twiggy." In *On Fashion*, ed. Shari Benstock and Suzanne Ferriss. New Bruswick, N.J.: Rutgers University Press, 1994.

Douglas, Susan J. *Where the Girls Are*. New York: Random House, 1995.

du Noyer, Paul. *The Story of Rock 'n' Roll*. New York: Schirmer Books, 1995.

Friedenberg, Edgar Z. "The Modern High School: A Profile." *Commentary*, November 1963, 373–80.

Friedlander, Paul. *Rock and Roll: A Social History*. Boulder, Colo.: Westview Press, 1996.

Gitlin, Todd. *The Sixties: Years of Hope, Days of Rage*. New York: Bantam, 1989.

Gottleib, David, and Ann Lienhard Hiensohn, eds. *America's Other Youth: Growing Up Poor*. Englewood Cliffs, N.J.: Prentice-Hall, 1971.

Grossman, Lloyd. *A Social History of Rock Music: From Greasers to Glitter Rock*. New York: David McKay, 1976.

Grover, Kathryn. *Teenage New Jersey 1941–1975*. Newark: New Jersey Historical Society, 1997.

Halberstam, David. *The Children*. New York: Random House, 1998.

Hanson, Mary Ellen. *Go! Fight! Win! Cheerleading in American Culture*. Bowling Green, Ohio: Bowling Green State University Popular Press, 1995.

Heller, Celia S. *Mexican-American Youth: Forgotten Youth at the Crossroads*. New York: Random House, 1966.

Henninger, Daniel, and Nancy Esposito. "Indian Schools." *America's Other Youth: Growing Up Poor*. David Gottlieb and Anne L. Heinsohn, Editors. Englewood Cliffs, N.J.: Prentice-Hall, Inc., 1971, 105–10.

Horn, Maurice. *100 Years of American Newspaper Comics*. New York: Gramercy Books, 1996.

Jackson, Kathy Merlock. "Frankie and Annette at the Beach: The Beach Locale in American Movies and Its Dominance in the 1960s." In *Beyond the Stars 4*, ed. Paul Loukides and Linda Fuller, 121–35. Bowling Green, Ohio: Bowling Green State University Popular Press, 1993.

Kaufman, Bel. *Up the Down Staircase*. Englewood Cliffs, N.J.: Prentice-Hall, 1964.

Kunen, James Simon. *The Strawberry Statement*. New York: Random House, 1969.

Layman, Richard, ed. *American Decades: 1960–1969*. New York: Gale Research, 1995.

Lukas, J. Anthony. *Don't Shoot—We Are Your Children!* New York: Random House, 1969.

Mayerson, Charlotte Leon, editor. Excerpts from *Two Blocks Apart: Juan Gonzalez and Peter Quinn*. In *America's Other Youth: Growing Up Poor*. David Gottlieb and Anne L. Heinsohn, Editors. Englewood Cliffs, N.J.: Prentice-Hall, Inc., 1971, 3–20.

McCloud, Bill. *What Should We Tell Our Children About Vietnam?* Norman: University of Oklahoma Press, 1989.

Medved, Michael, and David Wallechinsky. *What Really Happened to the Class of '65?* New York: Random House, 1976.

Melinkoff, Ellen. *What We Wore: An Offbeat Social History of Women's Clothing, 1950 to 1980.* New York: Quill, 1984.

Nilsen, Alleen Pace, and Ken Donelson, eds. *Literature for Today's Young Adults.* 4th ed. New York: HarperCollins, 1993.

Palladino, Grace. *Teenagers.* New York: Basic Books, 1996.

Petersen, James F. "Make Love, Not War: Playboy's History of the Sexual Revolution, Part VII (1960–1969)." *Playboy* 45, no. 6 (June 1998): 86+.

Russell, Ethan. *Dear Mr. Fantasy.* Boston: Houghton Mifflin, 1985.

Saltzman, Harold. *Race War in High School.* New Rochelle, New York: Arlington House, 1972.

Schmittroth, Linda, ed. *Statistical Record of Children.* Detroit, Mich.: Gale, 1994.

Schrag, Peter. "The Schools of Appalachia." *America's Other Youth: Growing Up Poor.* David Gottlieb and Anne L. Heinsohn, Editors. Englewood Cliffs, N.J.: Prentice-Hall, Inc., 1971, 117–22.

"The Slang Bag." *Time* 85 (January 1, 1965): 56–57.

Steiner, Stan. Excerpts from *The New Indians.* In *America's Other Youth: Growing Up Poor.* David Gottlieb and Anne L. Heinsohn, Editors. Englewood Cliffs, N.J.: Prentice-Hall, Inc. 1971, 85–88.

"Teen-agers Speak Out on Teen-age Drinking." *Senior Scholastic* 85, no. 11 (December 2, 1964): 18–19.

"Tragedy Stirs Furor." *Senior Scholastic* 85, no. 6 (October 21, 1964): 18–19.

Wallechinsky, David. *The People's Almanac Presents the Twentieth Century.* Boston: Little, Brown, 1995.

Weller, Jack E. Excerpts from *Yesterday's People.* In *America's Other Youth: Growing Up Poor.* David Gottlieb and Anne L. Heinsohn, Editors. Englewood Cliffs, N.J.: Prentice-Hall, Inc., 1971, 129–46.

West, Elliot. *Growing Up in Twentieth Century America.* Westport, Conn.: Greenwood Press, 1996.

Wright, David. *America in the Twentieth Century: 1960–1969.* New York: Marshall Cavendish, 1995.

• 7 •

The 1970s

In popular culture, the Seventies are often considered a joke decade, defined by shag carpet, pet rocks, streaking, polyester leisure suits, and the thump-thump of Beethoven to a disco beat. Nevertheless, it was also a time when Americans looked seriously inward too, trying to assess the legacy of the Sixties. For older teens, it opened with the hail of National Guard gunfire which, on May 4, 1970, killed four college students at Kent State University while they held a rally to protest the Vietnam War. Colleges, and possibly even high schools, were no longer havens where kids could express themselves freely and where their parents could count on their physical safety. On the night of May 9, 1970, when hundreds of students held a vigil at the Lincoln Memorial to honor their dead, President Richard Nixon unexpectedly appeared among them, apparently in a sincere effort to understand their objections to his government, but his smiles and superficial remarks only underscored the impossibility of such understanding between the generations at this time.

POLITICS AND NATIONAL EVENTS

The flawed presidency of Richard M. Nixon forever marked Seventies politics. Swept into office for a second term by a landslide victory in 1972, having defeated the young people's antiwar candidate George McGovern of South Dakota, Nixon had already set in motion the events that forced his resignation. His vice president, Spiro Agnew, had to resign in less than a year because of financial improprieties. The Watergate story was breaking in the *Washington Post*. Although his efforts to open conversations with China won him the approval of the public, the 1971 leak to the press and public of the so-called Pentagon Papers, a series of documents about the handling of the Vietnam War, did nothing positive for his reputation. By 1974 he was out of office. By 1975 Saigon and Cambodia had fallen to the Communists, and Americans had, in effect, withdrawn from a war they could not win.

Watergate Scandal

The word Watergate has come to symbolize governmental dirty tricks, illegality, rumor, and the disgrace and resignation of a president. In fact, the Watergate is an elegant Washington, D.C., hotel, office complex, and apartment building which in 1972 housed the headquarters of the Democratic National Committee. On the night of June 17, 1972, five men broke into those headquarters in search of information that would damage the Democrats. When they were arrested, a story began to unfold which riveted, amazed, and disturbed the whole country. The complex tale has been told many times; the names of the participants are famous well into the Nineties. H. R. Haldeman, E. Howard Hunt, G. Gordon Liddy, John Mitchell, John Dean III, and John Erlichman all worked for President Nixon. By the end of the debacle, many of these, and others, had confessed in return for immunity to prosecution, or had resigned or been indicted for their part in the break-in and the subsequent cover-up ordered by Nixon. Nixon himself exacerbated the situation by firing the special prosecutor he had appointed, refusing to turn over tapes of White House conversations about the break-in, and then by allegedly engineering a gap in the tapes when he was finally forced to relinquish them. The tapes revealed a behind-the-scenes president who was profane, arrogant, pathologically suspicious of his "enemies," and willing to engage in trickery and deceit.

In May 1973, the House began its impeachment hearings into the matter. They were nationally televised, and Americans stayed tuned in huge numbers to see what the latest revelation might be. Ultimately the House Judiciary Committee decided to impeach Nixon, but he was persuaded to resign to spare the country the ordeal of a Senate trial. He resigned on August 8, 1974, and his vice president, Gerald Ford, became president of the United States. One of his first acts was to grant a full pardon to Nixon.

Washington Post reporters Carl Bernstein and Bob Woodward were among the first to understand the significance of the Watergate break-in; they worked tirelessly to report it ethically to the American public. Their stories, which have become journalistic history, made Americans newly aware of the importance of a free press—a bright spot in an otherwise dismal series of events in American public life.

Expiration of the Selective Service Act

A signal moment for American teen boys was the 1973 expiration of the Selective Service Act, the legislation that drafted all young men into military service. Throughout the century, boys had lived with the knowledge that the army might be a part of their lives somehow. When the government elected not to renew the draft, that obligation was lifted, and although boys must still register with the Selective Service, they are no longer automatically drafted. Their futures could now be planned differently.

The Carter Presidency

Gerald Ford's bid for his own elected presidency failed in 1976 when Americans elected Georgia farmer turned governor, Jimmy Carter, a soft-spoken Democrat who lacked experience with Washington's insider politics. His open Christianity and his directness of expression appealed to American voters who were soured by Nixon's dirty political tricks. Carter tried to encourage Americans to make sacrifices for their country.

Carter, concerned about the events taking place in the Middle East, worked to bring about meetings between Israeli and Egyptian leaders at Camp David, which resulted in a peace treaty between those two nations. When the political situation in Iran erupted in revolution and sixty-three Americans were taken hostage in the American embassy in Tehran in 1979, Carter avoided hasty action and worked for a peaceful solution to the crisis, which dragged on for more than a year before the hostages were released after Carter's successor, Ronald Reagan, took office.

Environmental Concerns

The first Earth Day, held on April 22, 1970, was honored by gatherings around the country and advertising efforts to make people aware of various local and national risks to the air, water, and forests. Advocates of composting, saving, recycling, and preservation encouraged all Americans to do their part. The decade saw the emergence of such environmental groups as Greenpeace and Friends of the Earth; a number of folk-rock stars—Arlo Guthrie, Joan Baez, and Harry Chapin, among others—added their voices to the movement (Stein 1985, 15–16). Unlike some of the activism movements of the Sixties, this one involved teens and young adults no matter what their politics.

Teens were also directly affected by the 1973 oil embargo imposed by the Organization of Petroleum Exporting Countries (OPEC) on the United States during the Arab-Israeli War (Bondi 1995, 128–30). Prices at the gas pump soared to new highs making Americans aware of their heavy dependence on fossil fuels and of the lack of alternatives. They also made Japanese cars more popular in the United States because they got better mileage to the gallon.

More serious personal dangers came to national attention with the Karen Silkwood case, the pollution of Love Canal, and the crisis at Three Mile Island. Karen Silkwood, a young woman working in a nuclear parts factory in Oklahoma in 1972, became convinced that the factory was not properly run. As she was going public with her accusations, she was killed mysteriously in a car accident, prompting suspicion that she being silenced. Love Canal, a community near Niagara, New York showed an alarmingly high incidence of cancer among its residents. After the air and water in the area had been repeatedly tested by local, state, and federal agencies, in 1978 the State Health Commissioner acknowledged the presence of toxic chemicals, apparently dumped in the Thirties and Forties (Bondi 1995, 489–490). The following year, the Three-Mile Island nuclear power plant near Harrisburg, Pennsylvania experienced a failure that almost led to meltdown. During the crisis nearby residents were assured that they were in no danger.

Women's and Minority Activism

The feminist movement moved ahead quickly during the Seventies, capitalizing with mixed success on the gains women made during the Sixties. Shirley Chisholm, the first black woman elected to the U.S. House of Representatives, announced that she was a candidate for president in the 1972 election. She knew she would lose, but she announced that she was only the first to try; many others would follow. Women entered state legislatures three times more frequently than ever before between 1969 and 1982 (Stein 1985, 13). The case of *Roe v. Wade* came before the U.S. Supreme Court in the early Seventies; in a decision that was a mixed victory for women, the Court in 1973 affirmed a woman's right to choose abortion in the first trimester of pregnancy, but created greater regulations in the second trimester, and even stricter regulation in the third trimester (Bondi 1995, 294). The federal Equal Rights Amendment, amending the Constitution to acknowledge women's equality with men before the law, started strong. Thirty states had ratified it by 1973; however, it did not gain the necessary numbers by the ten-year deadline, which was a severe disappointment to many women and evidence of how sensitive an issue women's rights remained.

New black leaders filled the gap left by the death of Martin Luther King, Jr.: Ralph Abernathy, Julian Bond, Andrew Young, and Jesse Jackson worked hard for civil rights throughout the decade. César Chávez mobilized farm workers, especially Hispanics, and, in 1975, won the guarantee of their right to vote for a union of their choice. Dee Brown's 1971 history of the American West through Indian eyes, *Bury My Heart at Wounded Knee*, made all Americans more sympathetic to the plight of Native Americans as they also fought for equality under the law. For six days in 1972, a group of Native Americans occupied the Washington building which housed the Bureau of Indian Affairs, as a protest against what they regarded as official neglect (Bondi 219). In 1973, a group of militant Native Americans instituted what came to be called the "Second Battle of Wounded Knee." In memory of the 1890 massacre of a group of Sioux in the South Dakota village of Wounded Knee, the militants once again occupied the village, holding off law enforcement officers for two months as a dramatic statement about the continuing mistreatment of the Native American in this country.

Although the Seventies were popularly dubbed the "Me generation," these movements show that many Americans were working with others to better themselves. Arthur Stein, in *Seeds of the Seventies*, comments that the key word in the Sixties was "counterculture"; in the Seventies it became "alternative": "Developing alternatives to existing institutions and values was emphasized rather than merely being against those which one did not like" (1985, 9).

Religion

The decade of the Seventies saw great fragmentation in religious practice, especially among teens. Some, of course, remained with their traditional church practice, but many were drawn to alternative worship based on Eastern cultures. Their presence in public parks, airports, and streets became a common sight during the Seventies. The Hare Krishnas and Buddhists offered various forms of meditation and chanting, as well as communal living which promised physical as well as spiritual security to searching young people; many of the converts to such religions were recovering addicts, but many others were disaffected Christians who believed the established Church had sold out to those in political power. Some of the groups adopted a more fundamental style of Christianity, based on a combination of Old Testament practice, New Testament faith in Jesus, and hippie gentleness and communal life. The followers were often referred to as "Jesus freaks." In some of these religions, drugs were occasionally used to achieve visions or as acts of faith.

Television comedian and writer Steve Allen explored such a group of believers firsthand when his son, Brian, then in his early twenties, joined the Love Family in Seattle in 1971. His book *Beloved Son* (1982) details his struggle to understand Brian's decision, one that ultimately seemed to bring Brian much happiness. Other parents, who had completely lost contact with their children who had adopted such religions, made efforts to recapture and "deprogram" their teens, getting them psychological help to free them from what they saw as a kind of hypnotic enslavement. The most worrisome of the cults, or at least the one which seemed to attract the most public attention, was that organized by the Reverend Sun Myung Moon, a Korean who attracted many hundreds of followers among the young. He required strict observance of a number of rules regarding marriage, diet, and living arrangements, as well as transferring all earthly goods to his church and ultimately to him.

Some of the groups were more openly political. The Rastafarians, a group which originated in Jamaica in the beliefs of Marcus Garvey, appealed to black youth because its message, spread through reggae music, spoke out for the homeless and underprivileged. The dreadlock hairstyle popularized by Bob Marley, the avoidance of alcohol, the use of marijuana, and the belief that Ethiopian emperor Haile Selassie was the Living God and that blacks are innately superior to whites, being descended from the Israelites, are a few of the tenets of Rastafarianism (Wallechinsky 1995, 733).

The Reverend Jim Jones began his ministry in the 1950s with a focus on public service, which attracted both black and white converts. He soon began to claim that he could raise the dead and cure cancer. He established a large congregation in California where his church, the People's Temple, offered many services and where Jones became a political figure with a rapidly growing following, the majority of whom were African Americans, in the Seventies. By then he had established a commune called Jonestown, in Guyana, in northern South America, and rumors were beginning to surface about his use of drugs to control his followers, among other punitive measures and crimes. In October 1977 he went to Guyana and sealed off his commune from the outside world, perhaps planning a mass suicide. When a team of investigators flew into Jonestown in November, they were prevented from leaving by gunfire. Several, among them three newspapermen and a congressman, were killed but others escaped. On November 18, 1977, Jones gathered his more than 900 followers, many of them children, and ordered them to consume fruit-flavored drinks laced with cyanide. Several, including Jones himself, were shot trying to escape.

Jesus Christ Superstar

It is a sign of the times that the most popular theatrical production and one of the most popular albums of the decade were the rock opera *Jesus Christ Superstar*, with music by Andrew Lloyd Webber and lyrics by Tim Rice. In this retelling of the story of Jesus, his disciples, and his crucifixion, the focus was on Judas as a man sincerely troubled by the hysteria surrounding Jesus. Webber and Rice composed dramatic and lyrical rock music for all the performers, among them the popular "I Don't Know How to Love Him," sung by Mary Magdalene as she struggles with her strange attraction to Jesus. In an unusual reversal, the music was released first as an album in 1971; its popularity led to the stage production soon afterward. Companies toured the country presenting the show to audiences everywhere, sometimes causing discomfort to traditional religious leaders who believed its depiction of Christ was irreverent. By 1973 a film version had been produced.

Patricia Hearst

Between February 4, 1974, and September 1975, Americans were fascinated, puzzled, and frightened by the saga of nineteen-year-old heiress Patty Hearst. She was kidnapped from her Berkeley apartment by a group calling itself the Symbionese Liberation Army (SLA), a revolutionary group that apparently espoused violence to bring attention to the plight of "the people." They requested a ransom of $4 million in food for the poor, which her parents paid. After a frantic two-month hunt for her, she released a picture of herself wearing a beret and holding a rifle; her name was now Tania. In May 1974, she was photographed brandishing an M1 rifle while robbing a bank in San Francisco, shouting out, "This is Tania, Patricia Hearst." Shortly thereafter, she released a long statement explaining her motives and insisting she had not been brainwashed. She denounced her parents and her fiancé, calling them pigs and herself a "good soldier."

When the SLA hideout was discovered and burned down during a shoot-out, the country waited to see if Hearst had died in the fire, but she had not been in the building. When she was finally captured, unhurt, a year later, she identified herself as an "urban guerrilla" and gave the closed-fist sign for revolution with her manacled hands as she was driven away, smiling for the cameras, in a police car. During her trial, she seemed to change back into Patricia. She was convicted of armed robbery and sentenced to seven years in prison. Her sentence was later commuted by President Carter. With the help of journalist Alvin Moscow she wrote a memoir of her experience in 1988 called *Patty Hearst: Her Own Story.*

TEENS AT HOME

The stereotypical Seventies home was a ranch-style split-level with a two-car garage, a den or rec room, shag carpet throughout (even in the bathrooms), and avocado-colored kitchen appliances. Teens in the family had their own rooms complete with stereo systems and poster-decorated walls and, increasingly, a telephone. Also increasingly, mothers worked outside the home.

Radio and Television

Radio for teens in the Seventies generally consisted of afternoon disc jockey formats which played Top 40 hits such as those by James Taylor or Elton John, or late night music shows playing alternative music like heavy metal or New Wave. Radios became more portable than ever; the small ones got even smaller with developments in transistor technology, but some teens preferred larger ones with powerful speakers that amplified bass sounds. These "boom boxes," which became a fixture on urban streets, are often associated with black youth (another name for them was "bro boxes," playing on African-American slang for "brother"). One of the curiosities of Seventies radio was New York disc jockey Ted Brown's experiment in getting drunk (Wilson and Wilson 1975, 146–48). In an effort to demonstrate the dangers of drinking and driving—or doing anything else that requires concentration—Brown drank a fifth of Scotch on the air, on July 4, 1974, and continued doing his show while police officers and a nurse monitored his blood alcohol level, pulse, and blood pressure. His slurred speech, slow reactions, forgetfulness (he was unable to remember his own phone number), and missed cues (his earphones were on backwards) were funny but dramatic proof of the damage alcohol can do.

The television drama that broke new ground for miniseries aired twice in the Seventies. In 1977 the twelve-hour version of Alex Haley's *Roots* kept television audiences fascinated for eight consecutive evenings as they watched the saga of a family of slaves taken from their home in West Africa in the 1700s through the end of the Civil War. In 1979 the fourteen-hour version took the family into the 1970s when author Haley, who had worked for years to trace his ancestry, heard the story of his ancestor from a storyteller in West Africa.

Lighter family television shows included *Gunsmoke, The Mary Tyler Moore Show, The Wonderful World of Disney*, and *The Sonny and Cher Show*, starring pop rock performers Sonny Bono and his glamorous, deadpan wife Cher, whose slinky outfits and comic talent made her a popular hit. *The Brady Bunch*, which ran from 1969 until 1973, was a comedy about a blended family. The older siblings, Marcia and Greg, had the usual teen troubles added to the adjustments they had to make at home. Eventually, in what seemed an inevitable transition during the Seventies, the family formed a rock band. *The Partridge Family* (1970–1973) also concerned a family rock group; young David Cassidy became a teenybopper idol thanks to his performances on this show. In 1976 Donny Osmond also attracted the adulation of young teen girls on the show *Donny and Marie*, on which he starred with his teenage sister until 1979. Jim Henson's Muppets, which had become popular with children during the Sixties on *Sesame Street*, entered prime-time television in 1976 with a series of clever shows starring such pop icons as Raquel Welch and Elton John.

On their own, older teens might prefer *Starsky and Hutch*, a violent show about two detectives in Southern California; *Hawaii Five-O*, with its beautiful settings and well-written plots which followed the criminal more than the detective work; or *Charlie's Angels*, about three glamorous girls doing undercover police work. Younger teens liked *The Six Million Dollar Man* and its spin-off *The Bionic Woman*, about two people with artificial, super-powered body parts who lend their skills to the government to fight crime and espionage. One of the most curious things about these shows was their suggestion of rapid action, especially super-fast running, by the use of slow-motion photography. The comic book character Wonder Woman had her own show from 1974 to 1977, starring Lynda Carter as the statuesque Diana Prince who could transform herself into the patriotic, crime-fighting super heroine.

Two of the most famous shows of the century debuted in the Seventies. They had broad appeal because of their intelligent scripts, excellent ensemble performances, and wry humor. *M*A*S*H*, based on the trend-setting 1970 Robert Altman film about medics in Korea, ran from 1972 until 1983 and continues well into the late 1990s in reruns; its final first-run episode was a national event. *All in the Family*, based on an English hit television show, centers around a bigoted husband and father, Archie Bunker, who is always running afoul of his more liberal wife, daughter, and son-in-law. Archie's insults and crude terms for ethnic groups were balanced by his basically soft heart. The show captured with wit and sensitivity the conflicts between adults who had grown up in the Forties when America was always right, and their Sixties children who hated the Vietnam War and worked for civil rights.

The number-one show for the 1976–1977 season, however, was quite different. *Happy Days* looked backward to the Fifties, when teens worried about dating and cars rather than about backing a political candidate. Set in the Midwest, it focuses on high school student Richie Cunningham (played by Ron Howard), who distinctly resembles the comic-book character Archie. The show's theme song was the Fifties hit "Rock Around the Clock," which played while the opening credits showed a 45-rpm record spinning in a juke box. The public's favorite character soon became "Fonzie," Richie's greaser friend, played by Henry Winkler, with his ducktailed and pompadoured hair, his black leather jacket and tight jeans, and his ultra-cool swagger. His trademark greeting—thumbs-up and "Aaaaaay!"—became a pop icon.

A spin-off from an episode of *Happy Days*, the 1978 series *Mork and Mindy* introduced comic actor Robin Williams to the public as an alien living in Boulder, Colorado, trying to understand the strange ways of humans. More serious science fiction fans rejoiced that *Star Trek* reruns were being carried by more than 140 American stations and in forty-seven other countries by 1976 (Brown 1992, 532).

Comic Strips

Three strips introduced in the Seventies provided humorous images of the lives of teens and young adults. "Funky Winkerbean," introduced in 1972 and continuing in the late 1990s, centers around Funky himself, the quin-tessential average high school kid at Westview High. He has the usual trou-bles with girls, teachers, parents, and buddies but generally comes out okay. Funky's creator, Tom Batiuk, turned to cartooning after a short career as a high school teacher, and he draws on his own experience for his gentle plots, sometimes returning to his old high school for ideas (Horn 1996, 126).

"Cathy," a chunky young woman with long straight hair and her heart on her shirt, first appeared in 1976 trying to live as a single girl and juggling dating, job, weight, sweetly interfering parents, and frequent trips to cloth-ing stores. Even while her frustrations mount, she remains cheerful, or at least wryly optimistic. One of the cleverest elements of the strip is Cathy's encounters with the latest fashions in shoes, dresses, or—every spring—bathing suits. Creator Cathy Guisewite uses her own experience as a single working woman; her popular, simply drawn alter ego appears, in the late Nineties, in books and greeting cards and on T-shirts as well as in the news-paper.

Garry Trudeau began publishing "Doonesbury" in 1970, while student unrest and protest were still on the front page. His strip brought together a group of college-student types: Mike Doonesbury, a bumbling under-graduate who makes poor grades and cannot get a date; B. D., a football player (and a reference to Brian Dowling, star quarterback at Yale) who always appears in his helmet and is often accompanied by his dizzy girlfriend Boopsie; Zonker Harris, a laid-back hippie and sometime disc jockey; and Mark Slackmeyer, the campus radical. Soon Uncle Duke was added—an aging swindler and druggie who is always hatching plots to make money illegally. Eventually the strip included a Vietnamese and a Congresswoman, among many others.

Trudeau's liberal political views continued to inform the strip through the Eighties, during the conservative Reagan and Bush administrations; Presi-dent Bush was often depicted as a blank space occupied only by a feather. Some newspapers believed Doonesbury was too political for the comic pages and printed it on the editorial page, a practice that continues into the Nine-ties with some papers. In 1975 Trudeau won the Pulitzer Prize for editorial cartooning, an award that irritated many professional editorial cartoonists, since, unlike them, he did not have to submit his work to editors for daily approval and was not limited to a single panel. His characters, nevertheless, throughout the Seventies and Eighties, have accurately reflected the changes in American life and politics since the upheavals of the Sixties.

TEENS AT SCHOOL

The social upheavals of the Sixties lingered in the high schools during the Seventies. In many areas, busing was controversial as communities struggled to attain racial balance. Drug and alcohol use created difficult situations

Senior class officers posing outside Pendleton High School, Pendleton, South Carolina, 1977. Reproduced courtesy of Pendleton High School.

when students came to class drunk or stoned. Complaints about the oppressive, rule-driven atmosphere in high school clashed with parents' need to know their children were safe when they went to school.

High School

On a typical school day, the schedule was divided into seven forty-minute periods. Students would move from room to room as they took different classes: English, social studies, foreign language, speech, mathematics, science, and so on. They sat in rows facing front, listening to the teacher's presentation. After-school activities included chorus, band, and athletics. Students were not allowed to wander the hallways; passes were generally monitored carefully. Often seniors took the privilege, legitimately or not, of leaving the school grounds for lunch or a break. Student smoking was confined to the restrooms and monitored, successfully or unsuccessfully, by teachers. In some schools, students were tracked: placed into special sections or subjects depending on their test scores.

In the early Seventies, University of Michigan Professor Philip A. Cusick attended a high school daily for six months as part of a study to delineate the difference in perspective between a teacher and a student in a typical high school. What he noticed most was the students' dependence on their friends, in class and out. The athletes formed a particular group of boys who tended to make their own rules. Boys who flunked classes, who stole or who forged credit card signatures, or who cut classes routinely, formed a group. The same students tended to get power and maintain it, in student-run shows and in student government. Students had a lounge, but instead of providing unity it generated problems of noise, messiness, and disagreement with the administration on how it should be maintained. Cusick was very aware of a few students who were "isolates," friendless and often the butt of jokes. Most students were often simply unaware of other students who were not in their particular groups: the students "are left to create their own world, and it is a social world of groups, cliques, and friendships. In that setting, to be an isolate is extremely difficult" (1973, 173). As an organization, Cusick believed, the school was no help because it excluded students from real decision making.

Middle School

Although it had begun in the Sixties, the middle school became an established phenomenon during the Seventies. The concept of the junior high school emerged in the early decades of the century, as a kind of "introduction" to high school. Before this, schools were divided into six elementary grades and six high school grades (Wiles and Bondi 1993, 55). As school attendance increased through the century, as physical adolescence lengthened, and as students stayed in school longer, the different educational needs of, for example, students in the seventh grade and students in the eleventh grade became more noticeable.

By the Sixties new words had been invented for these younger students—"preadolescent," "tweenager," "transescent," "preteen"—and new methods of teaching them developed. The term middle school emphasized a separate identity, a school and group of students not "junior" to anything but in transition. By 1966 there were 499 middle schools in the nation. Between 1970 and 1981, the number increased from 1,001 to 6,003 (Kellough, Kellough, and Hough 1993, 7). The school might begin with grade 4, 5, or 6, and end with grade 6, 7, or 8, and would ideally be organized differently from either the elementary school or the high school. Its chief task was to ease these "tweenagers" through their personal and educational adjustments to adolescence (Wiles and Bondi 1993, 10–11).

TEENS AT WORK

The trends in student employment that had begun in the Sixties accelerated during the Seventies. The need for late-afternoon and evening part-time workers in food service jobs, department stores, and grocery stores was amply met by high school students seeking extra cash to spend on cars, gas, albums, movies, clothes, fast food, beer, and sometimes drugs. Most of these jobs were in the suburbs, where white, middle-class teens were plentiful; minority teens in urban areas, who might need to ride the bus to work or might need jobs for school or family, were most often out of luck. Nor did such work prepare students for the adult working world. Teens in these jobs mostly saw other teens and very seldom had any part in the management of the business, or even saw the boss. Working twenty hours a week, as some did, also made inroads on schoolwork. Some teens still babysat, worked in family businesses, acted as counselors in summer camps, or did volunteer work in addition to their school activities.

FASHION

By the mid-Seventies, the hippie look had lost much of its symbolism as a political statement and had become more widely fashionable. In high schools, dress codes were relaxed. Students who had remained true to the preppie look during the Sixties began to wear bell-bottom jeans and sport long hair or Afros. Ironically, however, this was also the decade when designer labels became more important to both boys and girls, especially on jeans. After all, comments Ellen Melinkoff, designers had to "keep the coffers flowing," so they made minor changes in their jeans so teens would have to buy new ones to keep in style: "Tight cigarette legs one year, stovepipes the next, then cuffed, then baggy, then baggy with a tight cuff, we played musical jeans. If you wore a pair for too long, you were out of it" (Melinkoff 1984, 178–79). Tom Wolfe, chronicler of the upper classes in the Seventies, called the styles of the early decade "Funky Chic," symbolized especially by the debutante in "blue jeans and her blue work shirt, open to the sternum, with her long pre-Raphaelite hair parted on top of the skull, uncoiffed but recently washed and blown dry" (Wolfe 1976, 199) and refusing to participate in the usual debutante balls.

Among more middle-class teen girls, mini dresses and skirts were more common; younger teens wore them with knee socks or panty hose and chunky shoes. Clingy jersey fabric became the favorite for such dresses. The maxi look—long skirts with boots, ethnic-print long dresses, or long coats worn over minidresses and high boots—appealed to older teens and young adults, as did close-fitting wrap dresses. Hot pants—very short, tight shorts in fabrics like velvet and satin—worn with boots were a brief fad for party wear, as were platform shoes. Shorts made from cut-off denim jeans made good casual wear. Actress Ali MacGraw made knit cloche hats popular; worn pulled low over the eyebrows, they showed off the long, straight hair that was stylish. Some girls even ironed each other's hair on an ironing board to achieve the look. Another popular hairstyle was the "shag" cut—layers of short hair over long. The most desired (but hardest to achieve) version of it was worn by actress Farrah Fawcett, whose style was widely imitated and

Ethnic fashion, Pendleton, South Carolina, teens, 1977.
Reproduced courtesy of Pendleton High School.

whose sexy, California-girl image appeared on one of the most popular celebrity posters of the decade. Diane Keaton's look in the 1977 film *Annie Hall* also created a popular clothing style for older teens based on loose-fitting menswear—trousers, vests, and ties, ideally worn with a rolled-brim hat pulled low on the forehead. Black girls and boys turned to natural or ethnic looks.

Boys' styles loosened up considerably during this decade. Along with bell-bottom jeans worn low on the hips and held with wide belts, boys wore tight-fitting shirts made of printed jersey in wild colors and patterns, or pastel cotton shirts which still fitted very close through the body and had very wide collars. Ties widened and became more colorful. Sneakers were good for casual wear and short boots for other occasions. Some teen boys also wore platform shoes. Longer hair meant that many boys as well as girls began using handheld blow-dryers to achieve the right hairstyle.

Although the classic suit-and-tie look for more formal occasions continued, the new "leisure suit" gave boys and men new options. Usually cut with slightly bell-bottomed trousers and tight through the hips, with wide jacket lapels, they required no tie—only a wide-collared shirt and sometimes a buttoned-up vest. Made of synthetic fabrics in light colors, even pastels

The prom, Villa Madonna Academy, Covington, Kentucky, 1972. Reproduced courtesy of Villa Madonna Academy.

or white, the look has become an instantly recognizable symbol of the Seventies, especially as worn by John Travolta in the movie about the disco craze, *Saturday Night Fever*. Prom wear often included a ruffled shirt with the standard tuxedo.

Girls who enjoyed going to discos, or who wanted to look as if they went to discos, also dressed up more for evening, in short, flounced dresses and high-heeled sandals that looked good on the dance floor. Some teens preferred the long, ethnic look for evening, with puffed sleeves, ruffles, and ribbons. Even with jeans, girls' underwear became more varied in color and fabric; the teddy, a one-piece undergarment that was usually decorated with lace and cut high on the leg, became popular in the Seventies.

SLANG

Teen slang in the Seventies was lively and diverse, characterized somewhat less by black street talk and drug patois than it had been in the Sixties, although there were still plenty of original expressions for drugs and their use. Marijuana might be called alfalfa, doobage, or tweed.

The television show *Star Trek* spawned the expression, "Beam me up, Scotty," used when you wanted to get out of an awkward situation; the response was "There's no intelligent life down here." Tom Dalzell describes specialized Seventies slang—Chicano, surfing, and Deadhead—as well, in his book *Flappers 2 Rappers*. Deadhead slang marked the user as a fan of the Grateful Dead rock group; their expressions captured the experience of a Dead concert—fans wearing their "Dead threads," the "runner" who sprints in to get the best seats for his friends, the "space dancers" who moved to the music, the "fanning" or "scrubbing" techniques Jerry Garcia used on his guitar (Dalzell 1996, 180–81).

In less specialized Seventies slang, a stupid or inept person was an airhead, dip, nerd, dingleberry, or dork. A weak person was a wimp. You might greet someone with "What it is?" or "Yo" or "What's going down?" Instead of goodbye you might say "Catch you later." If you were drunk you were blitzed, bombed, plastered, polluted, or juiced—probably on too much brew (beer) and later would probably barf (throw up). If you ate a lot, you had greased down, blimped out, or porked out. A pretty girl was a fox; if she had a great bod (figure), the frat rats were sure to check her out (fraternity guys were sure to look closely at her).

Tom Wolfe, whose fiction and essays captured the upper-class Seventies life, especially what he called the "Me" syndrome, explains that the Eastern prep school teen had his own style of speech, characterized by the "honk"—"lifting every vowel . . . up over the roof of his palate and sticking them into his nose and honking them out without moving his lower jaw" (1976, 217). Honks then were those prep school students who talked like that. "Wonks" referred to "all those who did not have the 'honk' voice—i.e. all who are non-aristocratic" (218). Prep school girls who were honks naturally preferred to date other honks.

LEISURE ACTIVITIES AND ENTERTAINMENT

Three of the distinctive fads of the Seventies were quite athletic. Jogging began its climb to the most pervasive health phenomenon of the late twentieth century, beginning the craze for aerobic—fat-burning—exercise and healthy foods. Along with the interest in Eastern religions and philosophy came a fascination with the martial arts—judo, karate, tai chi chuan, aikido, and others—which combine self-defense, exercise, and meditation. The unity of mind and body, the formality and ritual of the classes, and the excitement of battle give great appeal to these exercises, as well as the opportunity for both genders and all ages to participate. They were popularized on television in their more meditative forms in the series *Kung Fu* (1971–1973) and in the films of Bruce Lee and Chuck Norris, who emphasized the violent aspects of the martial arts. The silliest fad of the Seventies was streaking—running nude through a crowded public place. College boys did it on a dare, dashing through football stadiums at halftime trying to outrun the guards and police.

Just hanging around—or hanging out or goofing around—was still a major leisure activity for many teen boys, who, unlike girls, could enjoy a life on the streetcorner with their buddies without stigma. In 1975 and 1976 sociologist James P. Leary, who hung out with some teens in Bloomington, Indiana, observed that their hanging out was of two kinds. Several times a week, after 9 P.M., they gathered in the A & P parking lot, some in cars and trucks, to swap stories, listen to music, show off their driving, and smoke. Sometimes they were drunk. Sometimes girls would join their boyfriends or drive by in cars of their own. The conversation was loud and obscene, often bragging about girls, specifically about exaggerated sexual activity and conquests. It was a performance for the public, including the watchful police and the nervous storekeepers, and boys who were good at it gained popularity. Other evenings, though, they gathered in backyards or basements and told stories more for each other than the public, sometimes smoking marijuana as an accompaniment. Leary found it especially interesting that in these gatherings, the boys sometimes reverted to telling kids' jokes and stories, such as fractured nursery rhymes with dirty meanings, which they would never do in the parking lot (1980, 298–99). As he listened to these boys, he came to admire their conversational abilities: "Although existing apart from, and often in opposition to, the 'educated' middle class, these working class males are not cretinous louts; the breadth and sophistication of their verbal art argues otherwise" (299).

Dating and Sex

For the majority of Seventies teens, the dating pattern of boy asks/girl accepts continued. Being seen with the right person was generally more important than spending time with that person. Informal activities still consisted of cruising fast food places, going to movies, and parties at teens' homes, while formal dates usually centered around proms. The casualness of the Sixties made its way into dating life as well as into fashion for teens, and just "hanging out" and getting together in groups appealed to some teens more than one-on-one dates. Such activity was also cheaper for teens who had to earn spending money by working at part-time jobs.

For teens who used them, group activities also facilitated acquiring drugs and alcohol. Drug use was on the rise, jumping 13% between 1972 and 1979 among white twelve- to seventeen-year-olds (Mirel 1991, 1161). When teens in 1977 were asked what they felt the greatest problem facing them was, 27% said drug abuse (adapted from Chadwick and Heaton 1996, 220). Lloyd Johnston, writing for the Institute for Social Research at the University of Michigan in 1973, pointed out that drugs could no longer be considered a problem of minorities, nor could the stereotype of the drugged-out dropped-out high school user who ends up on the fringes of society be other than a misconception. Illicit drug use "has reached all sectors—rich and poor; rural suburban, and urban; black and white; college and non-college. The only sector with which we can primarily associate illicit drug use is the young—it is the phenomenon of a generation" (1973, 214–15). The question of whether to legalize marijuana was very much in the forefront, aggravating fears that its use would dramatically increase. Heroin use was already apparently on the rise among white, middle-class youth (Deschin 1972, 12–13).

Alcohol as a drug was sometimes pushed to back of the public mind because of publicity over marijuana, LSD, and hard drugs, but teens were certainly drinking. Sandra Scoppetone's 1976 teen novel *The Late Great Me* offers a disturbing image of a teen alcoholic. Some teenagers were joining Alcoholics Anonymous (Wilson and Wilson 1975, 139–42). In 1979 a survey reported that 38% of teens had consumed alcohol in the past thirty days, most of it beer although 10% reported drinking hard liquor (Adapted from Chadwick and Heaton 1996, 258).

Simon Frith, a reviewer of rock music, noticed the increase in what he called the "fantasy sexuality" of "girls at their youngest and least free stage . . . teeny boppers." They developed crushes on pop stars like David Cassidy and Donny Osmond, buying up magazines, T-shirts, and other idol-related merchandise as much as they bought the vaguely yearning songs the idols sang (1981, 226), but the rising birthrate suggests there was more than fantasy at work. Sex among younger teens, who for whatever reason did not use birth control effectively, resulted in an increase of one third in the birthrate for girls aged from ten to fourteen between 1966 and 1977 (Mirel 1991, 1162).

Among older teens, the explicit clothing and behavior of the "cock-rock" stars, such as Robert Plant of Led Zeppelin, introduced a blatant sexuality to the experience of the rock concert:

Cock-rock performers are aggressive, boastful, constantly drawing audience attention to their prowess and control. Their bodies are on display (plunging shirts and tight trousers, chest hair and genitals), mikes and guitars are phallic symbols (or else caressed like female bodies), the music is loud, rhythmically insistent, built around techniques of arousal and desire. (Frith 1981, 227)

Teen boys were being offered an image of aggressive male sexuality; girls could only watch and respond, becoming "groupies" in fantasy, or in some cases, reality, if they were able to make their way into the dressing rooms or cars of the performers.

Music and Dancing

Like many cultural elements of the Seventies, rock music spun off into a wide variety of styles, as if the intensity of the Sixties had kept a lid on it. Some see this fragmentation as negative—an inability to find the unity of motive that drove Sixties music. Others regard it as the freedom to choose, a multiplicity of voices that could not be heard before. Rock critic Simon Frith insists on the gender discrimination that marks much Seventies rock: "It is boys who form the core of the rock audience, become rock critics and collectors (girl rock fanatics become, by contrast, photographers). The rock 'n' roll discourse constructs its listeners in sexually differentiated terms— boys as public performers, girls as private consumers" (1981, 228).

Young teen girls enjoyed and screamed over Donny Osmond and David Cassidy. Among older teens, West Coast folk rock continued to be popular; Neil Young, Crosby, Stills and Nash, and James Taylor made room for Linda Ronstadt, Jackson Browne, and the Eagles. The Eagles' hits "Take It Easy," "Lyin' Eyes," and "Witchy Woman" put them at the top of the charts in the mid-Seventies, when they were selling "an incredible one million albums a month, a pace they managed to maintain for two years" (Goodman 1997, 245). Top 40 stations played Elton John, Billy Joel, Seals and Crofts, Stevie Wonder, and the Doobie Brothers. Bruce Springsteen was touted as the real comer, the "future of rock and roll" according to *Rolling Stone* (London 1984, 157), with his driving rock style and gravelly voice heard on his 1975 album *Born to Run*, although he did not live up to this promise. Barry Manilow appealed to those who wanted easy-listening, romantic ballads, as did Karen and Richard Carpenter, a brother and sister team. Richard was nineteen and Karen sixteen when they won a Hollywood Bowl musical competition; Karen was only nineteen when they signed their first major contract in 1969; soon her voice and his arrangements gave them huge hits in "Close to You" and "We've Only Just Begun." Like Manilow, they were talented musicians, but also like him, their music was often considered too "soft" for the times; nevertheless, they sold plenty of albums in the Seventies. Karen Carpenter died at age thirty-two in 1983, an early victim of what would soon become one of the most pervasive diseases among teen girls: anorexia nervosa. She literally starved herself to death.

New Wave, Art, Glitz, and Punk

Late night radio was most likely to feature New Wave or punk rock. New Wave is difficult to define; many different groups might wear the label. One feature is the use of technology—"tuned electric drums, reverb units, special studio techniques" (Dasher 1985, 88). The Talking Heads were the most famous of this group, which also includes The Cars and the British group The Police, whose lyrics and vocal leads were usually provided by the artist who called himself Sting. In the late Seventies, the university town of Athens, Georgia, became identified with New Wave sounds with the groups Pylon and B-52's.

Art rock was a theatrical form of rock which borrowed rhythms and motifs from both Western and some Eastern classical music. The Beatles began the trend in the Sixties, and it remained stronger in England than in America.

Stevie Wonder created a song cycle called "Journey into the Secret Life of Plants"; Emerson, Lake, and Palmer produced a rock version of Moussorgsky's "Pictures at an Exhibition"; and The Who had a triumph with their rock opera *Tommy*. Other groups dipped occasionally into this tradition as well, but it was pushed to its logical limits with the Heavy Metal groups, which traded on dramatic, often violent, stage effects: "The bizarre and grotesque aspects of rock reached new extremes in a number of groups that traded musical prowess for theatricality" (Dasher 1985, 88). Some called it "glitz rock." Kiss wore their faces painted in dramatic black-and-white designs, while the group Alice Cooper shocked and thrilled audiences by using boa constrictors and beheading chickens on stage, accompanied by "wall-shaking, ear-numbing, distorted, hyper-amplified" music, especially in a teen anthem called "Eighteen" (1985, 87–88). Led Zeppelin, a British group, probably the loudest, became the quintessential heavy metal group of the Seventies.

Punk rock, also a British contribution, was not just loud, but angry and "against everything" (86). The Sex Pistols set the aggressive tone with their first single, "Anarchy in the UK" and went on to embarrass the record company with its obscene language in interviews. Johnny Rotten, the lead singer, "was one of the few terrific anti-heroes rock and roll has ever produced: a violent-voiced bantam of a boy who tried to make sense of popular culture by making that culture suffer the world outside—its moral horror, its self-impelled violation, its social homicide" (Gilmore 1998, 150). By 1978 the group had disbanded and another member, Sid Vicious, had murdered his girlfriend. Their angry form of music, their bizarrely tinted spiky hairstyles, their black leather clothes, and their fad of piercing their bodies with safety pins have gone on to influence many other groups during the Seventies and Eighties, as well as many teens who want to express their disdain for society through their physical appearance.

Disco

Without doubt, when it comes to music, the Seventies are best known as the disco era. For those who value the Sixties tradition and take rock music seriously, disco was an aberration best forgotten. Certainly the trend did not last long, and the music it produced was only mildly interesting. For a while, however, probably as a reaction to Sixties music which called for political action rather than dancing and relaxation, it provided some fun and a chance to wear your best clothes and move with style.

The term, a shortened form of discotheque, a play on the French word for library, *bibliotheque*, was used to describe a place to dance to recorded music, smoothly blended by a disc jockey, so that the beat remained steady and the music never stopped. The dance style originated in Latino clubs where couples' dancing was a valued skill and social occupation, especially the style known as salsa. Van McCoy's recording "The Hustle" (1975) encouraged other teens to try the new steps and style. It had made its way into the mainstream popular clubs by 1977, fueled by John Travolta's performance in the film *Saturday Night Fever*. Travolta's dancing borrowed not only from Latino style but also from the athletic street dancing known as break dancing. The Bee Gees' soundtrack for the film, with the disco anthem "Stayin' Alive," was the best-selling album of 1978. The Trammps' hit "Disco Inferno" also provided plenty of opportunities for the strutting, the stylized steps, and the quick turns for both boys and girls that characterized disco dancing. Singer Donna Summer became "queen of disco" with her recordings of "Last Dance" and "Hot Stuff"; British rocker Rod Stewart contributed "Do Ya Think I'm Sexy?"

The music of disco reached some strange proportions when it transformed classical pieces by Beethoven or Mozart as well as standard pop songs into the steady 4/4 beat required for disco dancing. Perhaps the skill required of the dancers—they had to know specific steps, not just move around at will—made disco too complicated for real enjoyment among teens who just wanted to have fun and had gotten accustomed to the free-style dancing that came in with the Sixties. Moreover, the music lacked soul. Mechanically produced, it was a music "virtually without roots" (Paymer 1993, 86). It had "all the ingredients of a well-oiled machine" (London 1984, 146). So did what was called "robot dancing," which had a brief popularity in the mid-Seventies. Couples "wide-eyed and expressionless" moved and then stopped in place "like robots suddenly switched off." The group Devo, in goggles and jumpsuits, demonstrated the style in their performances (1984, 147).

Funk and Reggae

Disco was almost exclusively a white phenomenon; funk was the black version of disco. George Clinton was the artist most associated with funk and "funkadelic" music. His song "Think . . . It Ain't Illegal Yet" contained the line, "A mind is a terrible thing to waste."

Reggae, like punk, was born in response to social conditions among the poor. With punk, the impetus was blue-collar England; with reggae, it was the poor in Jamaica, many of whom immigrated to England, where things were not much better for them. The origin of the word is unknown, but the music's focus was clear. Reggae expressed concern for the homeless and poor through its lyrics, which were full of symbols from the Rastafarian religion and were accompanied by a steady rock beat similar to Jamaican "ska" music. Bob Marley and the Wailers is by far the best known reggae band to emerge during the Seventies. Marley himself was so politically active and outspoken, working tirelessly to bring a message of peace and unity to his fans, that he was almost assassinated in 1976. In 1978 he won the International Peace Medal, and died of cancer in 1981.

Country Music

Rock and roll had robbed country music of a good percentage of its audience in the Fifties, when the hybrid sound known as rockabilly began to attract teens. During the Sixties and Seventies, country music found ways to widen its audience once again. By softening the twang that characterized classic country, minimizing guitars, and even adding strings at times, record producers invented the Nashville sound. A number of country artists enjoyed new popularity as a result. Loretta Lynn became a country superstar during the Seventies thanks not only to her songwriting abilities: "the media caught on to her blunt yet thoroughly loveable personality, with not a hint of polish or packaging" (*Comprehensive Country Music Encyclopedia* 1994, 221). Married at age fourteen in 1949, Loretta knew firsthand about women's problems, and she spoke right up through her music (like "The Pill" in 1975) and on talk shows. In 1976 she published her autobiography, *Coal Miner's Daughter*, which became a hit film in 1980 and made her an even bigger star. Young Australian singer Olivia Newton-John had a string of country hits between 1973 and 1978; at the same time, she was topping the charts with pop tunes. She is the perfect example of a crossover artist; some of the more traditional country singers resented them, but such singers were a sign of the times.

Elvis

In 1977 Elvis Presley died at the age of forty-two, "a victim of drugs and self-indulgence" (London 1984, 145). He had spent his last years giving performances in Las Vegas, becoming almost a parody of himself with his increasingly obese body crammed into tight, sparkly suits and capes, his flirting with women in the audience, and his sweating vocals. For many, though, he was still the king. John Rockwell wrote in the *New York Times* that every rock singer owed something to Presley. Despite the more sophisticated artistry others might have brought to rock music, Rockwell said, Elvis

was and remained a working-class hero, a man who arose from obscurity and transformed American popular music in answer to his own needs—and who may possibly have been destroyed by the isolation that being an American celebrity sometimes entails. He was as much a metaphor as a maker of music, and one of telling power and poignancy. (Quoted in London 1984, 144–145)

Movies

A 1974 article written by Edwin Miller for *Seventeen* magazine warned teens away from the nostalgia that seemed to be afflicting Hollywood's Seventies image of teens: "Young people have become troublesome in recent years. Even nice kids. Who could seem more wholesome than little Linda Blair when first seen in *The Exorcist*? But on the verge of adolescence, she's suddenly possessed by the devil!" (1974, 144). Moviemakers re-create teens from the past: "If you have a teen-ager pinned down in the past like a butterfly under glass, you've got the upper hand" (128).

This is certainly an accurate characterization of a number of Seventies films, beginning with *American Graffiti* (1973), which focused on a group of teens graduating from high school in 1962 and made Harrison Ford a star. Nineteen seventy-eight brought *The Buddy Holly Story*, with Gary Busey playing the Fifties rock star; *I Wanna Hold Your Hand*, about a group of teens trying to get into the *Ed Sullivan Show* to see the Beatles; and *American Hot Wax*, which traced the career of Fifties disc jockey Alan Freed.

When Hollywood was not being nostalgic about teens, it was being horrific about them. *Carrie* (1976), based on a novel written by Stephen King, depicted arrogant teens who were thoughtless toward a mousy girl; she finally wreaks a violent revenge with her telekinetic powers. *Halloween* in 1978 set the tone for a whole series of horror films showing teens as victims of nightmarish psychopathic killers, a trend which continued well into the Eighties. *The Exorcist* (1973), based on a novel written by William Peter Blatty, one of the scariest films of all time, centers on a twelve-year-old girl experiencing demonic possession. Such films play on society's fears of adolescence and its incipient power to take over, as did *Blackboard Jungle* in the Fifties.

Although they were not teen films, three science fiction/fantasy films from the Seventies have become all-time hits with teen viewers. In 1977 George Lucas produced *Star Wars*, an action-packed space adventure starring Harrison Ford and Carrie Fisher that generated two sequels and many millions of dollars for its producers. The same year, audiences were fascinated and moved by Richard Dreyfuss's efforts to make contact with gentle alien beings in Steven Spielberg's imaginative *Close Encounters of the Third Kind*. In 1978 Richard Donner brought *Superman* to the big screen, starring Christopher Reeve as the Man of Steel. With a script by Mario Puzo (who wrote the novel *The Godfather*) and a huge budget, the film finally "succeeded in making comic book material respectable entertainment" (Daniels 1995, 175). Some critics complained about the film's three different sections and styles, but the action shots, excellent performances by actors in secondary roles, the remarkable flying scenes, and Reeve's charming comic touch made this film one of the hits of the decade.

Of course, the film that defines the Seventies for many is 1977's *Saturday Night Fever*, the story of a Brooklyn boy in a dead-end job who achieves stardom among his peers through his dancing abilities at the local disco. John Travolta's intense performance as Tony, and his spectacular dancing, along with the soundtrack by the Bee Gees, broke new ground in musical

John Travolta outdances Karen Lynn Gorney in *Saturday Night Fever*, 1977. Reproduced courtesy of The Museum of Modern Art.

films: instead of serving the story, the music largely created it—a trend that gathered steam during the Eighties and Nineties. Unfortunately disco also spawned what Leonard Maltin has called "perhaps the worst film ever to have won some kind of Oscar"—for Donna Summer's song "Last Dance"—*Thank God It's Friday* (1979).

Books and Reading

Some best-sellers of this decade reflect the flower-child legacy of the Sixties. In 1970 college professor Erich Segal wrote a short novel called *Love Story*, about an upper-class college boy in love with a free-spirited girl named Jenny, who dies at the end of the book. The book, a surprise hit, sold millions of copies and generated an equally popular movie starring Ali MacGraw as Jenny. Its catch phrase, "Love means never having to say you're sorry," was widely appreciated and parodied. Richard Bach's little story of a seagull searching for truth, *Jonathan Livingston Seagull*, topped fiction best-seller lists for both 1972 and 1973; it offered a gentle version of Eastern philosophy to American readers. The ethnic awareness which began in the Sixties increased with Alex Haley's 1977 novel, *Roots*, which traces the family of a slave from Africa through the Civil War. It also inspired a hugely popular television film.

In 1972 the libraries in Los Angeles explored what teens liked to read. Their survey results showed five books that were especially popular: Paul Zindel's *My Darling, My Hamburger*, Ann Head's *Mr. and Mrs. Bo Jo Jones*, Beatrice Sparks's *Go Ask Alice*, J. D. Salinger's *Catcher in the Rye*, and *Bless the Beasts and the Children* by Glen Swarthout. Books that they would recommend to others included S. E. Hinton's *The Outsiders*, Paul Zindel's *The Pigman*, J. R. R. Tolkien's *Lord of the Rings*, and Erich Segal's *Love Story* (Campbell, Davis, and Quinn 1978, 179–80)—an interesting mix of books from the Sixties, books written for the young adult market, and books written for adults. Series books continued popular in the Seventies as well, though few new ones were introduced. Teen taste, as in most things, appeared to be a little more varied than some of the media suggested.

The Seventies also saw the debut of Stephen King, who was teaching high school English in 1973 when word came that *Carrie* would be published. The character was based on a real person, a strange girl he had known when he was in high school. King's novel describes a mousy teen girl who is tormented by her schoolmates but finally exacts a dramatic revenge by using her telekinetic powers. According to King, "Carrie lives out a nightmare that all teenagers go through. Not being accepted by peers. And all high school kids are full of suppressed violence. . . . If it had any thesis to offer, this deliberate updating of 'High School Confidential,' it was that high school is a place of almost bottomless conservatism and bigotry" (Garrett and McCue 1989, 1:89).

Young Adult Literature and Censorship

The publishing phenomenon of Young Adult literature, which began in the late Sixties, reached its zenith in the Seventies as high school and public libraries mounted a campaign to reach young people who were no longer satisfied by "typical teen" romances and sports books. Sensitive and expert writers were attracted to the genre by publishers who avidly pursued the teen audience with more serious novels about teens with various personal and social difficulties.

Even a brief glance at Young Adult books published in this decade reveals a large number of what professionals would call classics of this fiction: *Run Softly, Go Fast* (Barbara Wersba 1970), *Dinky Hocker Shoots Smack* (M. E. Kerr 1972), *Summer of My German Soldier* (Bette Greene 1973), *A Day No Pigs Would Die* (Robert Newton Peck 1973), *A Hero Ain't Nothin' but a Sandwich* (Alice Childress 1973), *Rumble Fish* (S. E. Hinton 1975), *Is That You, Miss Blue?* (M. E. Kerr 1975), *Home Before Dark* (Sue Ellen Bridgers 1976), and *Father Figure* (Richard Peck 1978). One of the most disturbing of all was *Go Ask Alice* (1971), which purported to be the diary of an anonymous teen girl who became addicted to drugs. Its first-person depiction of a "nice" teen's slide into drugs and despair acknowledged the ease with which it could happen. (A few years later, writer Beatrice Sparks admitted that she had written the book [Nilsen and Donelson 1993, 70, 95].) In 1976 Sandra Scoppetone offered an entirely realistic image of a teen alcoholic in *The Late Great Me*. These books came to be called "problem novels" because they seemed to center on a teenager with a problem— divorce, drugs, alcohol—or problems associated with social life, sexual experience, and physical development. Not surprisingly, however, the books also came under fire by disapproving adult authorities, who were disturbed by the violence, the sexual frankness, and what they regarded as the crude language that appeared in some of these novels.

The major figures associated with this genre appeared during the Seventies; their books still find their way onto censorship lists well into the Nineties. Robert Cormier's *The Chocolate War* details events in a Catholic boys' school during a fund-raising sale. Violence occurs when one boy refuses to sell the chocolates, and the violence is apparently encouraged by one of the priests on the faculty. This is still one of the most controversial books marketed to teen readers. Cormier is, however, a sophisticated and skilled writer and his work is often taught in the schools despite the risks. Judy Blume's 1970 *Are You There, God? It's Me, Margaret* broke new ground for young teen girls who were interested in getting their periods and wearing bras as well as finding a religion that suited them. In 1975 she published *Forever*, the story of a teen girl's first serious love and her first sexual experience. Blume has been both the most popular author among young teen girls and the most frequently censored author in this genre, because of her frankness about sexual matters. Norma Klein's *Mom, the Wolfman, and Me* (1972) tells the story of an eleven-year-old girl whose mother had never married but who begins an affair with a man who owns a wolf hound. In 1980 she published *Breaking Up*, which is about a girl who learns that her divorced mother is a lesbian. Like Blume, Klein has a light touch along with her directness about sex, and like Blume, by the late Seventies, she found her books the target of increasing challenges from parents who did not want their children exposed to such reading.

With the increase in politically and religiously conservative groups (which the media dubbed the New Right), censorship began to increase in the latter half of the decade. In 1976 the Island Trees, New York, school board "unofficially" directed that a number of books they regarded as "anti-American, anti-Christian, anti-Semitic, and just plain filthy" be removed from the shelves of the school library. Among them were Kurt Vonnegut's *Slaughterhouse Five*, Alice Childress's *A Hero Ain't Nothin' but a Sandwich*, Richard Wright's *Black Boy*, and Beatrice Sparks's *Go Ask Alice*. When the review panel appointed by the board recommended returning the books but the board did not do so, a student, Stephen Pico, and several others brought suit against the board. The case eventually reached the U.S. Supreme Court, where it was the first such censorship case to be heard there. The decision of the justices was mixed, supporting the library's First Amendment rights but noting that the school board had the right to supervise the classroom curriculum (Nilsen and Donelson 1993, 526–28). By the early Eighties, the number of challenges to teen books had risen noticeably.

Comic Books

For many teens, comic books remained an important leisure activity—reading them, trading them, talking about them with fellow fans, and writing letters to the publishing houses complimenting or criticizing the artists or writers of their favorites. Comic fans—and they were not all boys—were among the most enthusiastic, dedicated readers among teens and young adults; their letters, as printed in the comic books, were intelligent and thorough critiques of character development, artistic style, and plot directions. Moreover, the comic writers and artists took them seriously and made efforts to incorporate their suggestions. Even *Girls' Love Stories* solicited advice from its readers on a plotline about an interracial love affair. According to the editors, the readers who "flooded the office" with their letters generally approved of the projected interracial marriage (No. 165, 1972).

In the early 1970s, Batman's sidekick Robin became a teenager. His appearance and his adventures reflected many Seventies concerns. Wearing bell-bottom jeans and a slim shirt, with his hair long, Robin entered "Hudson University," where he fought nasty fraternity guys, visited a commune, became a karate instructor, encountered some "Jesus freaks," and disguised himself as a black to spy on a rich man who treated blacks like servants. The message overall seemed to be that disparate groups needed to, and could, learn to get along with each other. At one point in these adventures, when his athletic prowess was noticed, a bystander remarks, "Wait til he's fully developed, in his twenties! He'll be even better'n Batman!" (No. 231, May 1971).

Some new characters became popular in the Seventies. Stan Lee's Spider Man, the Incredible Hulk, and DC's new offering, Swamp Thing. Both Hulk and Swamp Thing were horrific-looking creatures, transformed humans, who were "more hero than horror, and more to be pitied than feared" (Daniels 1995, 160). Both became great favorites not only with seasoned comic readers but with the public. Swamp Thing was soon featured in a 1982 film, and Hulk had his own network television series in 1978.

REFERENCES

Allen, Steve. *Beloved Son: A Story of the Jesus Cults.* Indianapolis: Bobbs-Merrill, 1982.

Bondi, Victor. *American Decades, 1970–1979.* Detroit, Mich.: Gale Research, 1995.

Brown, Dee. *Bury My Heart at Wounded Knee.* New York: Holt, Rinehart, and Winston, 1971.

Brown, Les. *Les Brown's Encyclopedia of Television.* Chicago: Gale Research, 1992.

Campbell, Patty, Pat Davis, and Jerri Quinn. "We Got There . . . It Was Worth the Trip." In *Young Adult Literature in the Seventies,* ed. Jana Varlejs. Metuchen, N.J.: Scarecrow Press, 1978.

Chadwick, Bruce A., and Jim B. Heaton. *Statistical Handbook on Adolescents in America.* Phoenix, Ariz.: Oryx, 1996.

Colbert, David, ed. *Eyewitness to America.* New York: Pantheon, 1997.

Country Music Magazine, ed. *The Comprehensive Country Music Encyclopedia.* New York: Random House, 1994.

Cusick, Philip A. *Inside High School: The Student's World.* New York: Holt, Rinehart, and Winston, 1973.

Dalzell, Tom. *Flappers 2 Rappers: American Youth Slang.* Springfield, Mass.: Merriam Webster, 1996.

Daniels, Les. *DC Comics: Sixty Years of the World's Favorite Comic Book Heroes.* Boston: Little, Brown, 1995.

Dasher, Richard T. *History of Rock Music.* Portland, Maine: J. Weston Walsh, Publisher, 1985.

Deschin, Celia S. *The Teenager in a Drugged Society.* New York: Richards Rosen Press, 1972.

Drew, Bernard A. *The 100 Most Popular Young Adult Authors: Biographical Sketches and Bibliographies.* Englewood, Colo.: Libraries Unlimited, 1997.

Eble, Connie. *Slang and Sociability: In-Group Language Among College Students.* Chapel Hill: University of North Carolina Press, 1996.

Frith, Simon. *Sound Effects.* New York: Pantheon, 1981.

Garrett, Agnes, and Helga P. McCue, eds. *Authors and Artists for Young Adults.* 6 vols. Detroit: Gale Research, 1989+.

Gilmore, Mikal. *Night Beat: A Shadow History of Rock and Roll*. New York: Doubleday, 1998.

Goodman, Fred. *The Mansion on the Hill: Dylan, Young, Geffen, Springsteen, and the Head-on Collision of Rock and Commerce*. New York: Random House, 1997.

Halliwell, Leslie, with Philip Purser. *Halliwell's Television Companion*. 2d ed. London: New York: Granada, 1982.

Horn, Maurice. *100 Years of American Newspaper Comics*. New York: Gramercy Books, 1996.

Johnston, Lloyd. *Drugs and American Youth*. Ann Arbor: Institute for Social Research, University of Michigan, 1973.

Kauz, Herman. *The Martial Spirit: An Introduction to the Origin, Philosophy, and Psychology of the Martial Arts*. Woodstock, N.Y.: Overlook Press, 1977.

Kellough, Richard, Noreen Kellough, and David L. Hough. *Middle School Teaching*. New York: Macmillan, 1993.

Leary, James P. "Recreational Talk Among White Adolescents." *Western Folklore* 39, no. 4 (1980): 284–99.

London, Herbert I. *Closing the Circle: A Cultural History of the Rock Revolution*. Chicago: Nelson-Hall, 1984.

Maltin, Leonard. *Leonard Maltin's 1998 Movie and Video Guide*. New York: Signet, 1997.

McDonnell, Janet. *America in the Twentieth Century: 1970–1979*. New York: Marshall Cavendish, 1995.

Melinkoff, Ellen. *What We Wore: An Offbeat Social History of Women's Clothing, 1950 to 1980*. New York: Quail, 1984.

Miller, Edwin. "What's Hollywood Saying to You, or Why Nostalgia?" *Seventeen* 33 (September 1974): 128+.

Mirel, Jeffrey. "Adolescence in Twentieth-Century America." In *Encyclopedia of Adolescence*, ed. Richard Lerner, Anne C. Petersen, and Jeanne Brooks-Gunn. New York: Garland, 1991.

Nilsen, Alleen Pace, and Ken Donelson, eds. *Literature for Today's Young Adults*. 4th ed. New York: HarperCollins, 1993.

Paymer, Marvin E. *Facts Behind the Songs: A Handbook of American Pop Music from the Nineties to the '90s*. New York: Garland, 1993.

Stein, Arthur. *Seeds of the Seventies: Values, Work, and Commitment in Post-Vietnam America*. Hanover, N.H.: University Press of New England, 1985.

Wallechinsky, David. *The People's Almanac Presents the Twentieth Century*. Boston: Little, Brown, 1995.

West, Mark I. *Children, Culture, and Controversy*. Hamden, Conn.: Archon, 1988.

Wiles, Jon, and Joseph Bondi. *The Essential Middle School*. New York: Macmillan, 1993.

Wilson, Morrow, and Suzanne Wilson. *Drugs in American Life*. New York: H. W. Wilson, 1975.

Wolfe, Tom. *Mauve Gloves and Madmen, Clutter and Vine*. New York: Farrar, Straus and Giroux, 1976.

The 1980s

Those who reached their teens in the late Eighties and early Nineties came to be known as Generation X, a label apparently invented by novelist Doug Coupland (himself of that generation) which expressed the public's mystification about their music, casual drug use, political apathy, cynicism about work, and taste in clothing. With the increased spending power of teens in the affluent Eighties—they could spend a staggering $45 billion per year on nonessential items—major industries, such as clothing, cosmetics, music, automobiles, and sports, fastened their attentions on the teen market with greedy enthusiasm, hiring marketers to poll them endlessly to determine their tastes and habits. Teen Research Unlimited of Northbrook, Illinois, established in 1982, was only one of the agencies devoted to polling teens. The resulting masses of figures are contradictory and difficult to put into context, but they are also often interesting and sometimes surprising.

POLITICS AND NATIONAL EVENTS

The decade opened with an event that shocked and saddened America's young people, as well as their parents who had grown up in the Sixties. In December 1980 Beatle John Lennon was shot to death outside his New York City apartment by Mark David Chapman. Lennon had spoken out strongly against the Vietnam War, but he had settled into a pleasant life with his artist wife, Yoko Ono. In fact, they had just released a joint album when he was killed. Chapman, who evidently had been stalking Lennon for some time, quoted from J. D. Salinger's *Catcher in the Rye* at his murder trial. He wanted to be like Holden Caulfield and protect little kids from evil. He was convicted and continues to serve time in Attica State Prison.

A step toward healing one of the nation's wounds occurred in 1982 when the dramatic memorial sculpture to American servicemen lost in Vietnam was dedicated. Designed by a twenty-one-year-old Yale architecture student, Maya Ying Lin, the huge wall of black granite carved with the names of 58,000 dead and missing now attracts many thousands of visitors each year, most of whom stand quietly with their memories or their sadness, or trace with their fingers the names of family members or friends who died or were lost.

In January 1981 Ronald Reagan took office and was soon dubbed the "Teflon president"; he seemed, no matter what, to remain serene, untroubled and untouched by any negative events or opinions around him. The American people seemed to forgive him everything and the press loved him. He had been a bona fide movie star and had the looks to prove it. His cheerful recovery from the assassination attempt in March 1981 by John Hinckley—in a bizarre attempt to attract actress Jodie Foster's attention—served to endear him even more. From the night of his inauguration, when he wore tie and tails and his wife a glittering white designer gown, he exuded a sense of well-being. He represented a decade of apparent prosperity in which the rich got richer, but, unfortunately, the poor got poorer. The national debt skyrocketed. As Stephanie Coontz points out, the national attention to teen spending deflected attention from the "real binge consumers . . . the corporations that engaged in trillions of dollars' worth of buyouts . . . and the government" (Coontz 1992, 274).

One of Reagan's first acts was to free up $8 billion in frozen Iranian assets in exchange for the release of the fifty-two hostages remaining in Iran (see Chapter 7). By the time George Bush took office in 1989, it was clear that the United States, in violation of the law, had engaged in arms dealing, selling weapons to Iran and hiding the profits by using them to support the Contras, a Nicaraguan rebel group.

Financial issues seemed more immediate to most Americans during the Eighties. Upper- and middle-class Americans enjoyed spending and buying more than ever, driving the stock market up. Savings and loan banks lent out money on inadequate security to keep up with the demand for credit. On October 17, 1987, the stock market took such a dive that some called it a crash and named the day Black Monday. Many large and small investors lost a good deal of money. Some stock market manipulators, including Ivan Boesky and Michael Milken, were prosecuted for their crimes; nevertheless, the savings of many Americans were gone.

The *Challenger* Spacecraft

The space shuttle *Challenger* lifted off at Cape Canaveral, Florida, around 11:30 A.M. on January 28, 1986, and within a few seconds, while millions of Americans watched on television, exploded and plummeted into the sea near Florida. No one survived. Especially devastating to students and teachers was the loss of Christa McAuliffe, a New Hampshire social studies teacher who had won the privilege of traveling on the shuttle by writing an essay on how the ordinary person contributes to history. After her journey into space, she was to have traveled around the country informing the public about the space program. The apparent cause of the explosion was eventually traced to a faulty O-ring, a protective seal around one of the boosters, which failed due to cold temperatures at launch time. The investigation also revealed that the National Aeronautics and Space Administration (NASA) may have rushed the launch. The space program was halted for two years during the investigation but resumed in 1988 with the launch of the shuttle *Discovery*.

The Image of Eighties Teens

Teens surveyed in 1985 generally appeared to be focused on money; having a good job, preferably in a large corporation, was very important to them. They wanted the American Dream: "fulfillment in marriage, children, a good job, and material comfort" ("Survey Shows" 1985, 80). They were also frightened. They worried that they might contract AIDS (acquired immune deficiency syndrome) and that there might be a nuclear war. In 1988 they still were pessimistic about the future: 62% believed that life would be difficult, racial discrimination would continue, and a nuclear war could happen (Schultz 1989, 32). Many had friends with eating disorders; a few knew someone with AIDS. Hispanic and black teens worried that they would not be able to find jobs—not an idle fear considering the lack of opportunity for such teens. The suicide rate for teens, which had tripled in the last thirty years, was now up to 6,000 per year ("Teen Suicide Clusters," 1989, 342).

The number of crimes involving teens had also risen; many of them were startlingly violent and not always committed by minority teens as suggested by stereotype. By 1989 the U.S. Supreme Court had ruled in such cases that some juveniles could be punished by death for violent crime. The cases of Kevin Stanford of Kentucky and Heath Wilkins of Missouri were heard by the Court. The seventeen-year-old Stanford had brutally murdered a female gas station attendant in a robbery. Wilkins had repeatedly stabbed a woman in a convenience store during a robbery (Sanders 1989, 48). A number of others on Death Row had committed their crimes as teens. As of 1997, thirteen states had banned the death penalty for crimes committed while the perpetrator was a juvenile; in twenty-six states, a perpetrator sixteen or older at the time of the crime may be sentenced to death (Jacobs 1997, 169).

AIDS and Ryan White

The first case of AIDS in the United States was reported in 1981. By the end of the decade, AIDS was regarded as a full-blown epidemic but was still mysterious to some degree in its transmission and patterns. Sexual contact, however, was known to be central to its spread, as were needle sharing among drug users and, to a lesser degree, transfusion of HIV-infected blood. Because most of the early victims were male homosexuals, some regarded it as a disease peculiar to that population, perhaps even a moral punishment for their sexual preference. As other cases appeared, it soon became clear that AIDS could appear in heterosexual men and women, in teenagers, and in children.

Since young people were apparently a population likely to engage in un-informed sexual activity or drug use, massive advertising campaigns were mounted to inform teens about the dangers of unprotected sex; television ads ran on network shows and schools undertook programs to inform students about the disease and its transmission. Rap song contests, teen-to-teen counseling, and teen theater troupes were all used to inform teens (Dworkin 1989, 29). Where once the fear of unwanted pregnancy was the chief reason for using condoms or for avoiding intercourse, now it was the fear of AIDS and a miserable death. The National Adolescent Health Survey conducted in 1989 proved the success of these efforts: high percentages of students understood the dangers associated with unprotected sex, although some still thought that "washing after having sex" could prevent infection ("Results," 1989, 2025). Other surveys revealed that the fear of acquiring the disease was a central one in Eighties teen life.

HIV-infected students presented a difficult problem for the schools. If they bore the human immune deficiency virus which usually led to AIDS, their blood and other bodily fluids could infect others. Many parents were frightened that healthy students could catch it. Some of the most difficult things for HIV-positive people to bear, especially the young, are the isolation and irrational fear that accompany public knowledge of their condition. When Ryan White, a hemophiliac, acquired the disease in 1985 through the blood-clotting medication he took, he was thirteen. He planned to go to school, to go on with his life as best he could, but he found himself embroiled in court battles to get back into school. When he finally won that legal right, he faced the prejudice and fear of his classmates. They told jokes about him, claimed he bit people, said he spit on the vegetables in the lunchroom, and vandalized his locker, writing "FAG" on his school supplies (Colbert 1997, 551).

His case inevitably attracted the media; he became a national symbol of the mysteries and injustices of the disease. In 1988 Ryan testified before a Presidential Commission on AIDS, describing his ordeals and the thousands of letters of encouragement he had received from all over the world. He had faith that people's attitudes could change, and he was glad to have helped that happen. When he died in 1990 at age eighteen, his funeral was a national event that reminded Americans not only of the dangers of AIDS but also of the need for compassion toward those afflicted.

TEENS AT HOME

Despite some dismal statistics about crime and drugs among teens, the image of the grumpy, disaffected teenager distancing himself from home life was not borne out by all statistics during the Eighties. According to a major survey in 1988, American teens were generally happy with their lives at home. Of those surveyed, 81% said they trusted their parents, and 39% said they wanted to emulate their parents (Schultz 1989, 32–34). Other surveys showed that, although about 25% of teens believed their parents were too strict, and another 25% thought they were too lax, many more thought their parents got it right. Many also believed that a grandparent or other relative was very important in their lives.

By the late Eighties, teens were also becoming more food conscious at home. One survey showed that 93% of female teens did the family grocery shopping, especially in homes where both parents worked, and they were educating themselves about brand names, cholesterol and fat content, and prices (Blumenthal 1990, 3). These mature concerns were offset by the amount of fast food and snack foods teens bought—burgers, fries, corn chips, ice cream, cookies, soft drinks. The microwave oven made fast food much easier and drastically changed the way teens cooked and ate. On the other hand, anorexia and bulimia were beginning to plague many teen girls as a result of an unhealthy obsession with thinness. These two extremes of behavior suggested that, as a large group, teens were not always such savvy food consumers. The insidious diseases of anorexia and bulimia were beginning to affect teen girls in increasing numbers, and public awareness of the problem escalated quickly in the Nineties.

In their rooms at home, teens were likely, in the Eighties, to have a stereo and a shelf full of albums, a radio, a telephone, a typewriter, a watch, a camera, a bike, an electric shaver, a closet full of clothes (many with designer labels), tennis racquets, video games, skates, or a skateboard, and so on. Some more affluent teens might have their own television. Sixteen percent of teens owned cars, and 10% owned personal computers (Horner, 1984, 42), and these numbers had increased by 1989. Many of these items were purchased with teens' own money, from part-time jobs or from allowances, and on most, the brand name was important—teens responded to advertising as well as to friends' advice. In all, surveys indicated that teens, in the late Eighties, spent between $40 and $45 billion per year on such items (Horner 1984, 42).

Radio and Television

After a poll conducted in 1988 on teen listening habits indicated that 79% of teens spent more time listening to the radio than their parents, *Publishers Weekly* declared radio the "medium that most widely separates the generations" (Wood 1988, 132). The transistor radio was an essential part of teen life by the Eighties, and on it, by the mid-Eighties, most teens listened to Top 40 stations and rock stations. For many teens, thanks to the smaller radios, listening at home was a private activity. It was a way to escape the demands of family interaction at times, rather than a way to cement the family together, which it had done in the Forties and Fifties. Even handier was the cassette player, on which teens could play cassettes of their choice rather than relying on a disc jockey; their portability also made them easy to take to friends' houses or in the car. By the end of the decade, compact disks were also beginning to appear.

Television, on the other hand, remained largely a family activity even for teens. One survey found that watching television was the second most popular activity after talking with friends; teens found it relaxing and time filling. As cable television became more available, they could watch not only the standard network fare but also reruns of silly comedies like *Gilligan's Island* and *The Flintstones*, or even Saturday morning cartoons like *Scooby Doo*, a perennial favorite among preadolescents. Teen girls sometimes watched soap operas in the afternoons; this was a favorite activity for some college students as well, and in response, the soaps began featuring more young actors and actresses in storylines that dealt with teen problems. Television in some surveys was also associated with boredom, lowered achievement at school, and the lack of a "positive mood," at least among teens who watched many hours per week (Schmittroth 1994, 868). Teens watched television anyway and became a truly television-nourished generation. Some speculate that young voters voted for Reagan in 1984 because he looked good on television; "only what is on television is what is real to them," said one commentator (Curtis 1987, 319).

VCRs and MTV

Of course, the video cassette recorder (VCR) was also changing teen viewing habits, offering more choices and more flexibility of time. By the end of the decade, many homes were equipped with a VCR, as well as cable television. The new Fox Network, deliberately targeting a younger audience than the established three networks did, increased teens' choices for viewing, but the major shift in teen viewing habits was brought about by Music

Television, or MTV, a cable channel devoted to the video versions of the latest hits.

Film and television images accompanying pop music were not new; *Your Hit Parade* in the Fifties used this format, and many films, from Twenties movies to those of the Beatles, tried new effects to enhance or parallel the music. But MTV, which debuted on August 1, 1981, ushered in an era of collaboration among musicians, marketers, record and video producers, performers of all types, and audiences that has transformed the music business. MTV was the first twenty-four-hour cable channel devoted entirely to music; artists donated their videos free of charge for the exposure they got in return. (Some think that MTV virtually created Michael Jackson and Madonna, the two most popular performers of the Eighties.) The format used a "video jockey," or "vj" to announce and link the songs and videos; the style was disjointed and sometimes jarring both visually and aurally, borrowing the style of television commercials—in effect, MTV was one big commercial. Rock artists began producing videos at the same time they brought out the album, hiring the best photographers, costumers, choreographers, and makeup artists to achieve the look that would sell the music. Record companies worked with MTV to gain the maximum advertising for new songs, tours, and contests. The slogan "I Want My MTV!" began appearing on T-shirts nationwide, and by 1989 MTV was sending its English-language programs to twenty-five countries. According to president Tom Freston, "Youth culture in just about every nation revolves around music, fashion, and humor. Kids are not the same all over the world, but they resemble each other closely, more than any other generation in history" (Sellers 1989, 117).

From the beginning it was extremely successful. It was also extremely controversial. Some of the images that accompanied the music were more sexually suggestive than anything previously seen on television aimed at young audiences. One survey suggested that 25% of the national audience for MTV was under age fifteen ("What Entertainers Are Doing to Your Kids," 1985, 46). Duran Duran's "Girls on Film" from 1981, showing nearly nude models pillow fighting, was banned from many of the stations that were beginning to run MTV (Ward, Stokes, and Tucker 1986, 593). It also became gradually obvious that the channel was avoiding black artists. Although it was willing to experiment with barely known white artists, even the best-known black musicians were excluded from MTV's playlist (1986, 594). Only when Michael Jackson's popularity became so overwhelming that to exclude him might lose MTV some valuable contacts in the business did MTV begin to feature blacks.

Popular Eighties TV Shows

Three classic family comedies appeared on television during this decade. *The Cosby Show*, which ran from 1984 to 1993, was, for many Americans both black and white, an eye-opening depiction of an affluent black family. Bill Cosby's humor softened the show's focus on the sensitive way to raise kids, especially the teens in the family, and when its spinoff, *A Different World*, followed one of the daughters to college, it was the first time some black teens had realized that college was an option for them as well. *Family Ties*, which aired between 1982 and 1989, at first focused on the split between Sixties hippie parents and their conservative Eighties teen children—a daughter, Mallory, who lived to go to the mall and a son, Alex, who espoused all the Republican virtues that the parents most hated. As the show's success continued, the focus shifted more to the kids themselves as they grew up and soon featured a third teenager, younger daughter Jennifer. Michael J. Fox, who played Alex, became a popular star as a result of the series. Perhaps as a reaction to all the yuppie affluence in such sitcoms, comedian Roseanne Barr began her own show, *Roseanne*, in 1988. Unlike the other popular family shows, this one revolved around a clearly working-class family, with parents who did not look like clothing models, a messy house and kitchen, small rooms, unstylish furniture, and mouthy kids. Some audiences were appalled at its often grating honesty and humor, but it showed that a family who had to struggle for a paycheck could love and nurture its kids just as effectively as a more affluent one.

Among adventure shows, *CHiPS*, which had begun in the Seventies, was popular with teen viewers for its handsome star Erik Estrada and for its exciting motorcycle chases along the California highways. *Magnum P.I.* (1980–1988), which starred Tom Selleck as a Vietnam vet and private investigator in Hawaii, featured a rock theme composed by Mike Post. Music and a tropical setting were also featured in the police drama *Miami Vice* (1984–1989); the often thin plots usually concerned drug deals, but the show was most popular for its look. Its pale neon colors in sets and costuming and its filming style set to a hard-rock score imitated MTV's obvious artifice. The loose linen jackets with white T-shirts worn by its stars Don Johnson and Philip Michael Thomas became a popular fashion. *Star Trek* fans rejoiced when *The Next Generation* finally aired in 1987. The new show drew its early plots directly from the Sixties series but then quickly found its own voice while maintaining the thoughtfulness-plus-action formula that was the *Trek* hallmark. The starship *Enterprise* had a sleek new look and a new captain (played by British Shakespearean actor Patrick Stewart) as the show warped far beyond the often-laughable special effects of the Sixties version.

Comic Strips

One of the most popular comic strips of the decade was the witty "Calvin and Hobbes," drawn by Bill Watterson, which appeared in the nation's newspapers—and in books, on T-shirts, and on car windows—from 1985 until 1995 when Watterson retired. Calvin was a mischievous boy who often talked like an intellectual adult; Hobbes was his stuffed tiger, who appeared full-sized and quite real to Calvin when no one else was around and who also spoke like a thoughtful, witty adult. Gary Larson's weird, single-panel cartoons in the series called "The Far Side" dealt with animals who lived like humans, cave men who went to school, dinosaurs who found humans in cereal boxes, and a myriad of bossy women in bee-hive hairdos and pointy-framed glasses. Larson had trouble getting started in 1979 because his cartoons made some people quite uncomfortable, and his work contin-ued to be controversial through the Eighties.

A gentler family strip which also began in 1979 and is still running is "For Better or for Worse," drawn by Canadian Lynn Johnston. The strip follows an ordinary family through their ordinary days, but it does so almost in real time, with the children in the family growing up gradually. Johnston has tackled some serious topics and, in fact, caused some discomfort among readers when Laurence, a friend of the teen boy, Michael, discloses that he is gay. Johnston was the first woman to win the Reuben Award from the National Cartoonists Society, and one critic has called the strip "one of the finest graphic narratives ever produced" (Horn 1996, 121).

Matt Groening got his start drawing comics for his college newspaper. His series of "Life in Hell" cartoons and strips which began in 1980 are among the wildest of strips to ever appear. They usually concern a skinny rabbit, Binky, who observes that school is hell, love is hell, and so forth, in a single panel or sometimes a series of panels that are full of tiny words or hieroglyphs or scrawls. Groening also created the animated family known as The Simpsons, which, after airing on television in 1989, became a hit in the 1990s.

Runaways and Homeless Teens

In the midst of the consumerism and emphasis on big money that the Reagan/Bush administrations invited, and the savings and loan scandals and the stock market crash of 1987, many Americans who never dreamed it could happen to them found themselves without a home. A number of teens voluntarily left their homes—usually because of problems with a parent or other adult in the home. When they did not go to shelters or could not be traced, their faces began to appear on milk cartons and billboards across America, and phone-home services which could put a teen in touch with home for free, no questions asked, began to advertise on television. Forty percent of those in shelters reported emotional conflicts at home as the reason for their leaving; a lesser but a significant percentage (26%–29%) cited physical or sexual abuse (Schmittroth 1994, 808). Violence and drug use also plagued the home situation for many such teens, who preferred living on the streets or in shelters, or, if they were lucky enough, in places of their own.

TEENS AT SCHOOL

In 1980 all but 3% of children aged from five to seventeen were enrolled in school. In that same year, 86% of them completed high school (Eccles, 1991, 4). These statistics were eagerly awaited, especially by people who had been in school during the Great Depression and remembered how valuable an education was and how difficult it could be to get one. Certainly, too, schools were providing more and better services for teens. Twenty-seven states mandated AIDS education in the school; others mandated life skills classes (Schultz 1989, 36). Teachers were trained in the latest learning theories; classrooms, where possible, were made more physically and intellectually open and the studies more challenging. The number of available extracurricular activities increased: music, dance, athletics of all kinds, speech, and drama. Academic and vocational counseling were part of the standard school services, as ubiquitous as the Scholastic Aptitude Test, which teens needed to take before college admission.

A sadder sign of the times was the increase in such services as birth control and psychological counseling for suicide prevention and incipient or full-blown drug addiction among the students. Schools still struggled with racial prejudices and with how to incorporate and to teach minority students. The peer group was still the dominant power in school, no matter how much the administration might wish otherwise. The dropout rate was still high, 26.1% in 1983. In that year, the average percentage of students who graduated from high school was 73.9; North Dakota was the highest at 94.8% and Louisiana the lowest at 57.2% ("School Dropouts" 1985, 14). Some states were experimenting with unusual legislation to counteract dropping out: students who did not stay in school lost their drivers' licences. In West Virginia, for example, any student under age eighteen who dropped out lost his license; the license might be suspended for ten consecutive days of unexcused absence or fifteen days of unexcused absence in the course of a semester (Pipho 1989, 502). The state expected to see a considerable improvement in school attendance as a result of the plan.

Criticism of Schools

Attendance alone could not make school a more useful experience, according to many Americans. When the National Commission on Education published a report in 1983 called *A Nation at Risk,* it excoriated American schools for producing students who had little academic skill and who spent their time in "soft" classes and extracurricular activities. The report, along with Education Secretary William Bennett's public pronouncements that American schools were lagging behind those in other countries, galvanized public criticism of the schools, especially high schools.

All of this put considerable pressure on the public high school, a place already beleaguered by overcrowding, continuing racial tensions, the needs of minority students, diminished funding, low teacher salaries, and rising college tuition. Now the public was demanding that schools raise academic standards, institute more testing to enforce the standards, and trim elective subjects to make room for more basic ones. Several states targeted extracurricular activities as the culprit and instituted what came to be called the "no pass, no play" rule: students who did not maintain a 70 average in all basic subjects could not participate in any extracurricular activities. In Texas, where football was an important part of high school life and revenue, the rule made itself felt when 15% of the varsity football players and 40% of the second-stringers, along with some cheerleaders and band members, were barred from participating in the sport. In one Maryland county, more than 40% of the students could not participate in extracurricular activities during the fall of 1985 ("School Athletes Hit the Books" 1985, 10).

The new rule pleased some, who felt that it put the emphasis back where it belonged—on academics. As one teacher groused, "Their priorities run something like this: peer group, job, car, leisure time, extracurriculars. Finally, but only with a lot of moaning and groaning, their studies" ("Debate," 1985, 27). Others worried that it harmed good students in activities like drama which depended on a small group effort in competitions and performances; when one student had to withdraw from the activity, the whole team might have to fold. More important, students who did poorly in academic areas might still enjoy school because of such activities and avoid dropping out. In the case of football, black students tended to be hurt more often than white ones.

"The Good High School"

Harvard sociologist Sara Lawrence Lightfoot made an effort to counteract some of the criticism of American high schools by publishing a thorough study of six that she thought were good. Two were urban: George Washington Carver in Atlanta and John F. Kennedy in New York. Two were suburban: Highland Park in the Chicago area and Brookline in the Boston area. Two were private: St. Paul's and Milton Academy, both in New England. Amid these diverse populations, she found a number of reasons why such schools were good, especially the mutual respect among the teachers, administrators, and students. Students want, she believed, "relationships with faculty that underscore the teachers' adulthood . . . [they] do not want adults to behave like peers or buddies" (1983, 351). The teachers she observed generally treated students as intellectual beings, willing to engage in serious conversation or debate about a particular topic.

Even in these schools, however, she found that students were essentially conservative; they gravitated to their own ethnic groups in the hallways and cafeteria. She observed tension between "tracks" of students, such as those in college prep courses and those in vocational courses. She noticed the multiple agendas that schools tried to adopt; the result was most often a sense of chaos and a lack of intellectual focus, especially in the public high school. Administrators in all the schools were "alarmed at the increasingly utilitarian view of education by all their students. From all backgrounds, students seemed more concerned with the learning of specific technologies that will equip them for work, college, and beyond" (366). She concluded,

For many students, high school stands uncomfortably between intellectual play and real work, and the no man's land stretching between them tends not to be very appealing. . . . Good high schools try to respond to the inevitable tensions that these adolescents produce and seek to create environments that will connect their students to the wider world and protect them from it. (368)

TEENS AT WORK

In 1986, 93% of high school students, in one national survey, said they had worked for pay. The situation was peculiar to America, declare researchers Ellen Greenberger and Laurence Steinberg (1986, 22). The growth of suburbia with its malls and fast food shops demanded part-time help, and teens were ready to supply it in return for spending money. One commentator observed, "You want to talk revolution? Not to this generation of adolescents. They have seen the future—and they want to buy it, not change it" (Trachtenberg 1986, 201).

Unfortunately, this privilege of salary applied primarily to white, middle-class youth. In April 1985 white jobless youth accounted for 14.9% of joblessness nationally; for black youth, the rate was 39% ("Teenage Orphans of the Job Boom" 1985, 46). Black youths tended to live in cities, where businesses were diminishing. In areas where bus or train service was poor, such teens could not get to the suburbs where jobs might be more plentiful. They might have also been shortchanged educationally, making them less desirable in a middle-class business, even fast food. Some enterprising black youth made their own jobs: break dancing in the streets for money or washing car windshields at intersections for tips. Others drifted into illegal drug trading. Training to encourage minority teens to learn other kinds of work was sadly lacking in the Eighties.

Not everyone thought that the time middle-class teens spent working was a good thing. Researchers Greenberger and Steinberg (1986) took a close

Sixteen-year-old George Doumar learns the family trade, Norfolk, Virginia, 1983. Reproduced courtesy of Albert Doumar.

look at the entire picture and found some depressing patterns. Working students did not necessarily do better in school or develop any sense of responsibility to either their work or their studies (115–119). The hours spent at work eroded the time spent doing homework, and some teachers colluded in the situation by requiring less homework because so many students worked (120). Since teens tended to spend what they made quickly, patterns of saving had all but disappeared. In their place was a commitment to luxury (200–201).

Even more disturbingly, working tended to contribute to certain types of delinquent behavior. In one of Greenberger and Steinberg's surveys, they found that one out of three of all teens in their first job had engaged in some kind of dishonesty about work: calling in sick when they were not, showing up for work high on drugs, giving away some of the company's goods to friends or taking them for themselves, and lying about the number of hours they worked (Greenberger and Steinberg 1986, 144–145). Certainly the kind of jobs teens could get tended to be repetitive and stressful, with little interaction with authoritative adults or decision-making power. Nevertheless, their response to this stress was all too often to find deviant means of blowing off steam.

Greenberger and Steinberg urged adults to make some improvements in working conditions for teens. They might be encouraged from time to time to participate in some decision making, for example, but they thought it was not likely that the "bad jobs" teens were in now could be turned into good ones (1986, 235). Instead, they suggested that the real work, the important work, of adolescence was growing up—a hard enough job in itself. They worried that the new teen workplace was causing teens to bypass this important process and remain stuck in adolescence for a long time, with disturbing results. For teens who did not absolutely need money for food and shelter, perhaps not working was the best solution.

FASHION

Reflecting the eager consumerism that dominated the decade, teens spent a lot of money on their clothes—and girls spent more than boys. One 1984 survey showed that boys between the ages of thirteen and fifteen spent almost $200 per year on clothing; girls that age spent $300. Older teens, ages sixteen to nineteen, spent more: boys, $425 per year; girls, $630 (Horner 1984, 42). It was also a decade where the distinction between boys' and girls' styles was less distinct; wearing pink, for example, was okay for both genders.

Part of the reason for these high spending figures was not quantity but quality. Teens were paying big bucks for designer labels including Izod Lacoste, Liz Claiborne, Gucci, Sassoon, and Sergio Valenti on clothes as well as accessories. Many times those labels were worn on the outside, as on Levi-Strauss jeans, Nike shoes and shorts, and Harley-Davidson shirts. Ralph Lauren's Polo brand was a major symbol of luxury and part of the preppie look that remained popular for many boys and girls: khaki pants and button-down-collar shirts. Athletic wear was now everyday wear: warm-up suits, T-shirts, visors, and sneakers. Athletic shoes became more varied and complex in construction and much more expensive, as Nike, Reebok, and others competed for the teen market.

Less conservative teens might prefer the hip-hop or break-dancing look—parachute pants, bandanas tied around the wrists and ankles, a loose sports jacket, and fancy high-top sneakers. Baggy sweat clothes or oversized shorts or jeans worn with a baseball cap and sneakers were also part of this style. The 1983 movie *Flashdance* popularized loose, curly hair and dancewear for girls: loose sweatshirts cut out at the neck and hem, leotards or tights, and leg warmers. Having a body that looked good in such clothes became increasingly essential for the fashionable girl; ballet and aerobic dance workouts helped. If teens really wanted to shock parents and teachers, they adopted the punk look, imported from England: a Mohawk haircut (shaved down the sides with a high shelf of hair down the middle) or spiked hair sometimes dyed green or orange, a whole row of earrings climbing up the rim of the ear (or more conservatively for boys, a single ear stud), and a black leather jacket. Some girls tried the "gothic" look: all black clothes, very pale face with dramatic eye makeup and black lipstick. Although at first it was rather sexy for younger or more conservative teen girls to wear them, Lycra leggings gradually became part of most girls' wardrobes because they were cheap, comfortable, and easy for most body types to wear with a tunic top.

Fashion fads for girls included very curly permed hair, pony tails worn on the side rather than the back of the head, Swatch watches, jelly bracelets, bangle bracelets, braided friendship bracelets, and anything in neon colors. Young tennis star Chris Evert created a fad for jewelry on the tennis court, especially a narrow diamond bracelet that came to be called a tennis bracelet. Well-to-do teen girls wanted the real thing—not, of course, to wear only on the tennis court—but there were also plenty of rhinestone or cubic zirconia versions available for girls with less money. Michael Jackson's white socks and single glove were imitated, and younger teen girls went wild over Madonna's uncoiffed hairstyle, her crocheted gloves, her miniskirts and bare midriff, her many necklaces and pendants, her bustier, and her eye makeup—most of which they had to experiment with away from the eyes of parents. A pair of sunglasses was absolutely essential for cool style, especially if they were Ray-Bans and, if you were a guy and had a two-day's growth of beard, they made you look like Don Johnson of the television hit *Miami Vice*.

Fallout from the Sixties had made proms un-cool during the Seventies, but Eighties teens took proms to new highs of formality and glamour. Boys wore their tuxes with pride, and girls spent hundreds of dollars on just the right dress, which, in the Eighties, would probably have ruffles, lace, net, sequins, and yards of skirt maybe held out with a hoop underneath. Many were strapless; some were slender-fitting around the hips. Dyed-to-match shoes and big hair—hair teased up into a large pouf and worn with flowers, bows, or mini-explosions of net—completed the look. Big hair was now easy to achieve thanks to mousse, a product that increased the hair's volume and held it in place with the addition of hair spray.

SLANG

The Eighties teen enjoyed an explosion of rich language associated with various elements of youth society: rap and early hip-hop music, Valley girls, television personalities such as Wayne and Garth of the *Saturday Night Live* skits or even the Flintstones.

Rap had a variety of words for money (booty, bucks, dead presidents), for guns (steel, click, piece, flamer), for relaxing (chilling out, mellowing out, kickin'), for the police (the Man, b & w [for black and white police cars], blue jeans), and for aiming insults at someone (to dis, dog on, toast, or riff on). The Valley girl was a caricature of the consumerist Eighties—more interested in going to the mall than going to class. She was a California girl—white, well-off, and living in the San Fernando Valley outside Los Angeles—and her nasal voice and vocal rhythm became an Eighties joke, but some of her expressions were original and vivid enough to last. Something she liked was bitchin, tubular!, gnarly, or awesome. If she agreed with you she said, "For sure!" (pronounced "fer sherrrr") and if she did not like something, it was grody, or even worse, grody to the max. Her most intense expression of dislike was, "Gag me with a spoon!" She was vividly portrayed by Tracey Nelson as "Jennifer" on the 1982–83 television show *Square Pegs*. Tom Dalzell insists that, despite the persistent caricature in comedy shows, television, and movies, the Valley girl was real: "a case of life imitating art imitating life" (1996, 183).

Wayne and Garth, two engaging teen characters, were played by Mike Myers and Dana Carvey on the television comedy show *Saturday Night Live*. They introduced the expression "Not!" to teens—a concise way of pointing out that what you just said was false—and the word "Babe" and many variations on it as a reference to good-looking girls (maximum babe, babe-alicious, etc.). They also helped popularize, once again, the term dude (a task shared by the films *Fast Times at Ridgemont High* and *Bill and Ted's Excellent Adventure*). *The Flintstones*, a Sixties cartoon about a stone-age suburban family, introduced the terms "wilma" and "betty" for a homely girl and a pretty girl.

Eighties terms for something good were def, rockin', smokin', or intense. If you were amazed at something, it blew you away. A good-looking guy was a stud muffin; studly was an adjective for something good in a masculine way. A good-looking girl was a honey. Someone weak was a wuss or dweeb. If he sat on the sofa watching television all the time, he was a couch potato. If he was really disgusting, he was a butthead, and if he always tried to ingratiate himself with the cool people (or with teachers), he was a brown-nose. Something phony was bogus, something tacky was cheezy, and someone who imitated someone else was a wannabe (such as a "Madonna wannabe"). As usual there were many words for cool: happening, radical, wicked, etc. If something was outdated, over, or ended, it was history ("Yeah, he was my boyfriend, but he cheated on me so now he's history"). You could say goodbye with "I'm history" or "Later, dude."

LEISURE ACTIVITIES AND ENTERTAINMENT

The Eighties was a decade of toys for teens, for those who could afford them. The VCR, the music cassette and the Sony Walkman to play it on, an extension telephone, the transistor radio (growing smaller and smaller) or the boom box version (growing larger and larger), a skate board, a dirt bike, and perhaps a car were joined in 1982 by video games. Kids took to

Pac Man and Space Invaders with addictive glee, spending many quarters in the mall arcades testing their skills against their friends'. More serious teens took up Dungeons and Dragons, a fantasy board game based on medieval knights, dwarfs, and monsters; it required thought and role-playing, and some teens became so occupied with it and so intense about it that some adults wondered if it were dangerous. A brief fad in the early Eighties for those who loved puzzles was Rubik's cube (named for its Hungarian creator), a cube made up of smaller colored cubes which you moved with your thumb to solve the puzzle.

Plenty of teens could not afford such toys. A basketball and a little space, and perhaps a net, were essential to inner-city boys. Break dancing was a form of exercise, play, and competition all in one. Painting graffiti on city walls and trains also invited competition to see who had the best style of graphic art. In parks and parking lots, black ghetto teens pooled their resources and "set up turntables, speakers, and a mixing board, tapped into a lamppost for electricity, and developed styles of rap singing and scratching (manually maneuvering the record on the turntable to create witty, rhythmic musical effects) until in the late eighties the streets became too violent to bring expensive equipment outdoors" (Dargan and Zeitlin 1990, 3).

In rural areas, pleasures were simpler yet. Girls still enjoyed slumber parties and boys still arm wrestled and got into play fights. Square dancing, telling fortunes, and courting games like Spin the Bottle and Post Office made good party fun, although they were perhaps not quite as innocent as they had been in the Forties and Fifties. Drinking games might be used at parties where adults were scarce. In the back of the school bus, kids might try a game of Credit Card, where they passed a piece of plastic to each other using only their lips (Lich 1989, 233).

Alcohol, Drugs, Cigarettes

In cities and towns where teens had cars, they gathered in clubs where they could listen to rock music and dance. Most clubs sold alcohol even though, theoretically, they were forbidden to sell liquor to patrons under eighteen. Fake IDs made it easy to get in. Many teens drank alcohol regularly, especially beer, but overall alcohol use apparently declined somewhat during the decade. In 1982, 42% of teens surveyed said they had consumed alcohol in the past thirty days; the percentage dropped to 21% in 1989. Still, the number of alcohol-related car accidents involving teens prompted Congress to pass a law encouraging all states to raise the drinking age to twenty-one; states that did not comply would receive less federal funding for highway improvements (Jones 1989, 3).

The recreational use of drugs, begun during the Sixties, continued unabated in teen culture in the Eighties. A major survey conducted in 1985 of high school seniors showed that marijuana was the most used illicit drug among teens, followed by amphetamines. Even more alarming was the increased use of cocaine: 17% said they had tried cocaine at some point, and 7% had used it in the month prior to the survey ("Teen Drug Use," 1985, 310). Cocaine deaths nationwide, for all ages, rose in 1984 to 617, a 77% jump in one year ("Teen Drug Abuse," 1985, 16). First Lady Nancy Reagan made one of her priorities a "Just Say No" campaign aimed at getting teens to refuse drugs—a solution alarming in its naiveté but one that got plenty of publicity.

Since the emphasis on the cancer-causing properties of cigarettes, teen smoking had been a major target of community and government agencies. For a brief time in 1985 another kind of cigarette was even more dangerous, even though it purported to be less harmful. Some teens tried smoking "kreteks" or cigarettes imported from Indonesia which contained tobacco and cloves, a craze which began on the West Coast in 1980 and continued all the way across the country to New York. They produced varying symptoms, from nosebleeds and nausea to large pulmonary cysts. A seventeen-year-old in California died after smoking one while he was recovering from flu ("Cloven Smokers," 1985, 63), prompting other teens to seek help for their addiction to them.

Dating

The "rating and dating" system hung on during the Eighties, especially in more conservative parts of the country like the South. In the classic pattern, boys did the asking and paying, girls did the accepting—especially of the responsibility to look good and act pleasant—and the usual activities were movies, dinner, or dancing at a club. Girls increasingly asked boys out and shared expenses or the responsibility for transportation, but this was an area of tension in the dating game. Lesley Nonkin in *Seventeen* magazine opined that this was "one of the more pressing and controversial teen issues these days" (Nonkin 1986, 224). Girls were caught in what might be called the "liberation lag": encouraged toward independence, yet uncertain about how and when to exert their new freedom. One girl commented, "Today, unless a boy calls you up and says, 'I'm taking you out on a DATE,' you don't know if you're supposed to pay or not" (1986, 224). Seventy-five percent of girls Lesley Nonkin surveyed thought that it was okay to ask guys out on a first date, but only 47% had actually tried it. Forty percent felt the bill was the boy's responsibility; even when the girl asked the boy, almost half of the girls surveyed thought the boy should still pay.

Study dates were a pleasant but distracting way to do homework; the unspoken aim for many couples was to finish the evening by necking or petting. Just hanging out at friends' houses watching television or videos and eating pizza was a favorite group or individual activity. Informality was the rule, except at the prom, which experienced a surge of popularity during the Eighties. As with so many other aspects of teen life during this decade, the prom became a place to spend money conspicuously. The pre-prom dinner, the flowers, souvenir photos, and increasingly the limousine, as well as new clothes, ran expenses into the hundreds of dollars. Many featured promenades or parades where teens could display their finery as they entered the dance. Post-prom parties, where the kids shed their fancy clothes for casual wear, were all-night affairs, ending with breakfast. The amount of drinking at these parties could and did result in accidents and injuries, prompting some parents to pay willingly for the limousine so the kids would not have to drive. Schools and parent groups encouraged and planned non-alcoholic parties, with only minimal success.

In at least two high schools during the decade, the prom became a focus of media attention when students fought for and won the right to attend their prom with a same-sex partner. In Cumberland, Rhode Island, in 1980, after a year-long battle, a judge ruled that eighteen-year-old Aaron Fricke's freedom could not be sacrificed to the threat of unruly behavior by other students ("A Rhode Island Town," 1980, 98–99). In 1986, in Salinas, California, teen girls Marie Hawkins and Stephanie Salgado won the right to attend their prom together after a judge found no good reason other than tradition for the school to prevent them from doing so (Burkett 1986, 30).

Sex and Pregnancy

Sexual intercourse among teens seemed to be on the rise. In 1988 twenty-five percent of sexually experienced teens aged from fifteen to nineteen said they had sex several times a week, 19% had sex once a week, and 33% had sex two or three times a month (adapted from Chadwick and Heaton 1996, 280). The frequency of explicit scenes in movies and videos aimed at teens may have had an impact; losing one's virginity seemed to be an increasingly public index to maturity, at least among teen girls and boys who quizzed each other about it. However, thanks to publicity about AIDS, teens used condoms more than they had since the Fifties, when the raised round dent in a boy's billfold was the classic signal of his readiness. One survey showed that condom use had doubled between 1979 and 1989, and that more boys were using them for first-time sexual encounters than in the Seventies ("Teen Boys Get Condom Sense," 1989, 63).

Despite increased condom use and AIDS education, for a variety of reasons passionately debated in the government and the media, teen pregnancy reached what some thought were epidemic proportions. In March 1985 the Alan Guttmacher Institute, which promoted family planning, released a major study of teen sexual behavior and pregnancy rates that concerned many Americans ("A Teen-Pregnancy Epidemic," 1985, 90). It compared American teens with teens from five other countries and found that their pregnancy rate was almost double that of their peers in the other countries. It

Table 8.1
Birthrate Statistics Showing a Pattern That Indicates That More Teenage Girls Are Keeping Their Babies

	Birthrate (per 1,000 women)	Ratios of out-of-wedlock births (per 1,000 births)
1980	53.0	476
1983	51.7	534
1984	50.9	556
1985	51.3	567
1986	50.6	595
1987	51.1	619

Source: Adapted from Bruce A. Chadwick and Jim B. Heaton, eds., *Statistical Handbook on the American Family* (Phoenix, Ariz.: Oryx 1992), Table D3-6, 122.

also found that American girls were less likely to use contraceptives than those in the other countries. Many had no knowledge of diaphragms; others bought the pill but either took it incorrectly or just left it in a drawer because it was too much trouble. Still others had unprotected sex for a variety of reasons: boredom, loneliness, ignorance, or the desire—conscious or unconscious—for a child. Increasingly, teens preferred raising the baby themselves to entering into an undesired marriage. In the Fifties, when a single teen girl was pregnant, she would go into hiding and give the baby up for adoption at birth, or she and the boy would marry under pressure. The trend in the Eighties was for the girl to keep the baby and raise it herself, usually with a lot of help from her parents. This pattern was more common in the black community than in the white (where economic privilege made a safe abortion an option). The inverse relationship between the birthrates and the ratios of out-of-wedlock births demonstrates this pattern (see Table 8.1).

The Guttmacher report speculated that one reason for these patterns might be American prudishness toward talking frankly about sex, in comparison to the more open climate in other countries. The Reagan administration did not help. Even though a blue-ribbon congressionally chartered study group recommended that contraceptives be made available to all teenagers, Reagan and his conservative colleagues remained adamant: contraception should not be given to teenagers (McBee 1986, 8). For a time, the administration pushed through the so-called squeal rule which required federally funded clinics to notify parents within ten days if they had prescribed birth control to minors ("Children Having Children," 1985, 82). According to the supporters of this bill, disseminating birth control information to teens would make kids eager to have sex; it would also suggest implicit approval of sexual activity among the young, and it would increase abortions (even though half of unwanted pregnancies already ended in abortion).

Birth control information, it was said, should be dispensed by parents and parents alone. Kids should "just say no" to sex as well as drugs.

Faye Wattleton, president of Planned Parenthood, commented, "Just saying no prevents teen-age pregnancy the way 'Have a nice day' cures chronic depression" (Wattleton and Edelman 1989, 140). It was a highly complex issue involving educational, psychological, racial, religious, and economic concerns as well as sexual ones. Various private agencies mounted programs to cope with the problem. Planned Parenthood, always at the forefront of such efforts, continued to supply family planning information to those who asked for it. The National Council of Negro Women created the Adolescent Mothers Initiative Program in New Orleans to prepare young mothers for jobs, and they worked in other ways to address the multiplicity of issues surrounding teen pregnancy (Height 1985, 84). A new kind of solution to part of the problem, just beginning in the late Eighties, was the education and preparation of teen fathers, a group who had been often ignored but many of whom genuinely wanted to be part of their children's lives ("Children Having Children" 1985, 90).

Music and Dancing

Some of the gentler hits of this decade were sung by the groups The Police, Duran Duran, Hall and Oates, and Men at Work and by soloists Phil Collins, Whitney Houston, Janet Jackson, and Paula Abdul. In the new techno-funk style—a strong beat backed up with electronic sound—Cyndi Lauper, with her strange soprano voice and even stranger clothes and hair, had a hit with "Girls Just Want to Have Fun" and its accompanying video. Prince's "1999" and "Purple Rain" were also in the techno-funk style, as were Michael Jackson's "Thriller" and "Billie Jean." Madonna's "Material Girl" also received plenty of airtime. Many teens still enjoyed soft rock, such as that sung by Lionel Richie, Stevie Wonder, and other stars in the Motown tradition. The Talking Heads made the transition from late Seventies punk into something looser, something more in the black tradition, and they had big hits with their single "Burning Down the House" and their album *Speaking in Tongues*. Their concert film *Stop Making Sense*, directed by Jonathan Demme, has been called "the most elegant rock movie ever made" (Ward, Stokes, and Tucker 1986, 605).

Heavy metal (a term coined by beat icon William Burroughs, according to Charles T. Brown [1992, 217]) evolved into something more than noise in the Eighties with groups such as Guns 'n' Roses, which had a big hit with "Sweet Child o'Mine," and Def Leppard with their album *Pyromania*, which appealed to a younger audience more than earlier heavy metal did. Mötley Crüe and Van Halen also weighed in with hit albums late in the decade. The signature of such groups was still volume, however, and many adults worried that teens who listened to a lot of heavy metal might suffer hearing loss.

During the Eighties, Athens, Georgia, home of the University of Georgia, also became the cradle of alternative rock when the small town and its growing number of clubs produced the groups REM and the B-52's. By the end of the decade, Top 40 stations were playing alternative rock.

Rap

The roots of rap go deep—into the rhythm of black English, into soul music, rhythm-and-blues sounds, and the style of James Brown. George Clinton's group Parliament, with their funkadelic sounds and witty lyrics, set the stage in the late Seventies for the growing popularity of rap in the Eighties. The style had been around in the urban ghettos in the mid-Seventies, when black teen boys took their turntables out on the street to enjoy "scratching"—turning the record by hand to make a scratchy, rhythmic sound to which they could move and recite lyrics. Those lyrics, using clever and surprising rhyming patterns which snapped connecting ideas into focus, usually described the violent, angry life of the inner city. According to Dalzell, "Like the first generation of rock and roll in the 1950s, rap had an unmistakably seditious and menacing edge, both in its celebration of ghetto life and in its defiant youth stance. And, like rock and roll, it seized the attention and interest of young people" (1996, 199–200).

"Rapper's Delight" by the Sugar Hill Gang was the first rap single to gain public airtime, in 1979, but soon other groups were recording this music of the streets, which often used beats and phrases from other recordings—a technique called "sampling." Run DMC and LL Cool J were the most popular black rappers of the mid-Eighties and they toured together in 1983, but white performers, such as Vanilla Ice and the Beastie Boys, were trying it too. M. C. Hammer, in the late Eighties, produced a rap style, enhanced by his skillful dancing, which was more accessible to a general audience; he became a popular spokesperson for a number of commercial products (Brown 1992, 265).

Break Dancing and Slam Dancing

Like rap, break dancing got its start in the streets of the urban ghetto, largely as a form of mock fighting. As one dancer put it, "When you got mad at someone, instead of saying, 'Hey, man, you want to fight?' you'd say, 'Hey, man, you want to rock?' " (Dargan and Zeitlin 1990, 3). Its incredible athleticism, skilled choreography, and demands on the body drew crowds of viewers to cheer on and applaud the daring feats of spins and flips accompanied by sharp hand moves performed to the rhythms from a boom box, portable tape player, or radio. Dancers wore loose jeans and jackets or sweat clothes, along with high-top sneakers. Sometimes they performed on a spread-out cardboard box to protect their backs and shoulders as they spun on them. Breaking moved for a brief time into the white culture but remained a passing fad there. It affected hip-hop dance styles, however, which were in turn picked up by popular performers. Rock bands performed increasingly athletic moves on stage, and the hit movie *Flashdance* featured some breaking moves in its musical numbers.

Slamming was equally athletic but more dangerous and less skilled. Usually performed at punk concerts, it required dancers to throw themselves from a high place—preferably the stage if they could get onto it—into the crowd, which would catch them and pass them around. It was also called moshing, and the target space was the mosh pit. Its exuberance was sometimes drug induced, and sometimes the crowd did not catch the slammer, causing injuries.

Michael Jackson and Madonna

Few pop stars have fascinated the public—and played to public tastes in such surprising and highly original ways—as Michael Jackson and Madonna did in the Eighties. Their success coincided with the coming of music video, and whether they helped cement MTV's success or whether MTV was in large measure responsible for theirs is a question impossible to answer. Both got maximum mileage from all aspects of Eighties rock: music, dance, costuming, marketing, video and still photography, and concert stage. Like Elvis and the Beatles, they have been so thoroughly analyzed in popular and academic media that we can only review them briefly here.

In his dynamic early performances as a child with his brothers in the Jackson Five, Michael Jackson was obviously an unusual talent, vocally mature beyond his years. He recorded his first solo album in 1972 when he was fourteen. In the Eighties, although he toured with his brothers, he emerged as a remarkable lone performer—singing, dancing, and getting involved in every aspect of his videos and recordings. The girlishness of his voice and face, combined with the open sexuality, not to say the remarkable skill, of his dance moves, made him appealing to young teens and older alike. Unlike teenybopper stars, and very much in the Elvis tradition, Jackson also marketed a mean streak, a suggestion of aggression and evil that made him even more appealing and mysterious.

When he was twenty-four, all of this came together in "Thriller," which topped the charts in 1982 and every version of which—recording, album, video—broke all records. Paul Friedlander declared "Thriller" "the biggest-selling album in history at over 40 million copies" (1996, 268); it had something for everyone, from danceable songs with a strong beat to romantic ballads beautifully crooned to guest performances by other stars (musicians Paul McCartney and Eddie Van Halen and actor Vincent Price, who was famous for his work in B-grade horror films). The video for the title song, produced by director John Landis and featuring expert choreography and dancing by Jackson and a chorus of dancers, told a horror story of an encounter with the supernatural in which Jackson may or may not have been part of the evil (ambiguity has always been Jackson's stock in trade). The dance style combined Broadway moves like those in *West Side Story* with a hip-hop style and Jackson's trademark sliding backward step, the moonwalk (widely imitated by young teens nationwide). Friedlander calls "Thriller" one of the "defining popular music moments of the eighties" (269).

Jet magazine, on January 14, 1985, proclaimed Jackson the "number one hero of high school students across the country, according to the annual Heroes of Young America poll taken by the World Almanac" ("Michael Jackson Named U.S. Teens' Top Star" 1985, 57). Jackson's subsequent music, although skilled and varied, has not topped this success, and his strange personal life eclipsed his performances in the Nineties.

Madonna, on the other hand, has grown more successful, perhaps because of her chameleonlike ability to remake herself into a variety of public personae. Born, like Jackson, in the late Fifties, she grew up Madonna Louise Ciccone and wanted a career in dance. Her early recordings revealed an average voice in mildly pleasant danceable songs, but when she recorded "Material Girl" and "Crazy for You" (which was number one in 1985), she showed she had other possibilities. Her appearance, too, became a matter of public interest. In "Material Girl" she capitalized on her similarity to the glamorous Marilyn Monroe, but in other videos she created a hodge-podge look of funky leggings, midriff-baring mesh tops, fingerless gloves, multiple pendants, disheveled hair pulled up in a scrunchy band, bra straps showing or a black bra under a white shirt (until now, for most girls a fashion felony), tightly laced black leather bustiers. She changed her hair color and style as well as her clothes to create multiple images of herself in first one video (or movie) and then the next. She was the ultimate popular fashion icon, what most teens in American culture enjoy to a lesser degree and what the fashion industry encourages: always trying something new and different. One scholar, accounting for Madonna's popularity with young people at this particular time in history, opines, "High school in particular is a period in which young people construct their identities, attempting to 'become someone.' " Along came Prince, Boy George, Michael Jackson, Cyndi Lauper, and Madonna, who "undermined traditional gender divisions and promoted polymorphic sexuality . . . [and] made it OK to be silly and weird, or at least different" (Kellner 1994, 161–62).

Madonna was not only weird and different. Accompanying her fashion image is an image of strength and independence. Her videos—*Papa Don't Preach*, *Like a Prayer*, and *Express Yourself*—have crossed boundaries in sexuality, miscegenation, and religion in what seems to be a deliberate effort to shock, but unlike many other stars she remains in artistic control of what she does, even while she seems to be having a lot of fun. Feminists have expressed mixed reactions to her. On the one hand, her open seductiveness seems to be a throwback to the days when women dressed to be ogled by men. On the other, she seems to be running the show and she does some ogling herself. The most famous and often quoted comment in this vein about Madonna comes from writer Camille Paglia (not popular with many feminists), who in 1990 in the *New York Times* called her the "true feminist":

She exposes the Puritanism and suffocating ideology of American feminism, which is stuck in an adolescent whining mode. Madonna has taught young women to be fully female and sexual while still exercising total control over their lives. She shows girls how to be attractive, sensual, energetic, ambitious, aggressive and funny—all at the same time. (Quoted in Rubey 1992, 264)

Censorship Efforts and the Parents Music Resource Council

On December 3, 1979, in Cincinnati, Ohio, eleven teens were crushed to death when they tried to get into a concert given by The Who. Ten years after Altamont (see Chapter 6), adults realized in horror, teens were still placing themselves in danger because of rock music. As MTV began broadcasting more sexually explicit and violent videos, as rap expressed its fatalistic view of the city, as Madonna and Michael Jackson performed their suggestive dances and songs, rock music itself came under scrutiny as a probable cause of rapes, murders, suicides, and violent acts by teens. At this point, it collided with the First Amendment.

Congressional subcommittees began investigating, just as they had during the Fifties, while a group of Washington, D.C. women led by Tipper Gore, wife of Senator (later Vice President) Al Gore, formed the Parents Music Resource Council, an agency that urged the rock music industry to place warning labels on its products. During the 1985 hearings, multitalented rock musician Frank Zappa testified in defense of the industry, although his frankness about the money-making aspects of it seemed for the Senators to clinch its image of rampant greed with the young as its prey. Many producers said they were sensitive to the vulnerability of teens; many senators insisted that they were not advocating censorship, even while they searched around for some legal way to control rock music. Les Garland, MTV's head programmer, commented to *U.S. News and World Report*, "We're like an art gallery. We just put the paintings on the wall" ("What Entertainers" 1985, 48–49). Kids themselves wondered what all the fuss was about.

Two studies in the journal *Popular Music and Society* attempted to find out whether indeed rock music, especially the lyrics, harmed teens. One found generally that teens paid little attention to the lyrics, often misunderstanding or completely missing references to sex, and that the worrisome "back-masking" (hiding subversive messages in the music) could only be discovered with sophisticated recording techniques (Rosenbaum and Prinsky 1987, 79–89). The other study noted that the Congressional hearings tended to regard teens as a "homogenous mass" rather than a collection of individuals with varying tastes (Verder, Dunleavy, and Powers 1989, 75) and found that teens who engaged in delinquent acts did not choose as favorite songs those that described the acts. It also found personality differences between teens who listened predominantly to Top 40 rock and those who listened to heavy metal, suggesting that the music was not a cause but a reflection of their tastes—something teens could probably have told the subcommittees in 1985.

Bruce Springsteen and Rock for Charity

Although Bruce Springsteen seemed to have faded in the late Seventies after being touted as rock's biggest comer, he returned to superstardom in 1980 with "Hungry Heart." Then came *Born in the USA*, his 1984 album, which stayed at the top of the pop album charts for nearly two years (Friedlander 1996, 268). The title song seemed to be a patriotic hymn to America, but as usual with Springsteen songs, there is a veiled sense of disaffection and disappointment (Stuessy 1994, 374). "The Boss," as he was often called, was a working-class youth who had struggled to gain his fame, and he showed it not only in his songs but also in his political activism, donating some of the proceeds from his concerts to food banks, veterans groups, the homeless, and some activist trade unions (Friedlander 1996, 268).

As if to counteract the public outcry against the sex, drugs, and violence of rock music, a number of musicians joined together to hold a giant concert to benefit starving Africans. In 1984, Irish rocker Bob Geldof organized Band Aid in England, sending the proceeds to Ethiopia. The following year he helped organize Live Aid, an even bigger event. On July 13, 1985, a series of simultaneous concerts in London, Sydney, and Philadelphia was beamed out to more than one hundred countries. It featured such performers as Madonna, Paul McCartney, The Who, Phil Collins, Mick Jagger, Tina Turner, David Bowie, and a host of others. In September of the same year, country star Willie Nelson mounted Farm Aid, a giant concert in support of family farms. In 1988 a group of performers issued a challenge to "Free Nelson Mandela" with a huge concert in London's Wembley Stadium. The same year Amnesty International mounted its Human Rights Now! tour which played in six American cities and cities in other countries, such as Zimbabwe, where human rights were at risk. While such mega-events brought attention to worthy causes, they also made money for their participants and underwriters. The taped versions might also be edited, so that the general public might not see some of the more political statements made by the performers (Friedlander 1996, 267).

Movies

Although not a movie made for teens, 1983's *Risky Business* offered an image of teen behavior that has come to be associated with the affluent Eighties. Tom Cruise plays a bored, wealthy teen boy left alone for a few days, during which he mimes being a rock star (playing "air guitar" in a scene that has become a movie classic) and becomes involved with a young prostitute. The film made a star of Cruise.

But teens could command movies of their own. In 1981 they made up

The Breakfast Club: John Hughes's 1985 film starring "Brat Pack" actors Molly Ringwald, Anthony Michael Hall, Emilio Estevez, Ally Sheedy, and Judd Nelson. Reproduced courtesy of The Museum of Modern Art.

40% of movie audiences nationwide, and the number evidently did not diminish as the decade continued. They seemed to go to the movies regularly and in great numbers, viewing their favorites several times. Such possibilities were not lost on Hollywood; the very late Seventies and the Eighties became the heyday of the teen movie—that is, a movie that is not only about teens, but stars teens and addresses genuine teen concerns, ideally with some measure of seriousness.

Serious Teen Films

Several teen films that dealt with sex more explicitly than earlier films were aimed directly at the teen audience. *Little Darlings* (1980) concerns two girls determined to lose their virginity; in *The Blue Lagoon* (1980), Brooke Shields is a girl marooned on an island with a boy; some of the scenes were labeled soft-core pornography by critics because of their frankness. *Endless Love* (1981) also stars Shields in a film version of a teen novel about two young people obsessively in love. Sex was the general topic of conversation in the more light-hearted *Fast Times at Ridgemont High* (1982), a film about California high school kids based on a real school (Scott 1983, 35).

Other films dealt with issues of friendship, power, and economic status, both in school and out. Director John Hughes directed three classics: *Six-*

teen Candles (1984), starring Molly Ringwald as a girl celebrating her sixteenth birthday; *The Breakfast Club* (1985), also featuring Ringwald, about a group of teens spending detention together and learning about each other; and *Pretty in Pink* (1986), in which Ringwald plays a poor girl asked out by a rich boy. With these films, and with his National Lampoon comedies, Hughes established himself as the foremost director of teen films, able to capture the comic elements of teen life without sacrificing the more tender ones. He worked with real teen actors in order to achieve a measure of honesty in their portrayals of their characters, and, in the case of *Sixteen Candles*, deliberately aimed for a female point of view:

This genre is predominantly about males, and sex is a predominant theme. I think they tend to ignore the families. When you're 30, you forget that at 16 sex was not your primary motivation; you were much more interested in having a girlfriend or a boyfriend. . . . I just don't think 16-year-olds are being served well by my generation. (Quoted in Barth 1984, 46)

The other director most associated with the genuine teen movie is Francis Ford Coppola, whose collaborations with author S. E. Hinton produced such films as *Tex* (1982), *The Outsiders* (1983), and *Rumble Fish* (1983). His teen films have been praised as have his classic films *The Godfather* (1972) and *Apocalypse Now* (1979), for their camera work and dark sensitivity. "Why shouldn't kids have art films, too?" he asked in an interview and then speculated about the time when "a thirteen or fourteen-year-old is going to make a feature film in Super 8 and it's going to be great—we'll all be watching a 16mm or 35mm blowup in a theatre. It has to happen" (quoted in Scott 1983, 33). Hinton's "hard-boiled teenybopper tough guys, with warm but not soft hearts thudding gently under black leather carapaces" came alive under Coppola's direction of young actors Patrick Swayze and Rob Lowe (Scott 1983, 34).

Both Hughes and Coppola gravitated to the same team of young actors in their films. Because Emilio Estevez, Judd Nelson, Ringwald, Ally Sheedy, Anthony Michael Hall, Sean Penn, and Lowe seemed to enjoy each other's company off-screen, studio publicity capitalized on their friendship in film ads. They came to be called the "brat pack," a reference to the "rat pack," the hard-boozing crowd that surrounded Frank Sinatra in the Sixties, only these young kids were just beginning to be tough.

One of the most popular teen heartthrobs was Matt Dillon. Cast at age fourteen in *Over the Edge* (1979), Dillon was the guy both girls wanted in 1980's *Little Darlings*, and he starred in all three films made from S. E. Hinton's novels. He has often been compared to Fifties teen idols James Dean and Marlon Brando, but seemed more real—"a new breed of teenage actors who appear in films that represent kids as they are (or as they could be)" (Scott 1983, 35).

For black teens, the films of Spike Lee countered the all-white brat pack image of these films. *School Daze* (1988) fantasizes about life on an all-black college campus, and *Do the Right Thing* (1989) offers a picture of life in the Bedford-Stuyvesant area of Brooklyn.

Comedies and Slasher Films

Of course, all was not serious all the time in teen films—probably not even most of the time. In John Hughes's joyful 1986 film *Ferris Bueller's Day Off*, Matthew Broderick as Ferris spends the day cutting classes in outrageous ways. The series of National Lampoon films entertained teens throughout the decade, beginning with *Animal House* in 1978 and continuing through *Class Reunion* (1982), *Vacation* (1983), *European Vacation* (1985), and *Christmas Vacation* (1989). *Animal House* is still the classic of this genre, famous for its scene of John Belushi spewing mashed potatoes out of his mouth. *Time* magazine called it "the Godfather of gross-out," and it spawned many like it in the Eighties, all of which featured things like food fights, dirty jokes, spying on girls, and teen boys generally behaving as disgustingly as possible ("And Animal House Begat," 1985, 103). *Porky's* and *Porky's II* depict "the hormonal hell of adolescence" (Scott 1983, 35) with hilariously exaggerated accuracy; they both earned the status of blockbusters. The director of *Revenge of the Nerds*, Jeff Kanew, commented that these films were "basically about guys trying to get laid. . . . [The script] had a party scene, a peekaboo scene, a panty raid, a food fight, a beer-guzzling contest. . . . I didn't think anything was tasteless as long as it was funny" ("And Animal House Begat," 1985, 103). As *Time* put it, "Sometimes, when you are 14 or 15, say, bad is better than good, dirt is more appealing than clean, and a night at the newest gross-out is more fun than sitting at home watching television with Mom and Dad" (1985, 103).

A different kind of gross-out was the slasher film. Taking their cue from the cult 1976 film *The Texas Chain Saw Massacre*, with its sleazy, bloody violence, two film series featured sweaty suspense, horrible murders, blood and gore, and teens—especially teen girls—as victims. *Halloween* (1978) was the first—a relatively serious, small-budget film about a killer who strikes on Halloween. Its popularity right into the Eighties engendered a sequel in 1981 followed by several more variations, all of which are basically, according to film scholar Leonard Maltin, "just a sequential slaughter of teenagers" (1997, 552). *Nightmare on Elm Street* directed by Wes Craven and its four sequels were equally scary and equally focused on teenagers as victims, but its villain, the scarred character of Freddy Krueger, and its premise were more interesting: Freddy could somehow get into the dreams of the teens. The films, which featured interesting special effects, were smash hits at the box office.

Such films as these—the brooding, often violent brat pack movies; the utterly mindless juvenile comedies; and the slasher films—fueled the already lurking notion of what has been called the "Blank Generation" (Smith

1987, 70). Kids today, they seemed to imply, had little to live for, little structure in their lives except that which a gang or other kind of peer group can give; it was a "post-punk, pre-apocalypse condition," and suggested that "teendom is, for the vast majority, a wasteland of boredom, desperation, and lack of purpose. . . . Absurdist nihilism is the Eighties' prevailing style—an inverted glamor, adopted by kids as they indulge in the peculiarly narcissistic masochism of adolescent self-martyrdom" (Smith 1987, 70–71).

Batman

Nineteen eighty-nine was the year of the Batman movie. Starring Michael Keaton as the Dark Knight and Jack Nicholson as the Joker, with brooding sets by Anton Furst, direction by Tim Burton, and music by Danny Elfman, the result was a "spectacular black comedy about two maniacs on a collision course, with its subversive lesson that the one without the sense of humor is bound to win" (Daniels 1995, 203). It took ten years to make, but the visual and financial results were worth it. The film made $405 million worldwide; the set won an Oscar; and Jack Nicholson's portrayal of the Joker has become a classic.

Books and Reading

The nonfiction best-sellers of the Eighties reflect the decade's interest in affluence. Lee Iacocca's autobiography explaining his rise to the chairmanship of the Chrysler Corporation topped the lists in 1984 and 1985. A book by Thomas J. Peters and Robert H. Waterman Jr. called *In Search of Excellence*, popular at the same time, offers illustrations of success by America's best-run companies. *Jane Fonda's Workout Book* tapped into the fitness and aerobics craze among affluent women. Popular fiction tended more toward fantasy. Teen favorite Stephen King dominated the Eighties best-seller lists with *The Talisman*, *The Tommyknockers*, and *It*. Tom Clancy's political thrillers and Jean Auel's novels set in prehistoric times appealed to adults and older teens. Olive Burns's 1984 *Cold Sassy Tree*, although written for adults, had great appeal for teens, as did Ernest J. Gaines's *A Gathering of Old Men* (1983), a story of black life in the Depression South.

Young Adult Books

The problem novel of the Seventies began to subside, but several unusually talented writers took up the genre during the Eighties, giving it more resonance and flexibility. Bruce Brooks produced *The Moves Make the Man* (1984) and *No Kidding* (1989). Chris Crutcher published *The Crazy Horse Electric Game* (1987), and Walter Dean Myers published his novel of the Vietnam War *Fallen Angels* (1988). Suzanne Fisher Staples opened teens' eyes to adolescence in a nomadic culture with *Shabanu, Daughter of the Wind* in 1989, while Francesca Lia Block, probably the most original voice in young adult books to this time, introduced *Weetzie Bat* in 1989—a funny, touching, punk fairy tale capturing the glitz of life in LA along with the difficulties of being a teen in the Eighties, shadowed by AIDS and loneliness.

Established writers, including Robert Cormier, Cynthia Voigt, and Judy Blume, continued to produce excellent reading for teens. Blume aimed at an older audience than she had previously when she published *Tiger Eyes* (1981), about a girl coping with the senseless murder of her father. Voigt tells the story of a girl whose leg has been amputated in *Izzy Willy Nilly* (1986). Cormier followed his characters from *The Chocolate War* (1974) into a sequel in 1985—*Beyond the Chocolate War*—partly as a response to the large number of teens who wrote or called him wanting to know what happened next. In 1988 he published *Fade*, a remarkable blend of fantasy and realism, about a teen who finds he has inherited the ability to disappear. In this novel, as in *I am the Cheese* (1977), Cormier challenges young readers to follow a complex plot, while his depiction of a twilight world in which reality may not be what it seems is even more chilling.

Censorship

Attempts to censor teen reading escalated considerably in the Eighties. As Judy Blume put it, "Everything changed. The censors crawled out of the woodwork, seemingly overnight, organized and determined. . . . Challenges to books quadrupled within months" (quoted in Nilsen and Donelson 1993, 514). Blume, along with Norma Klein, had been targeted in the Seventies, but in the Eighties her particular brand of realism, especially on the subject of sex, seemed to urge nervous parents, librarians, and school boards into new action. In 1982 the American Booksellers Association noted that Blume had tied Soviet author Alexander Solzhenitsyn as the author with the greatest number of banned titles (West 1988, 82). In 1984 a case of attempted censorship attracted considerable media attention. In Peoria, Illinois, without issuing a formal complaint and without any prompting from parents, a library official and an associate superintendent of schools removed three Blume books from their district's library shelves: *Then Again Maybe I Won't*, *Deenie*, and *Blubber*. When this became public knowledge, many parents, librarians, writers, and civil libertarians spoke out in the media denouncing this action. As the story occupied more newspaper space, the school officials were forced to back down and return the books (1988, 83).

The case drew attention to the fear of any sexual references in books for young readers. Challengers seemed to believe that what kids read about, they were sure to do—that they knew nothing about sex and were not interested in it until they read about it in books. This attitude has persisted throughout the century, and while it stems at times from a sincere attempt to instruct and encourage the young in positive ways, it more often represents a deep fear of the power, sexual and otherwise, of the young. Public and very popular writers for teens, like Blume, are the easiest targets; trying to remove their books from kids' hands gives the challengers the illusion that adults are still in control of that power. Of course, young teen girls continued throughout the decade to buy Blume's books for themselves and to write her confiding letters about their physical and emotional confusion.

Popular Series Books

Series books have accounted for a large part of the teen market since the turn of the century, peaking in the Twenties and Thirties with the Stratemeyer Syndicate books. The Eighties saw a phenomenal renewal of teen and preteen series books, with publication numbers soaring into the millions. Ann Martin's Baby Sitters Club series, designed for girls from eight to thirteen, began in 1986; Martin had written twenty-nine of them by 1990, as well as other novels for older teen readers. Janet Quin-Harkin began her series of Sweet Dreams romances in 1981 with *California Girl*. She produced six of these by 1987 and then created the Sugar and Spice series, writing up to eight books a year to keep up with the demand. Christopher Pike wrote very different series books for teens, both girls and boys: horror thrillers, beginning with *Slumber Party* in 1985. He has been called the "junior Stephen King" and admits to loving King's work (Drew 1997, 361). His name, a pseudonym, is taken from the short-lived captain in the first *Star Trek* episodes, but his publisher will not reveal his true name. He has said that despite the horror and fear in his books, he "has a romantic idea of high school," and this is why he likes to write for teens (Drew 1997, 361).

The queen of Eighties series books was undoubtedly Francine Pascal. Pascal had written both fiction and nonfiction prior to 1983 (including a 1974 book with her reporter husband about Patty Hearst), but when she began the Sweet Valley High series in 1983 with *Double Love*, she created books with such appeal to the teen girl market that she had written sixty-one of them by 1990. The early Sweet Valley books trace the adventures of twins Elizabeth and Jessica through their difficulties with friends and boys; Pascal has said that the books were "the essence of high school. . . . The world outside is just an adult shadow going by. The parents barely exist. The action takes place in bedrooms, cars, and schools" (Drew 1997, 325). Her 1985 Sweet Valley High book *Perfect Summer* startled the publishing world by ending up on the *New York Times* best-seller list, the first time a young adult book, especially a girls' series book, had had such a distinction. Eventually Pascal stopped writing them herself and began to submit plot outlines to hired writers who produced the books under the pseudonym "Kate William" (Drew 1997, 326).

V. C. (Virginia Cleo) Andrews unexpectedly entered the teen series market with her 1979 gothic novel *Flowers in the Attic*, about four children from an incestuous marriage who are imprisoned in an attic and are cruelly abused by their grandmother. Eventually the older boy and girl fall in love. This book, although not designed for a teen audience, captured the imagination of teen girls nationwide; they demanded more books about the characters, and Andrews complied with four more, as well as *My Sweet Audrina* in 1982. Adult critics sneered at these books, calling them mawkish and ghoulish; one said they were "the female equivalent of stories about giant crabs and mutated slugs among their brothers," adding, "Perhaps it was the jewelry and the clothes. Perhaps it was the incest" (quoted in Drew 1997, 17). Throughout the Eighties, nevertheless, teen girls scoured libraries and bookstores for more of them. Andrews died in 1986 but the series has continued, now written by Andrew Niederman.

Comic Books

Comic books suffered a slump in sales during the Seventies, but the Eighties brought some major changes that helped both comic fans and the general public, who loved the famous superhero characters. Instead of marketing through magazine sellers, who often threw away unsold comics and who did not attract hard-core comic fans, publishers tried marketing through specialty shops where fans could shop for old and new comics. DC also revamped its heroes. The strange psyche of Batman was explored anew in the series the Dark Knight Returns, beginning in 1986. Superman, who had reached his fiftieth birthday, was reenvisioned in comics by emphasizing his human qualities as much as his super powers; he made the cover of *Time* magazine in March 1988. Wonder Woman began anew in 1987 with revised versions of the first series, this time more true to the underlying mythology of the Amazon.

And Robin died. The original Robin, Dick Grayson, had gone into a career of his own as leader of the Teen Titans. The character called Jason Todd had taken over Robin's role with Batman, but he had not developed into a likable character. Comics editors have always paid attention to their fans, but this time, in an unprecedented move, DC editors created a series called *A Death in the Family,* which ended with Robin caught in an explosion. The editors posed the question to their readers: should Robin live or die? Readers could vote by phone, for two days only (Daniels 1995, 201). Two different versions of the ending were prepared, and the editors awaited the results. The editors themselves were divided about what they thought would happen, but they did not expect such a close vote: 5,271 readers voted that Robin should live; 5,343 voted for his death. This was not a particularly large number of actual voters, but Americans everywhere followed the developments. Many media pundits thought the whole thing was a setup, or in bad taste, but they were all interested. Even the *Wall Street Journal* ran the story. The DC editor in charge got hate mail as if an actual murder had been committed, and he was harassed by upset fans. He later said the whole thing had impressed upon him how much the public had invested in these characters: "They have become postindustrial folklore, and part of this job is to be the custodian of folk figures. Everybody on earth knows Batman and Robin" (1995, 201).

Graphic Novels

Older teens enjoyed the new sophistication of complex comics which went far beyond Batman and Robin even in their new versions. In 1986 DC Comics brought out the Watchman series, which created a new breed of antiheroes for the end of the millennium. The multilayered tale could be interpreted in many ways, and it raised some serious moral and ethical questions that had no easy answers. The Sandman series used different artists and original and literary storylines for each issue, all embedded in myth. The label "comic book" seemed hardly big enough to describe these richly illustrated texts which resembled novels more than any other genre. The term "graphic novel" seemed more appropriate, especially for books like DC's 1989 Batman tale *Arkham Asylum*. The elegant artwork by Dave McKean and the disturbing story by Grant Morrison resulted in an "unprecedented success, selling 182,166 copies in hard cover and another 85,047 in paperback" (Daniels 1995, 209).

Magazines

During the Eighties, teen magazine readership divided by gender, as it had in previous decades. Boys read adult men's magazines, such as *Sports Illustrated* and *Playboy*, because they had no major magazines of their own. Girls, however, had *Seventeen*, still the leader by far in sales with a paid circulation of 1,737,622 in 1985 ("Teens Targeted," 1985, 50). Two new magazines were beginning to gain on *Seventeen*'s readership: *YM* (which previously had called itself *Young Miss* and is now *Young & Modern*) and *Teen*. Both offered a similar mix of fashion, information, and advice to teen girls, but none of these three featured ads for birth control products, and although they ran articles on sexuality and the body, birth control itself was still a very delicate subject.

Along came *Sassy*, which offered fashion and informational features but was much more frank about previously taboo subjects. It was so frank, in fact, that it drew the wrath of the religious right, which urged advertisers to cancel their ads in protest. Jane Pratt, *Sassy*'s twenty-five-year-old editor, said, "That was devastating, particularly to a new magazine. But we came through because so many teenagers loved our magazine and stayed with us" ("A Teen's Eye View," 1989, 21). *Sassy*'s circulation had reached 500,000 after only seven issues; teen girls who wanted more than advice on a prom dress loved it ("Trying to Silence Sassy," 1988, 45).

REFERENCES

"And Animal House Begat." *Time* 125, no. 15 (April 15, 1985): 103.

Barth, Jack. "Kinks of Comedy." *Film Comment* 20, no. 3 (May/June 1984): 44–47.

Blumenthal, Dale. "When Teens Take over the Shopping Cart." *FDA Consumer* 24, no. 2 (March 1990): 30+.

Brown, Charles T. *The Art of Rock and Roll.* 3d ed. Englewood Cliffs, N.J.: Prentice-Hall, 1992.

Burkett, Kathy. "Stepping Out." *Ms.* 15 (August 1986): 30.

Chadwick, Bruce A., and Jim B. Heaton. *Statistical Handbook on Adolescents in America.* Phoenix, Ariz.: Oryx, 1996.

———. *Statistical Handbook on the American Family.* Phoenix, Ariz.: Oryx, 1992.

Charney, Mark J. "It's a Cold World out There: Redefining the Family in Contemporary American Film." In *Beyond the Stars: Studies in American Popular Film.* Vol. 5, ed. Paul Loukides and Linda K. Fuller, 21–42. Bowling Green, Ohio: Bowling Green State University Press, 1996.

"Children Having Children." *Time* 126, no. 23 (December 9, 1985): 78–90.

"Cloven Smokers: Dangers in a Teen-age Fad?" *Time* 125, no. 2 (January 14, 1985): 63.

Colbert, David, ed. *Eyewitness to America.* New York: Pantheon Books, 1997.

Considine, David M. *The Cinema of Adolescence.* Jefferson, N.C.: McFarland, 1985.

Coontz, Stephanie. *The Way We Never Were: American Families and the Nostalgia Trap.* New York: Basic Books, 1992.

Curtis, Jim. *Rock Eras: Interpretations of Music and Society, 1954–1984.* Bowling Green, Ohio: Bowling Green State University Press, 1987.

Dalzell, Tom. *Flappers 2 Rappers: American Youth Slang.* Springfield, Mass.: Merriam-Webster, 1996.

Daniels, Les. *DC Comics: Sixty Years of the World's Favorite Comic Book Heroes.* Boston: Little, Brown, 1995.

Dargan, Amanda, and Steven Zeitlin. *City Play.* New Brunswick, N.J.: Rutgers University Press, 1990.

"Debate: Should Students Maintain a 2.0 Average to Participate in Extracurricular Activities?" *NEA Today* 3 (May 1985): 27.

Drew, Bernard A. *The 100 Most Popular Young Adult Authors.* Rev. ed. Englewood, Colo.: Libraries Unlimited, Inc., 1997.

Dworkin, Peter. "The AIDS Threat to Teenagers." *U.S. News and World Report* 107, no. 16 (October 23, 1989): 29–30.

Eble, Connie. *Slang and Sociability: In-Group Language Among College Students.* Chapel Hill: University of North Carolina Press, 1996.

Eccles, Jacquelynne S. "Academic Achievement." In *Encyclopedia of Adolescence*, ed. Richard Lerner, Anne C. Petersen, and Jeanne Brooks-Gunn. New York: Garland, 1991.

Friedlander, Paul. *Rock and Roll: A Social History.* New York: Westview Press, 1996.

Greenberger, Ellen, and Laurence Steinberg. *When Teenagers Work: The Psychological and Social Costs of Adolescent Employment.* New York: Basic Books, 1986.

Height, Dorothy L. "What Must Be Done about Children Having Children." *Ebony* 40 (March 1985): 76+.

Horn, Maurice. *100 Years of American Newspaper Comics.* New York: Gramercy Books, 1996.

Horner, Barbara G. "How Teens Spend $45 Billion a Year." *Co-Ed* 30 (September 1984): 42+.

Jacobs, Thomas A. *What Are My Rights? 95 Questions and Answers About Teens and the Law.* Minneapolis: Free Spirit Publishing, 1997.

Jones, Peter M. "Congress and You." *Scholastic Update* 121, no. 12 (February 24, 1989): 3.

Kellner, Douglas. "Madonna, Fashion, and Identity." In *On Fashion,* ed. Shari Benstock and Suzanne Ferriss. New Brunswick, N.J.: Rutgers University Press, 1994, 159–82.

Lich, Lera Tyler. "Children's Games and Socialization in the Texas Hill Country." In *Texas Toys and Games,* ed. Francis Edward Abernathy. Dallas: Southern Methodist University Press, 1989, 229–35.

Lightfoot, Sara Lawrence. *The Good High School: Portraits of Character and Culture.* New York: Basic Books, 1983.

Maltin, Leonard. *The 1998 Movie and Video Guide.* New York: Signet, 1997.

McBee, Susanna. "A Call to Tame the Genie of Teen Sex." *U.S. News and World Report* 101 (December 22, 1986): 8.

McNeil, Alex. *Total Television: A Comprehensive Guide to Programming from 1948 to the Present.* 2d upd. rev. ed. New York: Penguin Books, 1991.

"Michael Jackson Named U.S. Teens' Top Star." *Jet* 67 (January 14, 1985): 57.

Nilsen, Alleen Pace, and Kenneth L. Donelson, eds. *Literature for Today's Young Adults.* 4th ed. New York: HarperCollins, 1993.

Nonkin, Leslie Jane. "Check, Please." *Seventeen* 45 (March 1986): 224+.

Phillips, Louis, and Burnham Holmes. *The TV Almanac.* New York: Macmillan, 1994.

Pipho, Chris. "The Quick Fix or a Lasting Solution?" *Phi Delta Kappan* 70 (March 1989): 502–3.

Portnow, Beth. "Teleteens: The World Through Word of Mouth." *American Health* 8, no. 8 (October 1989): 90.

"Results from the National Adolescent Student Health Survey." *Journal of the American Medical Association* 261, no. 14 (April 14, 1989): 2025–26.

"A Rhode Island Town Survives Its Night to Remember as Aaron Takes Paul to the Prom." *People Magazine* 13 (June 16, 1980): 98.

Rollin, Lucy. "Guilt and the Unconscious in *Arkham Asylum. INKS: Cartoon and Comic Art Studies* 1, no. 1 (1994): 2–13.

Rosenbaum, Jill, and Lorraine Prinsky. "Sex, Violence, and Rock 'n' Roll: Youth's Perceptions of Popular Music." *Popular Music and Society* 11, no. 2 (Summer 1987): 79–89.

Rubey, Dan. "Voguing at the Carnival." In *Present Tense: Rock & Roll and Culture,* ed. Anthony deCurtis, 235–70. Durham, N.C.: Duke University Press, 1992.

Sanders, Alain L. "Bad News for Death Row: The Court Okays the Execution of Teenage and Retarded Criminals." *Time* 134, no. 2 (July 10, 1989): 48–49.

Schmittroth, Linda, ed. *Statistical Record of Children.* Detroit, Mich.: Gale, 1994.

"School Athletes Hit the Books . . . or Else." *U.S. News and World Report* 99 (November 4, 1985): 10.

"School Dropouts—State by State." *U.S. News and World Report* 98, no. 21 (June 3, 1985): 14.

Schultz, Jerelyn B. "AHEA's Survey of American Teens." *Journal of Home Economics* 81, no. 2. (Summer 1989): 27–38.

Scott, Jay. "The Wild Ones." *American Film*, April 1983, 30–65.

Sellers, Patricia. "The ABC's of Marketing to Kids." *Fortune* 119, no. 10 (May 8, 1989): 114+.

Smith, Gavin. "Pretty Vacant in Pink." *Film Comment* 23, no. 4 (July/August 1987): 70–77.

Stuessy, Joe. *Rock and Roll: Its History and Stylistic Development*. 2d ed. Englewood Cliffs, N.J.: Prentice-Hall, 1994.

"Survey Shows That High School Seniors Still Want Family, Jobs, and Money." *Phi Delta Kappan* 17 (September 1985): 80.

"Teenage Orphans of the Job Boom." *Time* 125, no. 19 (May 13, 1985): 46–47.

"Teen Boys Get Condom Sense." *Psychology Today* 23, no. 10 (October 1989): 62–63.

"Teen Drug Abuse—the News Is Bad." *U.S. News and World Report* 99, no. 21 (November 18, 1985): 16.

"Teen Drug Use: Ups and Downs." *Science News* 128 (November 16, 1985): 310.

"A Teen-Pregnancy Epidemic." *Newsweek* 105, no. 12 (March 25, 1985): 90.

"A Teen's Eye View." *NEA Today* 8, no. 3 (October 1989): 21.

"Teen Suicide Clusters: More Than Mimicry." *Science News* 136 (November 25, 1989): 342.

"Teens Targeted as Buying Power Increases." *Advertising Age* 56 (October 3, 1985): 50–52.

Trachtenberg, Jeffrey A. "Big Spenders: Teenage Division." *Forbes* 138 (November 3, 1986): 201+.

"Trying to Silence *Sassy*." *Time* 132, no. 12 (September 19, 1988): 45.

Verder, Paul, Kathleen Dunleavy, and Charles H. Powers. "Heavy Metal Music and Adolescent Delinquency." *Popular Music and Society* 13, no. 1 (Spring 1989): 73–82.

Wallechinsky, David. *The People's Almanac Presents the Twentieth Century*. New York: Little, Brown, 1995.

Ward, Ed, Geoffrey Stokes, and Ken Tucker, eds. *Rock of Ages: The Rolling Stone History of Rock & Roll*. New York: Rolling Stone Press, 1986.

Wattleton, Faye, and Marian Wright Edelman. "Teen-age Pregnancy: The Case for National Action." *The Nation* 249, no. 4 (July 24, 1989): 138+.

West, Mark I. *Children, Culture, and Controversy*. Hamden, Conn.: Archon, 1988.

"What Entertainers Are Doing to Your Kids." *U.S. News and World Report* 99 (October 28, 1985): 46–49.

Wood, Leonard. "Teenagers' Reading Habits." *Publishers Weekly* 234 (July 29, 1988): 132.

Wright, David. *America in the 20th Century: 1980–1989*. New York: Marshall Cavendish, 1995.

· 9 ·

The 1990s

Determining patterns of a decade before it has become the past is risky; however, with regard to teen culture, three patterns seem clear. All three, which began in the Eighties, are gathering speed and intensity in the Nineties. First is the number of statistics for teens. As a group they are the most polled, questioned, evaluated, scrutinized, and speculated about in the nation. There is even a special research agency devoted to asking them about themselves: Teen Research Unlimited, of Northbrook, Illinois. Part of this attention comes from the determination of corporations to market their goods to apparently voracious teen spenders; part of it is the national mystification—and deep fear—adults experience in regard to today's teenagers. Unfortunately, the statistics produce few answers to the real questions.

The second pattern is the blending of all aspects of teen fashion and media culture. It has become almost impossible to separate movies, television, books, music, and the World Wide Web from each other or from an array of consumer goods—clothes, shoes, snacks, gadgets, soft drinks, candy, fast foods, video games, cosmetics, and drugs. More than at any other time in this century, popular culture is unified and teens are unified by their popular culture.

The third pattern, on the other hand, is the fragmentation of American life generally and teen life in particular. Shifting family patterns, short-term living arrangements, multiple part-time jobs, increasingly clear ethnic boundaries and identities, the isolation that results from gangs and drug use—all of these have changed the way in which teens perceive the world and themselves. Their media and their consumer goods may seem joined,

Eighteen-year-old college freshman using the computer in a typical Nineties dormitory room. University of Oklahoma, 1997. Reproduced courtesy of Lauren Grubb.

but for many young people, their teen years pass like a series of scenes in a music video. Some approach the millennium with hope, others with a sense of drifting into a vaguely hopeless future not much different from today. They sum it all up in the popular dismissive term, "Whatever."

POLITICS AND NATIONAL EVENTS

The decade opened with war, but a war very different from any that had been experienced before. When in August 1990 Iraq invaded Kuwait, the United States, with the sanction of the United Nations and other countries, vowed to take military action. After months of buildup and threats, the war itself, called the Gulf War or "Desert Storm," took only three days in January 1991. It was, as historian Gini Holland says, a war made for television (Holland 1995, 1366): intense, dramatic, and fast, over in time for the commercial and leaving Americans who were not directly involved with a sense of unreality.

Other events in the closing of the Bush administration shed little glory on the government. The U.S. Supreme Court, in a 1989 decision, gave states even more control over abortion, encouraging antiabortionists to undertake more violent encounters at abortion clinics around the country. The spectacle of soldiers engaging in sexual harassment appeared on national television when the Tailhook scandal broke; women in the military revealed that at the 1991 convention of military flyers, the men had lined up and groped, grabbed at, and humiliated the women as they tried to walk through the hotel's hallways. Yet another spectacle was the televised hearings held in 1991 in the U.S. Senate when attorney Anita Hill stated that Supreme Court nominee Clarence Thomas had harassed her when she had worked for him in previous years. Thomas was eventually confirmed by the Senate, by a vote of 52 to 48, the narrowest margin in history for a Supreme Court Justice.

When election time rolled around, Democrat Bill Clinton of Arkansas challenged President Bush by focusing on the depressing economic situation of millions of Americans. "It's the economy, stupid," was the slogan his campaigners used to anyone uncertain of the issues. Americans voted him into office in 1992. An accomplished politician, Clinton brought youth and a Kennedy-like vigor to the office and a determination to change the way government worked. He also brought a wife, as savvy a politician as her husband, who was a professional woman, an attorney, and planned to continue her career. Their teenage daughter, Chelsea Clinton, born in 1980, has lived out her teen years as America's First Teen with remarkable poise and normalcy, enjoying dates, parties with friends, and travel with her parents. After high school graduation, she enrolled in Stanford University.

Some are calling this the decade of the woman. Clinton has made it a priority to put women into positions of power and to address women's issues. The Clinton cabinet and Congress are a multicultural, as well as a gender, mix. Janet Reno is attorney general; Donna Shalala is secretary of health and human services; Jocelyn Elders was surgeon general; Ruth Bader Ginsberg is the second woman appointed to the Supreme Court; Madeleine Albright is the secretary of state. The number of women holding seats in the Senate and House has increased. Although the issue of health care is one that involves every American, it was perceived as a "women's issue." Hillary Clinton chaired a task force to investigate the system, one that is riddled with high expenses, inequities, and mountains of red tape.

Despite these gains, however, and despite an improved economy, Clinton has become the second president in American history to be impeached. The charges resulted from his denial of an affair with a White House intern, Monica Lewinsky. Throughout 1998, news reports followed the accusations and finally the proof that Clinton had indeed engaged in sexual activity with Lewinsky and then lied about it to the public and the grand jury. With unprecedented frankness, private sexuality became public knowledge. *The Washington Post* surveyed a group of teens for their response to these revelations and found that they believed extramarital affairs are too common to be grounds for such intense political scrutiny. Although Clinton may not be morally perfect, they thought, neither are his accusers. Some were simply disgusted by the public fascination with sexual misconduct, and some black teens expressed anger at the Republicans for attacking a president who had improved the economy for them (Russakoff and Loose 1998, 1F). Clinton's trial in the Senate lasted twenty-one days in early 1999, and resulted in his acquittal on both charges: perjury and obstruction of justice. The votes divided pretty clearly along party lines but some Republicans voted to acquit.

Nineties Teens—Generation X and "Thirteeners"

Those teens born between 1946 and 1964 have been called the Baby Boomers, products of the postwar period when young soldiers returned home and married. The Boomers, who were the hippies and activists of the Sixties, are now the businessmen and women, politicians and professionals, of the Nineties. Teens born between 1965 and 1976 now wear the label Generation X, coined by novelist Doug Coupland. They entered their teens during the late Seventies and Eighties; all are, as of 1998, past the teenage years. The X label symbolizes the mystery of what they were really like, what they will ultimately contribute to society, why they had so little ambition, and why there seems to have been such a blank in the center of lives filled with rock music and conspicuous consumption.

What shall we call the generation born after 1977, who lived out most of their teen years in the Nineties? Some have called them Generation Y, some the Echo Boomers, some the Baby Busters, some the product of a Baby Boomlet. Journalists Neil Howe and William Strauss offer the term Thirteeners: they are

the thirteenth generation to know the US flag and Constitution. More than a name, the number thirteen is a gauntlet, an obstacle to be overcome. Maybe it's the floor where elevators don't stop, or the doughnut that bakers don't count. Then again, maybe it's a suit's thirteenth card—the ace—that wins, face-down, in a game of high-stakes blackjack. It's an understated number for an underestimated generation. (1992, 68)

Howe and Strauss see them as practical, clear-eyed survivors who know "how the world really works." Thirteeners, they say, see a bleak version of the future, one in which they will have to work harder for less than their parents and one in which, although they will go to college, they will also probably be mugged at some point, or worse. Ironically the X-ers who widened the generation gap between them and their parents in the Sixties are finding the gap between themselves and this next generation growing daily. The Thirteeners do not want to be like their parents, according to Howe and Strauss.

And yet, polls also show that many American teens respect their parents, practice their religion, stay in school, appreciate their teachers, and, although they are entirely aware of the dangers, have a sense of optimism about the future. They enjoy their ethnic diversity and their skill at technology. They are aware of their power in the coming millennium.

Teens in the News

Teen athletes captured America's attention during the Nineties. Teen golfer Tiger Woods captured several amateur titles before turning pro and winning the prestigious Master's Tournament in 1997 at age 21. Switzerland's Martina Hingis and America's Venus Williams are providing tennis lovers with exciting tournament action. In the 1998 winter Olympics, teen figure skaters Michelle Kwan and Tara Lipinski competed for top honors and turned in virtually flawless performances, with Lipinski winning the gold medal by a single point. At just fifteen, in 1998, Lipinski decided to enter professional skating rather than continue competing as an amateur.

In the early Nineties, Americans were fascinated by the Texas cheerleader murder plot. In the small town of Channelview, Texas, Shanna Holloway and Amber Heath were rivals for the high school cheerleading team. Shanna had been disqualified for the team because her mother Wanda had tried to influence the selection. Wanda Holloway evidently believed that Amber's mother was at fault, and she allegedly plotted to have her murdered. Wanda Holloway was tried in 1991 and found guilty, but the verdict was subsequently overturned on a technicality. The Heath family filed suit in 1992 and won a settlement in 1994. In 1996 Wanda pled no contest at a retrial and served prison time. Shanna herself graduated from the school with honors in 1996; she never tried out for the cheerleading squad.

Violent Teens

The Fifties' concern with juvenile delinquency has been matched and exceeded by the Nineties shock wave of teen violence. As of 1991, America had the highest teen homicide rate in the world. Murder was the third leading cause of death for white teens, and the leading cause of death for young black males (Price, Desmond, and Smith 1991, 225). It has become an un-funny joke to say that black teen boys are an endangered species. Drive-by shootings in ghetto areas have become common occurrences. Teens who live in tough neighborhoods and attend schools where fights are routine have begun arming themselves, not with the switchblades of the Fifties, but with guns. In 1991, 47% of black males had a pistol at home and 57% said they knew someone who took a gun to school; 87% said they knew someone who had been shot (1991, 225). A 1996 study conducted among teens in a detention center in Atlanta showed that 84% of those who owned guns acquired them before they were fifteen; most of them were given the gun without seeking it. Those who sought the gun were likely to become regular carriers (Ash et al., 1996, 1754). They felt safer with a gun and generally bought them on the street, where they are easily available.

Some teen violence is more difficult to fathom; it occurs not in the setting of the daily tension of the ghetto but in quiet rural or suburban, mostly white neighborhoods. Two wealthy brothers were convicted for the brutal 1989 murder of their parents; Lyle Menendez was twenty-two at the time of their 1990 arrest, and his brother Erik was nineteen. In 1992 seventeen-year-old Amy Fisher, a senior at John F. Kennedy High School in Merrick, Long Island, shot the wife of her middle-aged lover, Joey Buttafuoco. Some of this violent thrill seeking echoes the cases Benjamin Fine described in the Fifties in his book *1,000,000 Delinquents* (see Chapter 5), but the violence has escalated in scope and power.

Especially disturbing is the recent rash of school killings—not individuals killing individuals but teens committing random mass killings with automatic weapons. In May 1998, in Springfield, Oregon, fifteen-year-old Kip Kinkel killed his parents, rigged the house with bombs which he had learned to make on the Internet, and then shot up his school, killing two students and wounding twenty-two others. On March 24, 1998, in Jonesboro, Arkansas, thirteen-year-old Mitchell Johnson and eleven-year-old Andrew Golden shot at a number of students in their school. They crept up behind the schoolyard carrying automatic weapons they had taken from a relative's house. When the students emerged, they began firing, killing four girls and one teacher. The motive, apparently, was that a girl had rejected Mitch, who said at his hearing that he had meant to fire over their heads. A clear image of these two boys has not yet emerged, although both were evidently quite familiar with guns. Both have been sentenced—Mitchell on his fourteenth birthday—to incarceration until they reach age twenty-one.

Why are these things happening? Where has our culture failed our teens that some must act out in violent ways? These same questions plagued parents and authorities during the Fifties, but more teens seem to be losing their lives in the Nineties, and more teens seem to kill without remorse. Answers are not easy to find. Many Americans feel that our culture itself is saturated with violence, especially in the popular media. Television documentaries show explosions and shootings in realistic detail as never before; movies glorify heroes with powerful weapons who mow down all opposition in fiery destruction. Directions for building bombs have been available on the Internet for years. Young children play violent video games; teens enjoy laser tag or paint-ball, imitating, say, Bruce Willis in one of his violent roles. On the other hand, adults have blamed the media ever since teens first spent their wages on the nickelodeons in the early decades of the century. Movies and television are easier to see and control than the complex problems underlying poverty, drugs, racial prejudice, lack of educational opportunity, and the absence of decent jobs. Some theorists blame the dysfunctional family, a catchall term which has come to cover everything from parental alcoholism and sexual abuse, to divorce, to occasional arguments between teens and parents about curfews and sex.

Journalist William Finnegan believes that Americans have created this world for teens.

We jail the poor in their multitudes, abandon the dream of equality, cede more and more of public life to private interests, let lobbyists run government. Those who can afford to do so lock themselves inside gated communities and send their children to private schools. And then we wonder why the world at large has become harsher and more cynical, why our kids become strange to us. (1998, 351)

Race

Tensions between the races have remained and, at times, have exploded. In April 1992, white police officers stopped a black man, Rodney King, on the Los Angeles streets. When he showed some sign of resisting, they began to beat him. A bystander taped the incident on his videocamera, and the officers were brought to trial. When they were acquitted, the worst riots in American history erupted, killing fifty-eight people. Two of the officers were convicted later in a civil trial. During the riots, a white man, Reginald Denney, was pulled from his truck and beaten by black men, in an incident also videotaped. His attackers were given a mild sentence. The O. J. Simpson case also revealed deep racial divisions among Americans. In June 1994 the handsome, black football and film star was arrested for the stabbing murder of his ex-wife, Nicole Brown Simpson, and her friend, Ronald Goldman. After a sensational trial that began in January 1995 and lasted many months, during which many white Americans tended to think he was guilty and many blacks believed him innocent, he was acquitted by a predominantly black jury. Simpson's defense lawyers were able to show that the Los Angeles police had displayed racist attitudes. Simpson was brought to civil trial in 1997 for the deaths and ordered to pay millions of dollars in damages to the families of the victims. The case continues to divide Americans along racial lines.

Racially motivated violence among teens continues as well. In 1997, in a disturbing echo of the Emmett Till case of the Fifties, thirteen-year-old African American Lenard Clark was riding his bike in a mostly white Chicago neighborhood, when he was attacked and savagely beaten. After remaining in a coma for a long time, he is mentally impaired. Two teenagers and a twenty-year-old have been arrested for the crime. The "skinhead" movement has attracted some teens, mostly male. They shave their heads, adopt Nazi-like attitudes and dress, and embrace racist attitudes with pride. Journalist William Finnegan spent some time with such teens, members of the Nazi Low Riders in Southern California's Antelope Valley. One told him, "White supremacism just comes from growing up and seeing what's happening in society. . . . We're all just sitting out here on the corner while [blacks] are getting all the scholarships. . . . I haven't seen any of them show me they really deserve to be in this society" (1998, 289). Such hateful thought has found a home on the Internet as well, in places like the Aryan Dating Page, where teens with such tendencies can be recruited into the National Socialist White People's Party or other similar groups.

The government still does its share of discriminating, too. Along the Mexican border, for example, Mexican teens are under particular surveillance by the Immigration and Naturalization Services (INS), or the Border Patrol. Native-American author Leslie Marmon Silko describes the power of the Border Patrol: they have complete power to detain anyone for any reason, and any resistance is lawbreaking. They watch cars with white and brown-skinned people in them, they watch for Indio-Hispanics, they detain anyone who looks Asian. "In Phoenix," Silko says, "INS agents raid public high schools and drag dark-skinned students away to their vans. In 1992, in El Paso, Texas, a high school football coach driving a vanload of his players in full uniform was pulled over on the freeway and INS agents put a cocked revolver to the coach's head through the van window"—an incident which finally persuaded a federal judge to issue a restraining order against the INS in El Paso (Silko 1997, 108–11).

Nevertheless, a 1997 poll sponsored by *Time* magazine and the Cable News Network (CNN) indicated that teens are remarkably optimistic about race relations in America. Black teens know there are problems, but in their own lives, they call racism a "small" problem or no problem (Farley 1997, 88). They tend to believe that race relations will get better in America, and they have plenty of friends of other races. The poll also found that the stereotype of the black teen drug user from the projects is just that—a stereotype: in this poll 13% of white teens had used illegal drugs, as opposed to only 6% of black teens. More than 90% of both black and white teens said they were likely to go to college (1997, 90).

Teen Girls

The plight of teen girls in American culture has come to the forefront in the Nineties. In response to a 1991 study, published by the American Association of University Women, to see how its findings played out day to day, journalist Peggy Orenstein spent 1992–1993 visiting two California middle schools and interacting with students there, sitting in on classes and conferences and befriending several individual girls. She found that girls were taught often unconsciously by parents and teachers to be polite and quiet; boys were allowed to be, and ultimately were rewarded for being, noisy and aggressive. The most disturbing fallout from this pattern was the incidence of sexual harassment. Despite the clear message in the courts that such behavior is illegal, its appearance among young teens was still regarded as similar to the boys' exuberant behavior in the classroom: boys will be boys, just high spirits, a temporary behavior, girls should be patient, the boys will grow out of it. At the schools Orenstein visited, boys grabbed girls' breasts or crotches, yelled insults and made obscene gestures at them, and—less publicly—pressured them for sex. Girls who gave in to any of this immediately became "sluts" or "ho's"; girls who did not suffered boys' coldness. The boys who did it remained as popular and noisy as ever. A principal who instituted an aggressive policy of calling boys' fathers to discipline their sons who engaged in such behavior eventually conceded defeat when some parents complained and when the school's higher administration failed to back her up with the parents (Orenstein 1994, 112–30)—an old story that suggests the problem will not be solved solely by the schools.

In 1994 therapist Mary Pipher's book *Reviving Ophelia: Saving the Selves of Adolescent Girls* reached the *New York Times* best-seller list. Widely regarded as an important book for the Nineties, it relates story after story of girls who had come to Pipher for counseling for their difficulties with parents and friends, their confusion about sex, and their frequent disgust with their physical appearance. An increasing sign of their lack of self-respect was their tendency to mutilate themselves—a "frequent initial complaint" about teen girls (Pipher 1994, 157) which takes the form of cutting with razors, picking at their fingers with pins, or burning themselves. Although this practice is certainly not limited to girls—boys engage in it as well—Pipher regards it as "a concrete interpretation of our culture's injunction to young women to carve themselves into culturally acceptable pieces" (157), a reaction in particular to the stresses of the Nineties.

TEENS AT HOME

As more parents must work two or more jobs to supply even basic needs, teens are taking increasing responsibility for themselves at home. Sometimes this may be a lonely life; sometimes teens welcome the opportunity to pitch in and help with cooking, cleaning, and watching younger brothers and sisters. Boys as well as girls are learning to do household chores and cooking.

The lingering impact of divorce on teens has been reevaluated lately. Some findings indicate that teens whose parents divorced when they were children may suffer depression and act out with increased drug use and delinquent behavior. Some teens have to cope with choosing one parent over another, with confused and conflicted visiting rights, with loss of access to grandparents and other family members, and with loss of financial support from one parent or the other. The question has even been raised about whether a teen can "divorce" unsatisfactory parents, as in the case of a Florida boy who in 1992 successfully petitioned the court to allow him to stay in foster care rather than with either of his parents, who had neglected him for years (Jacobs 1997, 18).

While most parents of teens still try to protect their children by insisting on a curfew, the issue of the citywide curfew continues to surface in the Nineties, especially with the upsurge of teen gang violence, drug wars, and drive-by shootings. Some large cities have curfews, but there is evidence that most teen crime occurs in the afternoon rather than at night, when teens are out of school and not yet expected at home. Teens who are not involved in gangs or drugs often feel discriminated against by such laws.

Gadgets

For teens who live in urban and suburban environments, the enjoyment of electronic gadgets is a central element of home life. Televisions large and small with cable boxes and satellite dishes, all kinds of audio cassette and compact disc (CD) players, video games, the video cassette recorder, the computer, and the portable telephone have changed the way households function. The video camera, growing smaller and handier, has become an ordinary way for families to record parties and prom nights.

Microwave ovens, and the burgeoning industry of microwaveable foods, have changed the way families cook and eat; teens on their own at home or in dormitories can cook and eat a variety of foods. Takeout pizza has been joined by the wide availability of other kinds of take-out foods from the grocery, not just from fast-food emporiums. In a shift from the stereotypical hamburger-and-fries teen diet, many teens are becoming vegetarians. The "veggies" are passionate about animal rights and ecology, are well informed about farming practices, and are learning about tofu. They may still eat fast food, but more such restaurants are providing vegetarian options. One survey found that 35% of teen girls and 18% of boys thought vegetarianism was "in" (Kaufman 1995, 60). REM's lead singer Michael Stipe is only one of the celebrity vegetarians who give teens encouragement in their crusade—and often, they do crusade to get their families to adopt similar eating patterns.

Keeping in touch with friends and family has become easier. Portable phones have become practically standard issue for teens going off to college or on a car trip, and teens use them in malls, at concerts, and on the street as well as in the car. The supply of towers to relay portable phone conversations struggles to keep pace with the demand. Teens have also found phone cards handy; the teen, or the parents, purchase telephone time in increments of a few minutes at a time, without needing a personal number. Pagers are growing in popularity as well, moving from a device for employees to keep in touch with their central offices to gadgets for teens to reach friends quickly.

All of these gadgets cost money, of course, and are generally paid for by credit card. Credit card debt is a fact of Nineties life for adults, but it is inching down into teen culture, especially among teens in their first year of college. Credit card companies target such teen customers at a time when they are vulnerable: their first real independence from home, their need for various school-related goods, their desire to keep up with their new peers.

Radio and Television

In 1992, 92% of teens said that FM radio was still their major source for music listening, although 88% also said they used tapes and CDs as well (adapted from Chadwick and Heaton 1996, 229). Listening, a more private than family activity, became even more private with the increasing use of headphones. Technology has made radios, tape and CD players, and the headphones themselves so small that teens can use them in public—at the mall, sports events, even in school—when they prefer to tune in to their music instead of to what is going on around them.

Also in 1992, 73% of teens said they watched television almost every day (adapted from Chadwick and Heaton 1996, 224). Per household, the average watching time had risen to more than seven hours per day. Producers are obviously taking note because the number of shows featuring teens seems to have risen considerably. Cable television, which made multiple channels available, has given way to satellite television and many hundreds of channels to choose from—something for every taste: sports, music, religion, drama, comedy, cartoons, movies of all kinds old and new, twenty-four-hour news, twenty-four-hour weather, with new networks springing up each year. MTV is still the network most aimed at the teen audience with its music videos, interviews, nonstop ads for movies and all kinds of teen-oriented products, and its video jockeys, or vjs—such as Jessie, a wild-haired slacker dude who won a contest to have an opportunity to be a video jockey. The Fox Network continues to aim for twenty-something audiences and attracts many teens as well. Aimed at black teens, Black Entertainment Television (BET) combines music videos with frank talk shows featuring live teen audiences and call-ins, all in a very hip-hop style with Christian overtones. All these channels are within a click of the handheld remote control, all tapeable for later viewing on the videocassette recorder. The next development is digital television, offering very high quality ("high-definition") television reception. The television and receiver are still priced out of the range of most families, but as with the computer, that will probably change within a few years.

Comedies

Comedy has always been favorite television fare, and several Nineties comedy shows are produced specifically for teens. *Clueless* is a funny spin-off from the movie of the same name. *Sabrina the Teenage Witch*, which originated from the well-known "Archie" comic strip, concerns a girl with magic powers who tries to lead a normal teenage life. *Saved by the Bell*, a light-hearted look at high school life featuring the usual array of nice girls and boys, glamor girls and silly cheerleaders, geeks and hunks, ran from 1989 to 1993, then returned in 1996 with *Saved by the Bell: The New Class. Living Single* features a group of girls sharing a New York brownstone and plagued by guy problems. Nineteen-year-old recording star Brandy Norwood is featured in *Moesha*, a gentle comedy centering around a black, middle-class teen girl, her parents, friends, and schoolmates; Brandy also played Cinderella in a 1997 television remake of the Rogers and Hammerstein musical that featured a multiethnic cast. It was ABC's most-watched movie in over ten years (Weeks 1998, 13). Other teen comedies include *Boy Meets World* and *Sister Sister.*

Although not marketed to teens, two major-network comedy shows have attracted many teen viewers as well as a majority of the American adult viewing audience. *Seinfeld*, starring stand-up comic Jerry Seinfeld, premiered in 1990; by the time Seinfeld himself decided to end the show in 1998, it had won multiple Emmy Awards and many critics claimed it was probably the best television show of all time. It came to be known as the show about nothing, but it centered around four friends in New York who got into various scrapes and had many conversations about their troubles. *Friends*, which premiered in 1994, is about a group of six friends, three men and three women in their twenties, who deal with life and love in a humorous Nineties kind of way—by making the women stronger and more independent and the men more sensitive and willing to talk about their feelings (although the shows also poke fun at these very things). The general aimlessness of the characters in both of these shows, the superficial way in which problems are treated, the sexual frankness, and the coming together of young people into a surrogate family make these shows perfect examples of Generation X television.

Dramas

Teens watch plenty of dramas designed for adults and young adults, such as *ER, Law and Order*, and the acclaimed *I'll Fly Away* (1991–1993) which, set in the Sixties South, showed the human side of those racially tense times through stories about the teen children of a liberal attorney. Teen girls also enjoy daytime soap operas like *General Hospital, The Young and the Restless*, and *Guiding Light*, which now feature younger cast members in storylines that appeal to teens.

Dramas marketed to teen audiences include *Party of Five*, in which five kids survive on their own after their parents are killed; *Dawson's Creek*, which centers around kids in a small town, their school life, and their love life; and the highly acclaimed *My So-Called Life*, which began in 1994 and ran for only a year but continues to be successful in reruns on MTV. This series made a star of Claire Danes. The stories concern Angela, a middle-class teen girl, and her friends at school, at parties, and at home. It has a melancholy quality, a serious note about the pain of being a teenager, that comes through especially in Danes's voiceovers. It also shows, to a remarkable degree, the artifice of the popular good teen/bad teen dichotomy. Angela's friends range from the class "brain" to the class "bad girl" to a gay boy, but they all rely on each other and do things together, often things that Angela's parents do not know about. Family shows have come a long way since *Leave It to Beaver*.

Less realistic are *Buffy the Vampire Slayer*, *The Mystery Files of Shelby Woo*, and *The Secret World of Alex Mack*. All three feature engaging teen performers in well-written well-produced shows. Imported from Australia and available on satellite networks is *Heartbreak High*, an often gritty image of high school. Younger teens might enjoy *The Animorphs*, a series adapted from K. Applegate's popular novels and starring teen actors as the characters who can "morph" into animals. Two sexy young-adult nighttime soap operas also attracted older teens. *Beverly Hills, 90210* depicts such problems as date rape, alcohol and drug abuse, and suicide in a glitzy California setting; *Melrose Place*, a spin-off of *Beverly Hills, 90210*, addresses similar topics with a lighter touch. Both shows involve sexual escapades and jealousy among their elegantly dressed, beautifully coiffed characters.

Trekkers got double their pleasure in the first half of the decade when *Star Trek* producers introduced two new series. *Deep Space Nine* takes place on an orbiting space station with a variety of human and nonhuman species interacting much less amiably than those in earlier Trek series. Several years later, Trek writers introduced *Voyager*, in which a trial spaceship is suddenly warped across space and must find its way home again. The ship, called *Voyager*, is piloted by Elizabeth Janeway, played by Kate Mulgrew, the first female starship captain in the series.

The quintessential late-Nineties television drama is Fox's *The X-Files*. The series began as an offbeat show about whether aliens had visited Earth and whether the government knew it and was covering it up. *The X-Files* quickly became a cult favorite, and then a huge hit with general audiences, because of its intelligent scripts, expert special effects, and interesting stars: David Duchovny as FBI Special Agent Fox Mulder (his wry comments have come to be known as Mulderisms) and his partner, physician and skeptic Dana Scully, played by Gillian Anderson, whose intelligence, appearance, strength, and independence make her an especially appealing female character for teen girls. It is a mystifying show, with convoluted plots, unanswered questions, and hazy resolutions. It accepts the paranormal as existing with no explanation necessary, and it assumes that its audience is computer literate.

Cartoon Shows

Introduced on the Tracy Ullman Show in 1989, *The Simpsons* has become America's most-watched television cartoon, and the longest-running animated show in prime time. It follows clumsy dad Homer Simpson, his blue-haired gravelly-voiced wife, Marge, and their three children: Lisa (who plays a mournful saxophone), baby Maggie (always sucking on a pacifier), and ten-year-old Bart. They live in some surreal suburbs and deal with some surreal problems, yet they seem to have touched the hearts of American families. Bart has become a runaway favorite with teens and adults—a "brat for the ages," as Richard Corliss called him in a special issue of *Time* magazine devoted to major figures of the twentieth century. According to Corliss, Bart is "a complex weave of grace, attitude and personality, deplorable and adorable, a very 90s slacker who embodies a century of popular culture and is one of the richest characters in it" (June 8, 1998, 205).

The most controversial animated show of the Nineties was MTV's *Beavis and Butt-head*, in which two weird, apparently teenage characters who have various adventures, sit around and talk, usually in a vulgar way, and chuckle at themselves. They watch music videos and make fun of them—an interesting bit of self-mockery on the part of MTV (Morrow 1997). They are "illiterate, amoral, and antisocial" (1997, 5) but they also make hilarious fun of many late twentieth-century pretensions, especially political correctness. However, many observers thought the show was a seriously corrupting influence on young viewers. Supposedly an Ohio boy set fire to his house after getting the idea from a *Beavis and Butt-head* show. In response to the criticism, MTV moved the show to a later time and later took it off the air temporarily. The animated cartoon show *South Park*, which debuted in 1998 and centers on a group of school children who say and do crude things, has also attracted teen viewers.

Younger teens, and older ones interested in animation techniques, are taking note of the Japanese cartoons that are appearing now on American television. *Sailor Moon* is one example; Sailor is an ordinary teen girl called Serena, except when monsters appear. Then she becomes a lively fighter for justice, joining with three other female "Sailors." The cartoon appears partly Western and partly Japanese, but the action, according to *TV Guide*, is "mesmerizing" (Hiltbrand 1998, 36).

Talk Shows

Teens watch talk shows and also participate in them, especially on television specials about teen sex or family problems. The Black Entertainment Network features frequent talk formats for teens, and talk show hosts seem eager to get the teen perspective. A favorite talk show of girls and young adult women is *Oprah*. Oprah Winfrey has become a power in talk show television. Winfrey's warmth and frankness about her weight problems, her love life, and her experimentation with drugs all make her seem like a friend to the women in the audience and to those who watch. She is able to exploit television's blend of public and private (Tannen 1998, 198) and the result is an estimated 14 million viewers around the world.

However, in the late Nineties, talk shows have become dangerous places, too. In a development sometimes called "ambush television" or "ambush journalism," talk show guests—not famous people but average people with particular problems—are surprised on the air by someone they knew but did not expect to see, often in an attempt to provoke some kind of dramatic response that will thrill or shock the audience. People throng to appear on such shows to relate the most intimate details of their lives, apparently for the thrill of it rather than to seek any particular solution. For example, a pregnant teen girl appeared on one show flanked by the two boys who might have fathered her child. The most watched of these alternative talk shows in 1998 is Jerry Springer's, who sits back and encourages the wild physical antics, sometimes violent, of his guests.

The Internet

Nothing has changed teen life—indeed all life in the Nineties—as much as the Internet. This link-up of millions of computers from universities, libraries, businesses, and individuals all over the globe has, in only a few years, opened the world to teens in unprecedented ways, and they have been instrumental in creating that new world through their ability to manipulate the technology. According to Howard Rheingold, author of *The Virtual Community*,

The computer-using population [went] from a priesthood in the 1950s, to an elite in the 1960s, to a subculture in the 1970s, to a significant, still growing part of the population in the 1990s. Again, it wasn't the mainstream of the existing computer industry that created affordable personal computing, but teenagers in garages. And it was neither national defense nor the profit-motive but the desire to make a tool for changing the world that motivated the young entrepreneurs who built the PC industry. (1993, 67–68)

The Internet has changed the way families stay in touch with friends and relatives around the world; electronic mail, or e-mail, has replaced letter writing. The Internet is useful for information of all kinds: compact disc encyclopedias of general information, information about travel, facts about potential colleges, television schedules, and literally millions of web pages on every conceivable topic. Some of them are not especially reliable and, in fact, sometimes are weird or quirky since there is no restriction on who can post a web page. It has also become the world's biggest marketplace. Advertising for a host of products, movies, and television shows appears on the Internet, alongside the information you might seek on it, just as in a magazine, with headlines, pictures, sidebars, cartoons, and music, or announcements. Just browsing through the possibilities, or "surfing the 'net," as it is called, is riding a virtual tsunami. (See the appendix for web sites of interest to teens.)

Surfing the net brings teens unusual freedom from parental restrictions.

They can design their own Web pages to advertise themselves to other teens. They can play "MUDs"—multiuser games which resemble the popular Eighties fantasy game Dungeons and Dragons except that the game continues without stopping all over the world. Teens can enter and exit as they choose. With only a few clicks of a button, teens can view sexually explicit material. They can enter chat rooms, using their real name or a false one, where they can "talk" to other teens about anything. Many of the chat rooms become places to insult one another or make enticing or shocking sexual remarks as well as exchange likes and dislikes about film, video, and rock stars, and, occasionally, homework. This "virtual conversation" has its own rhythms and symbols that are recognized by experienced users, for example, :) indicates a smiling face and "im" means "instant message." Teens may also quiz each other about drinking, drugs, and sexual preference. Questions such as "Any horny women out there?" are typical. Such talk has always been common when teens get together and show off or test the limits of their companions' tolerance for shock, but there are differences here. Chat rooms are open twenty-four hours a day. Their anonymity encourages the freedom to say anything, to present oneself as anything. There is virtually no restriction on such conversation. There have supposedly been cases of teens falling in love over the Internet without ever having seen the other person. In some cases very young Web users pass themselves off as much older kids and run into trouble when a particular correspondent wants to meet them. Some users have been adults seeking sexual contact with teens or children (Rozen 1997, 76).

The Internet brings with it a form of addiction still unnamed. Some teens and young adults are spending many hours a day on-line, neglecting schoolwork, family, and friends as well as sleep and food. A psychiatrist from the University of Cincinnati studied several people (none teens) who were addicted, one of them a twenty-one-year-old who had disappeared from his college classes only to be found in the computer lab where he had been online for seven continuous days (Ritter 1998, A2). A less dramatic fascination with the computer which consumes time (and telephone bills) at home is still worrisome to many parents of teens, especially since the teens seem to manipulate the technology much better than they.

Of course, some people believe the computer divides the haves from the have-nots in American society. While affluent families can install separate phone lines so their teens can use the Internet at will, other teens are, so far, effectively barred from much of this aspect of teen life because they cannot afford a computer at home.

Comic Strips

Four new teen-oriented strips became popular in the Nineties. Bill Amend's "Fox Trot," which began in 1988, has continued to gain readers.

The Fox family consists of the father, the mother, and three kids: teens Peter and Paige and ten-year-old Jason. Peter eats voraciously but stays skinny; he's a terrible athlete but keeps trying to make the team. Paige is a lousy cook, hates homework, and loves going to the mall. Both teens put up with a lot from little brother Jason, a math and computer whiz, Trek and X-Files fan, and originator of hundreds of dirty tricks. Curtis, the star of his own strip, is a young, black, urban teen, very hip-hop in his ball cap worn to the side and his oversized sneakers and jeans. He cannot get his father to stop smoking or his little brother, Barry, to behave, or the love of his life, Michele, to give him the time of day. Of course, he cannot stand Chutney, the girl who loves him.

"Zits," a strip that debuted in 1997, revolves around a stereotypical white, middle-class, late Nineties, teen boy. Jeremy is grunge personified, with his unkempt hair, his loose plaid shirt, and his desire to form a rock band. He is also touchingly innocent at times, a victim of his dreams. His best friend is Hector, a Latino; although neither drives yet, together they have bought a VW bus and plan to restore it and travel around the country playing music to pay for the gas. Jeremy's parents are, naturally, bewildered by him. Finally, "Free for All" follows the adventures of two Generation X slackers in a very minimalist style similar to that of *Beavis and Butt-head*. Clay, fabulously wealthy, lives apparently in a high-rise condo with his ferret; he does little except think up devious ways to use his money and power (e.g., a private cloning operation) and maneuver his poor buddy, Jonny, into impossible situations (e.g., getting ambushed on the *Jerry Springer Show*). Jonny is occasionally a desperate voice for morality, but Clay usually does what he wants.

TEENS AT SCHOOL

In the Nineties, 98% of American teens were in school, completing the gradual shift from school as a choice for the very few in the early decades, to school as a major element in all teens' lives. Most states mandate school attendance until age sixteen, some until age seventeen or eighteen. Despite the popular perception of school as a place of boredom, irrelevance, tight controls and punitive attitudes on the part of teachers and administrators (such as in the films *Ferris Bueller's Day Off* and *The Breakfast Club*), a 1990 survey showed that a surprising number of tenth graders liked being there, for a variety of reasons (see Table 9.1).

The academic day is still divided into various periods, with students moving from class to class, sometimes with study periods intermixed. Many schools are trying a schedule that varies the days and times when a student's classes will meet, and many are trying more communal learning situations: assigning students projects that will require teamwork, a variety of skills and forms of information, and as long as several months to complete the project.

Jeremy, rock star wannabe, in a "Zits" strip from January 26, 1998. Reprinted with permission of King Features Syndicate.

Table 9.1
Why Tenth Graders Go to School

	White (%)	Black (%)	Hispanic (%)
Think subjects are interesting	68.8	79.1	74.5
Get a feeling of satisfaction	74.8	85.8	81.3
Nothing else to do	30.1	29.0	31.1
Need education to get job	96.5	96.7	96.8
To meet friends	85.5	66.1	80.1
Play on a team or belong to a club	55.3	49.3	45.3
Teachers care and expect each student to succeed	72.4	81.6	76.0

Source: Adapted from Bruce A. Chadwick and Jim B. Heaton, eds., *Statistical Handbook on Adolescents in America* (Phoenix, Ariz.: Oryx 1996), 128.

Making student films and videos is growing in popularity, occasionally with surprising results. One Pittsburgh student, Julia Love of Shadyside Academy, worked with her teacher to get grant funding for her film, *Women in the Wings*, a documentary about Pittsburgh women who worked in aviation in World War II. Her film has had several screenings and has, according to some, Academy Award potential (Rubinowski 1997).

Some schools are experiencing increased ethnic and racial blending. Annandale High School in Fairfax County, Virginia, for example, serves students from well over 100 countries, who speak more than 100 languages. A representative from the U.S. Department of Education says, "By the year 2025, 50% of all public school students will be minority students" (Quoted in Jones 1997, 2A). Such students must often struggle to learn English, and teachers must learn new ways to teach them. Annandale employs nine English-as-a-second-language teachers. The racial mix in schools, while friendly in many ways, in some schools can be a source of tension. Ethnic groups tend to isolate themselves in the cafeteria, at parties, at sporting events, and at club meetings.

Clothes can also be a source of tension. Dress codes continue to create friction in many schools, as administrators try to balance notions of what constitutes dangerous dress or dress that distracts students from the educational mission of the school, with students' First Amendment rights. Recently the furors have concerned wearing gang colors, body piercing such as multiple eyebrow and nose rings, and hair dyed pink or green.

The pattern that began in the Seventies of schools providing an increasing variety of services to students continues. Students receive counseling for

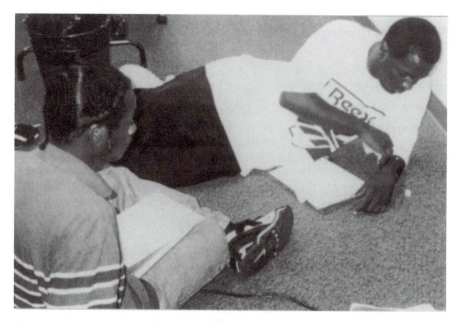

Learning probability theory with dice, T. L. Hanna High School, Anderson, South Carolina, 1997. Reproduced courtesy of T. L. Hanna High School.

career and college choice, for health problems, for addiction, and for psychological problems. Students with physical or mental disabilities must be provided an Individualized Education Plan and appropriate medical services (Jacobs 1997, 50–51). Students may enjoy art, music, drama, all kinds of sports, and all kinds of clubs, and many participate to some degree though many schools no longer offer some of these due to budget cuts (see Table 9.2).

The Computer

The computer has changed the appearance and emphasis of the middle and high schools in America. In affluent schools, classrooms may have computers available for most students. Word processing has increased students' writing skills and has made it possible to publish a great deal of student writing. Libraries are increasingly computerized, as are science labs and vocational skills areas, making the acquisition of information from a variety of sources much quicker. A poll of teachers taken in 1996 showed that teachers thought that computer skills were more important than biology, chemistry, physics, European history, the works of Steinbeck or Hemingway or Plato or Shakespeare (Oppenheimer 1997, 46). Internet links put students in touch with peers and resource people around the world.

Table 9.2
Participation of Tenth Graders in Extracurricular Activities

	White (%)	Black (%)	Hispanic (%)
Baseball/softball	16.0	13.7	15.7
Basketball	18.2	30.9	16.6
Football	14.7	22.6	16.0
Soccer	7.9	4.0	8.5
Swim team	4.1	2.8	3.3
Other team sports	14.5	11.3	13.5
Individual sports	23.9	21.9	17.9
Cheerleading	5.3	9.9	5.2
Drill team	3.6	9.4	5.2
School band/orchestra	21.7	22.3	14.1
School play/musical	11.0	12.1	9.3
Student government	7.3	7.4	5.9
Academic honor society	7.3	8.1	7.5
School yearbook/newspaper	8.5	10.5	7.3
School service clubs	11.7	10.4	9.9
School academic clubs	31.1	25.1	26.7
School hobby clubs	7.4	5.2	6.4
School FTA, FHA, & FFA	12.3	13.8	8.0

Note: Future Teachers of America (FTA); Future Homemakers of America (FHA); and Future Farmers of America (FFA).

Source: Adapted from Bruce A. Chadwick and Jim B. Heaton, eds., *Statistical Handbook on Adolescents in America* (Phoenix, Ariz.: Oryx 1996), 137.

Such dependence on the computer has been a mixed blessing. Schools must scramble to keep up with technology—not only to acquire it but to keep it running smoothly. Administrators are cutting art and music classes while spending thousands of education dollars on computers and the personnel to maintain them—that is, if they have the money in the first place. Ghetto, rural, or reservation schools may find it more difficult to acquire computers for their classrooms and libraries. If computer companies donate them, the schools must still find funding to install and maintain them. To use the computers that have been deposited in their classrooms, teachers must change the way they teach. Despite students' enjoyment of the computer, it does not automatically result in better grades or more creative thinking. Sherry Turkle, an MIT professor who has studied the computer's effect on children for several years and is fundamentally optimistic, nevertheless worries about students not thinking about anything but manipulating the software (Oppenheimer 1997, 56). Writing composition teachers notice a disjointedness in student essays that resembles the way information appears on the Web and a greater dependence on the superficial, unprocessed, and unregulated information that makes up most Web material. In a time when thousands of schools around the country need rooms, desks, books, and more teachers, the computer, despite its importance, will not be the ultimate solution to the problems facing education.

Drugs, Violence, and Pregnancy in the Schools

Schools are coping today with problems that simply did not occur in schools in the early decades of the century. Thomas A. Jacobs notes that, in the Forties, the top discipline problems in school were talking, chewing gum, making noise, running in the halls, getting out of turn in line, and not putting trash in the trashbaskets. In the Nineties, the top problem is alcohol and drug abuse, followed by pregnancy, suicide, rape, assault, arson, murder, vandalism, and gang fights (Jacobs 1997, 39).

By 1992, 3% to 11% of eighth graders were reporting that they had used alcohol or other drugs at or near the school during the previous year—not a large figure but a telling one (adapted from Schmittroth 1994, 363). Some high school students come to school regularly drunk or stoned on drugs, and many come armed with knives or guns. Bullies have been a staple of the school experience from time immemorial, but they may be more dangerous today. Metal detectors have become a fairly common sight in today's high schools, and the practice of assigning a policeman to the school to act as a counselor and disciplinarian is one way some schools are coping. In some schools, unannounced locker searches have become routine. Nevertheless, gang and drug-related fights erupt and bystanders get hurt. The number of killings and woundings in schools in the Nineties has alarmed the American public into holding many serious discussions about youth and violence (see section on Politics and National Events).

In previous years, too, an unmarried pregnant teen girl would have been prevented from attending school—by her own embarrassment if not by her parents. As late as the Seventies the school could legally ask her to drop out (Jacobs 1997, 81–82). Today, schools cannot legally bar a pregnant teen from attending school with her classmates. However, in Kentucky, two unmarried 1998 high school graduates with high grade-point averages were denied entry into the National Honor Society because they had children. The society does not allow "automatic denial" on this basis but says that "character" may be a factor. Those who denied the girls believed that their character was obviously flawed. Columnist Clarence Page commented:

That's not an unreasonable point in a country that has some of the highest teen pregnancy rates in the industrialized world. But doesn't a student who admits she made a mistake when she allowed herself to become pregnant show good character? Doesn't she also show good character when she decides to keep the baby instead of having an abortion? (*Greenville* [SC] *News*, August 12, 1998, 9A)

Stocking produce at the local grocery store, a typical Nineties part-time job for teens. Anderson, South Carolina, 1994. Reproduced courtesy of T. L. Hanna High School.

TEENS AT WORK

The point of view of the 1986 Greenberger and Steinberg study cited in Chapter 8 still affects discussions of teen workers. The Generation X slacker who works only to buy CDs and beer, who comes to work on drugs, who engages in petty thievery on the job, who cannot make change unless the cash register does it automatically, who just does not show up at times, has practically become a popular icon of cartoons and jokes, but it may have some basis in reality.

An article published in 1990 tries to counteract that image. In an attempt to get a more experiential perspective, researcher David L. Green interviewed several students, seniors in a rural North Carolina high school, about their attitudes toward their work. He found that, as in so many generalizations about teens, the reality was much more complex. The few teens he spoke to had a wide variety of reasons for working and attitudes toward working, but most were entirely positive. Teens felt that they were learning about people, money, and responsibility which schooling alone could not teach. Some worked because the family expected it, especially those who lived on farms, but they also saw it as having a positive effect: "For me, I work because it's a family responsibility and I also think it's important that when I go home in the afternoon that I have some sort of system, something that I have to do, to give me a sense of discipline" (1990, 431). Green concluded that work serves three important purposes for teens: transition from school to the larger world, structure for a teen's complex life, and social experience as well as material rewards (432). He warned against stereotyping today's teens and their work attitudes.

The Car

Cruising around in a car is still a favorite teen leisure occupation. In 1990, 56.1% of high school sophomores said they spent time this way at least once a week (adapted from Chadwick and Heaton 1996, 237). In the Nineties, however, teens are likely to cruise in a recreational vehicle (RV) or sports utility vehicle. Pickup trucks, vans, and minivans of all sizes and brands—Jeep, Ford Explorer and Windstar, Dodge Ram, Isuzu Trooper—dominate the automobile market. Teens whose parents can afford them can enjoy the benefits of camping, easily putting necessary gear into them and driving back into the woods, or just tooling around with plenty of friends inside. The sport of off-roading attracts teens who like to drive; they take a stripped down Jeep or similar vehicle to a dirt track or into the woods where the bouncing speed tests driving skills and provides dusty fun.

The American Automobile Association recently released sobering figures about accidents involving teens. One teen is killed every four minutes in a car wreck; although teens make up 7% of all drivers, they were involved in 14% of fatal crashes in 1995 and 20% of the total crashes in 1996 ("Put Brakes on Teen Driving," 1997, 3A). The association supports what it calls "graduated licensing": limiting sixteen-year-old drivers to daytime driving, encouraging drivers' education courses for all teens, offering first an intermediate license and then a full license only at age eighteen after a year's driving without accidents or convictions. Some states already have versions of this plan, which are aimed at making teens safer and more experienced drivers. A few parents are turning to computers to monitor their teens' driving. Personal tracking and recording systems, which can be attached to the car and then read out on a home computer, can tell how long a car has been driven and how fast, as well as its location at a given moment.

FASHION

For everyday wear and school, jeans and T-shirts still rule, for both boys and girls, but jeans are no longer just jeans. Early in the Nineties, when the grunge look was popular, jeans might be ripped out at the knees or even toward the top of the leg, to show the boxer shorts underneath. Later, jeans might be boot cut: narrow through the leg and widening slightly at the hem to flatter a high-heeled boot. As of 1998, very stiff jeans—"hard" jeans—

Arriving at school in casual style. T. L. Hanna High School, Anderson, South Carolina, 1996. Reproduced courtesy of T. L. Hanna High School.

rather than the well-worn ones are heavily advertised; they are sometimes ironed with a sharp crease down the front. Some are stove-pipe shaped: wide, very straight legs, a little floppy around the ankles. Khaki pants in the mid and late Nineties have begun to overtake jeans as school wear, also for both boys and girls. An interesting variation on jeans is overalls, a baggy style popular with teen girls. T-shirts for boys are still oversized and usually carry some kind of logo or saying. Girls might be more likely to wear a crop-top, a kind of T-shirt that ends above the waist or a "baby tee": a tight-fitting, tiny-sleeved T-shirt in a pastel color. Underneath, there might be a Wonder Bra to augment breast size. Shopping at lingerie stores like Victoria's Secret for brightly colored underwire bras and bikini panties has become a standard mall activity for girls. Bra straps are allowed to show; in fact, it is fashionable—although no bra at all is okay too. The cool accessory for school is a backpack, and very small ones are even used for dressy occasions. The major cosmetic accessory is nail polish—no longer in natural pinks or beiges but deep metallic greens, purples, and fuchsias.

Oversized pants, shirts, shorts, and sneakers—the hip-hop look—were hot in the early Nineties for teens, but the look has drifted down to younger teens and preteens, while older teens are becoming more conservative in their dress. Ironically, as white teens adopted the hip-hop look or

Seattle's grunge style (low-riding jeans and loose flannel shirts tied around the waist), black teens led the way back into the preppie look, marketed especially by the Gap, Tommy Hilfiger, and Eddie Bauer. Athletic wear— warm-up suits and sweats—is still comfortable and popular with most teens. Teens who are into the rave subculture, however, adopt the baggiest pants possible, very wide at the hem, and wild hats of all kinds.

For dressier wear, although miniskirts are still fashionable, girls now might choose ankle-length slim skirts or dresses of sheer fabric, aiming for a long, slim look top to toe. Ties for teen boys, which may be fairly wide, may also feature a cartoon character—Bugs Bunny or Sylvester the Cat, or perhaps something nostalgic like the Cat in the Hat from the famous Dr. Seuss book most teens loved as children. But boys also have the option not to wear ties; plain-necked shirts with small standing collars, closing with a single button, have been made popular by Hollywood stars who wear them with dress suits and tuxedos.

The prom is still *the* dressy occasion for teens. Rather than donning the ruffles and net of the eighties, girls are choosing long, slim dresses, often in black. They might be sequined, like the pageant dresses Miss America candidates wear, and they might have halter tops for real glamour. Boys have more options for tuxes, too; black is still standard but now a tux might be burgundy or gold.

Shoes, Hair, and Hats

Sneakers are still the most popular casual shoe, but sneakers are not just sneakers anymore. High-tops and low-tops, fancy soles with all kinds of configurations of color and shape, and now platform sneakers have all attracted teen feet. Chunky shoes are the favorite shoe style for girls: thick platform soles, thick heels one or two inches high, and squared-off toes. The most trendy are Doc Marten's, thick oxford-style shoes originally made in England. Slides—shoes you just slide your feet into—dominated the summer market in the mid-Nineties; they may be platform or flat-soled (or even sneaker-style) and may be worn with shorts, pants, or slim floaty dresses or long slim skirts with baby T's—an outfit that might be topped with a cloche hat pulled close around the face. For the "envirohip" teen, Teva sandals are cool and healthy; they fasten with Velcro over thick, soft rubber soles.

White girls' hair has become simpler than it was in the Eighties—no more teasing or "big hair"—medium length and well cut. The most popular style of the mid-Nineties was worn by Jennifer Aniston of the television show *Friends*: long in back, cut in tendril-like layers around the face, with fullness and bounce. Even when hair is pulled back off the face, a few strands are left undone on the face. Some girls still prefer short, sleek styles and variations on a bob, held on occasion with small barrettes or bobby pins. Longer

A braided hair style. T. L. Hanna High School, Anderson, South Carolina, 1997. Reproduced courtesy of T. L. Hanna High School.

hair might be pulled up in a large clip. Some girls try more alternative styles that involve braids, dreadlocks, and streaks of neon pink or green. In a dramatic change from the Sixties natural look, black girls' hair may be very highly styled with cornrows—rows of braids close to the head—or with very long braids, in the styles worn by comedian Whoopi Goldberg and teen singer Brandy Norwood, augmented with extensions—synthetic strands of hair in many colors, hooked or woven into the natural hair. Some techniques involve glue or needle and thread (or even a tiny sewing machine) to attach the extra hair. Strands of hair or tiny braids lined with bright beads has long been a favorite style among African American girls, and made more popular by Nineties teen tennis star Venus Williams. Now white girls are trying it as well, especially on a few strands of hair around the face. The French twist is popular with both black and white girls for a sleek, more formal look.

Boys' hair has more variety of style than ever before. Boys may wear long hair pulled into a pony tail as in the Sixties. They may wear their hair long on top and in front, and shaved up the back and on the sides for a "bowl cut" look. They may grow it long then cut it off straight around, just off the shoulders or a bit shorter. They may bleach part of their hair or, if they are into punk, dye it green or pink like basketball star Dennis Rodman. Black teen boys might wear a very close cut with a shape or word or number shaved into their hair, or they might wear short dreadlocks. One of the most popular looks is a completely shaved head. While the white skinheads (associated with neo-Nazi ideology) might have introduced the look, basketball star Michael Jordan popularized it with black teens; his image is one that all teens, black and white, find attractive. The popularity of shaved heads has had one touching result; in several instances, nationwide, when teens have a friend who has undergone chemotherapy and lost his hair, they will shave their heads as an act of support and concern.

Among black boys, a knitted, close-fitting cap works well with some hairstyles. However, for blacks and whites, most boys' hair is hidden, most of the time, under a baseball cap. The baseball cap has become an icon of the Nineties, worn by both boys and girls. It may have an extended bill in front and a logo. Among middle-class suburban teens who want to appear part of the subculture, the bill will be slightly crunched and the cap will sport a logo from a gas station or some other average-joe kind of place. (This is sometimes called a "gimme cap," since such places occasionally give the caps away for free advertising.) If the wearer wants to appear upwardly mobile, the bill might be suede and the logo a Nike swoosh. If boys are into hip-hop style, they will turn the cap around so that the bill is in the back. Some occasionally wear it to the side. The constant presence of the cap is sometimes an irritation to parents and teachers, since the boy (or girl) seems to be hiding under it or not concerned enough with common courtesy to take it off. Some schools have tried to outlaw the wearing of hats in class, but it is probably a losing battle.

Thinness and Kate Moss

The fashion industry has been the target of much criticism for encouraging teen girls' desire for thinness. Since the early Nineties, the favored models in high-fashion magazines and designers' studios have been extremely young, extremely tall, and extremely thin, with cropped off, unstyled hair, little makeup, and a pale, abstracted look which has been termed the "waif" look. The "Twiggy" look of the Sixties prompted some of the same distress, but the increasing seriousness of eating disorders among the young has increased the concern in the Nineties.

When designer Calvin Klein began featuring eighteen-year-old Kate Moss (5'7", 105 lbs) in his ads for 1993, Moss became the center of the controversy, especially when she appeared topless in some of them. Her picture seemed to be everywhere—on billboards and in books as well as in magazines. James Wolcott in the *New Yorker* magazine speculated:

Why her? Perhaps it's the baby bump of her stomach, which suggests a begging bowl ("Feed me," people scrawled across the Calvin Klein ad posters that featured her) or the way dresses drip off her like seaweed. Whatever the reason, Moss became the dartboard for every point to be made about bad female body image (1995, 102).

Many girls expressed appreciation for Moss's look, especially constitutionally thin girls who were accused of being anorexic when they really wanted to gain weight. For a time, Moss was featured in a Web site, "Waif Central Station," where many girls from all over the world wrote in to say they loved her look.

The furor over weight and health made teen magazines take notice; many now feature articles on healthy eating and body image, urging girls not to diet for thinness. Actress Elisa Donovan recently wrote about her anorexia for *Teen People* magazine, noting that she heard a six-year-old girl worry about looking fat: "With feminism these days, girls think they can do anything, which is great. But the pressure to be thin and beautiful is still there" (1998, 77). The models featured in these magazines, right alongside articles about healthy eating, are still rail-thin, and the clothes marketed to teen girls—long, slender dresses, baby T's—require a slim figure. To complicate the image, lingerie styles stress underwire bras—a necessity for large-breasted women but hardly essential for slender teen girls. Such underwear is supposed to be visible and sexy. These mixed messages may do little to stem the trend of dieting to thinness among teen girls, although the respect for such teen athletes as Martina Hingis and Venus Williams and the "athletic aesthetic," as it is now being called, may help. Of course, as long as girls see their mothers—and many fathers—obsess about weight and thinness, they will have a hard time sorting out what's right for them.

Tattoos and Body Piercing

Tattooing and body piercing have been staples of preliterate or aboriginal cultures for centuries. In America in the twentieth century, tattooing has until recently been mostly associated with males in the military, in homosexual circles, and in the biker culture. When pop star Cher began advertising her multiple tattoos in the Seventies and Eighties, however, the idea seemed to catch on with girls, especially white, middle-class girls. A tattoo on the shoulder or ankle could be discreet but daring, no doubt likely to drive parents crazy. It has become a fad of the Nineties, although it may be giving way to body piercing, since pierces are easier to get rid of should the fashion change.

In America, women have been piercing their ears for many years; in some elements of our culture, baby girls' ears are pierced. By the Sixties, pierced ears were the norm. With the punk movement in the Eighties, more body parts might be pierced, and ears might be pierced many times. In the Nineties, the body piercing trend has attracted many teen girls. Although by state law, one must be eighteen or older for piercing, much younger girls are doing it—doing it to themselves or finding a friend or a professional willing to do it. Navels, eyebrows, noses, and lips are the most common spots for piercing, and the kind of piercing jewelry one may choose to accent the pierce is available in a wide variety. Less common is the piercing of the nipples, tongue, or genitals, and plenty of hardware is available for these sites too.

Joan Jacobs Brumberg, author of *The Body Project*, suggests that American teens' interest in body piercing might be due partly to the "homosexualization" of American popular culture today—an increasing fascination with and enjoyment of the clothes, humor, music, and lifestyles of homosexuals, no matter what one's sexual preference. Body piercing "is a provocative symbol of a powerful revolution in sexual mores and behavior" (1997, 132). In the case of teens, it is also a kind of in-your-face rebellion against the kind of good looks associated with the white, middle-class clean-teen image. In the case of pierced genitalia or nipples, however, it seems more private, something a girl says is just for her secret pleasure and that of her boyfriend:

In an era when the distinction between the public and private has all but disappeared, some teenage girls apparently feel the need to decorate their genitals in order to have *something* intimate—in effect, to claim some degree of privacy in a world where the body has been made public. . . . When underwear has become outerwear, as it has in the past decade, adolescents of both sexes are likely to become confused about the nature of intimacy. (1997, 136)

SLANG

Characterizing slang in the Nineties is like driving blind; however, we can say with some certainty that the hip-hop culture and rap music continue to influence teen language. Close friends from your neighborhood are homeboys from the 'hood. If you live in a 'hood, you don't live in the 'burbs (suburbs). Your car is your ride, your room is your crib, and someone in authority is a suit. You won't take it when someone "disses" you (insults you or disrespects you). A cool guy is probably someone really *not* cool. If you're really relaxing, you be easin'. "You da man!" means you're the best.

In the patois of white teens, a disgusting person is a slimebucket; a stupid person is a donut hole or a gumbyhead (after the lanky green comic strip character). A boring party is a Maybelline waste (a waste of mascara). A good-looking girl is a hottie; a good-looking guy, a beef-a-roni. A woman with big hips is a wide load, and someone who wears unfashionable clothing is a polyester. Your response to something really dumb, whether you said it or someone else did, is "Duh." The best word to just dismiss something is "Whatever," and if you are mystified by something, such as a question on a test, you are clueless. "Way!" is the answer if you disagree with someone who says "No way!" or way can also mean very, as in "He's way smart."

A favorite late Nineties exclamation is "Dang!" If you want to agree with something, you might say, "Tell me about it!" or "Think it ain't!" Anything you don't like sucks. Tom Dalzell points out that this word is the most "highly recognized slang term in use among high school students today." It has lost its sexual meaning almost entirely (1996, 225).

The other word that marks Nineties teen slang is "like," the ubiquitous word that means almost, said, really: "He's, like, 100 years old"; "So I'm, like, 'but I don't want to go out with you.' " Dalzell calls this word a "stream of consciousness toggle switch between direct and indirect quotation, between thought and speech, between objective and subjective, and between real and perceived—the ultimate 20th century speech mechanism" (190–91).

The television cartoon character Bart Simpson, a great favorite with teens for his sly rebelliousness and essential innocence, has contributed several expressions to teen slang. "No way, man!" means it is not possible, and "Don't have a cow, man!" means calm down. The television and movie characters Wayne and Garth contributed, among other expressions, "Party on!"—meaning chill, enjoy, have a great time, be cool. The McDonald's hamburger franchise gimmick of tacking the prefix *Mc* onto everything they sell has opened the way for many expressions for something you want to trivialize. One popular expression is McJob—a perfect description of the low-paying jobs that teens tend to have.

Not exactly slang, but an interesting visual development in language, is the use of letters or numbers for words—R for are, 2 for to—or unusual spellings to indicate different meanings: phat means something good, kewl means *really* cool, and boyz are black ghetto boys. Rock groups have helped to popularize this with the names of their groups and song titles, as probably did the toy store chain Toys R Us. It is also common on the computer; for example, "O u r so dum."

LEISURE ACTIVITIES AND ENTERTAINMENT

Lots of teens' leisure time is spent in front of the television; listening to music is a close second. When they share leisure time with friends, they usually hang out, cruise in the car, eat pizza, or go to the movies. Teens in urban areas who are affiliated with gangs spend their leisure time with gang members. White, middle-class girls still get together for slumber parties. Mexican-American girls look forward to their *quinceanera*, their fifteenth birthday party, a huge and often expensive traditional coming-of-age celebration. Some cost many thousands of dollars. Teens' favorite games include the Gameboy, a handheld computer game with a variety of challenges and handy for traveling, and at parties, the old Sixties game of Twister where people contort themselves on a plastic sheet. Fads include the "virtual pet," a small computer game that asks to be fed, just as a pet might. Carrying around bottles of water—especially "designer water" such as Evian—is a particular fad, and perhaps a healthy one, among girls.

Raves

The most distinctively Nineties kind of party is the rave. Beginning as an exclusively subcultural, even secret event, the rave has crept aboveground in some places. Like many other popular cultural phenomena, its structure may vary widely, but raves always seem to involve dressing up in unusual ways, dancing, and using drugs. They apparently generate themselves spontaneously, and usually last all night. The name probably comes from the way those who attended such parties "raved" about them. Teens who attend raves wear extremely wide, baggy pants or loose dresses, or T-shirts with childlike emblems on them like Scooby Doo or the Cat in the Hat (Kahn-Egan 1998, 36). They must also have certain props with them: a book bag, water, a toy of some kind, Vicks Vaporub, and things to suck on—lollipops or pacifiers. The place for the rave might have a room for toys and games such as Twister, and a room where the music is softer and there is rest instead of dancing. The drug of choice is X, also called Ecstasy or Roll (methlenedioxymethamphetamine). A DJ usually supplies the music and there may be laser light shows. Like slam-dancing at punk concerts, the whole rave experience is geared to abandonment and to feeling intimate with strangers. The difference is that the rave seems also to be a place to regain, even though artificially, a sense of childhood fun.

Drugs, Cigarettes, and Alcohol

Generation X and the Thirteeners have grown up with drugs. They have watched countless television commercials in which someone feels lousy and moments later, after taking a pill, feels wonderful. They have watched parents and friends take antidepressants like Prozac, or various recreational drugs. Rock music and drugs seem to go together; concerts become veritable drug markets. Drugs are sold openly on the street in many parts of the country despite their illegality, for relatively low prices. Selling is not limited to boys trying to escape ghetto poverty; it is also an avocation among middle- and upper-class teens, who can find ways to obtain drugs from physicians and then sell them to friends.

Marijuana is a fact of life. Although experts agree that it is not in itself addictive, habitual pot smoking generally leads to trying other drugs. Cocaine was the drug of the Eighties; heroin seems to be the drug of the Nineties. More insidious and just as alarming is the use of commercial household sprays for "huffing": concentrating the fumes in a bag and breathing them, a practice that quickly causes brain damage and death. Gasoline fumes can also be inhaled for a dangerous high, known as a "wall-hit." Pills—tranquilizers and methamphetamines of all kinds—are easy to buy on the street or can be obtained by deceiving doctors and clinics and getting prescriptions. By 1996 the Department of Health and Human Services found that teens used drugs 105% more than they did in 1992. Monthly use of hallucinogens rose 100% among twelfth graders; pot smoking rose 150% (Gordon 1996, 1A). There are no particular racial or socioeconomic differences among drug-using teens. For those who choose it, fighting addiction becomes a way of life for teens who face fatigue, depression, the stress of school, various forms of abuse, peer pressure, and boredom.

Smoking cigarettes also seems to be on the rise, after a drop in 1992, even while tobacco companies are being hauled into court, accused of increasing the addictive properties of their product. Cigars have become chic among adults, and teens are beginning to try them as well (see Figure 9.1).

Teen alcohol use may also be rising, an especially troublesome problem since many teens drink and drive. Many drinkers are under the driving age. One statistic indicated that 2,000 kids who entered treatment for alcohol abuse were under the age of thirteen (Guttman 1997, 9). In 1997 actress Bonnie Root, who portrayed a teen alcoholic in a television movie, admitted that she too had been an alcoholic by age fifteen (1997, 9). Typically parents do not realize there is an addiction until serious behavior problems arise; teens can be very good at covering up addictions.

Sports

Although the Generation X image of teens as couch potatoes and druggies is a pervasive one in newspapers and magazines, plenty of teens are enjoying themselves in challenging sports. The classic sports of tennis, swimming, golf, horseback riding, soccer, softball or baseball, and basketball still attract many teen boys and girls. High school sports programs have expanded to include many sports that both genders can enjoy. More girls play basketball, for example. Volleyball, especially at the beach, and aerobic dancing can be enjoyed by boys and girls together. Surfing still rules on the West Coast. In the West, Midwest, and South, rodeo sports attract boys and girls. In South Carolina, teen participation in rodeo, through high schools, has grown 50% since 1994 (Sturrock 1998). To relax, many teens like to go tubing—floating down a river in an inner tube, often trailing a six-pack of beer. More energetic teens might try kayaking or white-water rafting through some mountain rapids. Hiking and camping are also ways to be alone with friends and get some exercise.

Nineties sports have become less traditional. They include in-line skating, skateboarding, and riding stunt bicycles. These sports lend themselves particularly to urban environments. To encourage competition in them (and to attract advertisers of course), the ESPN television network, devoted solely

Figure 9.1
Use of Cigarettes in the Past Month by Youths (Age 12–17) 1985–1995

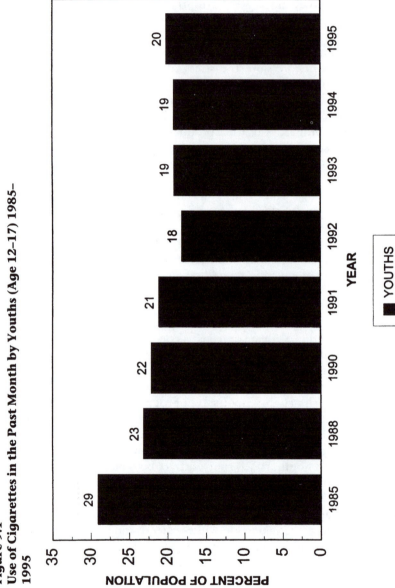

Notes: Selected years are those years for which data are available. Because these estimates are based on a sample, they may differ from figures that would be obtained from a census of the population. Each data point reported is an estimate of the true population value and subject to sampling variability.

Source: National Center for Health Statistics, Health, United States, 1995. U.S. Bureau of the Census, Statistical Abstract of the United States, 1994–95.

to sports, has created the "X Games," a kind of "street-sport Olympics" in which skaters, bike riders, and skateboarders "fling themselves over ramps and rails doing impossible flips and twists, sometimes careening 20 feet in the air, with nothing much to cushion the fall except wheels, knee pads and skin" (Rhodes 1998, 27). There are few rules and no required routines—typical of the "slacker aesthetic"—and the contestants seem to be in it for the fun of it rather than winning it. Prize money is growing nonetheless as the viewing audience and the number of sponsow. Fourteen-year-old Jenny Curry of San Luis Obispo, California, competes all over the world on her in-line skates and makes thousands of dollars a month. Some boys are being offered contracts worth $180,000 per year (Rhodes 1998, 30). Indoor climbing is also a part of the X Games, in which teens climb walls made of artificial rock. Katie Brown of Kentucky, age seventeen in 1998, won a gold medal at the X Games. Chris Sharma, who began climbing at age twelve, in 1997 at age fifteen won part of the World Cup of climbing (Biondo 1998, 8). Snowboarding, a cross between skiing and surfing, has overtaken skiing as the most popular snow sport among teens. It is, says William Finnegan, "infinitely cooler" than skiing. "It is an attitude, an argot, a look. The look is grunge, basically, with some gymnastic, speed-demon undertones" (1998, 229). A growing sport among California teens as well as teens abroad is laser tag, in which teens enjoy zapping each other with light beams as they circle through a maze.

Dating and Sex

For the most part, the rating-and-dating pattern continues: boy asks, transports, and pays; girl accepts and dresses appropriately. A date is a public activity where being seen is as important as seeing. A movie, a club for dancing, dinner, or a party are still the chief activities, although some teens are still confused at times about who should ask and who should pay. Going steady is still more acceptable than having many dates with many different people. Since the Fifties, the rule has generally been one boyfriend or girlfriend at a time, even for very young teens. The definition of a seriously long-term relationship may be changing. In April 1998 *Teen People* featured three "marathon love match" couples who were "going the distance"; two had been together a year. Going steady for even a month is pretty serious. With all the pressures on dating, perhaps more enjoyable are group dates, just hanging out, and get-togethers at teens' homes.

What boys and girls seek in a good date has not changed much; the emphasis is still on the superficial. A recent cross-cultural study asking adolescents between eleven and sixteen about their opposite-sex ideal showed that American teens ranked being fun, being sexy, and having a lot of money as the most important elements (Gibbons 1996, 531+). The chief difference is probably the use of the word *sexy*. In the early and middle decades, teens might have used a different term: *itty, smooth, neat*. But in the sexually frank Nineties, teens can be more direct, although *sexy* probably has a broader meaning than that implied by the word itself. Plenty of teens find intelligence and good manners almost as "sexy" as good looks, and today, they may find them in someone of a different race. It has become increasingly common to see interracial couples at dances and parties.

Dating has also become sometimes dangerous. The occasional instance of boys forcing sexual attentions on their dates is nothing new, but as feminism has encouraged girls to take pride in their bodies, to "own" them, teen girls now speak out more often about "date rape" or "acquaintance rape," and they are more willing to identify such boys and prosecute them. In one such case a fifteen-year-old girl, at a high school in Northern California, accused three boys of raping her at an after-prom party. All three were sentenced to ninety days in jail and three years of probation, in addition to taking a course on violence prevention (O'Connor 1998, 47–49). The publicity given lately to violent males and battered women has also made teen girls more aware of the dangers of a violent or potentially violent boyfriend or date. Starting in 1997 the "Smart Date" Web site allowed teens to register their dating plans for the evening, with the information released to authorities only if a missing person report is filed (Temple 1997, 1B). Even more alarming has been the "date rape drug," Rohypnol, a new drug that has been slipped into girls' drinks rendering them unconscious and unable to resist or even to remember what happened. Girls are being warned to be especially careful about what they drink at parties and bars.

Many parents find it increasingly difficult to talk to their children about sex because such conversations must begin so much sooner than expected and because they realize the children already know a great deal—or at least appear to—although they may be misinformed. Teens increasingly turn to television as a major source of information for them, in dramas as well as informational shows. Premiering in 1998, Warner Brothers' (WB) *Dawson's Creek*, a television drama centering around teens, has already become famous for its sexual frankness; for example, one of its characters lost her virginity at age twelve but is trying to live it down. "Dr. Drew," who offers frank sexual advice on MTV's call-in show *Loveline*, tries to offer teens advice which takes relationships into account, not just sexual technique.

Homosexual teens are finding life in the Nineties marginally easier, perhaps because of the positive media attention coming from such disparate sources as the publicity about gays in the military, House Speaker Newt Gingrich's sister Candace's admission that she is gay, and television star Ellen Degeneres's show in which she announced she was gay. More teens are admitting their orientation to their parents and friends and becoming active in gay rights organizations. Columbia University researcher Joyce Hunter told *Time* magazine that "the change has been enormous" since she began her work on this topic in the Seventies; 3% to 10% of U.S. teens now say they are gay, lesbian, bisexual, or uncertain of their orientation, whereas very few would admit it in earlier decades (Cloud 1997, 82). Churches and schools are beginning to be more sympathetic to gays, although verbal abuse is still something such teens must prepare for, as well as loss of some long-standing friendships.

AIDS and Pregnancy

The specter of AIDS, which continues to haunt the Nineties, was made even more vivid by the AIDS quilt. The quilt, the idea of a San Francisco man, contained, as of 1997, more than 70,000 names of those who have died from the disease, stitched by family, friends, and lovers (Colbert 1997, 559). It was assembled for the first time in 1996, and portions of it have traveled the country raising people's awareness of the tremendous death toll of the disease and enabling some to mourn those they have lost to it. It continues to grow.

Studies are constantly assessing whether teens are getting the message about the dangers of unprotected sex. Once the concern was the risk of unwanted pregnancy; now it is the risk of disease and death. Teens are still likely to engage in such sexual activity and to share needles when taking drugs; the indications that the disease is spreading among young adults suggests that they are contracting it when they are in their teen years. Not surprisingly, one study found that a "high level of conventionality" was the best predictor of whether a teen would use contraceptives. Teens who valued achievement, did well in school, had good parental support and friends who shared their beliefs, and did not engage in "problem behavior" would be most likely to practice birth control (Hollander 1996, 289).

The number of teen pregnancies seems to be dropping since the Eighties, but it is still too high for the comfort of many legislators, some of whom have begun fashioning laws to prosecute unwed mothers and fathers. Idaho is particularly strict, as are some counties in California (Diamond 1997, 8), although whether these approaches will work remains to be seen. Other efforts are gentler and probably more realistic. Social agencies are trying to educate teens about sexuality, responsibility to families and children, and the difficulties of parenthood. Author Jeanne Warren Lindsay, who specializes in this topic, has produced a series of books on teen parenting, for which she has interviewed many teen couples, wed and unwed. Her books offer straightforward, readable advice about caring for newborns, coping with parents and in-laws, and dealing with everyday life—buying groceries, keeping up with a checking account, and so on.

The huge toll that unwanted pregnancy can take on many lives was illustrated by the case of Amy Grossberg and her high school boyfriend, Brian Peterson. In 1996 Amy gave birth in a Delaware motel room to their baby after hiding her pregnancy from her parents and friends. Brian put the baby in a trash bag and threw it in a bin behind the motel. Amid accusations that neither was telling the whole truth, they both received jail sentences in 1998 for the killing: 2.5 years for Amy, 2 years for Brian. In another notorious case, in 1996, a thirteen-year-old boy fathered the child of his thirty-five-year-old married teacher, Mary K. Letourneau. She received a suspended sentence for second degree child rape, but when she shortly thereafter became pregnant again by the same boy, she was sent to jail for 7.5 years. She continues to protest her sincere love for the boy.

Music and Dancing

In the Nineties, labels such as "Top 40," "Underground," and "Alternative" have lost their meaning. The music itself has become so varied and so blended that identifying one particular sound or group with one particular movement is almost impossible. This trend is reflected in the most distinctive music-making technique of the decade. Begun in the Eighties, the technique of sampling had a major impact on music production in the Nineties. Established stars from earlier decades re-released some of their hits adding different tracks and instrumental combinations. Rap artists constantly "sampled" older songs—using bass tracks from them and adding other lyrics, tracks, and rhythms on top.

Rap

Without doubt, rap is the defining music of the Nineties. In both 1992 and 1993, 26% of teens polled said it was their favorite (adapted from Chadwick and Heaton 1996, 229). Between 1997 and 1998, rap sales increased 31% (Farley 1999, 56). As music, rap is minimal at best: a heavy bass line and beat, with rhyming lyrics usually spoken rather than sung. Those lyrics, however, have opened the world of ghetto culture in a way that nothing else has before. Havelock Nelson and Michael Gonzalez describe an Ice Cube album from 1990: "From dealers chillin' in front of the projects to rival gangs spraying them with bullets, from the din of children roaming through the streets of shattered glass to a group of pregnant girlies gulping cheap, sweet wine in front of the local 7-Eleven. . . . Welcome to the nightmare" (quoted in Stuessy 1994, 388). Soon the Nineties produced an even more extreme rap style: gangsta rap, exemplified by the groups Public Enemy and N.W.A. (Niggas with Attitude), performers like Ice T, Dr. Dre, and Snoop Doggy Dogg, and songs that angrily urge killing as a response to any kind of threat.

The lives of the performers seem to reflect their music. In 1993 Snoop Doggy Dogg, under investigation for a gang murder, surrendered to police after presenting an MTV award. Rapper Tupac Shakur was shot in a mugging in 1994; in 1996, he was shot to death in his limousine. He had been feuding with another rapper, Biggie Smalls, who died in a shooting himself in 1997. Rap concerts have been marred by violence—gun battles, riots, and the shooting of a seventeen-year-old who had just come to pick up a friend (du Noyer 1995, 277). Brushes with the law have also involved obscenity charges against the groups Marilyn Manson, who tears pages from a Bible in its act, and 2 Live Crew, who simulate sex play in their shows and whose single "Me So Horny" was banned from airplay and declared obscene by judges in Florida and South Carolina. Seven record shop owners in Greenville, South Carolina, were arrested for selling the record, which sold millions. Paul Friedlander analyzes rap's appeal:

Like white working-class youth finding power in the heavy metal identity, it is easy to see how disenfranchised Black youth could concur with these macho expressions of power and bravado. It is also clear that rap's characterization of American society as oppressive and unfriendly found support across broad segments of the African-American community. (1996, 275)

Most rap is distinctly male, but a few women entered the scene, partly as an aggressive response to the tendency of male rappers to characterize all women as "bitches" and "ho's." After a hit album *All Hail the Queen* in 1989, Queen Latifah has moved from rapping to acting with her role in television's *Living Single* and in a feature film. Sister Souljah made some hard, angry raps but also has made a name for herself as a spokesperson for blacks and for women, and she runs a New York City social program for inner-city children established by male rapper Puff Daddy. The group Salt 'n' Pepa takes a strong feminist stance in their music, and although not strictly rappers, the female group En Vogue has reacted similarly in songs like "My Lovin' " and "Free Your Mind."

The backlash against gangsta rap has taken the form of an effort to rate the content of concerts, just as movies and music have become rated. Legislation in South Carolina and Michigan has been proposed that would ban teens under age eighteen from attending concerts deemed too violent or obscene. The music industry objects, saying such control infringes on the First Amendment; others say such legislation is probably unenforceable.

Grunge and Underground Rock

The grunge music and style originated in Seattle, and the group Nirvana became its icon. Their single "Smells Like Teen Spirit" was a big hit—"a distinctive roar of alienation with a catchy chorus, the song was quickly adopted as the anthem for the grunge generation which grew up in their wake" (du Noyer 1995, 280). The video for this song, set in a high school basketball gym, features slam-dancing teens and tattooed cheerleaders. Also from Seattle, grunge band Pearl Jam's albums have sold in the millions; their early hit "Jeremy," which describes a suicidal teen, established them as the voice of teen angst for the Nineties. Visually, they looked the part, with loose shirts and oversized shorts. Smashing Pumpkins offers more melodic grunge with their elaborate musical arrangements and in albums such as *Melon Chollie and the Infinite Sadness.*

Underground music centered around the rave movement and the kinds of drugs associated with it. At these dances, under the influence of the drug Ecstasy (an amphetamine), teens like very fast techno music with a hard beat, but they also like to relax in different rooms with what is called "ambient techno," a smoother sound similar to the psychedelic music of the Sixties. One of the hallmarks of the decade was the popularization of what had previously been underground. As Paul du Noyer explains it,

In the Nineties, virtually all branches of what would have once been considered "underground" in previous decades came roaring overground to dominate youth culture on both sides of the Atlantic. . . . Groups like Nirvana, Pearl Jam, and Soundgarden suddenly made the poodle-haired, spandex-trousered heavy metal bands of the Eighties seem dated and absurd. (1995, 258)

Grunge fans suffered a shock when Nirvana star Kurt Cobain committed suicide in 1994 at the age of twenty-seven. His life had been plagued by depression and drugs. He grew up in Aberdeen, a poor, small town in the state of Washington, and, although he was talented, he was a mystery to those who knew him. His success seemed to intensify his drug problems and his attraction to guns. He died in Seattle on April 8 of self-inflicted wounds. A fifteen-year-old freshman at Aberdeen High, a grunge fan, commented, "I realize that Kurt Cobain had a few more problems than we might, but him doing this, it kind of cheated us in a way. We figured if someone like him could make it out of a place like this . . . it was like he might have paved the way for the rest of us" (Gilmore 1998, 445).

Alternative Rock, Rhythm and Blues, Ska, and Swing

What was once mainstream rock has merged with what was once considered underground, or at least less "pop," to produce what, for want of a better term, is now labeled "alternative" rock. It probably originated with college radio stations which played a different kind of music from that played on commercial stations, but now commercial stations play it as well.

The group REM, which had been relatively underground during the Eighties, moved into popular airtime in 1991 with their album *Out of Time*; the single "Losing My Religion" became a hit around the world. In 1992 they produced *Automatic for the People*, named for a diner in Athens, Georgia. In contrast to rap, punk, and heavy metal, REM has retained its connections to Athens, to a kind of folk tradition, to carefully worked music, and to its moral stance on environmental issues. U2, an Irish group, has moved in the Nineties to a more technological stance, represented by their 1992 tour during which the stage was loaded with television monitors tuned to global news programs which ran constantly during the show. U2's 1993

Zooropa album was a collection of improvised sound checks recorded at rehearsals.

During the Nineties, in a new development, girls are buying rock music almost as much as boys, affecting sales and the kind of music produced. They help make such female singers as Jewel, Celine Dion, Alanis Morrissette, Sarah McLachlan, and Fiona Apple stars, and the Lilith Fair—a tour featuring all female performers—into a national success. They also like the Backstreet Boys. Younger teen girls turn out in mammoth numbers for Hanson, three brothers from Tulsa, Oklahoma. In 1998, riding on the smash success of their hit song "MMMBop," Isaac, seventeen, Taylor, fifteen, and twelve-year-old Zac play to huge international crowds of screaming girls, the likes of which have not been seen since the Beatles. Like the Beatles, Elvis, and Frank Sinatra before them, they have genuine talent, although their blond good looks and upbeat songs prompt some to dismiss them as a teenybopper-type Partridge family. Part of this trend is the late Nineties girl group from England, the Spice Girls. They are a marketed product rather than serious musicians (as were the Monkees at the beginning of their career in the Sixties), but they have captured the imaginations of American girls with their funky fashions and "girl power" message, although the "power" seems mostly to refer to the freedom to wear what you want. Each Spice Girl has a nickname, such as "Posh" or "Baby" which reflects her fashion style; together they are a wild visual mix.

Rhythm and blues has a new teen star. Usher Raymond, just nineteen, after winning a teen "star search" contest, has made two best-selling albums and has performed with Janet Jackson (Zaslow 1998, 15). Ska music is also enjoying a renewal, especially on the West Coast, where bands mix old reggae and ska beats with more recent punk and pop. The album *Sublime*, by the group of the same name, and the group No Doubt have contributed several hits in this style.

The big surprise of the late Nineties is the return of swing. With bands like the Squirrel Nut Zippers popularizing the sounds of the Forties, and television ads for Gap clothing showing Nineties teens doing wild jitterbugs to the music of The Brian Setzer Orchestra, the past seems to have returned.

Country and Christian Rock

Only a few years ago, LeAnn Rimes was a North Texas kid singing for friends, but thanks to her remarkable maturity of voice and manner, in 1998, still not yet sixteen, she released two CDs which have sold in the millions and has had two big hit singles: "Blue" and "How Do I Live?" Although young woman performers are not new to country—Tanya Tucker was also a teen phenomenon—Rimes seems to be part of a new trend of young performers singing in a softer style which appeals to girls.

One of the phenomena of the Nineties is Christian rock. It features ska sounds, hard rock sounds, and highly danceable tunes of all sorts; it is, in fact, virtually indistinguishable from most other rock music except for the lyrics, which extol the joys of Christian faith. It is played on Christian radio stations and at clubs devoted exclusively to this kind of music, such as the Powerhouse Club in Greenville, South Carolina, where eleven-year-olds can dance alongside college freshmen and groove to the message. Christian bands such as My Friend Stephanie play here to sellout crowds.

Dance

Beginning in the Eighties with punk music, slam dancing, or moshing, became the most distinctive form of teen dancing. Previously performed mostly at alternative music clubs, today it has worked its way into more popular arenas, though it is still associated with hard rather than soft rock. Teens have even been seen slam dancing at Disney World. Slamming involves the organization of a "pit," or group of dancers moving tightly together to the music, while individual dancers throw themselves from a height (usually the stage) into the pit and are caught and passed around. It requires teamwork; at the same time, it encourages exuberant individuality of movement. It is an unusual combination of chaos and organization, with some unwritten rules, such as keeping your arms to yourself, going with the flow, and not dropping someone on purpose. Part of its charm is its danger: there is always the potential for fights or injury. When it works, it is exhilarating and tribal, and, as one eighteen-year-old girl said, it satisfies "a need for human physical contact among people who are not intimate friends" (quoted in Simon 1997, 167). A researcher theorized, "Regardless of where it occurs, as a metaphorical expression the performers are realizing and demonstrating the hope and the *possibility* that along with speed, chaos, and violence can come individuality, human contact, and order" (Simon 1997, 173).

The legacy of freedom and individuality, beginning with the Lindy and the jitterbug and evolving through the individual dances of the Sixties, continues today with the free-style dancing that accompanies less hard-core rock. Shagging—a smooth jitterbug couples dance—is still popular among Southern teens especially on the beach. At proms, slow-dancing couples embrace each other with both arms in a kind of free-style, intimate, shuffle step. Salsa music still inspires Latino teens—and others who like a more challenging style to these rhythms—to perform intricate, fast steps. Line dancing, which does not require partners but does require a knowledge of the step patterns (the Electric Slide is the most popular and best known) is found at proms as well as at clubs where country music is featured. The Texas two-step is a popular country couples' dance, performed with an easy, gliding rhythm moving in a large circle around the dance floor, preferably wearing tight jeans and cowboy boots.

Movies

The Nineties have enjoyed a number of big movies. One of the more absurd examples of bigness is the 1998 remake of the hokey 1954 Japanese import *Godzilla*, in which a huge lizard terrorizes civilization. The product tie-ins and ads are more amusing than the movie itself. Big can also mean sweeping scenery, exciting action, big-name stars, and big box-office profits. Denzel Washington's portrayal of Malcolm X in Spike Lee's excellent 1992 biography of the black leader does not minimize the complexity of Malcolm's life and death. Steven Spielberg's *Schindler's List* (1993), filmed largely in Poland, traces the history of a man who, after sympathizing with the Nazis, saved hundreds of Polish Jews from extermination. Leonard Maltin called this movie "staggering . . . looks and feels like nothing Hollywood has ever made before" (1997, 1169).

Visually big (though less thoughtful than those mentioned above) were *Dances with Wolves* (1990), *Jurassic Park* (1993), and the biggest of the big: *Titanic* (1998). James Cameron's well-researched movie about the famous ship, billed as the most expensive movie ever made, re-creates in meticulous detail the last hours of the *Titanic*'s sinking. In leading up to this tragedy, Cameron interweaves a story of two young lovers, the rich girl–poor boy combination. It is this element that impels teen girls to see the movie over and over again to watch Kate Winslet and Nineties teen heartthrob Leonardo DiCaprio swear their love to the romantic strains of Celine Dion's music. DiCaprio entered show business at the age of fourteen in a television commercial and at seventeen joined the cast of television's *Growing Pains*. Now twenty-three, like teenybopper idols before him such as David Cassidy, he projects a nonthreatening sexuality.

Like another Leo before him (Leonard Whiting in 1968), DiCaprio has played Romeo on the screen. Director Baz Luhrmann re-created the classic play in a postmodern, punk style, set in a burned-out cityscape using space-age weaponry instead of sword play, subjugating language to image MTV style, and titling it *William Shakespeare's Romeo & Juliet* (1996). Starring as Juliet is Claire Danes, a teen actress highly respected for her work in television's *My So-Called Life* and as Beth in the newest film version of *Little Women*.

In fact, genuinely young stars in movies aimed for teen audiences seem to be dominating Hollywood in the mid-Nineties. Just as in the Fifties, when teens went to the movies frequently and studios poured out cheaply made films for them, Nineties teens are the audience Hollywood wants to reach. Demographics show that the teen population overall is on the rise again, after a slight drop in the Eighties, and teens are going to the movies in record numbers, according to *Time* magazine (Corliss, August 3, 1998, 66). Some of these are comedies: *Clueless* (1995), about airhead Beverly

Leonardo DiCaprio and Claire Danes as *Romeo & Juliet*, 1996. Reproduced courtesy of The Museum of Modern Art.

Hills teen girls (and loosely based, surprisingly, on Jane Austen's *Emma*); 1998's *Can't Hardly Wait*, starring Jennifer Love Hewitt; and the latest gross-out, *There's Something About Mary* (1998), starring Cameron Diaz. *Dazed and Confused* (1993) is a nostalgic film set on the last day of school in 1976, and 1998's *The Wedding Singer* is set in the 1980s. The television-nourished generation of teens, who like to watch reruns on the Nickelodeon network, have also gotten a barrage of Nineties films based on television shows: *The Addams Family*, *The Brady Bunch*, *Leave It to Beaver*, and *The Fugitive*.

Also like the Fifties, and continuing the trend that swept the Eighties, most of the B-movie hits are horror or slasher films. (We might note in passing, however, that the favorite adult film of the Nineties was *Silence of the Lambs*, a 1991 horror film about a terrifying, cannibalistic criminal.) *Scream* and its sequel *Scream 2*, *I Know What You Did Last Summer* and its sequel *I Still Know What You Did Last Summer*, and *Disturbing Behavior*, about a group of clean teens turned into robots, all attracted teen audiences in droves between 1996 and 1998, making big profits for a relatively small investment on the part of the producers. Jamie Lee Curtis, star of the first *Halloween* film in 1978, made a return visit to the horror genre by suggesting a sequel twenty years later: *H20* (1998), in which she is the head of a private school terrorized by the same killer who stalked her in the original movie.

Buffy the Vampire Slayer, from 1992, was more interesting and clever—Valley girl meets vampire—and it has become a hit television series, expensively produced and written with occasional ironic wit. In fact, many teen movie stars are the same ones who star on television soap operas and sitcoms; the relationship has become completely fluid. However, the competition in the search for young performers has also become difficult; one can be a hit one day on both the small screen and the large, and forgotten the next. Nineteen-year-old Katie Holmes, who stars on television's *Dawson's Creek* and in the film *Disturbing Behavior*, is philosophical: "I'm kind of a fresh-face type of deal. . . . It's not that I'm sexy, I know that! Whatever. I know it won't last forever, but I'm glad to be in my teens and doing these things" (quoted in Corliss, August 3, 1998, 68).

Books and Reading

According to one 1992 poll, over 23% of high school seniors stated that they had not read a single book for pleasure in the previous year; however, more than 36% said that they had read as many as five books, and more than 14% responded that they had read ten or more books for pleasure. Those who keep predicting the demise of reading seem to be wrong. Teens enjoy books of many kinds, especially mystery and suspense, with horror novels a close second. Girls prefer romance over science fiction and fantasy; the reverse is true for boys.

Among the decade's best-sellers, Alexandra Ripley's *Scarlett*, the 1991 sequel to Margaret Mitchell's famous *Gone With the Wind*, appealed romantically to older teen girls; their mothers were probably reading *The Bridges of Madison County*. Fans of fantasy enjoyed books written by Jane Yolen and Piers Anthony, and devoured Robert Jordan's Wheel of Time series—up to eight hefty volumes by 1998. Stephen King continued to serve up thrills with novels such as *Dolores Claiborne* (1993) and *Bag of Bones* (1998).

Since the emphasis in the Seventies on helping oneself to a better life physically and spiritually, plenty of self-help books have been published to show adults the way. With the Nineties frankness about teen sexual and emotional problems have come self-help books for teens on every possible topic, from homework to sexual abuse to suicide prevention. *Fighting Invisible Tigers* by Earl Hipp is a stress-management guide for teens; *When Nothing Matters Anymore* by Bev Cobain—rock star Kurt Cobain's cousin and a nurse—is a guide for depressed teens. *When a Friend Dies* by Marilyn Gootman helps teens cope with this particular situation. At the top of the *New York Times* best-seller list in 1998 is *Chicken Soup for the Teenage Soul: 101 Stories of Life, Love and Learning*, a collection of short inspirational essays written by therapists and teens on dating, love, relationships with parents and friends, and what it means to be successful. The Teenagers' Bill of Rights offered on pages 306–307 of *Chicken Soup* makes an interesting comparison with the Fifties Teen Bill of Rights (see Chapter 5). Most notable in this list is the mention of privacy, a concern absent from the Fifties version.

Young Adult Literature

Horror tales have made their way from the movie screen into hundreds of books for teens, beginning with Christopher Pike's books in the Eighties. Annette Curtis Klaus ushered in the Nineties with *The Silver Kiss*, a cross between a young adult realistic novel and a supernatural thriller. It concerns a girl coping with the impending death of her mother from cancer while falling in love with a good vampire. Unlike some other novels of the horror genre, this one is a serious artistic effort. Less skilled writers also churn out horror tales for teens, to such a degree that Patty Campbell, a young adult literature expert, worried in 1994 that such fiction "threatens to engulf, or at least color, the whole of adolescent literature" (1994, 237). R. L. Stine's Fear Street series is a case in point. The series began in 1990 in response to teens' demands for more such fiction; Stine abundantly satisfied the demand by writing sixty books in this series by 1995 (Drew 400–401). Stine, who once worked as a junior high social studies teacher in Ohio, comments, "I believe that kids as well as adults are entitled to books of no socially redeeming value" (Quoted in Drew 395). In his formula, the kids are threatened by something which may or may not be supernatural, and manage to find their own way out of the difficulty. Despite the concerns of parents and critics, as well as protests aimed at school libraries and bookstores, such books continue to sell well, and they exploit current trends such as the dangers of the Internet (e.g., can a person be murdered in virtual reality?) and the *X Files* premise that aliens are among us.

Established young adult writers continue to produce good realistic fiction centering on teen life. Cynthia Voigt's *When She Hollers* deals with a girl who must free herself from her abusive stepfather. Francesca Lia Block continued her Weetzie Bat series with such novels as *Witch Baby* (1991) and *Cherokee Bat and the Goat Guys* (1992), as well as moving into novels about other characters. Chris Crutcher's uncompromising look at teen problems continues to make him a popular writer, with books such as *Athletic Shorts* (1991). Robert Cormier, whose excellent writing has helped make young adult literature a respected field, published another novel set in a shadowy place between fantasy and reality, *In the Middle of the Night* (1995), in which a boy is drawn into danger and sexual excitement, and into his father's history, by a mysterious phone caller.

The need to understand other cultures is making itself felt in young adult literature with books such as the 1996 award-winning novel about Mexican-American teens, *The Parrot in the Oven*, by Victor Martinez. In a 1994 poll, teens also said they liked books about black heroes like Rosa Parks and Malcolm X, time-travel books like *Dream Spinner* by Joanne Hoppe, and science fiction such as *Jumper* by Stephen Gould and *Songsmith* by Andre Norton ("Young Adults' Choices," 1994). The increasing emergence of homosexual teens has also produced both fiction and nonfiction on this subject. Marion Dane Bauer has edited a collection of stories on this subject by a number of popular young adult authors called *Am I Blue?* (1994). One of the most unusual young adult books of 1995 is Shelley Stoehr's *Weird on the Outside* about a seventeen-year-old girl who enters the world of topless dancing. Stoehr has also written *Crosses*, about "cutting," the practice of carving designs into the skin, something teen girls—and some boys—have engaged in recently.

Magazines and Jane Pratt

The Nineties seems to be the decade of the teen magazine, although boys still seem to prefer *Rolling Stone, Playboy, Spin*, and *Sports Illustrated*, as well as specialty magazines like those for climbing or bicycling, for example. *Seventeen* still holds the largest circulation by far among girls, but it is no longer the only option. *Teen* and *YM* have been gaining readership as well as some maverick magazines like *Jump* and *blue jean magazine*, which is both written and produced by girls, for girls, and which tries to address issues other than fashion and dating.

The ground-breaking maverick magazine for girls, *Sassy*, which began circulation in the Eighties to a large number of grateful girls who appreciated its frank subjects and slangy style, died in 1996. Many devoted readers are just as glad now, because *Sassy* had already been robbed of its appeal. After troubles with advertisers over its sexual directness, the magazine was finally sold to the owners of *Teen*, who began changing its format to resemble the more conservative *Seventeen*—i.e., articles about counting calories. In late 1996, the publishers stopped publishing a magazine called *Sassy* and folded it into *Teen*.

Sassy's original editor, Jane Pratt, believes that *Sassy* forced its competitors to sharpen up, to acknowledge that teen girls were certainly interested in more than fashion and that they were probably having sex or at least were in need of some straight advice about it. Others accuse Pratt of hypocrisy, of trading on sensationalism while saying she was treating teens with respect (Smith 1992, 69). She turned what she learned about teens while doing the magazine into a book of her own, *For Real: The Uncensored Truth About America's Teenagers* (1995). The book contains a number of portraits of American teens of all kinds—cheerleaders, skinheads, musicians, gays—written exactly in their words, interspersed with excerpts from Pratt's own diaries when she was a teen. She tells adult readers, "What I've shown you of American teenagers may not have been the picture you wanted to look at. . . . They more than anyone are who we need to look to, learn from. To support and to give them the autonomy they need to make the changes that will affect their lives" (1995, 302–3).

The increasing number of frank articles about sex in teen girls' magazines has created problems for school libraries. One parent complained, "When I was growing up, *Seventeen* was a magazine that talked about hair and lipstick and kissing boys. When you read what's printed there now, it belongs in *Playboy*" (Bertin 1998). In 1998 a Hauppauge, New York, public school principal removed *Seventeen*, *Teen*, and *YM* from his middle school's library shelves because he believed they were not "age-appropriate," despite the advice of a committee of parents, teachers, and librarians (Bertin 1998).

Comic Books

Amazingly, Archie continues his "typical teen" antics at the end of the century in comics and in a thicker format: *Archie's Digest* and *Archie's Double Digest*. His innocence and his problems with girls, cars, parents, teachers, and buddies still appeal to teens, although his readers are younger than they used to be. His girlfriends, Betty and Veronica, also have their own comic, which includes an advice column on everything, especially "getting a guy to like you."

When Superman "died" in late 1992, comic fans were astounded. Experienced readers knew that he would probably be resurrected somehow, but less experienced readers were upset when national news media featured the story: "Superman's death was in every paper and magazine, on every news broadcast, and included as part of every comedian's monologue" (Daniels 1995, 218). The public seemed to lose something vital, as it had when Robin was killed in the Eighties. Six million copies of the comic book were sold. Of course, he came back, more muscular and tousled than ever, in October 1993.

Devoted readers of comic books still love the X-Men series, debuted by Marvel in the Sixties and revitalized in the Nineties. Marvel, too, has led the way in stories featuring black super heroes, beginning in the Seventies. The early Nineties showed an increase in such characters; Brotherman, Ebony Warrior, Horus, Meteor Man, Shadowhawk, Sustahgirl, and Night Thrasher are a few. These super heroes have grown more complex in their kinds of powers, in their employment, and in their interactions with families (Davenport 1997, 27). Unfortunately, they may also be disappearing because many independent comics producers have been bought out. The "commitment of comic book publishers to diversity was and is of secondary importance" to economics (1997, 27), and such characters will have to appeal to a wider audience with solid storylines and artwork if they are to survive. DC's Milestone series has tried to create such audiences through an increasing pool of multicultural artists and writers.

REFERENCES

Ash, Peter, et al. "Gun Acquisition and Use by Juvenile Offenders. *Journal of the American Medical Association* 275, no. 22 (June 12, 1996): 1754+.

Bertin, Joan E. "Do Teenage Girl Magazines Belong on Middle School Library Shelves?" *Newsday*, March 1, 1998, B7.

Biondo, Brenda. "Quick Climb to the Top." *USA Weekend*, February 13–15, 1998, 8.

Birdseye, Debbie, and Tom Birdseye. *Under Our Skin: Kids Talk about Race.* Photographs by Robert Crum. New York: Holiday House, 1997.

Brumberg, Joan Jacobs. *The Body Project: An Intimate History of American Girls.* New York: Random House, 1997.

Campbell, Patty. "The Sand in the Oyster." *Horn Book Magazine* 70, no. 2 (March/April 1994): 234–38.

Chadwick, Bruce A., and Jim B. Heaton. *Statistical Handbook on Adolescents in America.* Phoenix, Ariz.: Oryx, 1996.

Cloud, John. "Out, Proud, and Very Young." *Time*, December 8, 1997, 82–83.

Colbert, David, ed. "The Quilt." In *Eyewitness to America*, 559–562. New York: Pantheon, 1997.

Coontz, Stephanie. *The Way We Never Were: North American Families and the Nostalgia Trap.* New York: Basic Books, 1992.

Corliss, Richard. "Bart Simpson." *Time*, June 8, 1998, 204–5.

———. "The Class of '98." *Time*, August 3, 1998, 66–68.

Dalzell, Tom. *Flappers 2 Rappers: American Youth Slang.* Springfield, Mass.: Merriam-Webster, 1996.

Daniels, Les. *DC Comics: Sixty Years of the World's Favorite Comic Book Heroes.* Boston: Little, Brown, 1995.

Davenport, Chris. "Black Is the Color of My Comic Book Character." *INKS Cartoon and Comic Art Studies* 4, no. 1 (February 1997): 20–28.

Diamond, David. "When Having Babies Is a Crime." *USA Weekend*, February 14–16, 1997, 8.

Donovan, Elisa. "Starving for Success." *Teen People*, April 1998, 74–77.

Drew, Bernard A. *The 100 Most Popular Young Adult Authors.* Rev. ed. Englewood, Colo.: Libraries Unlimited Inc., 1997.

du Noyer, Paul, ed. *The Story of Rock and Roll.* New York: Schirmer Books, 1995.

Eble, Connie. *Slang and Sociability: In-Group Language Among College Students.* Chapel Hill: University of North Carolina Press, 1996.

Farley, Christopher John. "Hip-Hop Nation." *Time* 153, no. 5 (February 8, 1999): 54–64.

———. "Kids and Race." *Time*, November 24, 1997, 88–91.

Finnegan, William. *Cold New World: Growing Up in a Harder Country.* New York: Random House, 1998.

Friedlander, Paul. *Rock and Roll: A Social History.* Boulder, Colo.: Westview Press, 1996.

Gibbons, Judith, Randy R. Richter, Deane C. Wiley, and Debrose A. Stiles. "Adolescents' Opposite Sex Ideal in Four Countries." *Journal of Social Psychology* 136, no. 4 (August 1996): 531+.

Gilligan, Carol. *In a Different Voice: Psychological Theory and Women's Development.* Cambridge, Mass.: Harvard University Press, 1982.

Gilmore, Mikal. *Night Beat: A Shadow History of Rock & Roll.* New York: Doubleday, 1998.

Gordon, Marcy. "Twice As Many Teens Using Drugs As in '92." *Greenville* (SC) *News*, August 21, 1996, 1A.

Green, David L. "High School Student Employment in Social Context: Adolescents' Perceptions of the Role of Part-time Work." *Adolescence* 25, no. 98 (Summer 1990): 425–34.

Guttman, Monika. "Ex-Teen Drinker Shows Young People an Option." *USA Weekend*, September 12–14, 1997, 9.

Hiltbrand, David. "The Family Page." *TV Guide*, July 4, 1998, 36.

Holland, Gini. *America in the 20th Century: 1990–1999.* New York: Marshall Cavendish, 1995.

Hollander, D. "Contraceptive Use Is Most Regular if Teenagers Have Conventional Lifestyles." *Family Planning Perspectives* 28, no. 6 (November–December 1996), 289.

Horyn, Cathy. "Leonardo's Masterpiece." *Vanity Fair* 449 (January 1998): 72+.

Howe, Neil, and William Strauss. "The New Generation Gap." *Atlantic Monthly* 270, no. 6 (December 1992): 67–89.

Jacobs, Thomas A. *What Are My Rights? 95 Questions and Answers About Teens and the Law.* Minneapolis: Free Spirit Publishing, 1997.

Jones, Charisse. "Education Challenged by Diversity's Demands." *USA Today*, September 24, 1997, 1–2A.

Kahn-Egan, Chrys. "Degeneration X: The Artifacts and Lexicon of the Rave Subculture." *Studies in Popular Culture* 20, no. 3 (April 1998): 33–44.

Kaufman, Leslie. "Children of the Corn." *Newsweek* 126, no. 9 (August 28, 1995): 60–62.

Lindsay, Jeanne Warren. *Caring, Commitment, and Change.* Buena Park, Calif.: Morning Glory Press, 1995.

———. *Coping with Reality.* Buena Park, Calif.: Morning Glory Press, 1995.

———. *Teen Dads.* Buena Park, Calif.: Morning Glory Press, 1993.

Maltin, Leonard. *1998 Movie and Video Guide.* New York: Signet, 1997.

Morrow, Melinda. " 'But Beavis, Everything Does Suck': Watching Beavis and Butt-head Watch Videos." Unpublished essay. Clemson University, Clemson, South Carolina, November 25, 1997.

Nilsen, Alleen Pace, and Kenneth L. Donelson, eds. *Literature for Today's Young Adults.* 4th ed. New York: HarperCollins, 1993.

O'Connor, Colleen. "Prom Night Nightmare." *Teen People,* April 1998, 47–49.

Oppenheimer, Todd. "The Computer Delusion." *Atlantic Monthly* 280, no. 1 (July 1997): 45–62.

Orenstein, Peggy. *School Girls: Young Women, Self-Esteem, and the Confidence Gap.* New York: Anchor Books, 1994.

Owen, Rob. *Gen X TV: The Brady Bunch to Melrose Place.* Syracuse, N.Y.: Syracuse University Press, 1997.

Page, Clarence. "Teen, Unwed Mothers' Courage Rates Notice." *Greenville* (SC) *News,* August 12, 1998, 9A.

Phillips, Louis, and Burnham Holmes. *The TV Almanac.* New York: Macmillan, 1994.

Pipher, Mary. *Reviving Ophelia: Saving the Selves of Adolescent Girls.* New York: Ballantine Books, 1994.

Pratt, Jane. *For Real: The Uncensored Truth About America's Teenagers.* New York: Hyperion, 1995.

Price, James H., Sharon M. Desmond, and Daisy Smith. "A Preliminary Investigation of Inner City Adolescents' Perceptions of Guns." *Journal of School Health* 61, no. 6 (August 1991): 225+.

"Put Brakes on Teen Driving, AAA Says." *USA Today,* September 24, 1997, 3A.

Rheingold, Howard. *The Virtual Community.* New York: HarperCollins, 1993.

Rhodes, Joe. "Shock Jocks." *TV Guide,* June 20, 1998, 26–30.

Ritter, Malcolm. "Doctor Studies Internet Addiction." *Greenville* (SC) *News,* June 1, 1998, A2.

Rozen, Leah. "On the Internet." *Good Housekeeping,* November 1997, 76–82.

Rubinowski, Leslie. "Winging It." *Pittsburgh Post-Gazette,* October 19, 1997, G1+.

Russakoff, Dale, and Cindy Loose. "It's All So . . . Well, Childish." *Greenville* (SC) *News,* September 20, 1998, 1F.

Schmittroth, Linda, ed. *Statistical Record of Children.* Detroit, Mich.: Gale, 1994.

Silko, Leslie Marmon. *Yellow Woman and a Beauty of the Spirit: Essays on Native American Life Today.* New York: Touchstone, 1997.

Simon, Bradford Scott. "Entering the Pit: Slam-Dancing and Modernity." *Journal of Popular Culture* 31, no. 1 (Summer 1997): 149–76.

Smith, Dinitia. "Jane's World! Jane's World!" *New York* 25, no. 21 (May 25, 1992): 60+.

Stuessy, Joe. *Rock and Roll: Its History and Stylistic Development.* 2d ed. Englewood Cliffs, N.J.: Prentice Hall, 1994.

Sturrock, Staci. "Rodeo Drive." *Greenville* (SC) *News,* June 5, 1998, 1E.

Tannen, Deborah. "Oprah Winfrey." *Time,* June 8, 1998, 197–98.

Temple, Linda. " 'Smart Date' Web Site Designed to Help Young Women Feel Safer." *Greenville* (SC) *News,* September 22, 1997, 1–3B.

"Waif Central Station: Images of Kate." Web site. Accessed 3-1-97.

Wallechinsky, David. *The People's Almanac Presents the 20th Century.* Boston: Little, Brown, 1995.

Weeks, Janet. "Brandy's Big Moment." *TV Guide,* July 17, 1998, 13–14.

Wolcott, James. "Gathering Moss." *New Yorker,* September 18, 1995, 102–3.

"Young Adults' Choices for 1994." *Journal of Reading* 38, no. 3 (November 1994), 219–25.

Zaslow, Jeffrey. "Usher." *USA Weekend,* August 7–9, 1998, 15.

A Note on Statistics

Few statistics focusing on teens are available for the early decades of this century. Most early national surveys concern school attendance and family structure. Beginning in the Fifties, however, with the rising concerns about juvenile delinquency and the growing spending power of teens, surveys began to scrutinize teen behavior and tastes. By the Eighties, a flood of statistics on every aspect of teen life had appeared, a good portion of it funded by private corporations seeking to market goods to teen consumers. Some of this material is contradictory and based on small samples.

I have tried to achieve a range of reliable statistical information in this book and to place it in context whenever possible. In compiling this material I have relied on Stacey Willocks, of Clemson University's Department of Sociology, who adapted statistics and tables from the *Encyclopedia of Adolescence*, edited by Richard Lerner, Anne C. Petersen, and Jeanne Brooks-Gunn (Garland 1991), the *Statistical Handbook on the American Family*, edited by Bruce A. Chadwick and Jim B. Heaton (Oryx 1992), the *Statistical Handbook on Adolescents in America*, edited by Bruce A. Chadwick and Jim B. Heaton (Oryx 1996), and the *Statistical Record of Children*, edited by Linda Schmittroth (Gale 1994). Especially useful was Jeffrey Mirel's essay in the *Encyclopedia of Adolescence*, "Adolescence in Twentieth-Century America" (pp. 1153–1160).

A Note on Sources

Several sources helped me lay the groundwork for each chapter. *America in the Twentieth Century*, a ten-volume set published by Marshall Cavendish in 1995, treats the century decade by decade in books written by various authors. The series is generously illustrated and rich with detail in a very readable format. It expertly incorporates minority histories and concerns into the more general sweep of American history, and it appears to be designed specifically for teen readers. The American Decades series by Gale, for a more mature audience, covers a much wider range of material arranged by topic. David Wallechinsky's *People's Almanac Presents the 20th Century* (1995), designed primarily to be entertaining, was useful for double-checking general facts and dates and occasionally for alerting me to information about teens and about popular culture that did not appear in the more general sources. *Eyewitness to America*, edited by David Colbert (1997), is a collection of firsthand accounts of events in American history, beginning in 1492 and ending in 1994 (with an essay about one man's e-mail conversation with Bill Gates of Microsoft). Elliott West's *Growing Up in Twentieth-Century America* (1996) focuses on children more than on adolescents, but it is especially good on housing, school, and work patterns affecting young people. Mark West's study *Children, Culture, and Controversy* (1988) was informative about attempts to censor young people's reading and media. *Literature for Today's Young Adults*, the classic text edited by Alleen Pace Nilsen and Ken Donelson and now in its fourth edition, helped with the history of young adult literature and related educational patterns. .

The most useful information on teen culture itself came from a combination of sociological studies and trade books. Among sociological studies and histories, David Nasaw's *Children of the City* (1985) is an outstanding work, thorough and insightful, lively and intelligent. He followed it with *Going Out: The Rise and Fall of Public Amusements* (1993), also an excellent resource on how teens spent their leisure time in the early decades of the century. John Modell's *Into One's Own: From Youth to Adulthood in the United States 1920–1975* is a readable exploration of growing up an American, especially useful on the concept of dating. The classic sociological treatise on *Middletown* (1929), by Robert and Helen Lynd, still commands respect and makes interesting reading, especially on the teens of Muncie, Indiana, although the study encompasses the whole community. Two similar studies, apparently inspired by the Lynds, appeared in the Forties: Carl Withers, writing under the pseudonym James West, published *Plainville, U.S.A.* (1945) which explores a rural community, and August Hollingshead published *Elmtown's Youth* in 1949, which focuses directly on how social class affects teenagers in a "typical" American small town. *The Damned and the Beautiful* by Paula Fass (1977) is, despite its dramatic title, a thorough sociological study of college students in the Twenties and a readable modern classic in the field. E. A. Smith's study *American Youth Culture: Group Life in Teenage Society* (1962) covers a lot of territory and sounds a little judgmental at times but still has some good insights into mid-century teens. Connie Eble's linguistic study *Slang and Sociability: In-Group Language Among College Students* (1996) shows how slang creates group identity among young adults and helps them resist authority.

Among trade books, Grace Palladino's *Teenagers* (1996) traces the rise of teens as consumers, taking the establishment of *Seventeen* magazine as the signal moment of recognition that there was a profit to be made on teen culture. Journalist David Halberstam's lengthy but highly readable books *The Fifties* (1993) and *The Children* (1997) offer vivid portraits of the people and the controversies of the Fifties and Sixties, many of which Halberstam witnessed personally. A more vivid and often chilling look at today's teens is journalist William Finnegan's brilliantly written *Cold New World: Growing up in a Harder Country* (1998). Finnegan's overall focus is the increasing number of families who must struggle for economic security in the midst of the apparent affluence of the late twentieth century. As he shows so well, it is the teens who must bear the burden of knowing their lives will not be as secure as those of their forebears. A very different sort of book, yet offering similar vignettes of teens in their own world, is Jane Pratt's *For Real: The Uncensored Truth About America's Teenagers* (1995). Founding editor of *Sassy* magazine, Pratt reproduces teen speech and teen life of the late twentieth century in a sympathetic teen-magazine vernacular.

Useful academic journals include the *Journal of Popular Culture*, *Studies in Popular Culture*, and the *Journal of American Film and Television*, an excellent source on teen films. I found more help overall from *Time* magazine, which during its more than seventy years of publication has had its editorial finger on the pulse of teen culture. *Time*'s articles are informative, well-researched, and lively; they tend to maintain a good balance between an adult point of view and a sympathetic view of teens. *Seventeen* magazine remains a useful resource for teen girl culture, although it has plenty of competition in the Nineties. It is significant, perhaps, that no similar teen boy magazine seems to survive very long.

Tom Dalzell's wonderful *Flappers 2 Rappers: American Youth Slang* (1996) appeared just as I was beginning my work on this book. Intelligent, funny, and complete, it is a remarkable history of young America in itself, illustrated throughout with Dalzell's own wacky cartoons. I realized as soon as I saw it that I would be able only to suggest the richness of teen slang throughout the century; I could not begin to match Dalzell's work—nor his collection of the sexual and bathroom slang that makes up so much teen talk. Anyone who truly wants to understand teen America in the twentieth century needs to have Dalzell along for the ride.

Appendix: A Sample of Teen-Oriented Links to the World Wide Web

The rapidity with which the Internet continues to grow may make this sampling outdated quickly. These sites are offered here as examples only; they make up only a tiny percentage of the available sites, both serious and frivolous, for teens.

SCHOOL AND WORK

http://quest.arc.nasa.gov/women/	Discusses women at the National Areonautics and Space Administration; aimed at an audience of teen girls
http://www.finaid.org/	Helps teens seeking funding for college
http://www.CollegeEdge.com/	A college rating system
http://www.usnews.com/usnews/edu/	College ratings by *U.S. News and World Report*
http://www.petersons.com./ugrad/	Peterson's guide to undergraduate institutions
http://www.bellsouth.net/dp/educ/	Bellsouth's comprehensive resource for teens, on almost all subjects related to school
http://www.homeworkhelp.com/yahoo__index.htm	Comprehensive homework help for a small fee
http://wwwfuturescan.com/	Details about jobs and beginning careers

SPORTS

http://www.peg.apc.org/~balson/ — Information on sports around the country

http://library.advanced.org/11902/ — Information on baseball

http://espn.sportszone.com/ — All sports, all the time

LEISURE

http://prominence.com/java/poetry/ — An on-line version of the poetry magnet game

http://roller.coaster.net/ — Information on the biggest and best roller coasters nationwide

http://www.wallofsound.com/ — General music resource for musicians and music lovers

http://www.tvgen.com/ — *TV Guide* on the Web

http://www.dreamagic.com/roger/teencritic.html/ — Movie reviews by a fourteen-year-old girl who has been writing reviews of film and video since she was nine

http://www.nextlevel.com/righton/ — A teen magazine on the Web

http://www.spankmag.com/ — A teen magazine offering comedy, culture, and literature

http://www.nida.nih.gov.MarijBroch/Marijintro.html — Warning guide on marijuana use and abuse

DATING AND SEX

http://cgi.pathfinder.com/drruth/ — Dr. Ruth, sex advisor, answers questions on-line

http://www.breakupgirl.com/ — An on-line sympathy group for girls who have broken up with their boyfriends

http://www.lovecalculator.com/ — Calculates how compatible you are with someone of the opposite sex based on the letters in both your names

http://www.takecare.co.uk/ — Comprehensive online guide to safe sex, both protection and abstinence

TEEN ON-LINE FORUMS

http://www.teens-online.com/ — Web page made by teens for teens

http://www.teenspeak.com/ — Teen discussion groups

http://www.citykids.com/ — A not-for-profit, youth-driven multicultural organization providing leadership training and youth-to-youth communication programs

My thanks to Professor Tharon Howard of Clemson University and to Birma Gainor, a graduate student at Clemson, for helping me compile this list.

Index

Broad categories are used in place of multiple specific entries for items such as movie titles and book titles.

About the Author

LUCY ROLLIN teaches Children's and Adolescent Literature at Clemson University. She has published books on nursery rhymes, psychoanalytic approaches to children's literature, and film adaptations, and has edited the Oxford World's Classics edition of Twain's *The Prince and the Pauper*. She has published many articles on popular culture and on literature for young readers.